SPATIAL PLANNING SYSTEMS AND PRACTICES IN EUROPE

Ideal for students and practitioners working in spatial planning, the Europeanization of planning agendas and regional policy discussed in *Spatial Planning Systems and Practices in Europe* develops a systematic and methodological framework for analyzing changes in planning systems throughout Europe. The main aim of the book is to delineate the coexistence of continuity and change and of convergence and divergence with regard to planning practices across Europe.

Based on the work of spatial planning experts from 12 European countries, the authors underline the specific and context-dependent variety and disparateness of planning transformation, focusing on:

- the main objectives of the changes;
- the driving forces behind these changes and the main phases and turning points;
- the main agenda-setting actors; and
- the different planning modes and tools reflected in the different "policy and planning styles."

Along with a methodological framework, the book includes 12 country case studies and comparative conclusions covering a variety of planning systems within EU member states. According to the four "ideal types" of planning systems identified in the *EU Compendium*, at least two countries have been selected from each of the four different planning traditions:

- regional–economic (France, Germany);
- urbanism (Greece, Italy);
- comprehensive/integrated (Denmark, Finland, the Netherlands, Germany); and
- "land-use planning" (UK, Czech Republic, Belgium/Flanders).

The book also includes two additional case studies focusing on recent developments in eastern European countries, in particular Poland, and in southern Europe, in particular Turkey.

Mario Reimer is Scientific Researcher at the Ruhr University in Bochum (Urban and Metropolitan Studies) and at the Research Institute for Urban and Regional Development (ILS) in Dortmund.

Panagiotis Getimis is Professor of Spatial Planning and Policies at the Panteion University of Social and Political Sciences of Athens. He obtained his PhD in Spatial Planning and Policies from the Technical University of Berlin (1980). He is a founding member and co-director of the journal *TOPOS: Review of Urban and Regional Studies*. He is a member of the Board of Directors of the European Research Association and has been a member of the Editorial Board of the journal *Urban Research and Practice* since 2007.

Hans Heinrich Blotevogel is Professor Emeritus of Spatial Planning at Dortmund Technical University's Faculty of Spatial Planning. He obtained his PhD in Human Geography from the Ruhr University in Bochum (1972). He is a member of the Editorial Boards of the journals *Erdkunde*, *Archive for Scientific Geography* and *Raumforschung und Raumordnung*.

SPATIAL PLANNING SYSTEMS AND PRACTICES IN EUROPE

A comparative perspective on continuity and changes

Edited by Mario Reimer, Panagiotis Getimis and Hans Heinrich Blotevogel

Routledge
Taylor & Francis Group

LONDON AND NEW YORK

First edition published 2014
by Routledge
711 Third Avenue, New York, NY 10017

and by Routledge
2 Park Square, Milton Park, Abingdon, Oxon OX14 4RN

Routledge is an imprint of the Taylor and Francis Group, an informa business

British Library Cataloguing in Publication Data
A catalogue record for this book is available from the British Library

Library of Congress Cataloging-in-Publication Data
Spatial planning systems and practices in Europe : a comparative perspective on continuity and changes / edited by Mario Reimer, Panagiotis Getimis, and Hans Heinrich Blotevogel.
p. cm.
1. Regional planning--Europe. 2. Land use--Europe--Planning. 3. Intergovernmental cooperation--Europe. I. Reimer, Mario. II. Getimis, Panagiotis. III. Blotevogel, Hans Heinrich.
HT395.E8S75 2014
307.1'2094--dc23
2013025769

ISBN13: 978-0-415-72723-5 (hbk)
ISBN13: 978-0-415-72724-2 (pbk)
ISBN13: 978-1-315-85257-7 (ebk)

Typeset in Perpetua by
GreenGate Publishing Services, Tonbridge, Kent

Printed and bound in Great Britain by
TJ International Ltd, Padstow, Cornwall

CONTENTS

FIGURES

TABLES

CONTRIBUTORS

Hans Heinrich Blotevogel is Visiting Professor at the Department of Geography and Regional Research at the University of Vienna, Austria. He is Professor Emeritus of Spatial Planning at Dortmund Technical University's Faculty of Spatial Planning.

Giancarlo Cotella is Assistant Professor at the Inter-University Department of Regional and Urban Studies and Planning, Politecnico di Torino. In recent years he has been Visiting Professor at the University of Kaiserslautern, the Wroclaw University of Technology and the University of Tartu. He serves as Communication Officer on the Executive Committee of AESOP, the Association of European Schools of Planning.

Ole Damsgaard is Head of the EU Northern Periphery Secretariat dealing with territorial challenges and opportunities in the High North and the Arctic. In the past, he has held positions as Director of Nordregio (the Nordic Center for Spatial Development) and Director of the Danish Town Planning Institute. He has a background in human geography.

Rainer Danielzyk is Secretary General of the Academy for Spatial Research and Planning. Prior to this, he was Managing Director of Research at the ILS (Research Institute for Regional and Urban Development, Dortmund). He was also Professor of Spatial Planning and Regional Development at the Faculty of Architecture and Landscape at Leibniz University, Hannover.

Gülden Erkut is Professor of Regional Planning at Istanbul Technical University's City and Regional Planning Department, Faculty of Architecture. She was DAAD Guest Professor at Berlin Technical University, Urban Management Program, from May 2012 to May 2013.

David Evers is Senior Researcher on Spatial Planning at the PBL Netherlands Environmental Assessment Agency in The Hague and Assistant Professor at the University of Amsterdam. He holds degrees in Political Science (BA, Reed College) and Urban Planning (MA and PhD, University of Amsterdam). His research interests and publications include retail policy and development, the impact of European regulations on planning, territorial cohesion, planning law and institutional change.

Anna Geppert is Professor of Spatial Planning at the University of Paris-Sorbonne (France). Her research focuses on the evolution of the French planning system and, in particular, the development of strategic spatial planning at the urban as well as regional scale.

Panagiotis Getimis is Professor of Urban and Regional Policies, Department of Economic and Regional Development, Panteion University of Social and Political Sciences, Athens, Greece. From 1996 to 2007, he was Director of the Research Institute of Urban Environment and Human Resources (UEHR) at Panteion University. His research interests include urban policies, spatial planning, local government, and regional policies. He is a member of the Executive Board of the European Urban Research Association (EURA) and of the editorial board of the journal *Urban Research and Practice*. He has also been a Visiting Professor at UK (Oxford, Manchester) and German (Darmstadt) universities.

Georgia Giannakourou is Associate Professor of Planning and Environmental Institutions and Policies at the University of Athens, Greece. Her research interests and publications include European spatial planning, the EU impact on domestic planning institutions and policies, and various aspects of Greek planning law and policy.

Sari Hirvonen-Kantola is Lecturer in Urban Planning and Design, especially planning theory, practice and strategic urban planning at the Department of Architecture, Faculty of Technology, University of Oulu, Finland. She has a Licentiate on urban planning history, and in April 2013 defended her PhD thesis on integrative urban planning and development work.

Annette Kuhk is Postdoctoral Researcher in the Department of Architecture, Urbanism and Spatial Planning at the University of Leuven. She has degrees in business economics and communication science and holds a PhD in sociology. Her research interests are urban policies in Brussels, future exploration research and regional policies in Flanders.

Els Lievois is Postdoctoral Researcher at the Department of Architecture, Urbanism and Planning (University of Leuven) and Coordinator at the Policy Research Centre on Spatial Development. She also lectures on Spatial Analysis on the Masters in Tourism course at the University of Leuven.

Valeria Lingua is Research Fellow and Adjunct Professor in Spatial Planning at the Department of Architecture, University of Florence. She conducts research and professional activities focused on cooperative governance, with particular regard to the relationship between institutional processes and planning tools, from regional to urban levels.

Karel Maier is Professor of Urban and Regional Planning and Head of the Institute of Spatial Planning at the Faculty of Architecture, Czech Technical University, in Prague, Czech Republic.

Raine Mäntysalo is Professor of Strategic Urban Planning and Vice Head of the Department of Real Estate, Planning and Geoinformatics at Aalto University, Finland. He is also Adjunct Professor of Planning Theory and Communicative Planning at the University of Oulu, Finland.

Frank Moulaert is Professor of Spatial Planning at the Department of Architecture, Urbanism and Spatial Planning at the University of Leuven and Visiting Professor at the University of Newcastle (UK) and University of Lille (France).

Angelika Münter is Researcher at the ILS (Research Institute for Regional and Urban Development, Dortmund) and at the Faculty of Spatial Planning at Dortmund Technical University.

Vincent Nadin is Professor of Spatial Planning and Strategy at the Department of Urbanism, Faculty of Architecture, TU Delft, and Director of the joint Urban Systems and Environment Research Centre with South China University of Technology. He has been Visiting Professor at Leibniz University, Hannover, and at the National Cheng Kung University and National Taipei University, Taiwan. He is joint author of *Town and Country Planning in the UK* and *European Spatial Planning and Territorial Cooperation* (Routledge).

Mario Reimer is Postdoctoral Researcher at the ILS (Research Institute for Regional and Urban Development, Dortmund). His research interests are metropolitan and regional governance, planning cultures and strategic planning activities.

Jan Schreurs' research interests have always focused on place studies and typology—morphology studies related to creativity in and innovation by analysis and design. Ten years of practice as Director of Physical Planning at the University of Leuven and a degree in real estate add a strong sense of reality to his research motivations. Consequently, bridging gaps between theory and practice has always been a central pedagogical concern. He is currently involved as co-promoter in the research projects SPINDUS (research into spatial quality from a transdisciplinary perspective) and Steunpunt Ruimte (Flemish Policy Research Centre for Spatial Planning).

Loris Servillo is Postdoctoral Researcher in the ASRO Department at the University of Leuven. His research fields concern European spatial planning, with particular regard to EU policy debate and policy analysis at the EU scale; strategic spatial planning and urban regional/metropolitan management in Europe, with particular attention to local development approaches, integrated area-based programs and territorial governance processes; and institutional aspects of spatial planning, Europeanization and comparative analysis of planning systems.

Ervin Sezgin is Research and Teaching Assistant at Istanbul Technical University's City and Regional Planning Department, Faculty of Architecture.

Dominic Stead is Associate Professor of Urban and Regional Development at Delft University of Technology. His specialist interests include European spatial planning and governance, the European dimensions of transport policy, and issues of policy transfer related to spatial planning and transport decision-making.

Pieter Van den Broeck is part-time Senior Planning Practitioner at OMGEVING, a private consultancy firm in the field of spatial planning, landscape planning and architecture, and a part-time Postdoctoral Researcher in the Department of Architecture, Urbanism and Spatial Planning at the University of Leuven.

Wil Zonneveld is Professor of Urban and Regional Development at Delft University of Technology, Faculty of Architecture. His research focuses on strategic planning at the regional and national levels, the role of concepts and visions in strategic planning, and the Europeanization of territorial governance.

PREFACE

This book is based on the collective work of a European Research Group, launched in 2008 and coordinated by the Academy for Spatial Research and Planning (ARL) in Hannover, Germany. Experts on spatial planning from 12 European countries developed a systematic and methodological framework for the analysis of changes in planning systems and practices. All authors contributing to the book applied the framework to the preparation of their respective country chapters.

The authors refer to the strands of literature that deal with the comparative analysis of spatial planning institutional frameworks and policies, without sticking to former typologies elaborated in this field of research. Such typologies are rather used as a starting point through the selection and analysis of at least two countries belonging to formerly defined types of planning systems (see page xvii). During recent decades, a new focus on spatial planning research, enriched by evidence-based knowledge gained at the European level, has opened up due to new European policies and the development of the European territory. Issues of territorial cohesion and territorial cooperation have been highlighted. However, little has been said about overall changes in planning systems, their rigidity and resilience, and the different trajectories of transformation. Therefore, this book deals in particular with the influence of "Europeanization" on spatial planning systems, policies and practices. The authors distinguish between a planning system perspective on the one hand, and a planning culture perspective which describes concrete practices within the legal and administrative frameworks of 12 national planning systems on the other hand. They also consider the concept of planning cultures in a comparative perspective. While doing so, they focus on the different logics of planning practices, mainly those leading to transformations in the planning systems, and reflect diversified manifestations of planning practices.

With regard to former deliberations on planning systems, this book contributes to the detection of changing patterns in planning systems and practices that have emerged during the past two decades. Its innovative approach is based on the comparative analysis and explanation of changes and continuities in spatial planning across the diversity of planning systems in Europe. The authors underline the specific and context-dependent multiplicity and heterogeneity of planning transformation.

The intended readership of this book consists primarily of people concerned with questions of spatial planning and the Europeanization of planning agendas and regional policy in general, as well as those dealing with comparative approaches to planning systems, cultures and practices in particular. The disciplinary focus of the book addresses those working in the field of spatial and planning sciences, but will also be of great interest to practitioners involved in urban and regional planning and regional development (e.g. local and regional authorities). Since the issue of the transformation of planning is currently high on the institutional agenda of many research institutes and policymaking institutions, the book will attract both academics and policymakers in different European countries.

Concept and structure of the book

Our interest is especially inspired by the ongoing debate on the convergence and/or divergence of planning systems and practices in European member states. While the classic comparative analysis of planning systems mainly focuses on the static comparison of legal and administrative traditions, culminating in the description of coherent and homogeneous "planning families" (Newman and Thornley, 1996) or "planning traditions" (CEC, 1997), this book focuses on the transformations of planning systems that have taken place during the past two decades, critically explaining the heterogeneity and diversity of planning practices in different EU member states (Stead and Cotella, 2011). Our main aim is to delineate the coexistence of continuity and change and of convergence and divergence with regard to planning practices across Europe since the 1990s.

The book comprises the introduction, 12 country chapters and a comparative conclusion. The authors involved in this book cover a variety of planning systems of EU member states. Based on the various planning systems identified in the *EU Compendium of Spatial Planning Systems and Policies* (CEC, 1997) and in the most recent study by Farinos Dasi (2006), at least two countries have been selected from each of the four different "ideal types" or "planning traditions":

- regional–economic (France, Germany);
- urbanism (Greece, Italy);
- comprehensive/integrated (Denmark, Finland, the Netherlands, Germany); and
- "land-use planning" (UK, Czech Republic, Belgium/Flanders).

Two more case studies focus on recent developments in Turkey (South East Europe) and Poland (East Central Europe).

All contributions follow a multi-scalar analytical framework, and refrain from reducing their findings to the national level, but focus rather on challenges and driving forces from the supranational level (Europeanization, globalization) and deepen their analysis with consideration of the rescaling of planning powers (regions, municipalities). They refer to five dimensions of change (scope, modes/tools, scale, actors and style), providing a fruitful base for cross-national comparison and conclusions.

The introduction by Mario Reimer, Panagiotis Getimis and Hans Heinrich Blotevogel presents an approach to the comparative analysis of planning systems and planning practice, the particular potential of which lies in the bringing together of structural and action theory perspectives, thus allowing the "blind spots" of comparative research into planning systems to be avoided. They first discuss methodological considerations of previous comparative research into planning systems. Drawing on the debate about the Europeanization of spatial planning, they then present the idea of a contextualized or context-based analysis of spatial planning, before turning to discussion of several theses concerned with the development of European planning systems.

Chapter 2 by Ole Damsgaard discusses recent changes to the Danish planning system. It was developed in an incremental fashion throughout the 1980s and 1990s but without any major changes being made to its main principles or to the scope of planning. Significant transformation, however, did occur from 2000 onwards with the creation of the Planning Act 2000, which introduced the concept of municipal planning strategies. The actual behavior of the municipalities did not, however, really change until after local governance reform in 2007. The new merged municipalities then had to define themselves in a new regional context for the first time.

As Sari Hirvonen-Kantola and Raine Mäntysalo highlight in Chapter 3, local planning authorities in Finland have been granted an independent role. The decisive role of the local authority has been emphasized within the devolution of power in a more decentralized planning system, while the adoption of local, unofficial, complementary instruments, mainly found to be economically expedient, has been enabled. This generates institutional ambiguity, but it also allows the system to react flexibly to new possibilities.

The decentralization of planning is dealt with by Wil Zonneveld and David Evers in Chapter 4 with respect to the Netherlands. The Dutch Ministry of Housing, Spatial Planning and Environment – known by its Dutch acronym VROM – was recently dismantled. For the first time since 1965, "spatial planning" can no longer be found in the name of a Dutch ministry. This is a clear indication of fundamental changes in the planning system in terms of institutional linkages, content and scope.

Hans Heinrich Blotevogel, Rainer Danielzyk and Angelika Münter demonstrate in Chapter 5 that the institutional system of German spatial planning, implemented in the 1960s/1970s, has developed notable powers of persistence, despite the fact that there have been fundamental transformations in, for example, understanding state activities or in terms of the challenges that spatial planning aims to meet. Thus, in addition to the formal planning systems, informal planning instruments are increasingly gaining significance on all spatial scales. Nowadays, both hard and soft modes of control are combined with one another as modern territorial governance.

Chapter 6 by Anna Geppert addresses the case of the French planning system. Her main argument is that French spatial planning has shifted from the "regional–economic" to the "comprehensive/integrated" ideal type, to use the nomenclature of the *EU Compendium of Spatial Planning Systems and Policies* (CEC, 1997). The chapter is based on a review of planning policies and discourses and on case studies from the author's research activities during the past two decades.

Valeria Lingua and Loris Servillo discuss in Chapter 7 the modernization of the Italian planning system. A series of innovative efforts to modernize Italian spatial planning has taken place in the past two decades. Their experimental phases have concluded, allowing for a better evaluation of provided benefits, missed opportunities and misleading directions. The chapter focuses on this process of modernization, analyzing issues, targets and trajectories, in order to highlight the strengths and limitations of the current trend toward a reform of the planning system.

Panagiotis Getimis and Georgia Giannakourou describe in Chapter 8 the evolution of spatial planning in Greece after the 1990s. The chapter aims, in particular, to analyze the main problems and challenges that have led to major changes in the Greek planning system, to explain the dimensions and the directions of change, and to highlight the role of various actors and actor constellations in producing change and institutional innovation. Furthermore, it focuses on the impact of the current economic crisis on Greek spatial planning policies.

Focusing on the case of Flanders in Belgium, Pieter Van den Broeck, Frank Moulaert, Annette Kuhk, Els Lievois and Jan Schreurs explain in Chapter 9 how spatial structural planning in Flanders is under transformation. The authors analyze the social forces that have, until recently, nourished or hampered particular approaches to spatial planning, and connect these to the deeper causes of the institutional dynamics in which these approaches are embedded.

Since 1990, planning in the UK has changed significantly, though arguably fundamental characteristics remain unaltered. As Vincent Nadin and Dominic Stead show in Chapter 10, the early 1990s saw the end of the fiercely neoliberal administrations that generally weakened the role of planning. From 1997, a left-of-center Labour government led by Tony Blair moved quickly to devolve government competences including planning, creating more diversity in the way planning is practiced in the countries of the UK. Strong efforts were made in the 2000s to change the "culture of planning," with new instruments from 2004 intended to strengthen planning's strategic function and from 2008 to speed up decision-making on major infrastructure. From 2010, these trends were abruptly reversed with the revocation of strategic plans, a shift to "localism" and a thinning out of national policy.

Karel Maier deals in Chapter 11 with the changing Czech planning system. Although spatial change in the period of totalitarian control was entirely subordinated to central government, since 1990 onwards virtually all spatial change has been driven by individual choice, while the planning environment has been rather weak and often without clear vision, mission and objectives. The chapter deals in brief with the most significant features of recent and ongoing changes of and in planning, making reference to the historic constraints that influence it.

Institutional change and new challenges of spatial and strategic planning in Turkey is described by Gülden Erkut and Ervin Sezgin in Chapter 12. Based on a short description of the main historical periods, the authors analyze the socio-economic and legislative changes regarding spatial planning, and the main driving forces influencing planning changes, both internal (administrative reforms, neoliberalism) and external (EU accession process, globalization), providing information about legislative and institutional change and its *raison d'être*.

In Chapter 13, Giancarlo Cotella reflects upon the evolution of spatial planning in Poland since the fall of the Soviet bloc. After 1989, the Polish government rapidly dismantled the socialist planning structure to welcome a new, market-friendly economic system. Within a few years, territorial disparities exacerbated by the neoliberal, macroeconomic approach called for a revival of regional policy and the reintroduction of spatial planning at the national level. The growing role played by foreign investors and progressive accession into the EU were among the many driving forces leading to the adaptation of Polish spatial planning and the introduction of self-elected regional governments.

The comparative conclusion by Panagiotis Getimis, Mario Reimer and Hans Heinrich Blotevogel focuses on the common or diverse trends based on evidence and findings from every country, emphasizing the multiplicity of continuity and change. The question of the convergence or divergence of spatial planning systems and practices (see the debate on the Europeanization of spatial planning) should, they argue, give way to the question of the multiple trends of continuity and change.

References

CEC – Commission of the European Communities. (1997). *The EU Compendium of Spatial Planning Systems and Policies*. Luxembourg: Office for Official Publications of the European Communities.

Farinos Dasi, J. (2006). *ESPON Project 2.3.2, Governance of Territorial and Urban Policies from EU to Local Level, Final Report*. Esh-sur-Alzette: ESPON Coordination Unit.

Newman, P. and Thornley, A. (1996). *Urban Planning in Europe: International Competition, National Systems, and Planning Projects*. London: Routledge.

Stead, D. and Cotella, G. (2011). Differential Europe: Domestic Actors and their Role in Shaping Spatial Planning Systems, *disP*, *47*(3), 13–21.

thus allowing the "blind spots" of comparative research into planning systems to be avoided. We first discuss methodological considerations of previous comparative research into planning systems. Drawing on the debate about the Europeanization of spatial planning, we then present our understanding of a contextualized or context-based analysis of spatial planning, before turning to a discussion of several theses concerned with the development of European planning systems and practices.

We propose that, as argued by comparative research on spatial planning in Europe, convergence tendencies can be identified. However, at the same time very specific adaptation mechanisms and practices can be detected in the individual countries under investigation (Healey and Williams, 1993; Davies, 1994), but these cannot be attributed to a unitary logic. This book and the chapters it brings together aim to tease out the specific relationship between change and continuity in the planning practice of each of the individual countries under consideration and thus direct attention towards the "diversity of spatial planning systems and practices" (Stead and Cotella, 2011, p. 13).

2 Comparative spatial planning research revisited: some methodological remarks

Comparative approaches have a long history in the research of (European) planning systems (see Newman and Thornley, 1996; CEC, 1997; Booth et al., 2007; Nadin and Stead, 2008). Attempts to create typologies and classifications of national planning systems have been greatly valued, as is the case with the work of Newman and Thornley (1996), which today continues to be well known and much cited in the planning sciences. From the perspective of comparative research into planning systems, their work demonstrates impressive strengths, but it also repeatedly lays itself open to criticism. There is no dispute over their observation of a close relationship between legal and administrative framework conditions that have evolved over time and the individual planning systems. The social status of planning is thereby derived not only from the legal and administrative tradition but is also dependent on individual "models of society," as "ideal types used to generalize about the diverse values and practices that shape relationships between the state, the market and citizens in particular places" (Stead and Nadin, 2009, p. 283). Therefore, spatial planning systems are not exclusively dependent on the legal–administrative systems, but also on the different socio-economic, political and cultural structures and dynamics prevailing in each country. Historically, different domestic structures and internal dynamics have developed in each country; these comprise economic modes and cycles (growth, recession, crisis), state traditions (Loughlin and Peters, 1997; Loughlin et al., 2011), welfare regimes (Esping-Andersen, 1990), political cultures (March and Olsen, 1989; Lijphart, 1999), governance modes (Sorensen and Torfing, 2007; Heinelt, 2010) and actor constellations (Adams et al., 2011a). Reference is thus made here to the complex interaction of societal cultures, planning systems and location-specific planning practices.

It cannot be denied that "classical" research into planning systems has focused on comparing institutional frameworks and structures relevant for planning. This has been associated with a clear overemphasis on constitutional and legal framework conditions, leading to a disregard of the particular, the exceptional and the "micro practices" (Healey, 2010) within these frameworks. In this context Nadin (2012, p. 3), for instance, argues that "a focus on formal description may hide as much as it reveals," and Reimer and Blotevogel (2012, p. 10) emphasize that "it remains a matter of dispute whether planning reality is in fact fundamentally determined by its basis in law." Indeed, Newman and Thornley (1996, p. 39) themselves point out that, at least with reference to Europe as a whole, the equating of legal framework conditions with actual planning practices entails a certain degree of risk:

> So far an assumption has been made that if a country has a set of legal and administrative regulations that relate to planning then these will shape and control the way in which planning is carried out ... The appropriateness of this assumption, though, varies throughout Europe.

In light of the above, it becomes clear that comparative research into planning systems has – to draw on the term "territorial trap" coined by Agnew (1994) – fallen foul of a "structural trap." Conclusions about planning practices inherent to the system cannot be drawn from a comparison of legal–administrative framework conditions alone. Furthermore, it has thus far been assumed that the national level of analysis is suitable for the comparative consideration of planning systems. However, this "methodological nationalism" fails to recognize that national planning systems are differentiated at different scales. This is particularly true for federal systems such as that in Germany, where national framework conditions are more concretely defined at the level of the federal state and the organization of, for instance, regional planning varies greatly.

This recognition has led to recent calls for a multi-scalar and relational perspective (Getimis, 2012), one that sheds light on the complex interaction of structural framework conditions and localized practices in spatial planning. Furthermore, a multi-scalar comparative analysis, without neglecting the importance of institutional contexts, focuses on changes emerging in a concrete period, in actor arenas and "knowledge orders" (Zimmermann, 2009) at different scales of planning practices (at the local, urban, regional and cross-border level). Of particular interest in this context are the "intrinsic" logic of place and the overlooked aspects of actor networks, knowledge and policy styles (Getimis, 2012, p. 26). A focus on specific actor constellations is necessary in order to demonstrate the mechanisms of the inclusion and exclusion of actors and their interests. Furthermore, key actors have particularly prominent positions as gatekeepers to certain resources (positions of power, financial funds, strategically important contacts and networks). Actors are also carriers of specific knowledge (e.g. scientific/expert, steering/institutional, local/milieu knowledge) that is fed into the planning process or indeed deliberately withheld. The specific interaction of actors and interests in turn characterizes specific "policy styles," understood as "policy making and implementation style, reflecting deep-rooted values" (Getimis, 2012, p. 34). This underlines the importance of contextualized research in the planning sciences (Sykes, 2008).

In addition to the overemphasis of structural framework conditions and the distinct research focus on a national scale, it is noticeable that in the past static descriptions of the state of planning systems dominated. These were unable to capture dynamics or directions of development:

Comparative studies on spatial planning systems in Europe have highlighted important differences and similarities in spatial planning traditions, typologies and ideal types. However, they tend to emphasize different aspects of the institutional, legal and administrative contexts at one scale of analysis, mainly the national level, during a specific period. Thus, comparative analysis remains static and does not allow an understanding of the ongoing transformations of planning systems and the important role that actor constellations play in dynamic terms.

(Getimis, 2012, p. 26)

Questions concerning patterns of transformation of individual planning systems have attracted research attention only in recent years. In particular, the stepwise extension of the European Union has led to investigation of the ability of individual planning systems to react and adapt (see Adams, 2008; Stead and Cotella, 2011; Giannakourou, 2012). In this context, discussion about the influence of European spatial development policies on individual planning systems is also relevant, although the notion of a Europeanization of spatial planning seems somewhat exaggerated. Only a differentiated assessment of the mechanisms and effects of European spatial development policies can provide an accurate picture (Böhme and Waterhout, 2008).

Within comparative research into planning systems to date, there has also been a certain degree of neglect of the significance of cultural contexts for planning action. Planning culture has sometimes been seen as equivalent to "the values, attitudes, mind sets and routines shared by those taking part in planning" (Fürst, 2009), but the question of how, for instance, such an understanding of planning culture fits into the concepts of social cultures, planning systems and concrete planning practices described above has not been answered. Although recent comparative studies on planning cultures highlight important cultural aspects of planning (Knieling and Othengrafen, 2009), they lack operational and systematic methods of comparative analysis and remain at an abstract level. It is the exception to find integrated analytical perspectives that use the concept of planning culture to compensate for the aforementioned weak spots in the "classical" research of planning systems (see, for instance, Stead and Nadin, 2009; Othengrafen, 2012; Reimer, 2012).

The weaknesses in past comparative planning research discussed above are, in our view, striking and require new theoretical, conceptual and methodological approaches to a research object (planning systems) that is itself often ill-defined. Thus, Janin Rivolin (2012, p. 64) points out that "the lack of clear definition of the subject of comparison seems however to be the ultimate obstacle to more fruitful observations and evaluations." With this criticism in mind, we interpret planning systems as

dynamic institutional technologies which prescribe legal and administrative structures for spatial order and structure, for securing land uses and for development within a specific defined area and which are manifest at various different tiers, i.e. national, regional and local. Accordingly, they define corridors of action for planning practice which may however nonetheless display a good deal of variability.

(Reimer and Blotevogel, 2012, p. 14)

Two aspects are thus the key to an understanding of planning systems. First, they are in principle adaptable and they can react to external challenges. It should nevertheless be noted that the degree of flexibility depends on the context and, essentially, on the maturity and functionality of the system itself. Thus, existing structures can exhibit pronounced persistency that can only be broken up with considerable effort on the part of actors. Planning transformations are dependent on certain actors of change. If these have active support from facilitating institutions and political forces, then planning reforms can take place. In contrast, if there is a lack of supportive facilitating institutions and politicians hesitate to embark upon the high political cost of planning transformations, then an advance preparation phase of persuasion and bargaining may be necessary. Second, the planning system context – that is, the legal and administrative structures – does not define planning activities completely. At most, it specifies corridors of action within which planning practice can move.

3 Europeanization of spatial planning: convergence or divergence? Or both?

The research on Europeanization has contributed new insights and explanations on the relationship between agency and change and on the impact of supra-national politics and policies on domestic institutions (Risse et al., 2001; Giuliani, 2003). Europeanization, understood either as governance, institutionalization or discourse, introduced different mechanisms and modes of governance· hierarchy, bargaining and facilitated coordination (Radaelli, 2004). How domestic institutions assimilate new challenges driven by Europeanization and whether there are convergence or divergence trends are open questions depending on the specific country, the relevant policy sector and the time frame.

European planning systems cannot be understood as static and immobile sets of formal regulations for planning activities, but are rather socially negotiated, adaptive and dynamic constructs. In light of this understanding, we agree with Janin Rivolin (2012, p. 69) who defines a planning system as a "specific social construct featuring the establishment and application, in certain institutional contexts in time and space, of certain techniques of social order and cooperation directed towards allowing and ruling the collective action for the use of space."

The "institutional contexts" addressed here refer primarily to the "domestic institutions" (Börzel, 1999) of individual countries that in a situation of increasing Europeanization are subjected to great pressure to adapt. The idea of a European spatial development policy, as followed particularly by the strategically oriented documents of the European Spatial Development Perspective (ESDP) or the Territorial Agenda of the European Union (TAEU), generates a complex "catalyst environment" (Morais Mourato and Tewdwr-Jones, 2012) within which national planning systems must position themselves. It is to be expected that the reactions (adaptation mechanisms and/or resistance) of the individual planning systems will differ greatly from one another. Three basic approaches to European spatial development policy that influence the "catalyst environment" can be identified (see Sinz, 2000): (1) strategically oriented, informal approaches; (2) formal acts; and (3) monetary incentive systems. The debate on the Europeanization of spatial planning (see Dühr et al., 2007; Adams et al., 2011a; Zonneveld et al., 2012) has attracted lively attention over the past two decades and forms the focus of the following discussion on the adaptation processes and resistance of planning systems in the various fields. Particular attention is paid to the extent to which the process of Europeanization is leading to the convergence or divergence of planning systems.

3.1 Strategically oriented, informal approaches to European spatial development policy

The influence of spatially related European discourses on the national level is especially revealed in the fundamental European goals and "European language" being incorporated into national strategies of spatial development. Servillo (2010), for instance, talks of "discursive chains" and "hegemonic strategic concepts" in the context of the goal of territorial cohesion, a term that has made its way into the nationally oriented strategies of spatial planning. Territorial cohesion is strongly related to territorial governance, aiming at the voluntary coordination and networking of actors. The "Open Method of Coordination" and the "White Paper on Governance" influenced the European discourse for multi-level governance arrangements, promoting the principles of participation, accountability, efficiency and legitimacy (Heinelt et al., 2006; Heinelt, 2010). However, it can also be seen that there is a fine line between European rhetoric and reality (Adams, 2008). Strategic spatial concepts such as the ESDP or the TAEU are informal and legally non-binding and cannot be imposed hierarchically, but through "facilitated coordination" and "bargaining" mechanisms. As meta-narratives of European spatial development policy, they foster European spatial development goals that in the medium to long term strengthen the European idea and attempt to embed it in the national discourse. Quite apart from any legally binding effects, their aim is to develop paradigmatic influence and to shape the "shared mental models" of the actors involved. In the interests of European agenda setting, they expedite learning processes that initially aim to change the cognitive logics of the actors and can, but must not necessarily, lead to a gradual adaptation of formal structures.

3.2 Formal acts of European spatial development policy

European meta-narratives can develop a power and momentum that should not be underestimated; however, there is no obligation for the national level to take them into consideration. This is contrary to the legally binding tools of European spatial development policy – first and foremost regulations and directives – that represent the significant and hierarchically imposed control competence of the European Union. Prominent examples are the European Water Framework Directive and the Habitats Directive. With these instruments the European Union exerts, within certain fields, direct influence on spatial development in individual countries and can directly enforce targets related to spatial development. Nonetheless, the formal acts pursue a strictly sectoral and hierarchically oriented logic and do not allow for overall cross-cutting coordination such as that aspired to by the European meta-narratives (ESDP, TAEU).

3.3 Monetary incentive systems of European spatial development policy

In order to increase their effectiveness, the European meta-narratives described above are linked to monetary incentive systems. These include especially the European Union INTERREG program. Linking particular spatial development goals with financial incentives increases their acceptance in the individual countries. Particularly in the East European acceding countries, the coupling of higher-level structural goals on a discursive level with the European Union's structural funds has led to the massive adaptation of planning discourses and planning systems (see the contributions by Maier (Chapter 11) and Cotella (Chapter 13) in this book). In these countries, the fragility of the planning systems following the breakdown of socialist-influenced structures led to a particular willingness to accept market economy and rather neoliberal tendencies, which were (and are) more strongly represented here than in other north-west European planning systems. It is already becoming obvious that it is important to differentiate when assessing the effects of the "catalyst environment" of European spatial development policy on individual planning systems. The degree of influence of the European Union can only be adequately assessed by considering the combination of the various tools and incentive systems. Faludi (2003) refers in this context to a "package deal."

In addition to the three approaches of European spatial development policy described in sections 3.1, 3.2 and 3.3, the role of the ESPON (European Observation Network for Territorial Development and Cohesion) network is not to be underestimated. As a European-wide network that focuses on spatial monitoring in Europe, it acts as an anchor point between research and practice, not only by continually gathering and transparently processing spatially relevant data but also by forcing the development of cross-border networking and thus launching processes of learning. The extensive documentation of the ESPON-based research projects thus makes a significant contribution to the exchange of experience and policy transfer between the individual countries, although Stead (2012), for instance, rightly points out the limits to the exchange of best practices in this context. Fundamentally, however, the ESPON network ensures the necessary horizontal coordination between different countries and thus represents an important element in the complex network of "territorial knowledge channels" (Adams et al., 2011b) in the frame of European spatial development.

Against this background, it becomes clear that the Europeanization of spatial planning cannot be conceived as one-dimensional. It should rather be assumed that there are vertical and horizontal approaches that have an effect on national planning systems only in their entirety. Adaptation processes are correspondingly complex; they do not follow a unitary logic and thus cannot be subsumed wholesale as supposed convergence or divergence. In this context, the Europeanization of spatial planning can be understood as a dynamic and contradictory process of "top-down" and "bottom-up" European integration. The incremental formation of a European spatial planning agenda in the 1990s, focusing on "territorial cohesion," "territorial governance," "sustainability," "environmental protection," "accessibility," and "polycentricity" (ESDP, ESPON) has influenced the domestic spatial planning discourse in EU countries in different ways (Dühr et al., 2007). Different intensities and paces of adaptation of these concepts and priorities in domestic planning agendas and in concrete planning practices can be expected. Although the emergence of the EU spatial planning agenda played an influential role as a driving force in domestic planning reforms, this did not lead to a complete "harmonization" of spatial planning systems and practices across Europe.

The complexity of the European "multi-level governance" described here requires a perspective to be taken that, particularly in the context of comparative spatial planning research, accepts the varying abilities of planning systems and practices to adapt and thus resist the underlying compulsion to create typologies and categorizations. The diverse empowerment of domestic actors, either to push forward and facilitate planning reforms or to oppose and even blockade them, enhances a continuing divergence of planning systems and practices across EU countries. However, we argue that a partial convergence is emerging alongside the "rhetoric" of the European spatial planning agenda and the main objectives of liberalization and deregulation. It is necessary to uncover this diversity of planning systems in Europe and the associated planning practices in order to achieve a more precise assessment of the tendencies of convergence and divergence, signs of which are found on various spatial levels. This book aims to contribute towards breaking down the logic of categorization and the inescapably associated blindness towards context that are traditionally strongly rooted in planning research. Although European planning systems all need to find answers to similar spatial challenges and thus display a number of basic similarities in adaptation processes (Lidström, 2007), the question of specific adaptation mechanisms has not, so far, been satisfactorily answered.

4 Context matters: a multi-scalar analytical framework for comparative spatial planning research

The discussion about the Europeanization of spatial planning indicates the necessity of an integrated analytical approach that focuses on both the structural framework conditions (institutional settings) for planning activities and the concrete practices within individual systems (actors of change). It is necessary to investigate the preconditions under which spatial and institutional challenges lead to adaptations of planning system characteristics (including legal configurations, tools and spatially relevant discourses) and to ask how these adaptations are carried through in the frame of contextualized "planning episodes" (Healey, 2007). We propose an analytical approach that encompasses different spatial tiers (Getimis, 2012) to consider the mutual interpenetration of (1) spatial and institutional challenges for planning that operate above the national scale (macro level); (2) the structural nature of a planning system that is usually constituted on the national level (meso level) and its ability to adapt; and (3) the planning practices inherent to the system (micro level) that are temporally and spatially very diverse.

4.1 Spatial and institutional challenges on the macro level

A distinction should be made between spatial and institutional challenges on the macro level. In terms of spatial challenges, it is possible to identify a number of significant economic, social and ecological developments that have equal relevance for all European countries, even if they are then dealt with very differently.

Globalization and economic structural transformation are leading to intensified locational competition. This strongly competitive orientation triggers not only a new process of negotiation between policies promoting equity and those focused on development, but also spatial restructuring in the individual countries. Particularly interesting in this context is the strengthening of metropolitan regions as important nodes in the worldwide net of locations (see the contribution by Hirvonen-Kantola and Mäntysalo (Chapter 3) in this book). A further question of interest is the influence of neoliberal ideologies on processes of spatial development and the associated danger of an "economization" of spatial planning (Waterhout et al., 2012). Neo-liberalism enhanced the "market orientation" of spatial planning through privatization, outsourcing, deregulation and public–private partnerships (Allmendinger and Haughton, 2012). It is expected that the prerogative of competitiveness and market-led spatial planning will gain ground across all countries, although with varying manifestations. In terms of processes of social transformation, demographic developments in particular are leading to grave changes in European cities and regions. For example, shrinking and aging processes affect housing markets, settlement densities, land utilization and the provision of public services. From an ecological perspective, the issues of climate change and sustainable energy currently dominate the spatial planning policy agendas of many European countries. Thus, especially complementary to discussions about strengthening metropolitan locations, questions of sustainable and climate-sensitive development strategies for these spaces are being pursued. Indeed, the potential of green infrastructures is attracting great attention not only in Europe but worldwide (Thomas and Littlewood, 2010).

The institutional challenges of spatial planning are particularly related to the ability of institutional architectures to adapt. Here it is similarly possible to detect a number of "European trends." As well as the issue of the effects of European spatial planning policy on individual planning systems, these relate primarily to the complex restructuring and rescaling processes that represent a great challenge for established institutional structures. Of particular interest in this context is the way in which administratively defined spaces and responsibilities work with (or against) new spaces and strategies that tend to be "softer," that require no administrative or fixed boundaries, and that are established and abolished according to need ("soft spaces" with "fuzzy" boundaries; see Allmendinger and Haughton, 2009). Furthermore, in many countries different responses to the global economic and financial crises can be expected, which could drastically restrict the scope of spatially related activities, changing the "rationale" of spatial planning, such as the orientation towards market-led and pro-growth strategies, the outsourcing of planning services or the weakening of strict environmental regulations.

4.2 Adaptive capacities on the meso level: planning systems between rigidity and flexibility

The spatial and institutional challenges briefly outlined above pressurize planning system configurations to adapt. If the findings of political system theory are applied to the field of spatial planning (see Reimer and Blotevogel, 2012), the challenges presented here can be interpreted as "inputs" that the planning system must process. The processing capacity of a planning system is revealed through the extent to which institutional framework conditions for planning action, which are usually anchored in law, and the fundamental goals of spatial development, allow such challenges to be adequately dealt with.

The pressure on a planning system to adapt is particularly high when either the legal and administrative framework conditions are no longer sufficient to adequately deal with known spatial and/or institutional challenges or when a planning system is confronted with new and selectively perceived spatial and/or institutional challenges. Thus, for example, it can be generally observed that the classical, formal procedures of spatial development are often supplemented by informal approaches. Such approaches exhibit a greater flexibility and a non-binding nature that gives them the potential to operate in a manner that fundamentally de-escalates conflict. It is also becoming apparent that new spatial challenges are rendering new approaches, concepts and tools necessary that have not yet been sufficiently tested or institutionally embedded. Such challenges include climate change and the associated discussions about the sustainable development of cities and regions that are (again) being intensively conducted, having been revitalized, for example, by the concept of resilience.

It is apparent that planning systems fluctuate between phases of stability and instability. Changes in basic framework conditions, whether they are social, economic, ecological, technological or cultural in nature, demand great flexibility from planning systems, although a distinction should be made here between comprehensive breaks and gradual adaptation strategies. An examination of many East European countries shows that the forces of overall societal transformation prevailing after the break-up of the Soviet Union opened a window of opportunity in which the fundamental issue of the social value of planning was renegotiated (see Nedović-Budić, 2001). It can therefore be surmised that the East European acceding countries showed a greater willingness to open up the national spatial planning debate to the European meta-discourse and the spatial principles associated therewith. Of course the role played by financial incentives from the European structural funds is not to be underestimated here. In contrast, the north-west European planning systems are subject to more gradual adaptation processes, where the social value of spatial planning is not fundamentally questioned (although it is very variably interpreted).

As described above, planning systems serve as structural filters by processing spatial and institutional challenges. The processing mechanisms vary greatly. So, for instance, in a comparative investigation of planning practice in Finland (Helsinki) and Greece (Athens), Othengrafen (2010) finds that fundamental social traditions and values massively influence processes of spatial development. The situation in Finland is characterized by great acceptance of the public sector and a fundamental trust in state powers of regulation, while in Greece a skeptical view of the state traditionally dominates and informal and unconventional planning actions thus also play an important role.

Drawing on the work of Janin Rivolin (2012), it is possible to distinguish between four dimensions within a planning system: discourses, structure, tools and practices. These dimensions are closely interrelated and can be applied as explanatory variables for processes of planning system transformation. In the discursive dimension, socially relevant foundations for spatial policy emerge as "hegemonic strategic concepts" (Servillo, 2010) that describe "the prevalence of certain ideas, concepts and arguments in the frame of spatial planning" (Janin Rivolin, 2012, p. 71) and may thus be interpreted as "planning doctrines" (Alexander and Faludi, 1996; Faludi, 1999). They affect the "structures," i.e. "the overall set of constitutional and legal provisions allowing and ruling the operation of the planning system" (Janin Rivolin, 2012, p. 71). The structural framework conditions also define the tools of spatial planning themselves; as well as classical plans these include "control devices, monitoring and evaluation procedures and various forms of economic incentive, allowing altogether a wide range of opportunities for practices" (Janin Rivolin, 2012, p. 71). The complex interplay of discourses, structures and tools on the national level defines a corridor of action for planning practice inherent in the system, as discussed in more detail in the following section.

4.3 Planning practices and policy styles on the micro level

The variety of planning practice within the system can be ascribed to the fact that the corridor of action described above can be very variably used. For instance, Oc and Tiesdell (1994) consider the situation in Turkey and identify contrasting planning cultures in Istanbul and Ankara, although the planning system configurations are the same at the national level. This touches upon the "urban planning systems" (Healey and Williams, 1993), the specific "policy styles" (Jordan and Richardson, 1983) and "steering styles" (Fürst, 1997) through which locally and topic-related planning practices are differentiated. Against this background, we propose broadening the planning system perspective, i.e. the structural framework conditions which guide spatial planning practice with a planning cultural perspective. This we understand as the concrete forms of planning action within individual planning systems that usually manifest themselves on a local and regional scale (see Reimer and Blotevogel, 2012).

Getimis (2012) draws on urban sociological debates in this context, using the term "intrinsic logic" (Berking and Löw, 2008) to refer to the context-dependent and differentiated forms of planning practice. In this way, he takes up a planning theory debate that proposes context sensibility in the analysis and theory building of planning research (Howe and Langdon, 2002; Cardoso, 2005; Van Assche, 2007). While Van Assche (2007) draws closely on Luhmann's system theory approach, Howe and Langdon (2002) and Cardoso (2005), for example, refer to Bourdieu's cultural sociological ideas. These latter two pieces of work represent a suitable starting point for discussion of the particular intrinsic logic of planning cultures, which can be conceived as specific and contextual configurations of field and habitus.

Bourdieu understands a field as, in the broadest sense, the objective configurations that determine the behavior of actors in a social setting. In a field, actors unite who have specific interests and are positioned in a particular relationship to one another. Every field has its own logic and history (Bourdieu and Waquant, 1996). In a field, actors become active and carry out actions. Fields influence the habitus, that is, the durable dispositions of actors that consolidate as unconscious schemata of perception and action. From the perspective of planning research, fields represent a specific social system in which actors connected by a concrete planning context come together and position themselves. A planning field of this sort unites the objective structures relevant for the action at hand; this includes existing physical structures, the challenges of spatial design and the derived thematic fields of action, the planning tools available, existing monetary and social capital, and the relational positioning of actors and groups of actors to one another. This macro context is supplemented by individual micro processes of context construction that are dependent on the individual habitus of the actors involved, which in turn determines the perception of field structures and guides action in a field. The dialectic of (planning) field and habitus can only be understood within its own contextuality and describes the intrinsic logics of a planning culture. It is expected that the reconstruction and analysis of these logics in terms of postulated "reflexive planning analytics" (Howe and Langdon, 2002; Cardoso, 2005) will allow deeper insights into the realities of planning practice.

5 Methodological framework for comparative analysis: some hypotheses

The complexity of planning systems and planning cultures (the latter understood here as the manifestations of locally and topic-related planning practices within structural framework conditions) described above leads inevitably to the dismissal of sweeping assumptions of convergence. Such assumptions are usually related only to certain aspects of planning, for example to the homogenization of spatially related discourses on the European level or the gradual adaptation of structural framework conditions of spatial planning on the level of individual countries. In contrast, the relations between the levels described here and the various transformative abilities are hardly considered. This tends to result in a blocking out of the parallelism of continuity and change within individual systems. Consideration of individual planning episodes (Healey, 2007) within planning research investigations is thus imperative, as only such an approach reflects the relations and roles of individual actors, the application of particular tools and processes, and the complex power structures. Booth (1993, p. 220) argues that

> the way forward comes from looking at the nature of the planning process. The decision to locate a factory, the developing of a long term strategy for a conurbation, the securing of a planning gain, are all products of a pattern of decision making which reflects power structures within a particular society. The power structures are culturally determined and the relationship between actors, though shaped by their cultural inheritance, is nevertheless in a constant state of evolution. The procedures that have been developed to handle the decision making and the plans which are used, sometimes as end products, sometimes as staging posts, are in effect formalizations of this unwritten pattern of power. They are the winks and nudges to which meaning is ascribed.

Although the contributions in this book will not delve into qualitative microanalysis of planning practices, the analysis of planning transformations is not reduced only to the institutional settings at the national level, but includes characteristic examples of planning practices (planning cultures) at different scales, highlighting the specific actor constellations and policy styles.

Our methodological approach does not favor the dominance of any specific paradigm in planning theory (e.g. communicative turn or cultural turn). Instead, it focuses on neglected aspects, i.e. actor constellations, scale and policy styles, driven from different theoretical backgrounds, such as actor-centered institutionalism and the governance debate, radical geography and the politics of scale. This book is intended to further sharpen our approach.

In the following, we build on these theoretical discussions by proposing a number of conjectured "dimensions of change" that are repeatedly addressed and differentially considered by the individual chapters. We focus on five dimensions in particular: (1) scope and objectives of spatial planning; (2) modes and tools of spatial planning; (3) scale(s) of spatial planning; (4) actors and networks in spatial planning; and (5) policy and planning styles. These five dimensions constitute the common methodological framework for the comparative analysis of the countries examined. The entry point of the analysis is the meso level (national planning system); however, it extends both to the macro level (challenges and driving forces) and to the micro level (planning practices).

5.1 Scope and objectives of spatial planning: turn to strategy?

For over two decades, the increasing significance of strategy-oriented planning has been discussed within the planning sciences (Albrechts et al., 2003; Albrechts, 2004, 2006; Newman, 2008; Walsh and Allin, 2012). In a more recent paper, Albrechts (2013, p. 52) suggests conceiving of strategic spatial planning as

> a transformative and integrative public sector-led, but co-productive, socio spatial process through which visions or frames of reference, the justification for coherent actions, and the means for implementation are produced that shape, frame and reframe what a place is and what it might become.

According to his view, strategic planning is to be understood as a rather open procedure that can supplement classical and formally constituted planning but that in no way replaces it. Technical logics are consciously somewhat retracted and planning in a strategic sense becomes rather a process of navigation that aims to align short- and medium-term operative planning action with overall guidelines and to simultaneously search for adaptation possibilities that can emerge from changed framework conditions (Van Wezemael, 2010, p. 53). Strategic planning serves "the development of coordinated or integrated perspectives that transcend traditional sectoral policy divisions through a specific focus on the spatial impacts of sectoral policies" (Walsh and Allin, 2012, p. 377). Strategic planning is particularly fueled by the increasing competitive pressure between cities and regions that renders new spatial development strategies necessary. The search for new local and regional identities, the need for new and horizontally oriented networks, and the process of Europeanization – particularly in view of the conditions pertaining to funding – makes new, usually regionally oriented strategies and principles a prerequisite for the granting of finance (Albrechts et al., 2003).

Against the background of this theoretical discussion, a "turn to strategy" in spatial planning can be expected. The chapters brought together in this book discuss the extent to which strategy-oriented planning logics on the various levels described above have penetrated spatial planning, and investigate the nature of their relationship to the more traditional planning logics (i.e. formally constituted and legally regulated planning). Here, interesting tensions within and differences between individual countries can be expected, as the characteristic style, content and meaning of strategically oriented planning approaches can vary greatly. Thereby, their goals and contents become the focus of interest. Precisely which spatially related meta-narratives are taken up within the frame of strategically oriented planning approaches and to what extent this represents a break with the past is an open question. Thus, it is conceivable that the pressure of neoliberal reasoning could lead to the role and status of spatial planning being fundamentally questioned and market principles winning the upper hand, while more balanced approaches lose significance. The individual chapters in this book also repeatedly offer insights into the varying processes of "spatial strategy making" (Healey, 2009).

5.2 Modes and tools of spatial planning: towards informalization?

In the course of a general paradigm change towards strategic planning, a differentiation of instrumental tools can be observed. This refers particularly to informal modes of operation and tools (Briassoulis, 1997) that lie outside the institutionalized planning system and characterize the "wider sphere (or field) of planning" (Sartorio, 2005). New modes and tools emerge referring both to general and specific planning regulations and documents and to formal and informal arrangements for territorial governance, enhancing multi-actor participation and networking. Although a trend of increasing informalization of planning action can be confirmed, it seems likely that the specific relationship between formal and informal planning will differ between the countries investigated in this book. The blanket claim that planning practice is becoming increasingly informal hardly seems sustainable. Much rather it is to be expected that both the formal and the informal foundations for planning action are changing and that it is the balance and interaction between the two poles that is of decisive importance for understanding spatial planning. It can be postulated that informal tools become especially attractive when formal planning reaches its structural limits. Informal planning tools oil, as it were, the wheels of formal planning, ensuring its functionality. It should be noted that the emerging new complexities of planning tools are expressions of two different "models of planning" that can be linked to the terms "conformance" and "performance" (Janin Rivolin, 2008). The conformance principle emphasizes the technical and regulative character of a plan that is implemented via a clearly defined, hierarchical chain of decisions. In contrast, the performance principle (see Faludi, 2000) underlines the fact that, quite apart from their technical–regulative character, plans can also fulfill strategic and informative functions (Janin Rivolin, 2008). Both principles interpenetrate and supplement one another, and characterize the institutional settings into which spatially related action fits.

5.3 Rescaling planning power: between decentralization and recentralization?

Insights into the limitations of country-based control and management have promoted a search for new action spaces below that of the level of the nation state. The "rescaling of statehood" (Brenner, 2004) has led to a differentiation in action spaces, with metropolitan regions in particular gaining significance. As obvious nodes, they contribute towards increased visibility in interregional locational competition. However, it is also necessary to address the question of the institutional anchoring of these new spatial units and to determine the appropriate governance and organizational forms that can ensure their ability to act. The "changing geographies of statehood" (Brenner, 2009, p. 124) are leading to polymorphic spatial structures that are no longer compatible with an understanding of scales as ontologically fixed geographical configurations. Thus, Brenner (2001, p. 592; see also Swyngedouw, 1997, 2004; Smith, 2004) establishes that

> traditional Euclidian, Cartesian and Westphalian notions of geographical scale as a fixed, bounded, self-enclosed and pre-given container are currently superseded – at least within the parameters of critical geographical theory and research – by a highly productive emphasis on process, evolution, dynamism and sociopolitical contestation.

The perspective explicitly addressed here leads to the thesis that the differentiation of action spaces in individual nation states and the associated new spatial complexity do not represent a one-way street. It is rather the case that the processes of decentralization and recentralization of competences interpenetrate one another, resulting in new patterns and architectures of state control and spatial planning. Thus, it is often possible to observe processes of "experimental regionalism" (Gualini, 2004) that make the testing of new "spatial and institutional rationales" (Gualini, 2006) below the level of the nation state possible, and that can be viewed as a significant stage on the way to a new "spatial fix" (Harvey, 2001). It is furthermore noticeable that, in many places, the phase of "experimental regionalism" often gives way to a phase of "experimental localism" (see the contribution by Damsgaard (Chapter 2) in this book) or alternatively to a strong recentralization of competences.

The complex rescaling of political orders and planning responsibilities is accompanied by a trend towards "soft spaces" (Allmendinger and Haughton, 2009). Functional principles of spatial delimitation increasingly prevail over territorial spatial delimitations. This results in "soft spaces" that supplement the "hard spaces of formal planning" and so offset the mismatch "between the spatial scales at which such planning is undertaken and the more amorphous, fluid and functional requirements of development and sectoral integration" (Haughton et al., 2010, p. 52). Soft spaces thus also require a change of thinking among planners as "wishing space always to be hard is illusionary" (Faludi, 2010, p. 20).

5.4 Actors and networks: shifting power relations?

In the course of the recognition of the limitations of state control and the transition from government to governance, cooperative forms of action have moved to the fore. The governance concept describes ways of controlling society aside from the hierarchical patterns of state order. It symbolizes an antonym to government, whereby the latter term describes the state as a controlling authority that delimits itself from the market and from civil society, and uses the implementation and enforcement of classical instruments of control like law and money to steer social development along hierarchical regulatory structures.

Governance implies and requires the management of interdependencies. The cooperation of actors from the public sector, business and civil society – as described by the ideal type of governance – requires specific regulatory structures for collective action. It can be observed that the boundaries between public and non-public spheres are softening, and thus different expectations and interests are becoming the object of discussions and negotiations. This makes it clear that collective ways of decision-making must be explored and institutionalized in order to generate the ability to act.

Successful interdependency management is largely dependent on whether the actors involved are able to channel their very differing logics of action so that shared goals may be developed that then lead to constructive, if not always harmonious, cooperation. In the more complex arenas of actors, the interests and logics of action formerly defined by the state no longer hold a monopoly position. They have to assert themselves in critical discourse with business and civil society interests and must be generally negotiable. Governance thus requires a high degree of openness and flexibility vis-à-vis numerous positions.

Precisely this type of control mix is typical of governance, and networks are a significant feature (networks of "arguing" and networks of "bargaining"; see Heinelt, 2010). They seem to be particularly functional ways of coordinating collective action between various actors. Networks are rather weakly institutionalized. They allow horizontal coordination of action (Fürst, 2006, p. 44) and are said not to impinge upon autonomy. In the course of the network discussion, reference has repeatedly been made to networks being fundamentally free of hierarchy. They are then conceived as the antipole to hierarchical types of control and it is suggested that interactions within them are channeled between autonomous partners of equal rank. However, the claim that networks are free from power and hierarchy has something of a mythical character (Blatter, 2003). In networks there are also gatekeepers who occupy dominant positions and possess greater power in negotiations than others. Networks are inevitably also an expression of geographies of latent power (Börzel, 1998, p. 256). The role occupied by the state as a central agent of spatial development and how the state positions itself within the complex network architectures are of particular interest in this context. It can be postulated that the state deliberately relocates parts of its control capacities to other scales, whereby the extent of this relocation of competences varies greatly. Recent occurrences in the Netherlands certainly represent an extreme example: here the state seemingly has reduced its central control of spatial development (see the contribution by Zonneveld and Evers (Chapter 4) in this book).

5.5 Policy and planning styles: coexistence of heterogeneous planning styles?

Planning practices are influenced by the different policy styles and political cultures. Policy styles vary from "command and control" to "consensus-oriented" governance arrangements (Richardson et al., 1982; Fürst, 1997, 2009). Political cultures prevailing in each country can be "coalitional" (non-majoritarian decisions) or "contradictive" (majoritarian principle) (Lijphart, 1999). Planning reforms usually attempt to introduce innovative planning practices with a consensus-oriented planning style. However, changes concerning policy styles are very slow, while the coexistence of heterogeneous planning styles is expected to emerge in the manifestations of planning practices at different levels.

Taking a political science perspective, Zimmermann (2008) thoroughly investigates the question of whether cities can exhibit local policy forms and thus intrinsically logical structures that differ from locality to locality, or if it is rather the case that the strength of overall social developments leaves cities without independent maneuvering room for local action and with a strategy of passive adaptation as the only option. This latter scenario would then lead to a far-reaching homogenization of local policy forms. Zimmermann reaches the conclusion that intrinsically logical policy patterns and thus also the differing results of policy action within comparable framework conditions have long been part of the argumentative canon of local political research. He furthermore states that the discourse about the intrinsic logic of urban governance does not merely represent a revival of the autonomy and decentralization debates of the 1980s (Zimmermann, 2008, p. 214). The fact that planning action cannot be seen in isolation from political contexts makes it probable that intrinsically logical structures can be identified within planning practice on the local and regional levels. This conjecture is pursued within the individual chapters of this book.

References

Adams, N. (2008). Convergence and policy transfer: an examination of the extent to which approaches to spatial planning have converged within the context of an enlarged EU. *International Planning Studies*, *13*(1), 31–49.

Adams, N., Cotella, G. and Nunes, R. (?011a). *Territorial Development, Cohesion and Spatial Planning: Knowledge and policy development in an enlarged EU*. London: Routledge.

Adams, N., Cotella, G. and Nunes, R. (2011b). Territorial knowledge channels in a multijurisdictional policy environment: a theoretical framework. In N. Adams, G. Cotella and R. Nunes (eds) *Territorial Development, Cohesion and Spatial Planning: Knowledge and policy development in an enlarged EU* (pp. 26–55). London: Routledge.

Agnew, J. (1994). The territorial trap: the geographical assumptions of international relations theory. *Review of International Political Economy*, *1*(1), 53–80.

Albrechts, L. (2004). Strategic (spatial) planning reexamined. *Environment and Planning B: Planning and Design*, *31*, 743–758.

Albrechts, L. (2006). Shifts in strategic spatial planning? Some evidence from Europe and Australia. *Environment and Planning A*, *38*(6), 1149–1170.

Albrechts, L. (2013). Reframing strategic spatial planning by using a coproduction perspective. *Planning Theory*, *12*(1), 46–63.

Albrechts, L., Healey, P. and Kunzmann, K. R. (2003). Strategic spatial planning and regional governance in Europe. *Journal of the American Planning Association*, *69*(2), 113–129.

Alexander, E. R. and Faludi, A. (1996). Planning doctrine: its uses and implications. *Planning Theory*, *16*, 11–61.

Allmendinger, P. and Haughton, G. (2009). Soft spaces, fuzzy boundaries, and metagovernance: the new spatial planning in the Thames Gateway. *Environment and Planning A*, *41*, 617–633.

Allmendinger, P. and Haughton, G. (2012). The evolution and trajectories of English spatial governance: "neoliberal" episodes in planning. *Planning Practice and Research*, *28*(1), 6–26.

Berking, H. and Löw, M. (2008). *Die Eigenlogik der Städte*. Frankfurt: Campus Verlag.

Blatter, J. (2003). Beyond hierarchies and networks: institutional logics and change in transboundary political spaces during the 20th century. *Governance: An International Journal of Policy, Administration and Institution*, *16*, 503–526.

Böhme, K. and Waterhout, B. (2008). The Europeanization of planning. In A. Faludi (ed.) *European Spatial Research and Planning* (pp. 225–248). Cambridge, MA: Lincoln Institute of Land Policy.

Booth, P. (1993). The cultural dimension in comparative research: making sense of development control in France. *European Planning Studies*, *1*(2), 217–229.

Booth, P., Breuillard, M., Fraser, C., and Paris, D. (2007). *Spatial Planning Systems of Britain and France: A comparative analysis*. Abingdon: Routledge.

Börzel, T. A. (1998). Organizing Babylon: on the different conceptions of policy networks. *Public Administration*, *76*(2), 253–273.

Börzel, T. A. (1999). Towards convergence in Europe? Institutional adaptation to Europeanization in Germany and Spain. *Journal of Common Market Studies*, *37*(4), 573–596.

Bourdieu, P. and Waquant, L. J. D. (1996). *Reflexive Anthropologie*. Frankfurt am Main: Suhr-kamp Verlag.

Brenner, N. (2001). The limits to scale? Methodological reflections on scalar structuration. *Progress in Human Geography*, *25*(4), 591–614.

Brenner, N. (2004). *New State Spaces: Urban governance and the rescaling of statehood*. Oxford: Oxford University Press.

Brenner, N. (2009). Open questions on state rescaling. *Cambridge Journal of Regions, Economy and Society*, *2*(1), 123–129.

Briassoulis, H. (1997). How the others plan: exploring the shape and forms of informal planning. *Journal of Planning Education and Research*, *17*, 105–117.

Cardoso, R. (2005). *Context and Power in Contemporary Planning: Towards reflexive planning analytics*. London: University College London, Development Planning Unit (DPU Working Paper, 128).

CEC – Commission of the European Communities (1997). *The EU Compendium of Spatial Planning Systems and Policies*. Luxembourg: Office for Official Publications of the European Communities.

Davies, H. W. E. (1994). Towards a European planning system? *Planning Practice and Research*, *9*(1), 63–69.

Dühr, S., Stead, D. and Zonneveld, W. (2007). The Europeanization of spatial planning through territorial cooperation. *Planning Practice and Research*, *22*(3), 291–307.

Esping-Andersen, G. (1990). *The Three Worlds of Welfare Capitalism*. Cambridge: Polity Press.

Faludi, A. (1999). Patterns of doctrinal development. *Journal of Planning Education and Research*, *18*(4), 333–344.

Faludi, A. (2000). The performance of spatial planning. *Planning Practice and Research*, *15*(4), 299–318.

Faludi, A. (2003). Unfinished business: European spatial planning in the 2000s. *Town Planning Review*, *74*(1), 121–140.

Faludi, A. (2010). Beyond Lisbon: soft European spatial planning. *disP*, *46*(3), 14–24.

Friedmann, J. (2005). Planning cultures in transition. In B. Sanyal (ed.) *Comparative Planning Cultures* (pp. 29–44). New York: Routledge.

Fürst, D. (1997). Humanvermögen und regionale Steuerungsstile: Bedeutung für das Regionalmanagement? *Staatswissenschaften und Staatspraxis*, *6*, 187–204.

Fürst, D. (2006). Regional governance: ein Überblick. In R. Kleinfeld, H. Plamper and A. Huber (eds) *Regional Governance: Steuerung, Koordination und Kommunikation in regionalen Netzwerken als neue Formen des Regierens* (pp. 37–59). Band 1. Osnabrück: V&R unipress.

Fürst, D. (2009). Planning cultures en route to a better comprehension of "planning processes"? In J. Knieling and F. Othengrafen (eds) *Planning Cultures in Europe: Decoding cultural phenomena in urban and regional planning* (pp. 23–38). Farnham: Ashgate.

Getimis, P. (2012). Comparing spatial planning systems and planning cultures in Europe: the need for a multi-scalar approach. *Planning Practice and Research*, *27*(1), 25–40.

Giannakourou, G. (2012). The Europeanization of national planning: explaining the causes and the potentials of change. *Planning Practice and Research*, *27*(1), 117–135.

Giuliani, M. (2003). Europeanization in comparative perspective: institutional fit and national adaptation. In K. Featherstone and C. M. Radaelli (eds) *The Politics of Europeanization* (pp. 134–155). Oxford: Oxford University Press.

Gualini, E. (2004). Regionalization as "Experimental Regionalism": the rescaling of territorial policy-making in Germany. *International Journal of Urban and Regional Research*, *28*(2), 329–353.

Gualini, E. (2006). The rescaling of governance in Europe: new spatial and institutional rationales. *European Planning Studies*, *14*(7), 881–904.

Harvey, D. (2001). Globalization and the "spatial fix." *Geographische Revue*, *2*, 23–30.

Haughton, G., Allmendinger, D., Counsell, D. and Vigar, G. (2010). *The New Spatial Planning: Territorial management with soft spaces and fuzzy boundaries*. London/New York: Routledge.

Healey, P. (2007). *Urban Complexity and Spatial Strategies: Towards a relational planning for our times*. London: Routledge.

Healey, P. (2009). In search of the "Strategic" in Spatial Strategy Making. *Planning Theory and Practice*, *10*(4), 439–457.

Healey, P. (2010). Introduction to Part One. In J. Hillier and P. Healey (eds) *The Ashgate Research Companion to Planning Theory: Conceptual challenges for spatial planning* (pp. 37–55). Farnham: Ashgate.

Healey, P. and Williams, R. (1993). European urban planning systems: diversity and convergence. *Urban Studies*, *30*(4/5), 701–720.

Heinelt, H. (2010). *Governing Modern Societies: Towards participatory governance*. Oxford: Oxford University Press.

Heinelt, H., Sweeting, D. and Getimis, P. (2006). *Legitimacy and Urban Governance: A cross-national comparative study*. New York: Routledge.

Howe, J. and Langdon, C. (2002). Towards a reflexive planning theory. *Planning Theory*, *1*(3), 209–225.

Janin Rivolin, U. (2008). Conforming and performing planning systems in Europe: an unbearable cohabitation. *Planning Practice and Research*, *23*(2), 167–186.

Janin Rivolin, U. (2012). Planning systems as institutional technologies: a proposed conceptualization and the implications for comparison. *Planning Practice and Research*, *27*(1), 63–85.

Jordan, A. G. and Richardson, J. J. (1983). Policy communities: the British and European policy style. *Policy Studies Journal*, *11*(4), 603–615.

Knieling, J. and Othengrafen, F. (eds) (2009). *Planning Cultures in Europe: Decoding cultural phenomena in urban and regional planning*. Farnham: Ashgate.

Lidström, A. (2007). Territorial governance in transition. *Regional and Federal Studies*, *17*(4), 499–508.

Lijphart, A. (1999). *Patterns of Democracy: Government forms and performance in thirty-six countries*. New Haven, CT: Yale University Press.

Loughlin, J. and Peters, B. G. (1997). State traditions, administrative reform and regionalization. In M. Keating and L. Loughlin (eds) *The Political Economy of Regionalism* (pp. 41–62). London: Routledge.

Loughlin, L., Hendriks, F. and Lidström, A. (2011). *The Oxford Handbook of Local and Regional Democracy in Europe*. Oxford: Oxford University Press.

March, J. G. and Olsen, J. P. (1989). *Rediscovering Institutions: The organizational basis of politics*. New York: Free Press/Oxford: Maxwell Macmillan.

Morais Mourato, J. and Tewdwr-Jones, M. (2012). Europeanisation of domestic spatial planning: exposing apparent differences or unspoken convergence? In W. Zonneveld, J. De Vries and L. Janssen-Jansen (eds) *European Territorial Governance* (pp. 157–173) (Housing and Urban Policy Studies, 35, IOS Press).

Nadin, V. (2012). International comparative planning methodology: introduction to the theme issue. *Planning Practice and Research*, *27*(1), 1–5.

Nadin, V. and Stead, D. (2008). European spatial planning systems, social models and learning. *disP*, *44*(1), 35–47.

Nedović-Budić, Z. (2001). Adjustment of planning practice to the new eastern and central European context. *Journal of the American Planning Association*, *67*(1), 38–52.

Newman, P. (2008). Strategic spatial planning: collective action and moments of opportunity. *European Planning Studies*, *16*(10), 1371–1383.

Newman, P. and Thornley, A. (1996). *Urban Planning in Europe: International competition, national systems, and planning projects*. London: Routledge.

Oc, T. and Tiesdell, S. (1994). Planning in Turkey: the contrasting planning cultures of Istanbul and Ankara. *Habitat International*, *18*(4), 99–116.

Othengrafen, F. (2010). Spatial planning as expression of culturised planning practices: the examples of Helsinki, Finland and Athens, Greece. *Town Planning Review*, *81*(1), 83–110.

Othengrafen, F. (2012). *Uncovering the Unconscious Dimensions of Planning: Using culture as a tool to analyse spatial planning practices*. Farnham: Ashgate.

Radaelli, C. M. (2004). Europeanization: solution or problem? *European Integration Online Papers*, *8*(16). Retrieved from http://eiop.or.at/eiop/texte/2004-016a.htm.

Reimer, M. (2012). *Planungskultur im Wandel: Das Beispiel der REGIONALE 2010*. Detmold: Rohn.

Reimer, M. and Blotevogel, H. H. (2012). Comparing spatial planning practice in Europe: a plea for cultural sensitization. *Planning Practice and Research*, *27*(1), 7–24.

Richardson, J. J., Gustaffson, G. and Jordan, G. (1982). The concept of policy style. In J. J. Richardson (ed.) *Policy Styles in Western Europe* (pp. 1–16). London: Allen and Unwin.

Risse, T., Caporaso, J. and Green Cowles, M. (2001). Europeanization and domestic change: introduction. In M. Green Cowles, J. A. Caporaso and T. Risse (eds) *Transforming Europe: Europeanization and domestic change* (pp. 1–20). Ithaca, NY: Cornell University Press.

Sartorio, F. S. (2005). Strategic spatial planning: a historical review of approaches, its recent revival, and an overview of the state of the art in Italy. *disP*, *41*(3), 26–40.

Servillo, L. (2010). Territorial cohesion discourses: hegemonic strategic concepts in European spatial planning. *Planning Theory and Practice*, *11*(3), 397–416.

Sinz, M. (2000). Gibt es Auswirkungen der europäischen Raumentwicklungspolitik auf nationaler, regionaler oder kommunaler Ebene? *Informationen zur Raumentwicklung*, *3/4*, 109–115.

Smith, N. (2004). Scale bending and the fate of the national. In E. Sheppard and R. B. McMaster (eds) *Scale and Geographic Inquiry* (pp. 192–212). Oxford: Blackwell.

Sorensen, E. and Torfing, J. (2007). *Theories of Democratic Network Governance*. Basingstoke: Palgrave Macmillan.

Stead, D. (2012). Best practices and policy transfer in spatial planning. *Planning Practice and Research*, *27*(1), 103–116.

Stead, D. and Cotella, G. (2011). Differential Europe: domestic actors and their role in shaping spatial planning systems. *disP*, *47*(3), 13–21.

Stead, D. and Nadin, V. (2009). Planning cultures between models of society and planning systems. In J. Knieling and F. Othengrafen (eds) *Planning Cultures in Europe: Decoding cultural phenomena in urban and regional planning* (pp. 283–300). Farnham: Ashgate.

Swyngedouw, E. (1997). Neither global nor local: glocalization and the politics of scale. In K. Cox (ed.) *Spaces of Globalization: Reasserting the power of the local* (pp. 137–166). New York: Guilford Press.

Swyngedouw, E. (2004). Globalisation or "Glocalisation"? Networks, territories and rescaling. *Cambridge Review of International Affairs*, *17*(1), 25–48.

Sykes, O. (2008). The importance of context and comparison in the study of European spatial planning. *European Planning Studies*, *16*(4), 537–555.

Thomas, K. and Littlewood, S. (2010). From green belts to green infrastructure? The evolution of a new concept in the emerging soft governance of spatial planning. *Planning Practice and Research*, *25*(2), 203–222.

Van Assche, K. (2007). Planning as/and/in context: towards a new analysis of context in interactive planning. *METU Journal of the Faculty of Architecture*, *24*(2), 105–117.

Van Wezemael, J. (2010). Zwischen Stadtplanung und Arealentwicklung: Governance-Settings als Herausforderung für die Planung. *STANDORT, Zeitschrift für Angewandte Geographie*, *34*(2), 49–54.

Walsh, C. and Allin, S. (2012). Strategic spatial planning: responding to diverse territorial development challenges: towards an inductive comparative approach. *International Planning Studies*, *17*(4), 377–395.

Waterhout, B., Othengrafen, F. and Sykes, O. (2012). Neo-liberalization processes in spatial planning in France, Germany, and the Netherlands: an exploration. *Planning Practice and Research*, *28*(1), 141–159.

Zimmermann, K. (2008). Eigenlogik der Städte: eine politikwissenschaftliche Sicht. In H. Berking and M. Löw (eds) *Die Eigenlogik der Städte: Neue Wege für die Stadtforschung* (pp. 207–230). Frankfurt am Main: Campus Verlag (Interdisziplinäre Stadtforschung, 1).

Zimmermann, K. (2009). Changing governance-evolving knowledge scapes: how we might think of a planning relevant politics of local knowledge (special issue). *disP*, *45*(2), 56–66.

Zonneveld, W., De Vries, J. and Janssen-Jansen, L. (eds) (2012). *European Territorial Governance* (Housing and Urban Policy Studies, 35, IOS Press).

2

THE DANISH PLANNING SYSTEM 1990–2010

Continuity and decay

Ole Damsgaard

Chapter objectives

The Danish case demonstrates:

- the evolution of a planning system from a traditional, top-down coordinated land-use system to a bottom-up oriented system, where values such as stability and logic are replaced by dynamics and individualism.
- However, evolution did not take the form of a linear unidirectional process but rather involved many different and often contradictory steps.
- Two examples illustrate the process and the role of the two main actors, the state and the Association of Danish Municipalities (Kommunernes Landsforening).
- Today the municipal level is the most important planning level with considerable and still growing variation between the individual municipalities.

1 Introduction

The Danish planning system has changed significantly since it was first put in place in the 1970s. This transformation has occurred primarily via both major and minor changes undertaken in respect of the formal planning system and, to some extent, in relation to the format and content of plans.

At the same time the role and powers of the various actors involved, the planning authorities in particular, have also changed. In the 1970s, a three-tiered hierarchical system existed with the state at the "top" and the municipalities at the "bottom." Municipal plans had to be approved by the regions and the regional plans had to be approved by the state. The state played a leading role, formally through mandatory guidelines in regional and municipal planning and through national planning reports. National planning policy was implemented through the regional plans and through the fact that the regional plans were formally binding preconditions for the municipal plans.

Today, the municipalities have – in a formal sense – been given the freedom to plan in their own way and to develop their own planning concepts. The municipal plan and the planning process in the individual municipalities are each able to play very different roles. In some municipalities, the municipal plan has the character of a traditional land-use plan. In other

21

municipalities, the municipal plan can have the character of a broad spatial plan including economic, social and cultural themes, and the municipal planning process can be part of the annual budgeting process involving the entire municipal organization, including the political bodies.

Parallel to this, the role of the regions and partly also that of the state has also changed dramatically. Now, the regions only draw up regional development plans that are not formally bound by the regional visions, while the state plays a much more reserved role than was previously the case.

This cannot, however, be easily represented as a simple linear change process from a "top-down" to a "bottom-up" system. Instead, change has occurred incrementally in relation to a number of incidental developments, both major and minor. Powers and tasks have been shifted around between the various planning levels, while the core planning questions and/ or challenges set the background for discussions that took place between various actors in the process. Some of the most important changes, from the 1990s to the present, and the discourses surrounding them, will be discussed in this chapter.

2 The Danish planning system

2.1 A comprehensive integrated approach

The modern Danish planning system was, in 1997, labeled by the *EU Compendium of Spatial Planning Systems and Policies* as a comprehensive integrated approach (European Commission, 1997). According to the *Compendium*, Danish planning in the early 1990s was conducted through a very systematic and formal hierarchy of plans from the national to the local level, which coordinated public sector activities across different sectors but focused more particularly on spatial coordination than economic development (European Commission, 1997, p. 36). Here it can be added that the main feature of the Danish system at that time was its ability to coordinate land-use between sectors and across administrative borders. However, the ability of the system to coordinate other kinds of activities and policies with spatial impact was very limited. Thus, as a point of departure, the formal planning system can in general be described as a spatial planning system with an overwhelming emphasis on land-use planning[1] (CEMAT, 1983).

Since the 1970s, Danish planning legislation has been altered substantially on numerous occasions and, in 1992, a Planning Act came into force that saw a number of laws addressing various sectors and administrative levels being merged into one Act. The latest major change to the Planning Act took place during the period 2005–2007 in connection with a reform of local government structure.

2.2 The recent planning system

The municipalities have had the main responsibility for planning in urban areas as well as in the countryside since 2007, when the regional councils lost most of their previously held powers as planning authorities to the municipalities. Thus, as things currently stand, only the municipalities now have the power to draw up mandatory land-use plans, while the regional councils have been left with the secondary role of preparing a strategic and rather general plan for regional spatial development. This regional plan has the character of a vision for the region without binding the municipalities to specific details in any way.

Since the 1970s, the Minister for the Environment has been responsible for upholding the national interest through national planning (Danish Ministry of the Environment, 2007), a function that was further strengthened by the 2007 local government reform. National planning is mainly expressed through national planning reports, binding instructions, guidelines and intervention in municipal planning for themes and projects of international, national or regional interest. This means that the Minister for the Environment has, on behalf of the government, the power to veto municipal plan proposals that are deemed to contradict national interests. In addition, the Minister of the Environment has specific powers and responsibilities in respect of coastal zone and retail trade planning (Danish Ministry of the Environment, 2007).

The Greater Copenhagen Region has always had special spatial planning status. In the period from the early 1970s to 1990 and again from 1999 to 2007, the functional capital region was covered by various councils with the power to coordinate and guide urban development and with responsibility to ensure cohesion between urban development and the development of the public transport system. After 2007, central government took over this role.

3 Problems and challenges

3.1 Introduction

The development of the Danish planning system took place in light of the urbanization and the considerable urban sprawl that followed the period of economic reconstruction after World War II. Thus, the primary focus of the planning system was to delimit and manage this process of urban growth and to ensure that coherent urban development took place not only at local and municipal levels but also at regional and national levels. Another important task in this small and densely populated country was to protect existing farmland from competing land-uses (Von Eyben, 1977).

This classical functionalist planning role was supplemented by elements of a more participatory mode of planning and ideas of ecology and the protection of the environment. Such notions were rooted in discourses and norms articulated in Denmark mainly during the late 1960s and, of course, inspired by ongoing planning discourses in other Western European countries at that time. An important part of the planning discussion and the public critique of planning practice during the 1970s was dominated by academics and professionals (Gaardmand, 1993) and it was often claimed that the participatory and deliberating potential of the planning system was underused.

The following sections are mainly structured along the timeline highlighting important changes in Danish planning legislation primarily in 1992, 1997, 2002 and 2007, while also looking at the rationales and debates behind these changes. Two distinctive changes in the formal system and the discussions around these two changes are particularly examined as examples of how new challenges are met at different administrative levels and, in that context, the role and behavior of various actors. The two examples illustrate a shift from a strict, top-down regulation system to a more multi-level, governance-oriented system. As a supplement to the discussion around these two formal changes, a 2009 evaluation that assesses municipal planning strategies is also included.

Figure 2.1 illustrates the relationship between the national, regional and municipal levels of planning before 2007. Overall planning decisions are taken at the national level and the decisions are implemented through the lower administrative levels' planning activities.

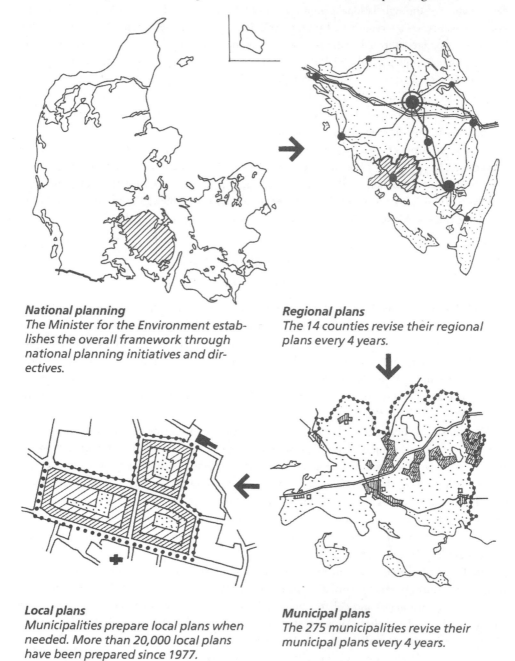

National planning
The Minister for the Environment establishes the overall framework through national planning initiatives and directives.

Regional plans
The 14 counties revise their regional plans every 4 years.

Local plans
Municipalities prepare local plans when needed. More than 20,000 local plans have been prepared since 1977.

Municipal plans
The 275 municipalities revise their municipal plans every 4 years.

Figure 2.1 Relationship between different planning levels

Source: Danish Ministry of the Environment (1995)

3.2 The 1992 Planning Act

During the 1980s, the planning discussion changed in character as local politicians supported by leading civil servants, planners from the municipalities and a few national politicians became more critical. Before, during the 1970s, as referred to above, the debate was dominated by professionals and academics and mainly addressed public participation. Now, arguments suggesting that planning had hitherto been too bureaucratic, too technically complicated and not transparent enough came to dominate the discourse. Furthermore, it was also claimed that the level of resources being used to maintain this complex system was simply unsustainable, particularly as the system itself was seen as being unsuited to addressing any future challenges and, from the municipalities' point of view at least, that local independence and the principle of subsidiarity were not being respected by the national planning bureaucracy (Gaardmand, 1993). One of the important actors in this discourse was the Kommunernes Landsforening (Associations of Danish Municipalities).

As a result, a simplification of the planning system was undertaken in 1992 where all planning legislation was merged into one Planning Act. Previously, sectoral planning concerning, for example, nature protection and the environment was carried out, resulting in a huge number of individual sectoral plans. After 1992, sectoral planning was integrated into the regional planning process, so, formally, only one plan (the regional plan) covered all kinds of land use activities outside the urban areas. This change caused the municipalities to frequently declare that the Planning Act of 1992 was meant to create a division of labor between the counties and municipalities such that the municipalities were now responsible for planning in the urban areas while the counties were responsible for planning in the countryside (Kommunernes Landsforening, 1998).

Another important simplification was that it was no longer necessary for the counties to give their approval to municipal plans or indeed for the state to approve regional plans. The hierarchy principle that no plan can conflict with another plan at a higher level was however retained, together with the counties' power to veto municipal plans that "directly conflicted" with regional planning. As a direct consequence, the National Planning Agency, on behalf of the government, became more detailed in their guidelines for regional planning. These guidelines were expressed as "national expectations for regional planning" and were launched before the revision of the regional plans, every fourth year.

3.3 The restructuring of the urban centers and retail functions

Despite economic recession and the fact that urban growth had been at a low level since the mid-1970s, the retail sector underwent tremendous structural change during the 1980s and 1990s. Centralization, new big external shopping malls outside the bigger cities and the development of new shop concepts had a visible impact on development, in parallel with the decline of the retail sector in the historic city centers.

In a report from 1996 produced by the National Planning Agency, it was foreseen that even medium-sized towns with 5,000–10,000 inhabitants could face an unsustainable future as centers with a traditional mixture of different kinds of private and public services (Miljø- og Energiministeriet, Landsplanafdelingen, 1996). A further observation that strengthened this forecast was that there was a considerable number of new projects for external shopping centers in the pipeline at that time, and that these more or less planned "new external centers" were all located in or near bigger city centers.

With this background in mind, the Social Democratic minister then responsible for planning, Sven Auken, appointed a committee, the main mandate of which was to consider how regional plans could seek to manage the future development of the retail sector and city centers so that smaller and medium-sized cities would be afforded a better opportunity to survive as centers. A further aim was that the environmental impacts of big external shopping centers, i.e. the rising transport needs in respect of private cars, could be minimized. Based on the recommendations of this commission, planning legislation was again changed in 1997.

According to the 1997 Planning Act, the counties were to carry out extensive and highly detailed planning concerning the future development of city centers, relating primarily to their localization and demarcation. The Planning Act further decided that regional plans should define existing and new centers according to their sizes in terms of the "square meter floor space" designated for retail activities and the maximum sizes of shops that could be accepted in the individual center. If maximum shop sizes above specific limits were not to be vetoed by the state, then the counties were now to be responsible for substantiating the proposals with facts. In general, the plans were to be based on evidence and specific evaluations of future needs for various kinds of retail shops (Miljø- og Energiministeriet, Landsplanafdelingen, 2000).

Furthermore, the new Planning Act decided on a temporary halt to new external centers and shops above certain (quite narrow) limits until sufficient planning had been carried out by the counties and followed up by the municipalities.

This very detailed instruction was clearly not in line with the "tradition" of how detailed the state should be in directing the planning activities of the counties and municipalities. First of all, planning legislation traditionally defines the responsibilities of the actors and formal procedures for the planning process together with some very general instructions concerning the contents of the plans, while the new Act contained highly detailed instructions concerning the methodology and required data, as well as the specific contents of the plans. Further, it can be argued that the instructions of the new Planning Act represented a rationalistic and quantitatively oriented, backward-looking style of planning. This style of planning was based on the understanding that retail and other services should be territorially organized in a hierarchical system and that the individual service center should reflect the size of its well-defined hinterland and its position in the hierarchy. Planning should thus act as a top-down corrective to market forces and ensure the individual citizen optimal access to services.

The new Planning Act was criticized by individual local politicians, particularly those representing the big cities with new projects in the pipeline, and by the big retail chains. The influential Kommunernes Landsforening was also very critical, but due to its members' often very different interests, it was generally unable to act with a clear mandate. However, the association did specifically criticize the fact that the counties should be left to demarcate the city centers, because they were of the opinion that this was a breach of the subsidiarity principle. Later, they launched a pamphlet (Kommunernes Landsforening, 1998) and took the initiative further by opening up a broader debate about the nature of the planning system as a whole (see below).

In this pamphlet, it was argued that the new law effectively froze urban development planning, that the law entailed a tremendous amount of bureaucracy and that it broke with the previously agreed "division of labor" between the municipalities and counties, etc. In addition, the association lined up ten specific examples of how the law's unintended consequences often gave rise to severe problems for cities of various sizes. Even for small centers, where the law was meant to act as a protection against the demise of the main retail centers, it was now shown to be the cause of some difficulties.

The new Act was, however, supported by organizations representing individual shop owners, local politicians mainly from rural municipalities, and by consumer and environmental organizations. Here, it is interesting to note that the arguments from the municipalities' side mainly addressed the question of power and not the questions of whether planning should or could counteract market forces or whether it was acceptable that certain areas could lose access to basic local services. The few planners who expressed their opinion in the public debate were mainly critical towards the new Act, for example arguing that the data needed for the planning process were too costly and indeed perhaps impossible to provide.

In conclusion, it can be argued that the minister and the National Planning Agency "won" this first round against the Kommunernes Landsforening. If the change in the Planning Act in 1997 is compared with the change in 1992, contrary directions of planning style change can be observed: the 1992 change represents a multi-level or bottom-up style of planning, while the 1997 change represents a top-down style.

3.4 The municipal planning strategies

Urban growth and the production of new houses in particular declined after the first oil crisis in 1973 and continued to decline throughout the following decades. In 1992, housing construction activities plummeted to the same level as that seen in the mid-1940s.

One explanation for this is that governments habitually used the level of public and private investment in building and construction activities as a tool to manage the impact of economic recession on society. The construction ban on public projects during this period combined with rising interest rates to fundamentally impact the production of new houses, while, at the same time, depressing demand (Gaardmand, 1993). The upshot of such policies was that the private housing market simply stopped functioning in such periods.

Another impact of the economic recession was the high level of unemployment generated during the 1980s and the first half of the 1990s. Many municipalities, however, used the high level of unemployment as a reason to continue planning and to lay out new areas for traditional industrial purposes, even though there was no market for the products that this activity produced. Together with the laying out of new areas for housing from the first generation of municipal plans, the result was a huge stock of planned urban areas that was simply not justified by the actual level of demand in the economy.

A survey produced by the National Planning Agency in the late 1990s concluded that several municipalities had enough room for the construction of enough new houses to cater for the next 25 years, while, in terms of construction for industrial and business purposes, some municipalities had enough room for expansion for the next 40–50 years, assuming that construction activities continued at the same level. The existence of so much room for urban development indicates that the land-use management system did not function properly and, in a worst case assessment, could lead to urban sprawl. At the same time, it could also be observed that a considerable number of the municipalities had not renewed their municipal plans every fourth year as laid down by planning regulation.

In fact, many municipal plans were more than ten years old and could be taken as no longer having any formal power as planning instruments. This fact was pointed out in a speech by Sven Auken, the minister responsible for planning, at the annual meeting of the Danish Town Planning Institute in October 1997. The speech was followed up by a bill in early 1998 that proposed that it should not be possible for municipalities to approve new local plans based on municipal plans that were older than four years (Miljø- og Energiministeriet, Landsplanafdelingen, 1999). If the bill had been passed through Parliament, it could have had quite a serious impact on the municipalities.

The Kommunernes Landsforening followed this bill with a number of activities, e.g. a debate paper launched in May 1998 (Kommunernes Landsforening, 1998). This paper was drafted by the association's administration but with help from a number of senior planners from the municipalities. The paper therefore had a certain professional "weight" besides the more political messages it espoused.

The political discourse of the document follows the line of previous statements given by the association, namely that the minister had disregarded the intentions behind the 1992 reform as far as the division of labor between municipalities and counties was concerned. Thus, planning in urban areas was a matter for the municipalities alone (Kommunernes Landsforening, 1998). This discourse cannot, however, be supported by any direct evidence in the legal texts or in the various guidelines produced by central government.

Furthermore, the association specifically emphasizes that the extended instructions concerning retail planning from 1997 were an example of how national instructions had resulted in a disproportionate level of bureaucracy.

The fact that more than 100 municipalities – out of 275 – had not renewed their municipal plans as laid down in the law was turned into a rhetorical question: perhaps the law was not in line with real planning needs and, if so, was it now time for a renewal of the entire body of law rather than simply time for the punishment of recalcitrant municipalities?

The notion of "real planning needs" was described with words like dynamic and quality-oriented planning. As such, the municipal plan could play a much more strategic role in relation to economic planning at the municipal level than in the previous situation where the state and the counties mainly focused on "minor formal and technical mistakes" made by the municipalities.

The relationship between planning and the citizens and, more specifically, the issue of public participation in the planning process was also highlighted. Instead of the usual complaint that public participation in the drawing up of municipal plans is too demanding in the light of the outcomes produced, the association wisely argued that because municipal planning had to be "automatically" undertaken in accordance with the renewal instructions every fourth year, and not when a real local need made it necessary, the law and the planning system itself undermined citizen interest and public participation. Planning at a kind of neighborhood level was proposed as a way to ensure a higher level of public engagement. This should supplement the formal municipal plan where the entire area of the municipality had to be covered, making the plan more general and abstract from a citizen's point of view.

Instead of entering into a public dispute with the association, the minister responded with the appointment of a new committee tasked to consider how municipal planning could be enhanced with a view to proposing specific changes in the text of the bill from earlier that year (Miljø- og Energiministeriet, Landsplanafdelingen, 1999). Seen from the Social Democratic minority government's point of view, the maintenance of good relations with the municipal association was at that time necessary because the government needed the association's support over the issue of public sector management in general and public expenses in particular. It is probably for this reason that the association was to be very well represented in the committee.[2]

The committee implemented the mandate through a rather open process during 1999. A number of seminars and meetings with different kinds of municipalities and roundtable discussions with experts and researchers were held, supplemented by surveys where all of the municipalities were involved. These initiatives were taken by the committee while the Kommunernes Landsforening ran their own parallel meetings. Thus, the committee's recommendations were already well anchored among municipal planners and politicians before they were given to the minister. It is also remarkable to note that the counties and their associations were quite passive during this process.

In the final report, the committee formulated ten main messages in respect of future municipal planning, which can be compiled in the following statements:

- The municipalities are different from one another and have differing needs in terms of planning; therefore renewal of the municipal plans shall take place as needed and can follow different tracks.
- Municipal planning is a question of politics and should be seen as a strategic and dynamic management tool.
- Public participation can be strengthened if participation is only used in cases where it is really needed.

Based on the proposal from the committee, the Planning Act was modified in 2000. The most important change was that the demand that municipal plans be revised every fourth year was replaced with the demand that the municipalities work out a strategy for municipal planning during the first part of every election period. This strategy was to be published and undergo the same public participation process as a proposal for a new municipal plan.

Hereafter, the revision could follow three tracks:

1   A total revision of the entire municipal plan following the previous rules.
2   A partial revision concerning one or a few specific themes or geographical areas.
3   The approval of the existing plan for another four-year period.

In general, the renewed Planning Act underlined the asymmetric development of the three planning levels. The municipalities gained the opportunity for a higher degree of diversity and also the possibility to become more individual and local-needs oriented. However, the counties' ability to conduct regional planning became something of a relic of the past, placed between the powerful municipalities on the one hand and the "top-down" detailed management of the state on the other.

Taking a bottom-up/top-down perspective, it is interesting to note that the 2000 Planning Act represented an extension of some of the bottom-up elements introduced by the 1992 Planning Act. This extension of bottom-up elements happened more or less parallel to the introduction of top-down elements concerning retail planning from 1997. In the fall of 2000, however, the Social Democratic Party lost the national election and a new liberal–conservative government was formed with support from a populist ultra right-wing party. A new era in Danish policy began that was to have a considerable impact on the Danish planning system. These impacts are reviewed below.

3.5 The local government reform of 2007

In October 2002, the new liberal–conservative government appointed a commission tasked with conducting a "critical evaluation" of local government structure and providing analysis for decisions concerning changes required in the public sector. The appointment came rather surprisingly after a relatively short public debate during the summer of 2002.

The commission delivered their report to the government in January 2004 with the inclusion of three alternative models for future administrative structure (Strukturkommissionen, 2004). Two overall objectives were present throughout the report: there should be a focus on the needs of the individual citizen and professional "sustainability" for the individual administrative and functional entity should be achieved. After a short public debate in June 2004, the government launched a fourth model that had already been agreed upon with the populist right-wing party (Dansk Folkeparti) so a parliamentary majority was ensured for the proposal.

The agreement defined three administrative levels and the division of labor between these levels. Furthermore, the agreement stated that the 14 counties should be merged into five new regions and that the future minimum size of the municipalities should be 30,000 inhabitants (Indenrigs- og Sundhedsministeriet, 2004). The municipalities were given half a year to come up with a proposal for how the future municipal demarcation should be structured or, more prosaically, who was to merge with whom? In early 2005, an agreement was made such that 270 municipalities could merge into 98 new units. This new structure was put into action on 1 January 2007.

In the meantime, the required changes to a large number of laws were adopted by Parliament so that tasks and competences were moved between the three administrative levels. The implication for the planning system was that power and planning tasks were transferred from the counties mainly to the municipalities but partly also to the state. The state took over responsibilities concerning the planning of the overall development of retail functions, planning of the coastal zone, water resource planning and responsibility for *Natura 2000* (an EU-wide network of nature protection areas), while the municipalities took over responsibilities concerning the urban pattern, retail, the environment and all the tasks associated with the overall planning of the countryside (Danish Ministry of the Environment, 2007).

The five new regions and the island of Bornholm[3] were given the responsibility to prepare regional spatial plans that were to outline a general development strategy for each region. According to a speech made in 2004 by the Conservative Minister of the Environment, Connie Hedegaard, the regional spatial plan cannot function as a mandatory binding plan for the municipalities, e.g. concerning land-use or other physical-functional issues (Themsen, 2008). In addition to creating regional spatial plans, the regions now serve the regional economic growth forums that are a partnership, including business, higher education institutions, the municipalities and the region. The regional economic growth forum guides the implementation of EU Regional Policy and the allocation of Structural and Cohesion Funds. The forum also has responsibility for working out the business development strategy for the region.

Following a partnership appointment, objectives for economic development were drawn up between the government and the regional economic growth forums. Here it is striking that these appointments were made directly with the growth forums and not with the democratically elected regional councils.

The regional spatial plans have to be in line with the business development strategy and they have to include the development strategies of the local action groups within the EU Rural Development Program.

There was remarkably little public debate concerning the changes made to the planning system in connection with the local government reform. In early 2004, the first indications from the government were that the new regions were to bear sole responsibility for the hospitals, and that the regions should have no right to levy taxes or to hold direct elections for the members of the regional council. But in the course of negotiations with the opposition (the Social Democrats), more tasks were allocated to the new regions and it was decided that the new regional councils should, after all, be directly elected (Jensen, 2008).

The Danish Town Planning Institute expressed a measure of mild skepticism. On the one hand, the regional spatial plans were evaluated as a promising element, while on the other hand the reallocation to the municipalities and the state of the counties' environmental and countryside planning tasks was criticized (Damsgaard and Rolandsen, 2004). It was argued that this could result in more fragmented and sector-oriented planning. The delimitation of the new regions was another point that was criticized, as important functional urban regions were split up into two or more regions. The worst case was that of the Greater Copenhagen Region which was divided between two different formal regions. As a consequence, the state gained power and responsibility for the coordination of planning in the functional capital region.

3.6 National planning after 2007

This new division of responsibility for the capital region was enforced with a planning report – *Fingerplan 2007* (see Figure 2.2) (Miljøministeriet, 2007) – which had the status of a national planning directive. The planning report makes reference to the classical *Finger Plan* of 1947 and continues the regional planning of the previous regional authority with mandatory guidelines for municipal planning of urban development, green areas and transport infrastructure.

5 KM

Figure 2.2 Fingerplan 2007
Source: Miljøministeriet (2007)

Fingerplan 2007 has the character of a classical land-use-oriented plan with detailed guidelines for the distribution of different land-uses and possibilities for laying out new urban areas in the individual urban fingers, etc. The plan divides the functional metropolitan area into a number of distinctive delimitated land-use categories, e.g. the central urban areas, the outer urban areas, the green structures and the rural areas. For each land-use category, a number of mandatory guidelines are formulated. This could be a close relation between transport infrastructure and localization of new jobs and service functions within the urban areas or that urban development within the green structures is prohibited. The layouts in the *Fingerplan* are mainly based on arguments made from a nature protection and landscape preservation point of view, rather than being seen from a broader regional development point of view where the recent role of the capital region in a national or global context is taken into consideration. The report can thus be generally said to lack strategic considerations, in particular concerning the future development of the capital region and the impact of the growing process of functional integration in the Øresund Region.

Another example of how national planning is to some extent replacing the historical role of regional planning can be found in the cooperation attempts of two major urban regions in Eastern Jutland and on Zealand. Here, partnerships between the municipalities and the national planning agency have developed visions for future urban and transport infrastructure development. A very strong focus on classical planning issues, urban development, transport and green areas is again clear, while broader strategic and spatial considerations are lacking, e.g. questions such as what is the future role of the urban region and how can the region cope in the future with growing national and global competition between urban regions and other major challenges.

This lack of overall national visions for the future spatial development of the country can also be seen in the national planning report from 2009. The report underlines that the municipalities, after the 2007 reform, have a very wide scope for planning (Miljøministeriet, By- og landskabsstyrelsen, 2009) and that the national planning report should politically define the direction of physical planning and the priorities for the planning activities of the municipalities and regions. However, the national planning report does not, in reality, fill this role. In a reply from the Danish Town Planning Institute (Dansk Byplanlaboratorium, 2009) to the public debate on the national report, it is stated that the report lacks specific messages on the future development desired by the government and that the report does not contain the necessary analyses of important trends and future spatial development. The Town Planning Institute, for example, mentions that the national planning report refers to the recently formulated national *Green Growth Strategy* as an important precondition for future national development but lacks any kind of consideration of the spatial impact of the implementation of the strategy.

An altogether different example of national planning can be found in the so-called *Plan09 Project*. The *Plan09 Project* is a partnership between the national planning agency and the private foundation Realdania, which financed the project. The objective of the project was to develop and enhance the planning competences of the municipalities after the 2007 reform. In the period 2006–2009, 27 projects were carried out in cooperation with 40 municipalities; the projects mainly addressed classical urban planning issues but also tackled issues such as public participation and strategic planning (Miljøministeriet/Realdania, 2009). In addition, the *Plan09* secretariat launched a large number of other initiatives: workshops, publications, studies, etc.

In short, Realdania is a non-profit foundation aiming at enhancing urban and architectural quality in Denmark. The capital behind the foundation was created in 2000 when the biggest Danish member-owned building society was bought by a private bank. Part of the deal was that the huge capital generated over generations by the members of the building society should be transferred to an independent foundation. The foundation is led by a board of directors elected by the (big) property owners, i.e. the social housing associations, some of the big municipalities and private property owners. The foundation allocates the returns from its capital, which total a considerable annual budget – bigger than the national budget for the same purposes.

Besides its non-profit activities, Realdania also invests parts of its capital directly in urban development projects, often in close cooperation with municipalities or big property owners. The foundation is known as being a demanding and agenda-setting partner when it invests; however, for many municipalities the direct economic support and investments from the foundation have become an important precondition for attracting other private and public investment and for the implementation of bigger urban development projects in general. The foundation therefore has considerable and direct influence on local and national planning decisions and to some extent wields the influence that used to belong to the state.

National planning after 2007 can be described as being less agenda-setting at the political level than was the case in the 1990s. The state has taken over the coordinating role in outlining future urban development in the Copenhagen Region; however, this has happened without any deeper consideration of the question of the future role of the capital region in the national and international context. At the municipal level, the state has focused on developing municipal competences and the quality of municipal planning in a partnership with the private foundation Realdania.

3.7 Planning at the regional and municipal levels after 2007

The first generation of the new regional spatial plans was launched in 2008 and was followed by municipal planning strategies for the 98 new municipalities. Based on four of the six regional spatial plans, the overall assessment is that the new, politically weak regional councils used the few instructions given to them by the state concerning the content and format of the new spatial plans as an opportunity to develop very diverse plans (Jensen, 2008), or rather planning documents very unlike the previous regional plans. Another observation is that the regional councils put significant effort into involving the municipalities and other important stakeholders throughout the entire process.

Content-wise, the new regional spatial plans typically addressed a few cross-cutting themes such as "the learning region" and "technology and networking" or "the global perspective" and "sustainable development" (Themsen, 2008). Furthermore, it was also observed that various themes on the contemporary political agenda were addressed in all the new plans, e.g. tourism and the experience economy were linked with nature and the environment or energy and climate, while rural development was linked to discussions on urban–rural relations. It was also striking that the new regional strategic plans did not focus on land-use or the urban pattern or, indeed, on other traditional planning issues.

An evaluation of the municipal planning strategies was made by the University of Copenhagen in 2009, commissioned by *Plan09*. The evaluation was based on a screening of the content of all the municipal strategies and detailed case studies of eight selected strategies representing different types of municipalities from across Denmark (Sehested et al., 2009). In line with the regional spatial plans, it can be observed that the various municipal planning strategies studied are very diverse in terms of concept and format.

On content, the strategies on the one hand reflect the catalog of themes that is now mandatory for municipal plans, but they are given very different weight from one municipality to the other. In relation to this, while the municipalities have taken over responsibility for the overall planning of the countryside, it is striking that of all 98 strategies only 40 percent address themes related to countryside development and nature protection in general.

On the other hand, the strategies in line with the regional spatial plans reflect different aspects of the contemporary political agenda, e.g. health, the experience economy, cooperation between business and universities, and different kinds of important events seen from the point of view of the municipality in question.

In contrast to the first generation of municipal planning strategies (Damsgaard and Rolandsen, 2004), the 2008 strategies are much more aware of the actual and potential territorial role of the municipality seen in a regional context and of being in competition with other parts of Denmark.

Based on the analysis of the eight case study municipalities, three different typologies of strategies can be identified: the narrow physically oriented strategy which primarily addresses decisions related to future physical development; the focused strategy that addresses a few development themes; and the holistic strategy that functions as an "overruling vision" and strategy for all other municipal policies and strategies. Seen from a management point of view, the three typologies are anchored differently in the municipal organization. For example, the physical strategy is anchored in the traditional land-use planning department, while the holistic strategy is anchored in a more central part of the organization close to the mayor and the overall management of the municipal organization.

Moreover, the municipalities studied have been able to involve local politicians actively in the process and, in line with one of the objectives of the 2002 revision of the Planning Act, it can be stated that the municipalities have succeeded in promoting political ownership of the planning process. It has thus been easy to involve politicians in the development of both the focused and the holistic strategies. In contrast to the situation with local politicians, the eight municipalities have not succeeded nearly so well in involving in their new strategies either the citizens in general or specific groups of stakeholders such as the business sector in particular.

3.8 Impact of the financial crisis

Denmark was initially only modestly impacted by the financial crisis of 2008–2009. However, the housing market in general cooled down and in the aftermath of the crisis some export-oriented industries experienced severe problems. Most well known from the Danish media was the case concerning the Vestas company, which decided to close down two wind turbine plants situated in peripheral parts of Denmark. The decision was used by different political groups as an opportunity to raise their voices on behalf of the periphery: the government and the state in general had to act if the periphery were not to experience total decline.

The liberal–conservative government responded in 2010 with a proposal giving the 30 or so municipalities in the periphery a more "liberal" and less restrictive set of formal planning rules in the coastal zone and in rural areas both in general and concerning the development of new large-scale retail functions. The bill was approved by Parliament in 2011. The argument from the government's side was that planning could be seen as an obstacle for economic development, particularly in the economically weakest municipalities. Less restrictive planning rules would help these areas to enhance their competitiveness compared with other parts of the country.

However, later in 2011 after the national elections, a new social democratic lead government took over and, in 2012, proposed that the specific planning rules for peripheral Denmark should be changed to take a less liberal direction. The argument again was that the government wants to help the periphery. This time it was suggested that the liberal rules concerning retail center functions might well be a threat to the existing and well-functioning urban centers in the periphery and that the more liberal rules in the coastal zone might jeopardize natural assets in these areas.

4 Dimensions and directions of change

4.1 Shifting objectives and the scope of planning

The Danish planning system was originally developed as a comprehensive integrated and land-use-oriented planning approach during the 1970s. This system was developed in an incremental fashion throughout the 1980s and 1990s but without any major changes being made to its main principles or to the scope of planning.

Significant change has, however, occurred from 2000 onwards with the creation of the 2000 Planning Act where the concept of municipal planning strategies was introduced. This meant that the scope of planning at the municipal level was formally extended beyond its traditional focus on the coordination of land-use questions and the management of urban development to encompass more proactive and strategic modes of planning. Nonetheless, the actual behavior of the municipalities did not really change until after the local governance reform in 2007, where for the first time the new merged municipalities had to define themselves in a new regional context.

An evaluation in 2009 recognized that the formal framework for planning is now used in very different ways by the individual municipalities, i.e. the character and the functions of the municipal plans have become ever more heterogeneous. Some municipalities use the municipal plan as a strategic instrument, others still use it primarily as a tool for land-use coordination, while yet others use it as an internal organizational tool in conjunction with the municipal budget. This tendency is likely to be still further strengthened in the future. Planning at the regional level totally changed in scope after 2007 when the five new regions were given responsibility for preparing so-called regional spatial plans. These plans are not land-use plans and have no formal power to coordinate the planning activities of the municipalities or other public authorities. The role of the new regional spatial plans is rather to function as a vision and inspiration for the development of the region in a broad sense, e.g. in relation to themes such as globalization and territorial competition.

In terms of national planning, two rather different trajectories can be identified after 2007. The first trajectory can be described as a very traditional physical functional mode of planning, e.g. the planning of the capital region – *Fingerplan 2007* – or the *National Planning Report* from 2009. The second trajectory can be described as taking the partnership direction, for instance where the government makes partnership agreements with the regional growth forums concerning future regional development, or the *Plan09* initiative where the national planning agency enters into a partnership with a private foundation with a focus on enhancing municipal planning.

4.2 Decentralization and re-centralization

During the 1980s and to some extent the 1990s, a process of decentralization can be seen to have taken place where power and tasks were moved from the state to the regions and the municipalities. In Denmark, however, this process occurred in such a way that the previous formal relations between the three planning levels were basically retained, as the state maintained the ability to regulate in detail planning at the regional and municipal levels.

One such example here was the change from a stage where the state had to approve in detail all regional plans and the regions had to approve in detail all municipal plans, to a stage where plans did not have to be approved at a higher level but where the state and the regions instead had the ability to veto lower-level planning if it contradicted national or regional planning. The veto right was in reality only used in cases where significant deviations emerged between plans at different levels.

Regions typically vetoed municipal plans in cases of new municipal proposals for urban development in protected natural areas of regional or national interest, or where environmental limits were not respected, e.g. in connection with the extension or new establishment of polluting or noisy activities.

During the 1990s, efforts to enact a certain amount of re-centralization occurred. This saw the state reintroduce an approach that relied on the highly detailed, top-down regulation of planning at the regional and municipal levels. The case of retail planning and the state's desire to compel the municipalities to renew their municipal plans every fourth year provide clear examples of this.

The 2007 local governance reform process can thus be conceived both as decentralization and re-centralization where, on the one hand, power and planning tasks were moved from the counties to the municipalities and, on the other hand, other planning tasks were moved from the counties to the state. For example, the state took over responsibility for coastal zone planning, the implementation of the EU Water Framework Directive and the overall planning of the capital region.

4.3 Changes in actors and power relations

During the 1970s and 1980s, the state played a major role both in a formal sense – by providing the regions and municipalities with detailed formal instructions for regional and municipal planning – and in a more informal way through the provision of non-binding guidelines for the format of the plans and the recommendation of planning methodologies.

During the 1970s, the public planning discourse was dominated by professionals and academics. Public participation and especially the question of whether the potential of public participation was being adequately used was a frequent theme. From the early 1980s, growing critique of the bureaucracy caused by the planning system arose, led by local politicians and leading municipal civil servants.

In parallel with the more active role of the municipalities, the Kommunernes Landsforening played a growing role both as a formal stakeholder in negotiations with the state concerning new national initiatives and as a major critic of both the regions and the state in the ongoing public debate over planning, specifically over the restriction of municipal planning. This role culminated in the late 1990s and in 2000 when first the changes of planning legislation concerning retail and later the lack of renewal of municipal plans led to the introduction of the concept of municipal planning strategies into planning legislation.

The case of retail demonstrates an example of planning practice in which multi-actor involvement can be observed. However, the minister responsible for spatial planning together with the National Agency for Spatial Planning took the initiative. The state was supported by the association representing individual shop owners and consumer organizations but was opposed by the municipalities, specifically by the Kommunernes Landsforening, and by the big retail chains. The regulation was discussed with the different parties but at that time the minister had the power and the will to implement the very detailed, top-down regulation of municipal retail planning. One result of the way the national level acted was that the municipalities and, more specifically, their association became more active and more aggressive in their discourse.

The second case concerning the renewal of the municipal plans and the introduction of municipal planning strategies was handled in a different and much more inclusive way on the minister's part, while the Kommunernes Landsforening managed to involve local politicians and leading municipal planners so that the final result of the process was based on a broad consensus.

One explanation of the growing influence and the increasingly proactive attitude of the Kommunernes Landsforening and of the more inclusive attitude of the state is that the social democratic minority government had at the time severe problems with the economy and needed a consensus with the municipalities on the issue of public finances. After 2001, a new political regime took over and the municipalities effectively lost this potential for influence, at least for a period.

The change of the Planning Act concerning retail is an example of a top-down style of planning, as the municipalities were overruled during the process and the resulting regulation contradicted the municipalities' understanding of their own role. In contrast, the change of the Planning Act concerning municipal planning strategies is an example of a much more bottom-up or, rather, multi-level style of governance where the municipalities had considerable influence on the final result. The result of the process gave opportunities for the planning system to be used in many different ways dependent on the individual needs and municipal differences, thus enhancing opportunities for local political engagement in the planning process. What is also remarkable is that these two changes were implemented over a short time span by the same government so that these two different styles existed – and to some extent are still practiced – side by side.

After 2007, the regions lost their formal power concerning spatial planning and the municipalities became the most important actors with very considerable scope for their individual planning. The municipalities in the capital region were the exception; here the state took over responsibility for overall spatial planning and coordination of land-use and infrastructure planning. The state took the initiative in *Fingerplan 2007* and in the establishment of partnerships with the municipalities in two other urban regions where the aim was to develop visions for future urban and transport infrastructure development. However, the state limits these activities to a narrow and quite static mode of land-use planning and does not include other more strategic and important spatial development issues.

Furthermore, the role that the private Realdania foundation plays has become increasingly noteworthy, particularly relating to the development of the quality of planning in the municipalities. This is a role that would naturally have been played by the state under the traditional system. Besides its non-profit activities, Realdania acts directly as an investor in urban development projects. This means that the foundation has a very powerful position and plays a double role, on the one hand aiming to improve the quality of the urban environment and on the other ensuring a good return on investment.

5 Conclusion

This chapter has primarily focused on the legal and institutional changes of the Danish planning system, including changes in scope, planning tools and the role of actors at different levels made especially in the period from 1990 to 2010. Further, the chapter focused on the discussions and discourses emerging from these changes.

As a system, Danish planning can be viewed as exhibiting a high degree of continuity up to 2000 where the traditional comprehensive land-use-oriented system was increasingly supplemented with a more strategic approach to planning, thus inevitably making the system more heterogeneous. After 2007, when Denmark's 14 counties were merged into five regions, the practice of regional planning has increasingly moved away from its traditional role as a land-use coordinator, while the municipalities have maintained the traditional approach to planning and, at the same time, have increasingly sought to make use of new partnership concepts.

As mentioned before (see section 3.8), a bill giving the municipalities in the periphery access to a more "liberal" and less restrictive set of formal planning rules was passed during spring 2011. This means, in practice, that three different variations of the Planning Act have to be followed in the 98 Danish municipalities: one variation in the capital region where the state coordinates the municipal planning; another variation in the peripheral municipalities where extended possibilities for development in the coastal zone are given together with the freedom to locate new retail centers everywhere; and a third variation of the Act in the rest of the country. The effect of this change together with the administrative reform of 2007 is that the logical coherent planning system described by the *EU Compendium of Spatial Planning Systems and Policies* in 1997 has now, 14 years later, totally decayed. The process can be perceived as one of simultaneous decentralization and re-centralization where the state and the municipalities have gained power but the regions have lost their spatial planning influence. Furthermore, the state has narrowed its own role and influence concerning the more qualitative content of the municipal plans and thus made room for the powerful foundation Realdania. For the municipalities, the new possibilities result in a higher level of political interest being shown in planning and huge variations between the municipalities in terms of the layout of the plans, their content and the way planning is used as a steering instrument.

Overall, when observed as a system, spatial planning in Denmark has become more fragmented and heterogeneous during the past 20 years. Notwithstanding, it is important to bear in mind that the economic, social and political context in which Danish planning has taken place over the past 20 years has changed dramatically. This, in effect, means that the challenges and opportunities faced, together with the values and the mindsets of the actors involved, cannot realistically be compared.

Notes

1 There are numerous definitions of spatial planning. One of the earliest definitions comes from the European Regional/Spatial Planning Charter (often called the Torremolinos Charter), adopted in 1983 by the European Conference of Ministers responsible for Regional Planning (CEMAT, 1983, p. 13): "Regional/spatial planning gives geographical expression to the economic, social, cultural and ecological policies of society. It is at the same time a scientific discipline, an administrative technique and a policy developed as an interdisciplinary and comprehensive approach directed towards a balanced regional development and the physical organisation of space according to an overall strategy."
2 There were eight members of the committee, three members from the national level, three members from the Kommunernes Landsforening, one from the Association of Danish Counties and one from the Municipality of Copenhagen, which at that time was not a member of the Kommunernes Landsforening. The Kommunernes Landsforening appointed their managing director, a head of department and a director from one of the big municipalities as their representatives, while the Association of Danish Counties appointed a civil servant without any rank as head or chief in the organization.
3 The island of Bornholm with its 50,000 inhabitants became a part of the capital region but kept its autonomous status concerning regional development policy.

References

CEMAT – Council of Europe conference of ministers responsible for spatial/regional planning. (1983). European Regional/Spatial Planning Charter. Retrieved from www.coe.int/t/dg4/cultureheritage/heritage/cemat/versioncharte/Charte_bil.pdf.

Damsgaard, O. and Rolandsen, S. E. (2004). *Plansystemet, hvordan virker det?* Copenhagen: Realdania Medlemsdebat.

Danish Ministry of the Environment. (1995). *Spatial Planning in Denmark* (p. 9). Copenhagen: Ministry of the Environment, Spatial Planning Department.

Danish Ministry of the Environment. (2007). *Spatial Planning in Denmark*. Copenhagen: Ministry of the Environment, Spatial Planning Department.

Dansk Byplanlaboratorium. (2009). Refleksioner over foslag til Landsplanredegørelse 2009. Retrieved from www.byplanlab.dk/?q=node/395.

European Commission. (1997). *The EU Compendium of Spatial Planning Systems and Policies, EU Compendium No 28*. Brussels: European Commission.

Gaardmand, A. (1993). *Dansk Byplanlægning 1938–1992*. Copenhagen: Arkitektens Forlag.

Indenrigs- og Sundhedsministeriet. (2004). *Aftale om strukturreformen*. Copenhagen: Indenrigs- og Sundhedsministeriet.

Jensen, J. U. (2008). En ny plan og en ny samarbejdsmodel. *BYPLAN NYT*, 2, 4–7.

Kommunernes Landsforening. (1998). *Forenkling og fornyelse på planområdet. Oplæg til debat med kommunerne om kommunernes fremtidige udvikling.* Copenhagen: Kommunernes Landsforening, Kontoret for Tekinik og Miljø.

Miljø- og Energiministeriet, Landsplanafdelingen. (1996). *Detailhandelsudvalgets rapport.* Copenhagen: Miljø- og Energiministeriet, Landsplanafdelingen.

Miljø- og Energiministeriet, Landsplanafdelingen. (1999). *Strategi og kommuneplanlægning. Rapport fra Udvalget om fornyelse i kommuneplanlægningen.* Copenhagen: Miljø- og Energiministeriet, Landsplanafdelingen.

Miljø- og Energiministeriet, Landsplanafdelingen. (2000). *Udviklingen i region-, kommune- og lokalplanlægningen for detailhandelsstrukturen.* Copenhagen: Miljø- og Energiministeriet, Landsplanafdelingen.

Miljøministeriet. (2007). *Forslag til Fingerplan 2007. Landsplandirektiv for hovedstadsområdets planlægning.* Copenhagen: Miljøministeriet, Skov- og Naturstyrelsen.

Miljøministeriet (2009). *Forslag til Landsplanredegørelse 2009.* By- og Landskabsstyrelsen.

Miljøministeriet/Realdania. (2009). *Udvikling af Plankultur I. 27 kommunale eksempler.* Copenhagen: Plan09.

Sehested, K., Groth, N. B. and Caspersen, O. (2009). Evaluering af kommuneplanstrategier: notat 3: case-beskrivelser – tværgående analyse – konklusion. *Arbejdsrapport Skov and Landskab*, 63/2009. Copenhagen: Skov and Landskab, Københavns Universitet.

Strukturkommissionen. (2004). *Strukturkommissionens Betænkning.* Copenhagen: Strukturkommissionen.

Themsen, B. (2008). RUP og stub. *BYPLAN NYT*, 2, 10–13.

Von Eyben, W. E. (1977). *Dansk Miljøret.* Copenhagen: Akademisk Forlag.

Further reading

Galland, D. and Enemark, S. (2013). The shifting scope of spatial planning: assessing the impact of structural reforms on planning systems and policies. *European Journal of Spatial Development*, 52.

Olesen, K. (2010). Danish strategic spatial planning in transition. 24th AESOP Annual Conference, Finland. Retrieved from http://vbn.aau.dk/files/43876932/Danish_strategic_spatial_planning_in_transition_Kristian_Olesen.pdf.

The Danish Nature Agency. (2007). Spatial planning in Denmark. Retrieved from www.naturstyrelsen.dk/Planlaegning/Planlaegning_i_byer/Udgivelser_og_vejledninger/Udgivelser/Udgivelser.htm#andre_sprog.

3

THE RECENT DEVELOPMENT OF THE FINNISH PLANNING SYSTEM

The city of Vantaa as an executor, fighter and independent actor

Sari Hirvonen-Kantola and Raine Mäntysalo

Chapter objectives

The objectives of the chapter are:

- to show that the Finnish land-use planning system established in 1958 has mainly been retained, but major changes can be identified concerning strategic land-use planning;
- to stress that the decisive role of the local authority has been highlighted;
- to illustrate that the focus of the Finnish land-use planning system has shifted from the viewpoint of planning substance into process;
- to conclude that, in order to enhance sustainability, institutional reforms and better instruments for integrated cross-sector planning, coupled with a two-way evaluation and continuous monitoring of urban and regional development, with relevant indicators of sustainability, are needed.

1 Introduction

This chapter describes the development of the Finnish planning system, examining changes and discussions about legislation, planning instruments used and the way these combine with planning ideologies, the national political context and economic opportunities.

As a feasibility study, a descriptive case study of 50 years of planning history in the city of Vantaa has been conducted (Hirvonen, 2005, 2007), and a study on integrative planning practices in Vantaa is also being carried out. The city grew from a rural commune into an inseparable part of the Helsinki Metropolitan Region (HMR). The city evolved simultaneously with the Finnish planning system, making it a revealing case – although the depiction is also specific since only one metropolitan region exists in Finland. This study describes the development of the planning system by building on a survey of critical literature, and elucidates the description with the results of the feasibility study.

We focus on the past two decades, but also introduce the relevant trajectories of the planning system prior to this. After describing the Finnish planning system, we discuss its contemporary challenges, and finally examine the future directions of development.

1.1 Development trajectories of the Finnish planning system

There are four major trajectories preceding and explaining the current state of the planning system: the establishment of the zoning system (1.1.1), the establishment of a planning hierarchy (1.1.2), the emergence of the land-use agreement system (1.1.3) and the decentralization of the service system (1.1.4).

1.1.1 Establishment of the zoning system

The zoning system was created to structure planning in the spirit of functionalism. Urban sprawl was becoming a problem around the capital, engendering the need for zoning private land. Independent municipalities finally gained a planning monopoly in 1968, but the first prerequisites for urban planning were established in the Town Planning Act which came into force in 1932 (Laki taajaväkisistä maalaisyhdyskunnista 1931/185). This became a necessity after World War II, when Finland needed to accommodate evacuees and undergo structural change from a rural community into an urbanizing country.

At this stage, the urban planning organization of Vantaa was nothing more than a spectator in a rural and unplanned suburb. The impetus to plan arose from technical necessities. A few planners tried to control wild land parceling, to bring some expertise to the commune so that it could deal with the regional cooperative planning organization that was led by the capital Helsinki, to support existing local industrial policies and to plan municipal engineering (Hirvonen, 2007).

1.1.2 Establishment of a planning hierarchy

The hierarchical political control system was established to execute plans in the spirit of rationalism. National planning began in 1956 with the establishment of the National Planning Agency. It was supposed to focus on land-use, but was broadened to cover education, industry, transport and social planning – namely into fields relevant for encouraging society to develop. Along with the beginning of the social planning system, the Building Act (Rakennuslaki 1958/370) established a hierarchical urban planning system in 1958, with strong central government steering and general planning guiding detailed planning. In the 1960s and 1970s, this rationalist and hierarchical system was supposed to deliver the super ideology of the Nordic social democratic welfare state (Vuorela, 1991, pp. 100, 102; Haimi, 2000, p. 171).

The methods of implementation were land-use planning, economic planning and sector plans, which were economically supervised (Vuorela, 1991, pp. 101–103; Haimi, 2000, p. 157). Rationalist planning was not practiced in all sectors of planning, but it was applied in general municipal planning and land-use planning (Haimi, 2000, p. 254). Planning work was organized hierarchically as well; the main goals in the municipalities were in target plans, which were set by politicians. In the period 1977–1995, the Communal Law (Kunnallislaki 1976/953) obligated local governments to make at least a five-year municipal plan (Haimi, 2000, p. 172), which was in close cooperation with land-use master planning (Airamo and Permanto, 1997, p. 62). Land-use planning was supervised by the central government from 1958 to 2000. Regional plans and general plans, as well as the majority of detailed plans, were ratified by the Ministry of the Interior and later by the Ministry of the Environment.

2.1 Levels of land-use planning

There is no national plan in Finland. The government formulates the National Regional Development Targets that specify the goals of the Regional Development Act (Laki alueiden kehittämisestä 2009/1651) and establishes the priorities of regional development measures at the national level for the government's term of office. The decision aims to strengthen regional competitiveness, which ensures that the regions can operate efficiently in an open economy. The aim is also to secure the basic infrastructure and the standard of service, and to create a regional structure that enables smoother economic development and employment throughout the country. The government also formulates the National Land Use Guidelines, which are advisory. They steer policy on land-use issues that are important for the whole country; they relate to the regional and urban structure, the quality of the living environment, communication networks, energy supply, natural and cultural heritage, and the use of natural resources (Ympäristöministeriö, 2009b).

One reason for establishing the National Land Use Guidelines is that, previously, national goals were inadequately and slowly transmitted to local planning through regional land-use plans (Puustinen and Hirvonen, 2005, p. 62; Ympäristöministeriö, 2009b). Among the central goals of the National Land Use Guidelines is the connection of the Helsinki-Vantaa Airport to the regional commuter rail network. Nevertheless, from the early 1990s to 2009, Vantaa had to wait for the decision on the biggest investment in its history, the Ring Rail Line which will connect Helsinki-Vantaa Airport, the adjacent Aviapolis business and retail district and substantial future residential areas to the Helsinki commuter rail network.

The actual land-use planning instruments include, in hierarchical order, regional plans, master plans and detailed plans (Table 3.3). All of them are legally binding – with the exception of master plans, which are optional in this regard. When a legally binding land-use plan is ratified, it replaces the higher-level plan in its area.

The regional plan is aimed at directing land-use planning at the local level. The plan has had special significance in adjusting national, regional and local aims. However, the effect of regional plans on municipal planning is rather weak (see e.g. Puustinen and Hirvonen, 2005; Jauhiainen and Niemenmaa, 2006, p. 83; Koski, 2007; Sairinen, 2009, p. 277; Ympäristöministeriö, 2009a; Mäntysalo et al., 2010).

Municipalities draft their own local land-use plans (master and detailed plans), and the powers of approval and ratification are given to the local municipal councils. The neighboring municipalities also have the option of drafting joint master plans. These must be approved by the regional council, a joint authority co-established by the municipalities, and then ratified

Table 3.1 The land-use planning system in Finland

	Planning authority	Planning instrument	Legal effect
National level	Government	National land-use guidelines	Advisory
Regional level	Regional councils	Regional plan	Binding
Local level	Municipal councils	Optional joint master plan	Optional
		Master plan	Optional
		Detailed plan	Binding

by the Ministry of the Environment. The master plan may be drawn up to cover all or a part of a municipality, or several municipalities jointly. The local master plans, which usually are given legally binding status, determine the overall land-use framework of the municipalities, thereby offering guidelines for the local detailed plans.

The detailed plans regulate development by defining building rights, efficiencies, dimensions and functions in detail, attached to landowning information. A detailed plan may cover whole residential districts or sometimes just a single plot. Plans can be initiated and paid for by both landowners and municipalities. Investors and the Ministry of the Environment expect speedy preparation of detailed plans.

2.2 Formal planning hierarchy challenged

Actual planning practice in Finland seldom conforms to the formal planning hierarchy. *Ad hoc* projects appear to counter the strategic guidelines defined at higher planning levels. There have been various case studies of clashes between project-oriented and strategic land-use planning (for example, Tulkki, 1994; Vesala, 1994; Jauhiainen, 1995; Mäenpää et al., 2000; Rajaniemi, 2006; Mäntysalo, 2008). In some cases, the clash has led to divisions between leading administrators and their departments, the planning department defending the planning hierarchy, and the building and real-estate department pressing for project-generated development (see Tulkki, 1994; Mäenpää et al., 2000; Rajaniemi, 2006).

On some occasions, the latter has also been the case in Vantaa. For instance, a shopping mall's total floor space, restricted to 45,000m^2 by the Ministry of the Environment in 1989, was interpreted to denote the floorspace of the actual store areas only, thus allowing the total floorspace of the building to become considerably bigger (Hirvonen, 2007, pp. 149–151). This resulted in the Jumbo shopping center, the second largest shopping mall in Finland at the time, a decision that knocked master planners as well.

2.3 Landowner rights

Landowner rights are exceptionally well protected in the LBA. At each planning level, the requirements for the contents of the plan include the avoidance of unreasonable harm to the landowner. Moreover, the landowner has a *basic building right* – a concept used in planning, although Finnish planning legislation does not use the concept or directly address it, thus rendering it hard to invalidate.

The basic building right is mostly interpreted as the right of a landowner to build detached houses in rural, sparsely populated settlements. A landowner in Finland has the right to build on his/her land if it is not limited in statutory land-use plans or by regulations concerning construction. This contrasts with the situation in many other European countries. For example, in Denmark and Sweden the mirror image of this right can be observed: only a statutory land-use plan or high-level exceptional permission would give the right to build or change the use of land in an irreversible way. The basic building right in Finland is reflected in the general liability of society to compensate when this right is lost. Besides local detailed plans, this liability is also valid in the legally binding local master plans and regional land-use plans, which can themselves create a basis for building permission (Planning System of Finland, 2007, p. 23).

2.4 Ideals of public participation

While the landowner's basic building right is only indirectly indicated in the LBA, the ideals of the public sphere are boldly pronounced in the general objective of the Act: "[T]he Act also aims to ensure that everyone has the right to participate in the preparation process, and that planning is high quality and interactive, that expertise is comprehensive and that there is open provision of information on matters being processed" (LBA 1 §, 2. Mom.). The range of participants to be included in the planning process has been broadened, and the demands concerning inclusiveness are high. The planning authority must publicize planning information so that interested parties are able to follow and influence the planning process (LBA 62 §). When launching the preparation of a new plan, a Participation and Assessment Scheme has to be drawn up and publicized. The scheme should cover participation and interaction procedures as well as processes for assessing the plan's impacts (LBA 63 §).

3 Problems and challenges

The basic challenges that Finland is facing include economic restructuring (de-industrialization and globalization), economic disparities within the country, finance for maintaining and developing infrastructure and services, and demographic changes such as ageing and the emerging question of immigration (Jauhiainen and Niemenmaa, 2006, p. 269). In the following sections, we concentrate on a few contemporary problems related to the Finnish planning system that have attracted a lot of debate and attempts at corrective measures.

3.1 Institutional ambiguity

The Finnish land-use planning system aims to produce statutory plans enabling urban and regional development. Planning is considered strategic, but there is a lack of coordination between different levels, sectors and planning and policy tools. Mäntysalo and Roininen (2009) conclude that urban development is becoming more complex and pluralistic, as are the prerequisites for guiding it. A major change is needed. The development work should be guided in both directions, up and down, and a shift to more holistic and cross-sector governance is needed (Mäntysalo and Roininen, 2009, p. 76). The OECD has also criticized Finland for its sector-oriented planning (Lau, 2010), since despite aiming at government-led integrated planning, the national sectoral planning system continued to be developed (Haimi, 2000, pp. 161, 169–170). There is no consistency between the sector plans; they serve different purposes and areas, and they have not been introduced simultaneously. There have been, for instance, sector plans for regional policy and for fishery (Haimi, 2000, p. 170).

Besides the statutory planning instruments, new strategic and program tools have been developed, better suited for operating in networked urban structures (Jauhiainen, 2012). Master plans are reduced to static zoning plans, overburdened with requirements for comprehensive analyses and assessments. Urban development typically manifests as separate programs (Wallin and Horelli, 2009, p. 112), such as the most significant urban policy program by 2006, Urban II, which included Vantaa in 2000–2006. The palette of planning tools should, however, be dealt with as a whole (Jauhiainen, 2012, p. 37). When the consolidation of planning tools with normative and economic guidance is neglected, institutional ambiguity is generated (Mäntysalo and Roininen, 2009, p. 76; Bäcklund and Mäntysalo, 2010; see also OECD, 2005; Jauhiainen and Niemenmaa, 2006, p. 222).

Vantaa, along with some other cities, has started ten-year programming of land-use plan implementation. The program is longer than that of economic planning, and it is based on land-use plan goals, opportunities created by plans, sector goals, resources and continuous monitoring. If all the factors are to be adjusted, it is vital that the projects affecting land-use are brought under control. However, regional planning has not particularly developed plan implementation programming (Laitio and Maijala, 2010, p. 18).

3.2 Out-of-town shopping centers

All the master plans in the history of Vantaa have highlighted the strategic subordination of land-use considerations to the international airport, the national highways and the municipal industrial policy. There was also a planning event, deriving from an old political decision in 1976: a large company had a plan drawn up and succeeded in arguing for a commercial center to be developed at the intersection of the E18 highway, the ring road III.[2] The landowners had an American mall concept in mind (retired master planning director Vappu Myllymäki, 24 November 2004, cited in Hirvonen, 2007, p. 175), to build first a shopping center, followed by a residential settlement. The Jumbo project led to the generation of yet another center in polycentric Vantaa, for which the rest of the urban fabric was not ready. Jumbo opened in 1999. Later, in the master plan of 2007, Vantaa developed the means to control different types of retail.

Unfortunately, the Jumbo project did not turn out to be exceptional in Finland. A recent survey reveals an alarming tendency for large-scale shopping centers continuing to be developed outside urban cores or areas designated for them in strategic regional plans (Ympäristöministeriö, 2009a). Here, the interests of one local government often contrast the view concerning the structural functionality and sustainability of the broader urban region (see Mäntysalo et al., 2010). Such solo activity by local governments concerning large commercial projects also emerged as one of the key problems of strategic land-use planning in a recent questionnaire by the Ministry of the Environment (Maijala, 2009). The weakness of Finnish regional planning in guiding commercial development is somewhat acknowledged in the Ministry of the Environment's report, where regional plans are characterized as being rather reactive concerning commercial development (Koski, 2007). However, this potentially critical idea is overshadowed by the positive statement that the guidelines for commercial development expressed in regional plans are well transmitted to planning at the municipal level (Koski, 2007, p. 26). This is, in fact, a reflection of the prevalent condition where regional planning is more or less reduced to the reactive collection of local governments' planning intentions, often lacking a proper regional perspective. The local governments, through their representatives in the regional council, together determine the regional guidelines to govern their own municipal planning. As a joint authority, the regional council is, after all, subordinate to its member municipalities.

Such development has generated lively debate on controlling large-scale retail projects, and the Ministry of the Environment has toughened up its policy. A dedicated committee was nominated in 2008 by the Ministry of the Environment to suggest corrective measures. It proposed the revision of the National Land Use Guidelines to include regional studies on the service network. Moreover, it recommended that the largest retail projects should be subject to Environmental Impact Assessment procedures (Ympäristöministeriö, 2009a, pp. 9–10). On 15 April 2011, an amendment to the LBA came into force (71 §), restricting the construction of large-scale retail projects outside core urban areas.

3.3 Lack of planning cooperation in urban regions

Competition in large shopping center projects between neighboring municipalities highlights the lack of inter-municipal planning cooperation, which potentially intensifies the fragmentation of the urban structure. The acceleration of Finnish urban sprawl (e.g. Ristimäki et al., 2003; Ristimäki, 2009) has led to the coining of the term "fennosprawl" (Ylä-Anttila, 2007), which refers to urban densities with closer resemblance to the Australian and North American condition than the European one (Newman and Kenworthy, 1998; Kosonen, 2007, p. 81).

Despite the efforts for strategic coordination between municipalities, there are tensions that remain (see also Sjöblom, 2010, p. 257), especially in the land-use sector. The capital of Finland, Helsinki, with its land resources and huge city planning office, differs drastically in its city-steered land-use policy from neighboring cities and towns, including Vantaa, which have fewer land resources and more landowner-oriented political cultures, stemming partially from their rural history. The ability to manage growth has been the vital political condition ensuring municipal independence is retained. In 1946, the rural commune of Vantaa reluctantly lost a third of its area to Helsinki as it was not able to cope with suburban planning. Since then, the city of Vantaa has promoted regional cooperation, considering collaboration a favorable alternative to municipal mergers (Hirvonen, 2007, pp. 84–85). The competitiveness of the city of Vantaa is also a symptom of the long-term inequality problems in regional responsibilities concerning housing the growing population, taxation and social coherence. The little brother of Helsinki wants to shine alongside the capital (see Mäenpää et al., 2000, p. 190; Kivistö, 2011).

Today, there is competition between the municipalities for national investments in infrastructure and other mega projects in different parts of the region. The urban structure of Vantaa has mostly been built since the 1950s. Since the late 1990s, there has been an increasing need to invest in renovation of the built environment – for example, in repairing schools and technical infrastructure (main analyst Raila Paukku, 9 December 2004, cited in Hirvonen, 2007, p. 185). This contributes further to municipal competition for enterprises, retailers and the so-called good taxpayer residents seeking a place to locate (see e.g. Jauhiainen and Niemenmaa, 2006, p. 264).

Competition among municipalities for investments and residents has resulted in intensified urban sprawl in the region. The industrial and residential areas in Vantaa are strongly separated, which complicates the planning of mixed-use areas (master planning director Matti Pallasvuo, 14 January 2005, cited in Hirvonen, 2007, p. 190). In Vantaa, the largest industrial area is affected by aircraft noise, and politicians have been reluctant to support residential infill plans in the area, such as consolidating the K2 Land Use Plan (proposed in 2004).[3] Nevertheless, in the master plan of 2007, the city of Vantaa chose a laborious densification of the existing urban structure, instead of reserving new districts. The city of Vantaa also questioned the capital-centered finger model and opted instead for a webbed polycentric urban structure consisting of living communities as a starting point, while consideration of the urban model of the HMR continued.[4]

The central government introduced an amendment to the LBA: *Capital City Region Master Plan § 46 a* (2008/1129), ordering the four core cities of the HMR – Helsinki, Espoo, Vantaa and Kauniainen – to draw up a joint master plan, but without a deadline for the plan. A recent study on metropolitan governance (Tolkki et al., 2011), published by the Ministry of the Environment, concludes that land-use planning and transport coordination should in fact include the wider network of cities in Southern Finland.

The problems of inter-municipal cooperation in the HMR are paralleled, with different intensity, in other urban regions in Finland. The Paras-Act (Laki kunta- ja palvelurakenneu-udistuksesta 2007/169) launched a reform of the municipal and service structure, aiming to unite small municipalities into coalitions better capable of bearing the economic weight of municipal service responsibilities, especially concerning the health and social service sectors. In urban regions, the municipalities are pushed by the Act towards intensified strategic planning cooperation, integrating land-use and housing and transportation consid-erations. However, the local willingness for mergers and strategic planning cooperation in the urban regions is rather weak (Haveri, 2006; Sjöblom, 2010, p. 258). There are politi-cal, institutional and economic path dependencies maintaining the status quo. For instance, travel-to-work areas typically include several municipalities, each depending on taxes and applying an industrial policy of its own. Thus, there is a risk that the Paras-Act will be imple-mented only superficially, generating joint plans for the urban region that appear strategic but fail to tackle problems such as uncoordinated competition for enterprises and residents between the individual municipalities of the region (Mäntysalo et al., 2010).

The new government, established in May 2011 after the parliamentary election, has started the preparation of a new "Structure Act" that would replace the Paras-Act. Concerning large- and medium-sized urban regions, the aim is to merge municipalities together and dismantle the various cooperation arrangements that have been established between independent municipalities for the provision of, especially, social and health ser-vices. The "Structure Act," including proposals for new municipal coalitions, was sent for comments in November 2012 (Valtiovarainministeriö, 2012). The new "Structure Act," motivated by the recent economic challenges, has called forth a profound discussion on the political foundation of basic services and on reorganizing the responsibilities of the Finnish municipalities.

4 Dimensions and directions of change

Zoning is only one part of land-use planning. Strategic planning and land policy conducted by municipalities are significant for the overall success of land-use planning. This involves not only the mere planning system, but planning practices as well (Puustinen and Hirvonen, 2005, pp. 62, 64). Vantaa has experienced hectic eras in which it attempted to absorb massive growth with minimal planning and implementation resources, adopting several complementary and unofficial planning instruments to manage growth, sustain institutional autonomy and reach for an acknowledged position as a global business district in the HMR.

4.1 The increase of complementary, unofficial planning

Typically, unofficial planning instruments are based on the public–private partnerships that Vantaa has actively been enhancing since the establishment of land-use agreements in 1964. The municipalities have been granted and recommended legal instruments for active land policy since the 1970s, but Vantaa, which owns only 35 percent of its surface area,[5] has acted as a pioneer in land-use agreements (business development director Leea Markkula-Heilamo, 10 December 2004, cited in Hirvonen, 2007, p. 196) and has been content to achieve the same results in this way (retired head of office Veikko Heino, 18 November 2004, cited in Hirvonen, 2007, p. 138). At the time of the hectic project development system, Vantaa required detailed neighborhood plans from developer-contractors to safeguard the quality of the resulting built milieu. Later on, the planning agency of Vantaa started to include detailed construction plans in the agreements to obligate developers. In recent years, planning has advanced to negotiations with developer-contractors, setting common goals and tying in partners right at the beginning of planning projects. The implementation of plans has been integrated with planning, and the detailed plan has become a type of project plan.

In order to plan in neo-liberal conditions, Vantaa has been using unofficial plans, which have developed into central instruments in planning practice. The increase of unofficial planning is pertinent (Airamo and Permanto, 1997, p. 40; Mäntysalo and Jarenko, 2012, p. 42). In the late 1980s, unofficial land-use agreements were about to displace the land-use planning system (Vuorela, 1991, p. 120) but, in 1995, Vantaa came up with the means to utilize business investments strategically. A project organization was established to link the urban planning system to an external network of urban actors. This led to the establishment of the prevailing partner organization, consisting of City Planning, Business Development and Financial and Administrative Services, which creates substantial cooperation between urban policy and land-use planning, harnesses land-use planning for the use of industrial policy, and, on the other hand, positions land-use planning centrally in the strategic planning organization and the bargaining network. Under these circumstances, the presentation of plans to the municipal council is considered central in the planning organization.

A key motivator for the LBA reform was the deep economic recession of the early 1990s. It became clear that the public sector could not afford to finance the welfare state alone. Different levels of the administration and the private sector needed to cooperate in terms of urban and regional development, planning and implementation (Jauhiainen, 1995, p. 277; Kurunmäki, 2005, p. 65). While the role of the state has been economically and strategically declining, the system has been calling for ever more local activity – both in terms of new responsibilities and possibilities. With the reform of the LBA, the authority of the local government in land-use planning was strengthened. This led to the generation of partnerships, consisting of independent municipal actors, related developer coalitions and NGOs (Suomen Kuntaliitto, 2008), as was the case in the integrative development project of the Leinelä housing area in Vantaa in 2004–2011. While consultants are increasingly being utilized, the role of the planning authorities in Vantaa has shifted towards planning management.

4.2 The rise of urban policies

The economic recession and the resulting problems in the municipal economy, as well as the intensified migration of the unemployed to the larger cities, activated the formation of urban policies and programs at the national level. In fact, in Finland "urban policy" referred to national-level activities creating measures to tackle urban problems through central government policies and programs (Kurunmäki, 2005, p. 70). Integration with the EU in 1995 and the attention paid to the European discussion on urban policy were catalysts for redefining urban policy as creating prerequisites for urban development (Jauhiainen and Niemenmaa, 2006, p. 179). Today, Finland drives growth-oriented and urban-based development policy, and is stepping into a new phase of network facilitation by renewing its urban policy tools. In 2006, urban regions applied to the Centre of Expertise Program and to the Regional Centre Program. New activities in nationwide networking are taking place (Antikainen and Vartiainen, 2006, p. 39)

The next phase is to network urban regions internationally (Antikainen and Vartiainen, 2006, p. 39). The most remarkable change in urban policy was the emergence of a metropolitan policy with the previous government in 2007. The HMR has been given priority as a region to guarantee the global competitiveness of Finland. As a goal, competitiveness, aided by the HMR and the other largest urban regions, has superseded the former emphasis on the balanced development of all regions (Antikainen and Vartiainen, 2006, p. 39).

The four core cities of the HMR, including Vantaa, and the surrounding municipalities have recently established boards and launched several strategy documents to secure the region's global competitiveness, social and cultural cohesion, and to coordinate land-use, housing and transport issues as well as regional services. Aware of the central strategic role of the HMR, the central government has launched a specific Metropolitan Policy Program, and a number of partnership agreements are being drafted between the central government and the municipalities. In 2007, the Greater Helsinki Vision 2050, an international ideas competition, was held to study different models for regional spatial structure and explore visions for cooperation. The competition was organized jointly by the 14 towns and municipalities of the HMR, together with the Ministry of the Environment (Greater Helsinki municipalities et al., 2007). The revision of the regional plan of the broader Uusimaa region is underway.

The urban development organization of Vantaa has been kept light and capable of responding quickly to the demands of investors. In the 1990s, Vantaa worked in close cooperation with the Ministry of the Environment, which used to ratify plans. Today, Vantaa benefits from being agile. In 1990, Vantaa identified the advantages of having the international airport and E18 Road (Vantaan kaupunki, 1990, p. 17) and, since 2001, a vision of Aviapolis, a premium class international business district located on the edge of Vantaa, has been successfully marketed. In this next generation hub including 33,500 jobs (a share of 33 percent in Vantaa), a Finland and China Cooperation Committee and Innovation Institute has been established to serve Finnish and Chinese enterprises. The institute, owned by the city of Vantaa, will work in cooperation with the marketing company Greater Helsinki Promotion Ltd (Tuomi, 2011) and the Uusimaa Regional Council for the benefit of a broad area, including the Baltic Sea region (Uusimaa Regional Council, 2011). Vantaa has claimed a new standing in the HMR and a role as an independent international actor.

municipalities were made responsible for their own expenses and income. At the time of the *EU Compendium*, strategic planning was still mostly undertaken by regional authorities (European Commission, 1997, p. 58). Today, local planning authorities have been granted an independent role, including strategic planning. Critically, one could conclude that with the devolution of planning power, the current planning system has abandoned the idea of a political control system that sets and implements goals through the hierarchical system, which was the initial aim of our system. On the other hand, the system has offered even global opportunities for strategically active municipalities.

The focus of the land-use planning system has shifted from planning substance to process, and new complementary, unofficial planning instruments are being developed. In general, the decisive role of the local authority has been highlighted within the decentralized Finnish planning system. This enables the system to react to new possibilities flexibly (Puustinen and Hirvonen, 2005, p. 62). The perceived challenges can be responded to by redirecting guidance and developing planning practices (Ympäristöministeriö, 2005, p. 155).

Early signs of re-centralization can be seen in the recent amendment of the LBA concerning large-scale retail projects, and in the preparation of the "Structure Act" aimed at municipal structures covering travel-to-work areas and the provision of social and health services. However, the relative weakness of the regional level in the strategic guidance of municipal land-use planning (see also Laitinen and Vesisenaho, 2011) and in regional resource programming does not serve efforts to counteract the continued dispersion of urban structures, jeopardizing sustainable urban development. In order to counteract "fennosprawl," we need institutional reforms, as well as better instruments for integrated cross-sector planning coupled with two-way evaluation and continuous monitoring of urban and regional development, with relevant indicators of sustainability.

Notes

1 Severe conflicts in land-use planning are dealt with in legal proceedings. The planning system is considered equally legally binding; Finland has had the reputation of being one of the world's least corrupt countries (Joutsen and Keränen, 2009).
2 See section 2.2.
3 The K2 Land Use Plan has recently proceeded. The plan has a major significance in regenerating a large industrial area in the central parts of Vantaa into a more mixed-use area, and thus connecting the Eastern and Western parts of the municipality.
4 See section 4.2.
5 The situation in 2004.
6 The continuous monitoring of sustainable development is challenging, since the indicators of sustainability are not yet internationally, regionally and inter-organizationally coherent. The six biggest cities in Finland, including Vantaa, have been developing a common practice for reporting environmental issues.
7 The first value mentioned is the culture of innovation: "Innovativeness refers to the ability to create changes that benefit Vantaa; to act as a trail-blazer; and the courage to seek new enhanced ways of arranging services for the citizens" (City Council of Vantaa, 2010). The third value is social belonging, referring to promoting citizens' social inclusion and joint objectives.

References

Airamo, R. and Permanto, T. (1997). *Yleiskaavoitus ja vaikutusten arviointi. Esimerkkinä Lahden yleiskaavoitus 1946–1996*. Helsinki: Ympäristöministeriö, Suomen ympäristö 88/1997.

Antikainen, J. and Vartiainen, P. (2006). A patchwork of urban regions: structures and policies in support of polycentricity. In H. Eskelinen and T. Hirvonen (eds) *Positioning Finland in a European Space* (pp. 30–40). Helsinki: Ministry of the Environment and Ministry of the Interior.

Bäcklund, P. and Mäntysalo, R. (2010). Agonism and institutional ambiguity: ideas on democracy and the role of participation in the development of planning theory and practice – the case of Finland. *Planning Theory*, 9(4), 333–350.

City Council of Vantaa. (2010, 15 November). *Vantaa's Balanced Strategy. Financial Plan 2011–2014*. Special publication. Retrieved from www.vantaa.fi/instancedata/prime_product_julkaisu/vantaa/embeds/vantaawwwstructure/65622_Erillisstrategia_EN_netti_1_.pdf.

Ekroos, A. and Majamaa, V. (2000). *Maankäyttö- ja rakennuslaki*. Helsinki: Oy Edita Ab.

European Commission. (1997). *The EU Compendium of Spatial Planning Systems and Policies*. Luxembourg: European Commission, Regional Development Studies 28

Greater Helsinki municipalities, the State of Finland and the Ministry of the Environment. (2007). *Greater Helsinki Vision 2050 – International Ideas Competition*. Retrieved from www.hel.fi/hel2/helsinginseutu/FINAL_GreaterHelsinki_200x200mm_english_03-09-2010_LOW.pdf.

Haimi, O. (2000). *Yhteiskuntasuunnittelun pitkä marssi. Suomalaisen sosiaalipoliittisen suunnittelun kehitys. Tapaus kuntien valtionosuusuudistus*. Doctoral dissertation. Helsinki: Helsingin yliopisto, Sosiaalipolitiikan laitos, Tutkimuksia 2.

Haveri, A. (2006). Complexity in local governance change: limits to rational reforming. *Public Management Review*, 8(1), 31–46.

Helsingin kaupunki and Vantaan kaupunki. (2006). *Urbaani tulevaisuus – Kaupunki kaikille. Urban II -yhteisöaloiteohjelman juhlakirja.*

Hentilä, H.-L. (2012). Tavoitteena hyvä elinympäristö ja kestävät yhdyskunnat – alueidenkäytön suunnittelun haasteita ja kehityssuuntia. In M. Airaksinen, H.-L. Hentilä, J. S. Jauhiainen, R. Mäntysalo, K. Jarenko, T. Määttä, M. Pentti, J. Similä and A. Staffans (eds) *Katsauksia maankäyttö- ja rakennuslain toimivuuteen* (pp. 50–62). Helsinki: Ympäristöministeriön raportteja 4/2012. Retrieved from www.ym.fi/download/noname/%7B0011C42D-E36A-43E3-A7A5-22E15FFCC42A%7D/30355.

Hentilä, H.-L. and Soudunsaari, L. (2008). *Land Use Planning Systems and Practices Oulu–Skanderborg–Umeå. InnoUrba*. Oulu: University of Oulu, Department of Architecture, Publications B 29.

Hirvonen, S. (2005). *Ruraali urbaani. Vantaan kaupunkisuunnittelun historia*. Vantaa: Vantaan kaupunki, Kaupunkisuunnittelu, Julkaisu 8/2005, C 18:2005.

Hirvonen, S. (2007). *Vantaan kaupunkisuunnittelun historia*. Licentiate thesis. Oulu: Oulun yliopisto, Arkkitehtuurin osasto.

Jauhiainen, J. S. (1995). *Kaupunkisuunnittelu, kaupunkiuudistus ja kaupunkipolitiikka. Kolme eurooppalaista esimerkkiä*. Doctoral dissertation. Turku: Turun yliopiston maantieteen laitos, Julkaisuja 146.

Jauhiainen, J. S. (2012). Aluekehitys ja maankäyttö- ja rakennuslain uudistamisen haasteet. In M. Airaksinen, H.-L. Hentilä, J. S. Jauhiainen, R. Mäntysalo, K. Jarenko, T. Määttä, M. Pentti, J. Similä and A. Staffans (eds) *Katsauksia maankäyttö- ja rakennuslain toimivuuteen* (pp. 32–41). Helsinki: Ympäristöministeriön raportteja 4/2012. Retrieved from www.ym.fi/download/noname/%7B0011C42D-E36A-43E3-A7A5-22E15FFCC42A%7D/30355.

Jauhiainen, J. S. and Niemenmaa, V. (2006). *Alueellinen suunnittelu*. Tampere: Vastapaino.

Joutsen, M. and Keränen, J. (2009). *Corruption and the Prevention of Corruption in Finland*. Finland: Ministry of Justice. Retrieved from www.om.fi/material/attachments/om/tiedotteet/en/2009/6AH99u1tG/Corruption.pdf.

Kivistö, P. (2011). Aviapolis – takapihasta näyteikkunaksi. *Vantaa suunnittelee ja rakentaa 2011*, 16–17.

Koski, K. (2007). *Kauppa maakuntakaavoituksessa*. Helsinki: Ympäristöministeriön raportteja 23/2007. Retrieved from www.ym.fi/download/noname/%7BDE61BB3A-F815-4C7A-A68B-BAAEE685709A%7D/32075.

Kosonen, L. (2007). *Kuopio 2015. Jalankulku-, joukkoliikenne- ja autokaupunki*. Helsinki: Ympäristöministeriö, Suomen ympäristö 36/2007.

Kurunmäki, K. (2005). *Partnerships in Urban Planning. "Development Area" in National and Local Contexts in Finland, Germany and Britain.* Doctoral dissertation. Tampere: Tampere University of Technology, Datutop 26.

Laitinen, J. and Vesisenaho, M. (2011). *Kaupunkiseutujen yhdyskuntarakenne maakuntakaavoissa. Arviointi valtakunnallisten alueidenkäyttötavoitteiden vaikuttavuuden kannalta.* Helsinki: Ympäristöministeriö, Suomen ympäristö 2/2011.

Laitio, M. and Maijala, O. (2010). *Alueidenkäytön strateginen ohjaaminen.* Helsinki: Ympäristöministeriö, Suomen ympäristö 28/2010.

Lau, E. (ed.) (2010). *Finland 2010: Working Together to Sustain Success.* OECD Public Governance Reviews.

Mäenpää, P., Aniluoto, A., Manninen, R. and Villanen, S. (2000). *Sanat kivettyvät kaupungiksi. Tutkimus Helsingin kaupunkisuunnittelu prosesseista ja ihanteista.* Espoo: Teknillinen korkeakoulu, Yhdyskuntasuunnittelun tutkimus- ja koulutuskeskuksen julkaisuja B 83.

Maijala, O. (2009). STRASI-hankkeen tilanne. In *STRASI work seminar.* Seminar conducted at the meeting of the Ministry of the Environment, Helsinki.

Majamaa, W. (2008). *The 4th P – People – in Urban Development Based on Public–Private–People Partnership.* Espoo: TKK Structural Engineering and Building Technology Dissertations: 2 TKK-R-VK2.

Mäntysalo, R. (2008). Dialectics of power: the case of tulihta land-use agreement. *Planning Theory and Practice,* 9(1), 81–96.

Mäntysalo, R. and Jarenko, K. (2012). Strategisen maankäytön suunnittelun legitimaation haaste maankäyttö- ja rakennuslaille. In M. Airaksinen, H.-L. Hentilä, J. S. Jauhiainen, R. Mäntysalo, K. Jarenko, T. Määttä, M. Pentti, J. Similä and A. Staffans (eds) *Katsauksia maankäyttö- ja rakennuslain toimivuuteen* (pp. 42–49). Helsinki: Ympäristöministeriön raportteja 4/2012. Retrieved from www.ym.fi/download/noname/%7B0011C42D-E36A-43E3-A7A5-22E15FFCC42A%7D/30355.

Mäntysalo, R. and Roininen, J. (eds) (2009). *Kuinka alueellista muutosta hallitaan – parhaat keinot ja käytännöt. Esiselvitys sektoritutkimuksen neuvottelukunnan Alue- ja yhdyskuntarakenteet ja infrastruktuurit -jaostolle (teema 3).* Espoo: Teknillinen korkeakoulu, Yhdyskuntasuunnittelun tutkimus- ja koulutuskeskuksen julkaisuja C 71.

Mäntysalo, R., Peltonen, L., Kanninen, V., Niemi, P., Hytönen, J. and Simanainen, M. (2010). *Keskuskaupungin ja kehyskunnan jännitteiset kytkennät. Viiden kaupunkiseudun yhdyskuntarakenne ja suunnitteluyhteistyö Paras-hankkeen käynnistysvaiheessa.* Helsinki: Suomen Kuntaliitto, Acta 217.

Ministry of the Environment. (2009). *The Future of Land Use is Being Decided Now: The Revised National Land Use Guidelines of Finland.* Retrieved from www.ym.fi/download/noname/%7B331CBF76-8C6B-4AAF-93E6-95DCCF1E2AC2%7D/58466.

Moisio, A. (2002). *Essays on Finnish Municipal Finance and Intergovernmental Grants.* Doctoral dissertation. Helsinki: University of Jyväskylä, Valtion taloudellisen tutkimuskeskuksen tutkimuksia 93.

Newman, P. and Kenworthy, J. (1998). *Sustainability and Cities: Overcoming Automobile Dependence.* Washington, DC: Island Press.

OECD. (2005). *Territorial Review of Finland.* Paris: OECD Publications.

Planning System of Finland. (2007). *COMMIN: The Baltic Spatial Conceptshare.* Retrieved from http://commin.org/upload/Finland/FI_Planning_System_Engl.pdf

Puustinen, S. (2006). *Suomalainen kaavoittajaprofessio ja suunnittelun kommunikatiivinen käänne. Vuorovaikutukseen liittyvät ongelmat ja mahdollisuudet suurten kaupunkien kaavoittajien näkökulmasta.* Doctoral dissertation. Espoo: Teknillinen korkeakoulu, Yhdyskuntasuunnittelun tutkimus- ja koulutuskeskuksen julkaisuja A 34.

Puustinen, S. and Hirvonen, J. (2005). *Alueidenkäytön suunnittelujärjestelmän toimivuus.* AKSU. Helsinki: Ympäristöministeriö, Suomen ympäristö 782/2005.

Rajaniemi, J. (2006). *Kasvun kaavoitus. Tapaus Raahe 1961–1996.* Doctoral dissertation. Kankaanpää: Messon.

Ristimäki, M. (2009). Autoriippuvainen yhdyskuntarakenne ja täydennysrakentamisen haaste Suomessa. In R. Sairinen (ed.) *Yhdyskuntarakenteen eheyttäminen ja elinympäristön laatu* (pp. 61–77). Espoo: Teknillinen korkeakoulu, Yhdyskuntasuunnittelun tutkimus- ja koulutuskeskuksen julkaisuja B 96.

Ristimäki, M., Oinonen, K., Pitkäranta, H. and Harju, K. (2003). *Kaupunkiseutujen väestömuutos ja alueellinen kasvu.* Helsinki: Ympäristöministeriö, Suomen ympäristö 657/2003.

Sairinen, R. (ed.) (2009). *Yhdyskuntarakenteen eheyttäminen ja elinympäristön laatu.* Espoo: Teknillinen korkeakoulu, Yhdyskuntasuunnittelun tutkimus- ja koulutuskeskuksen julkaisuja B 96.

Sjöblom, S. (2010). Finland: the limits of the unitary decentralized model. In J. Loughlin, F. Hendriks, A. Lidström (eds) *The Oxford Handbook of Local and Regional Democracy in Europe* (pp. 241–260). New York: Oxford University Press.

Söderman, T. and Kallio, T. (2009). Strategic environmental assessment in Finland: an evaluation of the Sea Act Application. *Journal of Environmental Assessment Policy and Management*, *11*(1), 1–28.

Soudunsaari, L. (2007). *Hyviä käytäntöjä etsimässä. Vertaileva tutkimus alankomaalaisesta ja suomalaisesta suunnittelujärjestelmästä ja kaavoituskäytännöstä*. DECOMB. Oulu: Oulun yliopiston arkkitehtuurin osasto, Julkaisuja B 28.

Suomen Kuntaliitto. (2008). *Julkisen ja yksityisen sektorin yhteistyö maankäytössä*. Helsinki: Suomen Kuntaliitto. Retrieved from www.kunnat.net/fi/asiantuntijapalvelut/mal/maankaytto/yhdyskuntasuunnittelu/tonttituotanto/yhteistyo-julkinen-yksityinen/Documents/JYMY_raportti.pdf.

Suomi.fi editorial team and State treasury. (2012). *Joint authorities*. Retrieved from www.suomi.fi/suomifi/english/state_and_municipalities/municipalities_and_local_government/joint_authorities/index.html.

Tolkki, H., Airaksinen, J. and Haveri, A. (2011). *Metropolihallinta. Neljä mallia maailmalta ja niiden sovellettavuus Suomessa* Helsinki: Ympäristöministeriö, Suomen ympäristö 9/2011.

Tulkki, K. (1994). Murtumia. *Kaupunkisuunnittelu taitekohdassa. Keravan keskustan suunnittelu 1990–91*. Espoo: Teknillinen korkeakoulu, Yhdyskuntasuunnittelun täydennyskoulutuskeskuksen julkaisuja C 34.

Tuomi, S. (2011). *Innovaatioinstituutin saavutuksia: Rahoitushanat avattu Kiinaan ja Airport Cluster nousukiidossa, Vantaa suunnittelee ja rakentaa 2011*, 18.

Uusimaa Regional Council. (2011). *A Partnership Agreement with China Development Bank Opens the Way to the Chinese Market for Companies in Uusimaa*. Retrieved from www.uudenmaanliitto.fi/?5525_m=8055andl=enands=7.

Valtiovarainministeriö. (2012). *Kuntauudistus*. Kuntarakenneuudistus kuntiin lausunnoille. Retrieved from www.vm.fi/vm/fi/05_hankkeet/0107_kuntauudistus/index.jsp.

Vantaan kaupunki. (1990). *Vantaan kehitysnäkymiä*. Vantaa: Vantaan kaupunki, Hallintopalvelukeskus, Tietopalvelut and Yleiskaavoitus C4:1990.

Vantaan kaupunki. (2004). *Vantaan kestävän kehityksen indikaattorit*. Vantaa: Vantaan kaupunki, Ympäristökeskus C17:2004.

Vesala, R. (1994). *Maankäytön suunnittelun strategiat ja käytäntö – Esimerkkinä Lahti*. Espoo: Teknillinen korkeakoulu, Yhdyskuntasuunnittelun täydennyskoulutuskeskuksen julkaisuja A 21.

Vuorela, P. (1991). Rakennetun ympäristön suunnittelun johtavista periaatteista Toisen maailmansodan jälkeen. In P. von Bonsdorff, C. Burman, H. Lehtonen, M. Norvasuo, J. Rautsi, Y. Sepänmaa, S. Säätelä and P. Vuorela. (eds) *Rakennetun ympäristön kauneus ja laatu. Esteettisesti ja laadullisesti korkeatasoinen fyysinen ympäristö ja uudet suunnittelutekniikat. Osa 1* (pp. 92–153). Espoo: Valtion teknillinen tutkimuskeskus, Tiedotteita 1234.

Wallin, S. and Horelli, L. (2009). Arvioinnin paikka alue- ja yhdyskuntasuunnittelussa? *Hallinnon Tutkimus*, *28*(5), 109–116.

Ylä-Anttila, K. (2007). FennosprOawl and network urbanism. In K. Ylä-Anttila and S. Alppi (eds) *Processing Utopia. City Scratching II* (pp. 112–119). Tampere: Tampere University of Technology, Institute of Urban Planning and Design.

Ympäristöministeriö. (1988). *Selvitys kaavoitustoimen kehittämisestä ja kuntien omavastuisen päätöksenteon lisäämisestä*. Helsinki: Ympäristöministeriön raportteja 1988.

Ympäristöministeriö. (2005). *Maankäyttö- ja rakennuslain toimivuus. Arvio laista saaduista kokemuksista*. Helsinki: Ympäristöministeriö, Suomen ympäristö 781/2005.

Ympäristöministeriö. (2009a). *Kaupan sijainnin ohjauksen arviointityöryhmän raportti*. Helsinki: Ympäristöministeriön raportteja 21/2009.

Ympäristöministeriö. (2009b). *Valtakunnalliset alueidenkäyttötavoitteet*. Retrieved from www.ymparisto.fi/fi-FI/Elinymparisto_ja_kaavoitus/Maankayton_suunnittelujarjestelma/Valtakunnalliset_alueidenkayttotavoitteet/Valtakunnalliset_alueidenkayttotavoittee(13419).

Further reading

Eskelinen, H. and Hirvonen, T. (eds) (2006). *Positioning Finland in a European Space*. Helsinki: Ministry of the Environment and Ministry of the Interior.

Havel, M. B. (2009). *Property Rights Regime in Land Development: Analysis of the Influence of Institutions on Land Development in Terms of Property Rights Theory*. Doctoral dissertation. Helsinki: Helsinki University of Technology, Faculty of Engineering and Architecture, Department of Surveying.

National Planning Systems: Finland. (2007). BSR INTERREG III B project "Promoting Spatial Development by Creating COMmon MINdscapes." Retrieved from http://commin.org/en/planning-systems/national-planning-systems/finland/1.-planning-system-in-general/1.2-basic-principles.html

4

DUTCH NATIONAL SPATIAL PLANNING AT THE END OF AN ERA

Wil Zonneveld and David Evers

Chapter objectives

Until the 1990s, Dutch spatial planning was widely seen as an almost perfect example of a comprehensive integrated approach towards spatial planning:

- The organizational structure, especially at the national level, was elaborate.
- The system was effective in steering the location of homes, especially in the 1990s.

After this time, the comprehensive integrated approach was gradually substituted by a kind of regional economic approach at the national level:

- Most national urbanization policies have been abandoned.
- Spatial quality – for a long time a key objective – is no longer considered a national interest.
- Economic development has become the main priority of spatial planning.

Dutch national spatial planning has changed course in more than one sense:

- Content: it is less concerned with integrating land-uses into a single national spatial vision.
- Governance: provinces and municipalities are given responsibility for urbanization.
- Geographical scope: much narrower, focusing on the economically most competitive parts of the country.

1 Introduction

Unnoticed by the wider public and the majority of professional planners, a symbolic event took place on 12 November 2010. Directly following a reorganization of the public sector by the new government taking office that year, the letters of the Ministry of Housing, Spatial Planning and the Environment – VROM according to its Dutch acronym – were scraped off the facade of the main building in The Hague (see Figure 4.1). Compared to the United Kingdom, where the name, scope, aim and composition of ministries are changed virtually every election period, ministries in the Netherlands are relatively protected from the caprices and vacillations of party politics and prime ministers. VROM was an institution in more than one sense of the word, and "spatial planning" (the RO in VROM) had been part of its name since 1965 (Siraa et al., 1995, p. 64). In the title of the new ministry – Infrastructure and the Environment – spatial planning is conspicuously absent.

The removal of the letters represents more than a symbolic act: it reflects the stated intent of the new government to "leave spatial planning more up to provinces and municipalities" (Coalition Agreement, 2010, p. 38). Within a year of assuming office, the new ministry published its new spatial planning strategy which minimizes planning at the national level (Ministerie van IenM, 2011). With this, the tradition of national urbanization policies such as growth centers, new towns, buffer zones, the Green Heart and VINEX[1] had come to a close (Faludi and Van der Valk, 1994; Zonneveld, 2007). To foreign eyes, these changes may seem drastic and sudden, but they are actually part of a gradual systemic change.

Since the early 1990s, the external institutional environment of national spatial planning has transformed fundamentally. National housing policy, once a key partner in helping spatial planning steer urban development, has largely been privatized (Salet, 1999). Agricultural policy, once instrumental in protecting rural areas from urban encroachment, has weakened under increased EU influence and reform. On the other hand, the powerful national transport and infrastructure department, whose relationship to planning was as much one of rivalry as partnership (Siraa et al., 1995; Priemus, 1999), has now merged with planning. The same is true for regional economic policy: this has become the main spatial policy thrust.

Figure 4.1 The end of national spatial planning?

In the same period, national planning has undergone significant changes from within. At the beginning of the decade, the research arm of the National Planning Agency (RPD) was transferred to an independent organization (Halffman, 2009; Roodbol-Mekkes et al., 2012). At the same time, the practice of passive or regulatory planning was criticized for being too reactive. Since then, planning has attempted to become more "hands-on" and development oriented (Gerrits et al., 2012). A major reform to the Spatial Planning Act in 2008 reshuffled powers, responsibilities and expectations between governmental layers, with the intent to simplify governance, speed up planning procedures and stimulate proactive planning. This was accompanied by a succession of administrations that, on balance, favored decentralization to centralization and deregulation to regulation, and introduced new legislative proposals attempting to further streamline the planning process.

Finally, the role of planning in Dutch society seems to have changed in this period as well. A general trust in government and faith in expert opinion – conducive to technocratic planning – has diminished, not unlike developments in many other countries (Albrechts, 2006). Citizens have become more vocal, and civil society more polarized. For the first time in its post-war history, national spatial planning no longer seems immune to this. Consensus on the necessity of national planning has eroded even within the ranks of planners and scholars. Urban growth (and therefore the need to manage it) is no longer self-explanatory and governance rescaling (rise of the regional and EU levels) has made the national level increasingly suspect as a locus for spatial planning.

What follows is a critical reflection on the current changes in Dutch national spatial planning in a historical context. Section 2 will examine the institutional conditions that gave birth to national spatial planning. This will be followed by a more detailed description of the exogenous and endogenous developments sketched out above (section 3). The current national policy document and the controversy surrounding it will then be addressed (section 4). The chapter closes with a reflection on the likely repercussions these changes may have in the future (section 5).

2 The institutionalization of Dutch spatial planning

As in most countries, planning in the Netherlands has emerged from, and in response to, a particular institutional structure. Planning issues rarely fit the mold of the public administration, and therefore involve multiple levels of government and usually different sectoral departments simultaneously. In order to fully understand the Dutch planning system and the current changes being made to it and from within it, one must have a clear grasp of the overarching state structure.

2.1 Decentralized unitary state

A tension between centralization and decentralization has been a constant factor in Dutch history. The Low Countries – including parts of present Belgium – have been characterized by powerful regions since the middle ages. The Republic of Seven United Provinces, which came into being in 1588 during the Eighty Years' War leading to Dutch independence, earned the nickname "The Republic of Seven Disunited Provinces" (Faludi and Van der

Valk, 1994, p. 33). Since its founding, the Netherlands has never willingly had a centralized government like those found in Spain, France and the United Kingdom, which also tend to produce a monocentric urban structure. Instead, cities and regions scattered throughout the Low Countries remained relatively independent and autonomous, and usually in mutual competition (Wagenaar, 2011). This situation changed when Napoleonic France occupied the Republic at the beginning of the nineteenth century and transformed it into a monarchy.

The revolutionary wind blowing through Europe in 1848 reached the Netherlands, but only as a mild breeze. The new 1848 constitution not only restricted the power of the king, but also embraced the principle of self-government. The country was divided into three tiers of government: national, provincial and municipal. Municipalities were considered autonomous except for certain powers reserved for the provinces or central government, and provinces also became self-governing entities. This system is drastically different from the English system, for example, in which local government only has competences explicitly granted to it by central government. The Netherlands is more or less a mirror image of this.

Still, the country is not a federation like Germany – a "decentralized unitary state" is the most common term used to describe this hybrid organization of public administration (e.g. Toonen, 1987, 1990). Co-government is the underlying principle: central government involves the provinces, municipalities or both in the formulation and execution of its policies. The underlying philosophy is that unity cannot be imposed from above, but must come from a plurality of forces hashing out their differences within an agreed-upon framework (Faludi and Van der Valk, 1994). In other words, the unity in the "decentralized unitary state" is brought about by consensus-building, an activity commonly known as polderen.[2] In the 1990s, the Dutch style of consensual democracy became internationally acclaimed and the "polder model" signaled as a best practice. Meanwhile, a domestic counter-discourse was emerging that depicted this system as slowing down effective decision-making. Excessive deliberation, it was argued, had produced a "viscous state" – one advancing as slow as molasses (Hendriks and Toonen, 2001).

2.2 Polderen and planning

The idea of the Netherlands as a decentralized unitary state run by consensual democracy has left its imprint on many policy domains. Obviously, spatial planning is one of them. The legal and institutional basis of the Dutch planning system is laid down in the Spatial Planning Act (WRO) of 1962, which came into effect in 1965. The legislative process leading up to this, which had been underway even before World War II, is indicative of the viscous state. The process took decades because it was very difficult to reach a consensus about the roles of the different layers of government in relation to each other and about the instruments of spatial planning in relation to the tasks and jurisdictions of policy sectors.

Following the WRO, national spatial planning was seen as predominantly coordinative. Rather than commanding its own budget, planning relied on financing from policy sectors such as transport, housing or agriculture. Nor was national spatial planning overtly regulative – the statutory powers to coerce lower tiers of government were rarely used. For national planners, the tools of the trade were primarily communicative: concepts, plans and vision documents were drawn up to capture the imagination of others, both within the sector departments at the national level (i.e. the "horizontal axis" of coordination) as well as at other levels of government (i.e. the "vertical axis"). Sometimes the power of these communicative instruments – especially concepts such as Randstad, Green Heart and mainport – stretched beyond government, spilling over into professional and academic circles, and society at large.

An important institutional practice to achieve this coordination was the National Spatial Planning Committee (RPC: *Rijksplanologische Commissie*).[3] The task of this committee was to develop a common policy framework for all the departments that influence spatial development. Members of the RPC occupied high positions in their departments, mostly at the level of director-general, but the secretariat was part of the Directorate-General for Spatial Planning. The monthly meetings of the RPC have never been open to the public or even members of parliament (Hajer and Zonneveld, 2000). More important than the lack of transparency was the fact that once bureaucratic consensus had been constructed behind the scenes, this served to limit the discussion on alternatives in the subsequent political debate.

The fact that Dutch planning cuts across so many governmental layers and departments and tries to arrive at a coordinated, comprehensive and integrated solution has earned it the epitaph of "comprehensive integrated approach" in the international literature. In fact, according to the synthesizing report of the *EU Compendium* project, the Dutch system epitomizes this approach because it is characterized by "a very systematic and formal hierarchy of plans from national to local level, which coordinate public sector activity across different sectors" (CEC, 1997, p. 36). While the coordination aspect is certainly true, one can take issue with the statement regarding a plan hierarchy. The relationships between the three governmental levels and their respective planning documents are rather subtle and fluid. In the Netherlands, there is no clear-cut hierarchy defined by a binding national plan. Instead, when making plans and designing policies, lower levels of government (re)interpret the plans and policies of higher levels of government. Consultation and negotiation is key to this process, and strongly recalls the Dutch tradition of polderen (Frissen, 2001). Although there have been many changes to planning in recent years and there is evidence that spatial planning has become more politicized (Boonstra and Van den Brink, 2007) and juridical, this consensual aspect has remained relatively constant.

2.3 Performance of national spatial planning

The way national spatial planning has functioned can be best illustrated by the example of urban development and containment policy. There is no consensus on whether this has been successful or not (e.g. Nozeman, 1990). Although Dutch national planning has gained an "almost mythological status" abroad (Faludi and Van der Valk, 1994), Needham (2007) points out that, in practice, many municipalities take advantage of the absence of clear-cut hierarchical lines to unilaterally realize their growth, development and building aspirations. Indeed, Bontje (2001) found that physical developments regularly fell short of national government targets. On the other hand, given the nature of national planning as coordination and communication, it is not so much *conformance* to planning goals which is important, but the *performance* of planning – the extent to which planning concepts, aspirations and ideology affect others (Faludi and Korthals Altes, 1994; Faludi, 2000; Korthals Altes, 2006). From the point of view of performance, the success of national planning should be measured by the extent to which key spatial concepts and planning approaches have been adopted outside the national planning department.

A conceptual cornerstone of national spatial planning from the early 1960s onwards has been the Green Heart, the Dutch version of a green belt policy (Zonneveld, 2007). Although the policy was not supported by an effective zoning regime, it gradually became accepted, especially by the three involved provinces. Sometimes these provinces were less strict about regulating municipal extension plans as central government would have liked, but nevertheless the Green Heart is more than words on paper: large parts of the area designated in the late 1950s as the central open space of the Randstad are still open. At times – especially in the 1990s – central government threatened to use its legal power to force lower levels of government to comply, but in the end did not. The main reason for this is because other governments had sufficiently internalized the concept of the Green Heart. In addition to the Randstad, the Green Heart is widely known by the larger public. There is an important difference between the two concepts: whereas the Randstad does not have strong defenders and over the years has merely become a place name, the Green Heart does. The strong support from civic society, NGOs and even the business community (see Figure 4.2) to keep this area green is indicative of strong performance via vertical coordination.

The combination of spatial planning and economic policy is another example of performance. Strengthening the competitive position of the Netherlands has been the predominant goal of spatial policy for over two decades. The Fourth Policy Document on Spatial Planning of 1988 identified a "main spatial economic structure" that included "mainports" as a key spatial concept, referring to the essential role of the Port of Rotterdam and Schiphol Airport in the Dutch economy (Ministerie van VROM, 1988), and this served as an argumentative basis for large public investments (Van Duinen, 2004). This could be interpreted as another success for Dutch planning: by allying itself with the institutionally powerful Ministry of Economic Affairs and Ministry of Traffic and Transportation, planning was able to tap into their resources (Hajer and Zonneveld, 2000), and at the same time managed to export its ideas – both the mainport strategy and the main spatial–economic structure had originated in the planning department – to these powerful departments (Zonneveld and Waterhout, 2007). In this sense, the Fourth Policy Document on Spatial Planning was a superb communicative act, one in which internalization comprised the basis for horizontal policy diffusion.

Not all of the concepts in the Fourth Policy Document on Spatial Planning performed well, however. A prime counter-example is the ABC policy, which was intended to guide the location of businesses. In order to promote compact development and public transportation, business locations were divided into three categories: A (central, near rail stations and limited parking), B (easily accessible by both car and public transportation) and C (peripheral, car-dependent) (Van der Cammen and De Klerk, 2012, pp. 393–394). Although the national government favored and invested in development in the first two categories, most construction still occurred at C-locations. The result was immediately visible: sprawling commercial structures along highways throughout the country (Hamers and Piek, 2012), an increasing share of which – partly due to the crisis – lies vacant. A major reason for the failure of the ABC policy is that it went against the prevailing planning practice whereby municipalities use cheap land to lure developers to build business parks within their jurisdiction. The poor vertical performance of the ABC policy shows that in spite of powerful principles and concepts

Figure 4.2 Advertisement in the Summer 2011 editions of the Amsterdam daily newspaper *Het Parool* placed by the chambers of commerce within the Green Heart praising its leisure opportunities (Programmabureau Groene Hart, 2011)

about sound spatial development, local self-interest can sweep these aside. Unless the right incentives are in place at the local level, spatial policies can easily and embarrassingly fail. This fact has become painfully evident since the 1990s as national spatial policy has struggled with institutional change and public-sector retrenchment.

3 Fundamental change within national spatial planning

In 1990, the National Planning Agency published a 25-year retrospective of its activities in its annual report, ending with the words:

> As far as public interest is concerned, spatial planning has nothing to complain about. On the contrary, society is insistently demanding that spatial planning promote economic development and safeguard sustainable development. To answer this call, planning powers should be strengthened.
>
> (Galle, 1990, p. 52; own translation)

Anyone familiar with the current state of Dutch national planning will marvel at how much has changed in two decades. National planning has lost its self-explanatory status, become politicized and is viewed by many as being as much part of the problem as the solution. On the other hand, planning has embraced its inherent pragmatism and focused more on facilitating the market than fighting against it. In this section, we will present our own retrospective of what has changed since these words were written.

3.1 Decoupling and recoupling of institutional linkages

As stated, Dutch national planning attempts to strategically coordinate the actions of others and, in so doing, largely relies on other departments' budgets as well. To be effective, it is essential to find complementary objectives or mutual interests. Over the years, various departments have fulfilled the role of "dual-harness interest" for planning (NSCGP, 1999, p. 16). Since 1990, the relationship between planning and these interests has changed fundamentally.

The link between housing and spatial planning goes beyond that of mere common interest. Modern planning in the Netherlands emerged with the Housing Act of 1901, which gave municipalities powers of compulsory purchase and the authority to designate streets and squares, and impose building regulations. At the national level, the connection between housing and planning was carried forward with vigor directly following World War II (Van der Cammen and De Klerk, 2012, pp. 185 ff.). As part of the same ministry, planning was charged with providing building locations to solve the acute housing shortages caused by wartime damage and the postwar baby boom. At first, locations were sought in existing cities but, by the 1960s and 1970s, planners turned to creating new towns and growth centers, taking advantage of massive housing subsidies. By the 1980s and 1990s, the focus shifted again to urban areas, with the compact city and VINEX policies designating building locations in and at the edges of cities (Ministerie van VROM, 1991). Although not all policy objectives have been reached – such as curtailing private car use – these policies can be regarded as highly successful (in terms of conformance) in that a substantial proportion of the total housing production in the Netherlands since the early 1970s has been realized at locations selected by national spatial planning. Under the VINEX regime (from the early 1990s onwards), the percentage is even above 50 percent (Korthals Altes, 2006).

Even under successive right-of-center government coalitions, spending on public housing had continued to rise. In 1990, following a critical parliamentary inquiry, the government decided to stop subsidizing the construction of public housing altogether (Boelhouwer and Priemus, 1990). Responsibility for housing the poor was transferred to housing associations, which were subsequently privatized. In the course of the decade, these housing associations increasingly assumed the role of a private company: branching out into new markets such as for-profit housing (and not just affordable housing), participating in complex financial constructions, undergoing mergers and acquisitions and selling off existing stock. On the one hand, this enabled the associations to reap unprecedented profits but, on the other hand, exposed them to new risks. This came to a head in the second half of the 2000s. The new practices attracted the attention of the European Commission, which suspected that the hybrid status of the associations was distorting competition since they continued to enjoy preferential treatment in land transactions and low interest rates (Tasan-Kok et al., 2011). The inquiry resulted in a mandatory separation of operations and increased regulation and control. At the same time, many of the investments made prior to the crisis backfired as returns fell far below expectations. At present, a number of housing associations are on the brink of bankruptcy.

For planning, this means there is less of a guarantee that new housing projects are realized at locations and in densities it considers desirable. The timing of housing development has also become less a matter of public policy and more a matter of market returns. In 2010, the separation was complete: the housing directorate-general was formally split off from planning and moved to another ministry.

The link between planning and agriculture is less cozy than that between planning and housing, and can be characterized as more of a convergence of interest than a common mission. The agricultural sector wished to retain control over rural areas in order to maximize crop production, and did so through a series of major "land readjustments" that consolidated ownership and rationalized the landscape (Needham, 2007, pp. 79–83). Profitable agricultural areas indirectly benefited spatial planning objectives of urban containment, as farmers were less eager to sell land for development. Like housing, the agricultural sector has changed dramatically since 1990. Policy is now largely determined by the European Union, which has been gradually phasing out production-based subsidies (Van Ravesteyn and Evers, 2004). Dutch farmers have responded by intensifying production (particularly livestock and horticulture) to remain profitable and diversifying activities (recreation, services and nature/landscape management) for extra income. As a result, agricultural interests have become less vehement about reserving land for crop production. At the same time, the Dutch countryside has become increasingly industrial in appearance as massive greenhouses and livestock sheds have begun to dominate many rural landscapes. This has further undermined the relationship with planning, which has traditionally sought to defend or impose a clear separation of town and countryside. In the mid-2000s, national planning embarked on a short-lived policy called Beautiful Netherlands to combat perceived eyesores in the landscape, including the protection of views from highways (Van der Cammen and De Klerk, 2012, pp. 401–409). At the same time, the planning profession seems to be admitting that the rural idyll no longer exists, and is increasingly viewing these areas in terms of their potential value for urban residents. The ambivalence towards agriculture is reflected in the public backlash against the construction of so-called megastables that hold over 7,500 pigs, 250 cows or 100,000 chickens – a completely rational development from a business point of view, but abhorrent to many on environmental, aesthetic or animal welfare grounds.[4]

Since 1990, environmental policy, and more specifically nature conservation, has partly filled the vacuum left by agriculture. A National Ecological Network (EHS) was designated in the 1990s, much of which is comprised of Natura 2000 habitats, and therefore protected by European law. One of the main elements of the EHS are "key corridors" designed to allow fauna to migrate from one protected area to another. While serving another purpose than urban containment policies such as the buffer zones, these corridors have assisted planners to guide development by designating certain areas as off-limits. A crucial difference is that environmental policies, most of which are European in origin, tend to reinforce sectoral frameworks, making it difficult for planners to freely balance competing land-use claims (Zonneveld et al., 2008). Although escape clauses do exist (e.g. projects that fail the Habitat Assessment can still be realized if there are no alternatives and an overriding public interest exists), in practice European sectoral policy is given priority over other interests. This has put pressure on the Dutch comprehensive integrated approach (CEC, 1997).

Of all policy domains, transport and infrastructure are arguably the most important for national planning. Because of this, it is highly interesting to see which institutional linkages have developed over the years. History shows this has not transpired smoothly, as illustrated by the disagreement surrounding the 1966 Second Policy Document on Spatial Planning. This document is renowned among planners for its powerful vision on the spatial structure of the country in 2000, featuring an intricate urban mosaic with an emphasis on the formation of urban regions – "network cities" in today's terminology – instead of autonomous cities and towns. But these ideas were almost totally disconnected from how planners at the Department of Transport saw the future layout of the country. The transportation planners felt that a vast and intricate tangential system of highways was needed to hook up the entire country to the transportation network. This was not what spatial planners had in mind: in their vision, public transit should play the leading role. Rather than reconciling the differences, the transportation planners simply projected their desired network of motorways onto the spatial planners' out-line of the urban system, which undermined the spatial concept (Siraa et al., 1995, pp. 44, 48). There were negative feelings on the other side as well. The growth center policy of the 1970s and 1980s created resentment in the Ministry of Transport. The transportation planners felt that they had been insufficiently involved in the selection of locations, even though they were the ones who would have to connect the new towns to the donor cities.

Finally, we can consider the institutional linkage with economic development policy. In the late 1980s, international competitiveness was adopted as a main objective of spatial planning. We have already discussed how spatial planning concepts such as the "main economic structure" and "mainports" were exported to economic development policy. This was followed by a "spatialization" of economic policy during the course of the 1990s. Rather than creating a new linkage, however, this actually undermined the political standing of spatial planning (for a full account see Hajer and Zonneveld, 2000). In the mid-1990s, the government set up the ICES (Interdepartmental Commission for the strengthening of the Economic Structure). This committee – lacking an official status – started to look into ways in which, after years of spending cuts, the government could contribute to economic recovery. The ICES recommendations to extend and improve physical infrastructure received a tremendous boost when the government decided to feed the policy with natural gas revenues. As it matured, ICES started to overlap more and more with national planning activities, especially the RPC. The alternative circuit formed by ICES worked within its own paradigm, which is more akin to the economic development style of planning than the comprehensive integrated approach, since it is not focused on strategic territorial frameworks but on investments in specific infrastructure projects. ICES was followed up by another program called ICRE (the last two letters stand for spatial economy), which was somewhat more amenable to spatial planning. Still, since the main decision-making support tools are heavily biased towards the calculation of economic benefits, qualitative criteria such as "spatial quality," which are part and parcel of planning but notoriously difficult to quantify, tend to be excluded from consideration (Marshall, 2009, p. 23).

There are clear signs that the gap is closing between planning, economic development and infrastructure. Since 1999, all investments from the budget of the Ministry of Transport, Public Works and Water Management have been made transparent through the annual publication of the ministry's Multi-Annual Plan for Infrastructure and Transportation (MIT). At the request of the Dutch parliament, the scope of the investment program was widened to include all major spatial investments of the national government. With this, the acronym MIT became MIRT: the new letter stands for *Ruimte* or space. More importantly, the selection criteria for investment were broadened to include spatial concerns. This resulted in "tying project decisions into a more spatialized understanding of goals across the big spending ministries" (Marshall, 2009, p. 26). One could argue that MIRT comes close to replicating the earlier linkages with housing and agriculture. But there is reason for concern as well. According to the official MIRT procedure, decisions on investments should be taken within the framework of one of the seven regional territorial agendas that have been developed by national and lower levels of government. Because of this, the MIRT process is heavily dominated by provinces and major cities attempting to obtain subsidies for their projects. Such a practice is deeply rooted in an administrative and political culture – to a certain extent the result of the fact that 94 percent of all taxes are collected by the national government, making local government highly dependent on central funding – which probably will not change significantly in the short term (Merk, 2004). The fact that the directorate-general of spatial planning has been integrated into the Ministry of Infrastructure and Environment seems promising, but the position of national spatial planning is extremely precarious and strongly overshadowed by much more powerful interests. Moreover, as we will argue now, the position of national spatial planning had weakened from within.

3.2 Rescaling and reform

Despite the auspicious self-assessment of national planning at the beginning of the decade (Galle, 1990), over the course of the 1990s dissatisfaction mounted within and outside the profession. First came criticism of the practice of "passive planning" in which governments simply waited for initiatives from others and evaluated them for consistency with land-use plans and spatial policy. This practice, it was argued, was out of touch with a reality of public-sector retrenchment, new demographic and economic challenges and the rise of a global network society (Hajer and Zonneveld, 2000). In particular, passive planning was blamed for slowing down the construction of homes. At the end of the decade, the respected Netherlands Scientific Council for Government Policy (NSCGP) argued for a new direction: rather than regulating development, the government should become actively engaged in promoting it (NSCGP, 1999). This had been achieved in part at the beginning of the decade by designating VINEX housing locations and creating partnerships for their realization but, as the VINEX policy wore on, it was increasingly felt that local governments and private parties should decide for themselves how to accommodate new housing.

By 2000, facilitating growth had become the central tenet of national spatial policy. Short-cuts through the planning system were implemented to speed up procedures on large-scale infrastructure projects (see Pestman, 2000), and the national government began delegating responsibility for urban development to provinces and municipalities. Although the notion of subsidiarity had already appeared in the Fifth Policy Document on Spatial Planning (Ministerie van VROM, 2001, p. 266), this became the guiding principle of the draft Spatial Memorandum, whose very title was "Room for development: decentralize when possible, centralize when necessary" (Ministerie van VROM et al., 2004). The policy was less regulatory than the Fifth Policy Document on Spatial Planning, which imposed a regime of green and red growth boundaries (Priemus, 2004).[5] In addition, no new housing developments were designated and the ABC policy for business locations was abandoned. Finally, the draft Spatial Memorandum announced the abolition of the national policy restricting out-of-town retail development.

The abolition of national retail policy is illustrative of the complexity of multilevel governance in the Netherlands. For approximately three decades, national planning restrictions had made it nearly impossible to obtain permission for out-of-town shopping malls, retail parks or supermarkets. By decentralizing responsibility, the government had hoped that this would stimulate development (Evers, 2001). Instead, provinces collectively decided to maintain the previous restrictive policy, often using the same terminology in their plans and policy documents. Several attempts by developers to create the first "mall of the Netherlands" soon ran afoul of consensus-oriented polder politics. The first proposal for a development at the junction of the A2 and A15 motorways – a strategic location at the crossroads of the country – was blocked by the province of Gelderland following objections from neighboring municipalities, while a second initiative in Venlo in the southeast met a similar fate. A third proposal in Tilburg in the south of the country caused so much uproar that the municipality held a public referendum to resolve the issue. In this case, the citizens themselves voted down the proposal, fearing the demise of their city center. This example effectively demonstrates that deregulation does not automatically follow from decentralization and that the pro-development stance of the national government is not always followed through in planning practice. In short, the performance of retail policy liberalization was rather poor.

In addition to a national policy encouraging development, the formal planning system was adapted to make the public sector more proactive. This was done by a major revision of the

1965 Spatial Planning Act (WRO). The political sensitivities surrounding the new planning act, combined with the collapse of several government coalitions, delayed the legislative process considerably. The new Spatial Planning Act (Wro) came into effect in 2008 – ten years after the recommendations on which it was based were published.[6] Like its predecessor, the Wro does not address substantive planning issues like in Germany, but only establishes the rules, responsibilities, procedures and instruments of the planning system. The Wro contained far-reaching reforms to these rules, replacing a weak hierarchical plan structure with one in which all three governmental tiers (national, provincial, municipal) have access to the same legal instruments – including the binding local land-use plan. Under the new system, a province or even the national government can unilaterally draw up a local plan and impose it upon a municipality (Needham, 2007). In practice, this usually occurs for infrastructure or non-controversial matters, but there are a few isolated cases where provinces have done this to try to bring about comprehensive urban development against the wishes of municipalities. So far this has met with limited success (Evers and Janssen-Jansen, 2010).

Another important change to the planning system is the abolition of the evaluation of land-use plans by provinces and the national government, the foundation on which the practice of passive planning rested. Higher tiers of government are instead expected to act proactively by establishing general rules in a legally binding ordinance beforehand. If a local plan conforms to the stated requirements, it gains the rule of law as soon as it is approved by the municipal council; no approval is needed from a higher tier of government. The abolition of plan review led many in the planning community to believe that a proliferation of uncontrolled development was imminent. The opposite proved the case: many provinces drew up ordinances that introduced or perpetuated a highly regulatory planning regime. In fact, some ordinances ban virtually all development outside existing centers, and contain clauses to allow exceptions to be granted by the province. This effectively restores the provincial review system under the previous law. While certainly not in the spirit of the Wro, these practices did follow the letter of the law, attesting to the pliability of the formal system to promote either centralization or decentralization (Evers, 2013). It also shows once again that the Dutch planning system is not a unified system across the administrative levels and provides room for diversity – different planning cultures even – at the provincial and municipal levels.

4 Current developments, challenges and controversy

The forces at work since 1990 that have contrived to destabilize national spatial planning have intensified in recent years. Even though it can be regarded as a continuation of a long-term political trend, the coalition agreement presented on 30 September 2010 was still met with disbelief by Dutch planners. After years of perceived decentralization of policy, many were hoping for a guiding vision from central government. Instead, almost no words were wasted on spatial planning: this was to be left up to lower tiers of government as much as possible. To add insult to injury, the official position on housing was to encourage small-scale development in the Green Heart (Coalition Agreement, 2010, p. 61). In the fall, the government announced that it would commence work on a new policy to replace the Spatial Memorandum.

4.1 The National Policy Strategy for Infrastructure and Spatial Planning

Given that it generally takes several years to draft a national spatial policy, the fact that the newly formed Ministry of Infrastructure and the Environment succeeded in producing a draft strategy within a few months while in the midst of a major bureaucratic reorganization is remarkable. At a little over 100 pages, it is far more succinct than the many policy documents it replaces.[7] This is also its intent: the draft National Policy Strategy for Infrastructure and Planning (*Structuurvisie Infrastructuur en Ruimte*: SVIR) stressed that the national government will only act if national interests are at stake, and these interests have been kept to a bare minimum. Specifically, the number has dropped from 39 to 13 (only one of which directly concerns urbanization). The document goes further than the credo of its predecessor (decentralize when possible, centralize when necessary) by making decentralization appear like a goal in itself. The opening lines are indicative:

> To make the Netherlands competitive, accessible, livable and safe, we need to change tack in our spatial planning and mobility policy. Excessive layers of government, complex regulations and compartmentalisation are all too common. Central government therefore intends to bring spatial planning as close as possible to those directly affected (people and businesses), and leave more to the municipal and provincial authorities (decentralization as the first option). This will mean less focus on national interests and simpler regulations. The government expects subnational governments to also strive for more simplicity and integration in the area of spatial policy.
>
> (Ministerie van IenM, 2011, p. 10; own translation)

The heading of this passage, whose tone and content consciously distances itself from half a century of Dutch national planning, is: "changing tack." The statement about bringing spatial planning as close as possible to citizens and businesses is a clear example of this. The resemblance to David Cameron's "big society" is no accident: both the prime minister and the minister in charge of spatial planning belong to the Liberal Party, the Dutch equivalent of the British Conservative Party (Lord and Tewdwr-Jones, 2012).

Most national policies designed to steer urban development have been abolished by the SVIR (see Table 4.1). Many of these had been in place for decades, such as the buffer zones. What had traditionally been a key national interest in national planning – the location of new housing – has been dropped as well. Instead, the SVIR states that "only in the urban regions around the mainports (Amsterdam and Rotterdam) will the national government make agreements about the programming of urban development" (Ministerie van IenM, 2011, p. 12; own translation; "urban development" refers mainly to housing). However, the word programming only refers to the number of houses and not to their location, as in preceding decades. The only national interest that refers to planning specifically is the "ladder for sustainable urban development" (Ministerie van IenM, 2011, p. 55), which introduces a three-step procedure for planning new urban functions.[8] There are mixed expectations as regards the effectiveness of this policy, as it simply requires that a procedure is followed rather than calling for substantive results. In other words, the policy expects performance but does not demand conformance. Tellingly, the SVIR announced that the national government would no longer be checking plans for compliance, arguing that its relationship to other governments should be based on trust. This is, of course, highly consistent with the overall objective of easing restrictions on development but, again, a clear break with the past.

It is also interesting to note that, in general, urbanization concepts are being replaced by economic ones – virtually all of the new policies in the SVIR are geared towards stimulating economic growth. This may be an indication that the Netherlands, once the exponent of the "comprehensive integrated approach," is moving towards the "economic development approach" in the European classification of planning types. Another indication is that many policy objectives – "national interests" in the current terminology – referring to quality have been dropped. Examples are landscape quality, cultural heritage quality, leisure quality and spatial quality (Ministerie van IenM, 2011, pp. 94–99). The fact that spatial quality, which tries to strike a balance between efficiency and sustainability, has been abandoned as a principle is significant, as it is closely tied to the comprehensive integrated approach. Another net effect of these policy changes – especially the aim to eradicate impediments to development – is that restrictions beyond the span of control of the Dutch national government (especially EU environmental directives) become de facto more visible and determinative of the national spatial structure (Evers, 2012).

4.2 Reactions and performance

In the quotation from the draft SVIR, the last line explicitly refers to the desire of the national government that lower tiers emulate its ambitions to simplify spatial policy. There is an obvious tension in this document between the decentralization (or abolition) of national policy and the will of provinces to regulate spatial developments via legally binding ordinances. In an administrative agreement with provinces and municipalities, the national government reit-

Table 4.1 Change in spatial planning policies

Discontinued Spatial Memorandum (2004) policies	New SVIR (2011) policies
Urban bundling (more than half of development must occur in designated bundling areas)	Top-sectors (aid to nine economic clusters)
Intensification (about 40 percent of new development should occur within the built-up area)	Priority regions (involvement in development of Amsterdam and Rotterdam metropolitan areas and Eindhoven)
Location policy for businesses and retail (in centers or near multimodal transport)	Sustainable urban development ladder (three-step approach to urban development)
Basic environmental quality levels	Olympic Games
Urban networks (development of)	
National landscapes (restricted urban development)	
Urban renewal policy	
Buffer zones (development restrictions within)	
Recreation around cities (funds for)	
Concentration of intensive agriculture	

erated its stance and policy choices regarding spatial planning (Administrative Agreement, 2011, p. 40). It remains to be seen to what extent the sub-national governments incorporate this philosophy into their own policies. As demonstrated above, decentralization does not necessarily beget deregulation. There are certainly provinces that are unwilling to ease restrictions on development in the way the national government is advocating. Time will tell if the national government will seek to impose its governance philosophy on provinces and municipalities via a general administrative order. An indication that this will probably not happen is given by the fact that the sentence in question in the draft SVIR was dropped in the final version (Ministerie van IenM, 2012).

There are already some interesting issues as regards the performance of the SVIR (Kuiper and Evers, 2011). An obvious example is the ladder for sustainable urban development. The SVIR requires that land-use plans must describe how the ladder was applied in their explanatory notes. However, there is no assurance that development will occur in conformance with the intent of the ladder, namely sustainable urban development, as any explanation is theoretically valid. Another issue to be watched closely is the "key connections" in the EHS. Previously, the national government had stimulated the acquisition of land in these areas but, in 2011, moved beyond decentralization and deregulation by mandating that the land be sold back to farmers. Whether or not sub-national stakeholders would have heeded this call is moot; the key connections were reinstated after the 2012 elections. Finally, there is every indication that provinces are no more likely to abolish restrictions on out-of-town retail development following the publication of the SVIR than they were after its abolition in the previous national policy document.

5 Conclusion

The national government is retreating from spatial planning. Most national urbanization policies have been abandoned in the SVIR, and spatial quality is no longer considered a national interest. Even more than before, economic development is the main priority of spatial planning. For this reason we have concluded that, at least at the national level, the comprehensive integrated approach is being substituted by a kind of regional economic approach. Interestingly, national planning has not taken on one of the key characteristics of the regional economic approach found in other countries: balanced development. Instead, funding is focused on what are seen as the most competitive areas of the country (in the draft version of the SVIR this was only the regions around Amsterdam, Rotterdam and Eindhoven, but it was expanded to seven regions in the final version; see Figure 4.3). So there is convergence with respect to Europe as well as divergence: convergence because economic goals are dominating, divergence because fair distribution of economic development across the country (one dimension of what is often called territorial cohesion) is not what the present policy seeks to achieve.

National Spatial Network

Competitive

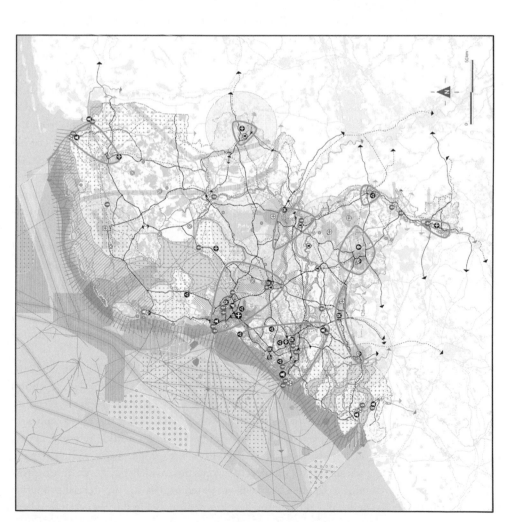

Urban region with a concentration of key sectors

Mainport Schiphol

20 Ke noise contour

Rotterdam Mainport

Brainport Southeast Netherlands

Greenport

Zuidas development

International city of peace and justice

(Potential) site for power plant, from 500MW

(Potential) site for nuclear power plant

High-voltage power line, from 220 kV

New high-voltage power line (approximate route)

Pipeline zone

Pipeline

Existing offshore wind farm

Designated area for offshore wind farm

Potential area for offshore-onshore grid link

Area with high potential for wind power

Accessible

Railway station for High-speed/international trains

Civilian airport of national importance

Seaport of national importance

Inland port of national importance

Potential route for new road on main road network (not yet established)

Potential route for new line on main railway network (not yet established)

National or international main road network

National or international main railway network

National or international main waterway network

Liveable and safe

Main water system

Management of coastal foundation

Primary flood defence

Maintain unrestricted view to horizon

Cultural heritage site on (tentative) World Heritage list

Natural heritage site on World Heritage list

Other property or site on (tentative) World Heritage list

Revised national ecological network on land

Military restricted zone

Radar activity

Military air base

Military air base with civilian use

Naval base

Major military training area and/or artillery range

Figure 4.3 National spatial structure

The fact that the Dutch national planning system no longer nicely fits into the category of the comprehensive integrated approach is related to much wider developments. One can safely say that the system of Dutch spatial planning expanded as part of the construction of the welfare state. Basic principles such as affordable housing for all, balanced spatial–economic development of the country, a balanced urban system (the famous planning concept "concentrated deconcentration" as an expression of this) and open, rural areas as public spaces – including the Green Heart – are the expressions of spatial planning as a particular offshoot of the Dutch welfare state. A clear indication that the current changes are unprecedented is the disappearance of the Green Heart as a national policy concept. As the Green Heart was the cornerstone of what has been called a planning doctrine (Faludi and Van der Valk, 1994), its disappearance marks the end of this doctrine (Faludi, 1991, 1999; Faludi and Van der Valk, 1997; Roodbol-Mekkes et al., 2012). The present objectives, concepts and instruments towards stimulating economic development could become a new doctrine, given a certain durability over time. But it would be difficult to call it a *spatial* planning doctrine unless it becomes more place-based.

Dutch national spatial planning has therefore changed course in more than one sense: (1) content: it is no longer comprehensive; (2) influence over lower levels of government: what was binding in the past has been handed over to provinces and municipalities; and (3) geographical scope: much narrower.[9] These changes may be abrupt and unprecedented in their intensity, but should not come as a surprise. Although spatial planning had been a fairly de-politicized policy domain, it would be naïve to assume that the system could be shielded from the restructuring of the welfare state in which it was historically rooted, and from the profound changes occurring in Dutch society. Since the 1990s, the polder model has eroded as society has become more politically polarized, and with it support for a technocratic activity oriented towards consensus and compromise has eroded as well. The changes were foreshadowed in statements during the second half of the 1990s that planning should become more "selective" – in terms of issues and geographical scope – and more oriented to stimulating development instead of controlling it. But the current changes are far more radical than the reforms advocated by the National Scientific Council for Government Policy at the end of the 1990s (NSCGP, 1999). The current change in course is also the result of a political decision to curtail national planning in terms of objectives, concepts and instruments, and to transform what remains of it into a policy sector aimed at improving the competitive position of the most competitive regions of the country. Unlike the NSCGP's report to reform planning, the current policy course has generally been met with suspicion by the planning community (Warbroek, 2011).

In April 2012, a month after the publication of the final version of the SVIR, the government fell and new elections were called for September that year, resulting in a coalition government comprised of the Labour Party and Liberal Party.[10] The reason for the elections was disagreement about EU austerity measures. The Netherlands is not the only country in Europe where the crisis and European budgetary controls caused a transition in government. But the current and ongoing crisis has impacted territorial development as well. We have already mentioned rising vacancies in commercial properties, which puts even more pressure on the financial system since quite a few banks invested heavily in commercial property. More importantly, it has undermined the urban development model in the Netherlands where financial gains by the municipality from commercial property are reinvested in public housing and urban renewal. Throughout the country, urban development, on which the public sector has become so dependent to finance services, has come to a grinding halt. On the one hand, this could place a natural brake on disorderly development. On the other hand, this may place pressure on the planning system to ease restrictions on development even further.

Notes

1 The Dutch acronym VINEX comes from *Vierde Nota over de Ruimtelijke Ordening Extra* [Fourth Policy Document on Spatial Planning Extra], an addendum of the 1988 document. The term VINEX has entered popular consciousness, being used to describe 1990s suburbia.

2 This verb is derived from the noun polder, the water management unit used for most of the country and neighboring parts of western Belgium. Reclaiming land and building defenses to keep areas protected from the sea was only possible through cooperation and by balancing different interests at the level of the polder, and was not the result of top-down grand schemes.

3 The RPC does not exist anymore. In 2007, it merged with a similar body for environmental policy, the RMC. The new entity was called the Committee on Sustainable Built and Natural Environment (CDL). The rationale behind the merger was to streamline negotiation and deliberation structures in the Dutch government and to combat compartmentalization. Although both the RPC and the RMC had been working quietly behind the scenes – as was a main criticism – the silence surrounding the CDL is even more impressive. There are no CDL evaluations available to the public, and it is highly unlikely that this will change.

4 See: www.animalfreedom.org/english/information/megastables.html (accessed 23 March 2013).

5 Green boundaries are defense lines drawn around valuable green areas; red boundaries are drawn around built-up areas and mark the boundary of urban growth.

6 We follow here the Dutch convention of making a distinction between the old Spatial Planning Act (*Wet Ruimtelijke Ordening*, WRO) and the new (Wro) by the capitalization of its acronym.

7 These are, in Dutch, the *Nota Ruimte*, *Structuurvisie Randstad 2040*, *Nota Mobiliteit*, *Nota Mobiliteitsaanpak*, *Structuurvisie voor de Snelwegomgeving*, *Agenda Landschap*, *Agenda Vitaal Platteland* and *Pieken in de Delta*.

8 The three steps of the ladder are as follows. First, authorities should determine whether a regional need (i.e. market demand) exists. Second, infill development should be considered before greenfield locations. Third, new multimodal locations should be preferred above car-dependent sites. This approach has already been used in practice, with mixed results, for business parks.

9 The last of these was tried before in the 1988 Fourth Policy Document's proposal to focus stimulation policies on the western part of the Randstad. This led to political outcry and a policy modification to widen the scope of beneficiaries. The same fate seems to have befallen the SVIR: the number of regions with top sectors has been increased from three to seven.

10 At the time of this writing, no major change has been carried through by the new government; the SVIR remains official policy. The controversial abolition of key connections in nature policy by the previous administration was however overturned.

References

Administrative Agreement. (2011). *Bestuursakkoord 2011–2015*. Vereniging van Nederlandse Gemeenten, Interprovinciaal Overleg, Unie van Waterschappen en Rijk.

Albrechts, L. (2006). Shifts in strategic spatial planning? Some evidence from Europe and Australia. *Environment and Planning A*, *38*(6), 1149–1170.

Boelhouwer, P. and Priemus, H. (1990). Dutch housing policy realigned. *Journal of Housing and the Built Environment*, *5*(1), 105–119.

Bontje, M. (2001). *The Challenge of Planned Urbanisation*. PhD dissertation, University of Amsterdam.

Boonstra, W. J. and Van den Brink, A. (2007). Controlled decontrolling: involution and democratisation in Dutch rural planning. *Planning Theory and Practice*, *8*(4), 473–488.

CEC – Commission of the European Communities. (1997). *The EU Compendium of Spatial Planning Systems and Policies*. Luxembourg: Office for Official Publications of the European Communities.

Coalition Agreement. (2010). *Freedom and Responsibility*. Coalition Agreement VVD-CDA, 30 September.

Evers, D. (2001). The rise (and fall?) of national retail planning: towards an abolition of national retail planning in the Netherlands. *Tijdschrift voor Sociale en Economische Geografie*, *93*(1), 107–113.

Evers, D. (2012). *The Significance of European Policy in the Context of Decentralization of Planning: The Case of the Netherlands*. Paper presented to AESOP conference, 11–15 July, Ankara.

Evers, D. (2013). *Formal Institutional Change and Informal Persistence: The Case of Dutch Provinces Implementing the 2008 Spatial Planning Act*, Environment and Planning C (accepted).

Evers, D. and Janssen-Jansen, L. (2010). *Provincial Diversity: A Preliminary Assessment of the Implementation of the Dutch Spatial Planning Act of 2008*. Paper presented to PLPR Congress, 10 February, Dortmund.

Faludi, A. (1991). Rule and order as the leitmotif: its past, present, and future meaning. *Built Environment*, *17*(1), 69–77.

Faludi, A. (1999). Patterns of doctrinal development. *Journal of Planning Education and Research*, *18*(4), 333–344.

Faludi, A. (2000). The performance of spatial planning. *Planning Practice and Research*, *15*(4), 299–318.

Faludi, A. and Korthals Altes, W. (1994). Evaluating communicative planning: a revised design for performance research. *European Planning Studies*, *2*(4), 403–418.

Faludi, A. and Van der Valk, A. (1994). *Rule and Order: Dutch Planning Doctrine in the Twentieth Century*. Dordrecht: Kluwer.

Faludi, A. and Van der Valk, A. (1997). The Green Heart and the dynamics of doctrine. *Journal of Housing and the Built Environment*, *12*(1), 57–75.

Frissen, P. (2001). Consensus democracy in a post-modern perspective. In F. Hendriks and Th. A. J. Toonen (eds) *Polder Politics: The Re-invention of Consensus Democracy in the Netherlands* (pp. 61–75). Aldershot: Ashgate.

Galle, M. (1990). 25 jaar realisering van ruimtelijk beleid [25 year implementation of spatial policy]. In *Ruimtelijke Verkenningen 1990 [Spatial Reconnaissances 1990]* (pp. 12–52). Den Haag: Rijksplanologische Dienst.

Gerrits, L., Rauws, W. and De Roo, G. (2012). Dutch spatial planning in transition. *Planning Theory and Practice*, *13*(2), 336–341.

Halffman, W. (2009). Measuring the stakes: the Dutch planning bureaus. In W. Lentsch and P. Weingart (eds) *Scientific Advice to Policy Making: International Comparison* (pp. 41–65). Opladen: Verlag Barbara Budrich.

Hajer, M. and Zonneveld, W. (2000). Spatial planning in the network society: rethinking the principles of planning in the Netherlands. *European Planning Studies*, *8*(3), 337–355.

Hamers, D. and Piek, M. (2012). Mapping the future urbanization patterns on the urban fringe in the Netherlands. *Urban Research and Practice*, *5*(1), 129–156.

Hendriks, F. and Toonen, T. A. J. (2001). *Polder Politics: The Re-invention of Consensus Democracy in the Netherlands*. Aldershot: Ashgate.

Korthals Altes, W. (2006). Stagnation in housing production: another success in the Dutch "planner's paradise"? *Environment and Planning B*, *33*(1), 97–114.

Kuiper, R. and Evers, D. (2011). *Ex-ante evaluatie Structuurvisie Infrastructuur en Ruimte [Ex-ante Evaluation of National Policy Strategy for Infrastructure and Spatial Planning]*. Den Haag: Netherlands Environmental Assessment Agency.

Lord, A. and Tewdwr-Jones, M. (2012). Is planning "under attack"? Chronicling the deregulation of urban and environmental planning in England. *European Planning Studies*, *20*. doi:10.1080/09654313.2012.741574A.

Marshall, T. (2009). Infrastructure and spatial planning: Netherlands working paper. Oxford: Department of Planning, Oxford Brookes University. Retrieved from http://planning.brookes.ac.uk/research/spg/projects/infrastructure/resources/NLWPmay182009final.pdf.

Merk, O. M. (2004). Internationale vergelijking omvang decentrale belastingen: Nederland in middenpositie [International comparison of decentralized taxes: the netherlands takes a middle position]. *BandO November 2004*, 21–23.

Ministerie van IenM – Infrastructuur en Milieu. (2011). *Ontwerp Structuurvisie Infrastructuur en Ruimte [Draft National Policy Strategy for Infrastructure and Spatial Planning]*. Den Haag: Ministerie van IenM.

Ministerie van IenM – Infrastructuur en Milieu. (2012). *Structuurvisie Infrastructuur en Ruimte [National Policy Strategy for Infrastructure and Spatial Planning]*. Den Haag: Ministerie van IenM.

Ministerie van VROM – Volkshuisvesting, Ruimtelijke Ordening en Milieubeheer. (1988). *Vierde Nota over de Ruimtelijke Ordening* [*Fourth Policy Document on Spatial Planning*]. Den Haag: Ministerie van Volkshuisvesting, Ruimtelijke Ordening en Milieubeheer.

Ministerie van VROM – Volkshuisvesting, Ruimtelijke Ordening en Milieubeheer. (1991). *Vierde Nota over de Ruimtelijke Ordening Extra* [*Fourth Policy Document on Spatial Planning Extra*]. Den Haag: Ministerie van Volkshuisvesting, Ruimtelijke Ordening en Milieubeheer.

Ministerie van VROM – Volkshuisvesting, Ruimtelijke Ordening en Milieubeheer. (2001). *Vijfde Nota Ruimtelijke Ordening deel 1: Ontwerp* [*Fifth Policy Document on Spatial Planning part 1: draft*]. Den Haag: Ministerie van Volkshuisvesting, Ruimtelijke Ordening en Milieubeheer.

Ministerie van VROM – Volkshuisvesting, Ruimtelijke Ordening en Milieubeheer, Ministerie van LNV – Landbouw, Natuur en Voedselkwaliteit, Ministerie van VenW – Verkeer en Waterstaat, and Ministerie van EZ – Economische Zaken. (2004). *Nota Ruimte* [*National Spatial Strategy*]. Den Haag: Ministeries van VROM, LNV, VenW and EZ.

Needham, B. (2007). *Dutch Land Use Planning*. The Hague: Sdu Uitgevers.

Nozeman, E. (1990). Dutch new towns: triumph or disaster? *Tijdschrift voor Economische en Sociale Geografie*, *81*(2), 149–155.

NSCGP – Netherlands Scientific Council for Government Policy. (1999). *Spatial Development Policy*. Summary of the 53rd report, Netherlands Scientific Council for Government Policy Reports to the Government. The Hague: SDU Publishers.

Pestman, P. (2000). Dutch infrastructure policies. In J. Van Tatenhove, B. Arts and P. Leroy (eds) *Political Modernisation and the Environment: The Renewal of Environmental Policy Arrangements* (pp. 71–95). Dordrecht: Kluwer Academic Publishers.

Priemus, H. (1999). Four ministries, four spatial planning perspectives? Dutch evidence on the persistent problem of horizontal coordination. *European Planning Studies*, *7*(5), 563–585.

Priemus, H. (2004). Spatial memorandum 2004: a turning point in the Netherlands' spatial development policy. *Tijdschrift voor Economische en Sociale Geografie*, *95*(5), 578–583.

Programmabureau Groene Hart. (2011, Summer). Advertisement by the chambers of commerce within the Green Heart praising its leisure opportunities. In *Het Parool* [Newspaper].

Roodbol-Mekkes, P. H., Van der Valk, A. J. J. and Korthals Altes, W. K. (2012). The Netherlands spatial planning doctrine in disarray in the 21st century. *Environment and Planning A*, *44*(2), 377–395.

Salet, W. (1999). Regime shifts in Dutch housing policy. *Housing Studies*, *14*(4), 547–557.

Siraa, T., Van der Valk, A. J. and Wissink, W. L. (1995). *Met het oog op de omgeving: Een geschiedenis van de zorg voor de kwaliteit van de leefomgeving* [*In View of the Environment: A History of Care about the Quality of the Environment*]. Het ministerie van Volkshuisvesting, Ruimtelijke Ordening en Milieubeheer (1965–1995). The Hague: Sdu Uitgevers.

Tasan-Kok, T., Groetelaers, D. A., Haffner, M. E. A., Van der Heijden, H. M. H. and Korthals Altes, W. (2011). Providing cheap land for social housing: breaching the state aid regulations of the single European market? *Regional Studies*, *47*(4), 628–642. doi:10.1080/00343404.2011.581654.

Toonen, T. A. J. (1987). The Netherlands: a decentralised unitary state in a welfare society. *West European Politics*, *10*(4), 108–129.

Toonen, T. A. J. (1990). The unitary state as a system of co-governance: the case of the Netherlands. *Public Administration*, *68*(3), 281–296.

Van der Cammen, H. and De Klerk, L. (2012). *The Selfmade Land: Culture and Evolution of Urban and Regional Planning in the Netherlands*. Houten/Antwerpen: Spectrum.

Van Duinen, L. (2004). *Planning Imagery: The Emergence and Development of New Planning Concepts in Dutch National Spatial Policy*. PhD dissertation, University of Amsterdam.

Van Ravesteyn, N. and Evers, D. (2004). *Unseen Europe: A Survey of EU Politics and its Impact on Spatial Development in the Netherlands*. Rotterdam/Den Haag: NAi Uitgevers/Ruimtelijk Planbureau.

Wagenaar, C. (2011). *Town Planning in the Netherlands since 1800: Responses to Enlightenment Ideas and Geopolitical Realities*. Rotterdam: 010.

Warbroek, B. (2011). Planologie zonder plan [Planning without a plan]. *Binnenlands Bestuur*, 21 May, 28–35.

Zonneveld, W. (2007). A sea of houses: preserving open space in an urbanised country. *Journal of Environmental Planning and Management*, *50*(5), 657–675.

Zonneveld, W. and Waterhout, B. (2007). Polycentricity, equity and competitiveness: the Dutch case. In N. Cattan (ed.) *Cities and Networks in Europe*: *A Critical Approach of Polycentrism* (pp. 93–104). Montrouge: John Libbey Eurotext.

Zonneveld, W., Trip, J. J. and Waterhout, B. (2008). *The Impact of EU Regulations on Local Planning Practice: The Case of the Netherlands*. Paper presented at the ACSP-AESOP 4th Joint Congress, 6–11 July 2008, Chicago.

5

SPATIAL PLANNING IN GERMANY

Institutional inertia and new challenges

Hans Heinrich Blotevogel, Rainer Danielzyk and Angelika Münter

Chapter objectives

The objectives of this chapter are:

- to explain the institutional system of German spatial planning, which is organized as a decentralized, multi-level system and is rendered very complex by the federal structure of the country;
- to discuss old and new problems of spatial planning in Germany, such as equivalent living conditions, the relationship between metropolitan spaces and rural regions, and demographic change;
- to highlight that on the one hand the institutional system of German spatial planning has developed notable powers of persistence, while on the other hand informal planning instruments are increasingly gaining significance in tackling the challenges spatial planning aims to solve;
- to show that, nowadays, both hard and soft modes of control are combined with one another as modern territorial governance.

1 Introduction

In international comparisons of national planning systems, Germany is often regarded as the motherland of comprehensive spatial planning. It is indeed the case that regional planning associations intended to guide settlement development and transport infrastructure were founded very early (for the greater Berlin area in 1911 and the Ruhr area in 1920). Furthermore, in 1935 under the National Socialist regime, a hierarchical system of spatial planning came into being that aspired to range from the national level to the cities and municipalities (Blotevogel and Schelhaas, 2011). After the Second World War, two German national states emerged, with the individual *Länder* (federal states; singular *Land*) of the Federal Republic of Germany in the West having extensive legislative authority. After long and controversial discussions, a countrywide system of spatial planning was implemented in the 1960s and 1970s; this was characterized by the strong position given to the municipalities and the *Länder*. Following German reunification, the West German multi-level system of spatial planning was extended to cover the new *Länder* in the East. The institutional system

Table 5.1 The German multi-level system of spatially relevant policies

	Spatial planning	Regional policy	Agricultural policy	Environmental policy	Transport policy
Europe (EU)	European Spatial Planning (ESDP, Territorial Agenda)	Regional Policy (ERDF, ESF, Cohesion Fund)	Rural Development Policy (EAFRD)	Environmental Policy, e.g. FFH-Area	Transport Policy, esp. TEN
Federal level	Federal Spatial Planning (BMVBS, 2006; ROG, 2008)	Joint Scheme GRW; NSRF for EU Regional Policy	Joint Scheme GAK; Rural Development Policy	Nature Conservation and Environmental Policy	Federal Transport Planning, esp. BVWP
State level (*Land*)	Federal State Planning (e.g. State Development Plan)	Bundling of European and National Regional Policies, Operational Program	Rural Development Policy	Nature Conservation and Environmental Policy, Landscape Planning	Federal State Transport Planning
Region	Regional Planning (Regional Plan)	Regional Development Concept	Integrated Rural Development ILEK, Leader	Landscape Structure Plan, FFH-Area	Regional Mobility Concept
Municipality	Municipal Development Planning, Local Land-Use Planning	Municipal Business Promotion	Integrated Rural Development, Village Renewal	Environmental Planning, Landscape Plan, Green Space Planning	Municipal Mobility and Transport Planning

Notes:
EU level: ESDP = European Spatial Development Perspective; ERDF = European Regional Development Fund; ESF = European Social Fund; EAFRD = European Agricultural Fund for Rural Development; FFH = Fauna and Flora Habitats; TEN = Trans-European Networks. *Federal level*: GRW = Gemeinschaftsaufgabe Verbesserung der regionalen Wirtschaftsstruktur (Joint Federal and *Länder* Scheme Improvement of Regional Economic Structure); NSRF = National Strategic Reference Framework; GAK = Gemeinschaftsaufgabe Verbesserung der Agrarstruktur und des Küstenschutzes (Joint Federal and *Länder* Improvement Scheme for Agricultural Structure and Coast Protection); BVWP = Bundesverkehrswegeplan (Federal Transport Infrastructure Plan). *Regional level*: ILEK = Integriertes ländliches Entwicklungskonzept (Concept for Integrated Rural Development); Leader = Liaison entre actions de développement de l'économie rurale (Link between actions for the development of the rural economy).

Source: own compilation by Blotevogel

The strategic stipulations for regional policy are established on both state levels, that of the *Länder* and that of the Federal Government, and, especially on the supra-state level of the EU, with graduated levels of specification. Action programs are drawn up on the level of the *Länder*, or – to use EU terminology – the regions. These programs have to fit into the framework program of the federation and that of the EU. The projects and development measures are usually co-financed by the *Land* concerned, the EU and – to a lesser extent – by the federation and the municipalities. This more or less reflects the various influences on the structure of regional policy: the EU establishes the most important strategic guidelines, while in Germany the *Länder* play a decisive role in operational implementation.

Further detailed discussion of spatially relevant sectoral policies or sectoral planning is not possible here due to space constraints. Multi-level system structures are also characteristic in these other policy fields (Table 5.1), although the significance of the individual levels varies considerably. Important in this context is which policies have been "communitarized" and how the division of responsibilities between the federation and *Länder* is regulated by the Basic Law. As is well known, agricultural policy is communitarized, so that the provisions from Brussels play a decisive role here. However, for the implementation of the so-called second pillar of agricultural policy, which is concerned with the development of rural areas, the local and regional levels are particularly important. In recent decades, the EU level has also had significant influence on environmental policy, for instance with the FFH (Fauna and Flora Habitats) Directive and the strategic environmental assessment.

In contrast, landscape planning, which in Germany has always been closely linked to spatial planning, is rather a concern of the local and regional levels. The situation related to transport planning is quite different. Here, the federal level produces the Federal Transport Infrastructure Plan, adopted as a law, which stipulates the extension and renewal requirements of federal transport infrastructure, i.e. for the highways, rail lines and waterways (but not for airports).

Both between the policy and planning levels, i.e. vertically, and between the spatially impacting policies, i.e. horizontally, many interactions and coordination problems exist that manifest themselves, for instance, as thematic overlaps, insufficient agreement and unclear reciprocal effects. Empirical evidence about the intended and non-intended spatial effects of practicing or not practicing coordination between sectoral policies is generally deficient, but several investigations have at least examined the extent to which sectoral policies contribute to the spatial policy principle of equalizing regional disparities, or to what extent they can be attributed with having a spatially polarizing effect. The results are remarkably unambiguous: most federal policies and particularly those that are highly financed have a clearly corrective effect, benefitting rural and structurally weak *Länder* and regions. This is the case for social and employment policies as well as for defense policy, transport policy, fiscal equalization policy, urban development and housing policy, higher education policy, agricultural policy and, of course, also for regional policy. Only research policy has a clearly contrary effect, favoring the structurally strong regions as that is where the vast majority of research institutions are located (BAW and IW, 2009, p. 84). Färber et al. (2009) show that in particular the effects of urban development promotion and housing benefit conform to these goals and contribute towards interregional equalization, and the East German *Länder* profit particularly from the positive effects.

As part of the Spatial Planning Report (most recently BBR, 2012), the Federal Office for Building and Regional Planning regularly informs about the distribution of spatially impacting federal funds among the *Länder*. According to these reports, based on per head residential population, *Länder* with particular structural problems receive greatly disproportionate shares of federal expenditure on spatially relevant policies. This concerns all five of the new *Länder* in eastern Germany and the city states of Berlin and Bremen. In particular, fiscal equalization policy and social and labor market policies strongly benefit the structurally weak regions. Furthermore, transport policy and regional policy also have a clearly equalizing orientation (BBR, 2012, p. 220).

A problem that has hardly begun to be solved is the strategic coordination of the various spatially impacting structural funds and development policies. The development policies are sectorally "pillarized," i.e. strategically and organizationally speaking they primarily follow a departmental principle: they are in the first instance differentiated according to function and only in the second instance according to spatial levels. However, they impact jointly on individual spatial levels or at times even work against one another when intended and non-intended effects offset each other. This problem is particularly virulent on the regional level, that below the *Länder*, because departmental coordination is undertaken on the federal level and on the *Länder* level in the context of the individual governments, while on the regional level corresponding instruments of coordination are largely lacking. In the large states, the district authorities can in part assume coordination tasks, but at times separate informal instruments, such as regional development concepts and regional management authorities, are also deployed on the regional level.

The coordination of spatially impacting policies in terms of their spatial effects has to be judged as wholly insufficient. With the exception of explicitly spatially related policies such as fiscal equalization and regional and spatial policy, the spatial dimension of most sectoral policies only plays a subordinate role. The systematic coordination of programs of the most important spatially impacting policies such as regional policy, agricultural policy, energy policy, infrastructure policy and social and labor market policy seems particularly urgent. This should also include the spatially impacting policies of the *Länder*, whereby here education and higher education policy is of special importance.

3 Old and new challenges

3.1 Challenge 1: equivalent living conditions and the relationship between metropolitan spaces and rural regions

The production and/or safeguarding of equivalent living conditions in all sub-spaces has always been a central concern of German spatial planning. The contrast between prosperous agglomerations and structurally weak rural areas influenced spatial policy for many years. However, this topic lost significance in the 1970s and 1980s, as many rural areas became largely consolidated and many cities were hit by deindustrialization and emigration. After German unification in 1990, as the grave structural weaknesses of the new *Länder* became obvious, the principle of equivalent living conditions gained a new immediacy. Despite massive investments in infrastructure, housing and urban development, high investment incentives for the industrial sector and other financial transfers, the gap in economic performance between the West and East has scarcely lessened.

In the 1990s, the principle of equalization and equivalence therefore remained central, but with two new emphases. The amendment of the Spatial Planning Act in 1998 brought with it a new version of the general principles, in that it introduced the notion of sustainable spatial development as a paramount normative orientation of spatial planning, although the principle of equalizing regional disparities continued to be important. The second new emphasis concerned the greater focus on growth and competitiveness in federal spatial planning. The

MKRO substantiated these ideas by designating "European Metropolitan Regions" in 1995 (BMBau, 1995). They defined metropolitan regions as

> spatial and functional locations with outstanding functions on an international scale that impact beyond the national borders … As motors of societal, economic, social, and cultural development it is hoped that they will maintain the performance and competitiveness of Germany and Europe and contribute towards accelerating the process of European integration.
>
> (BMBau, 1995, p. 27)

The group of metropolitan regions originally numbered six and then seven, and in 2005 the MKRO resolved to enlarge it to a total of 11. Metropolitan regions are regional development confederations in which public and private actors participate. In many of the metropolitan regions, strategic goals are documented in regional development concepts. Typical fields of action are the economy (infrastructure, locational marketing), science and knowledge (research, transfer) and quality of life (culture, leisure). However, their political relevance varies greatly from region to region.

A further step towards emphasizing growth and competitiveness in spatial planning was undertaken by the MKRO in the "Concepts and Strategies for Spatial Development in Germany" (BMVBS, 2006). This document is not formally binding but is intended to influence federal sectoral policies in respect of their spatial effects, and also provides the *Länder* with orientation with regard to content for amendments to their spatial plans. The document contains three guiding principles, whereby the guiding principle "Growth and Innovation" occupies a prominent first place. In line with the so-called Lisbon goals of the EU, this guiding principle emphasizes the contribution of spatial planning to the promotion of growth, innovative strength and competitiveness. The metropolitan areas are seen as playing a particularly important role in driving development, while the rural areas are presented as "stabilization areas" and likewise as "growth areas." While this does not represent a U-turn for spatial planning, a new normative emphasis can be identified in that the traditional equalization objective is supplemented and thus ultimately qualified. As the intensive and at times controversial debates about the guiding principles from 2006 show, the issue of equivalent living conditions remains topical, even if the problem of regional disparities is considerably more complex than is suggested by public discussions of the much acclaimed antagonism between metropolitan and rural areas.

The principle of equivalent living conditions is the subject of controversial discussion. This derives from the fact that it concerns an indeterminate legal concept that requires interpretation through academic–political discourse. The way in which it is understood is thus inevitably socially constrained and time-bound; misunderstandings and misinterpretations are virtually bound to occur. Two criteria are of central importance here (see ARL, 2006): (1) sufficient opportunities to participate in the labor market and earn a living (this is primarily concerned with regional economic performance levels and the regional labor market situation); and (2) possibilities to access facilities providing basic services. Here, the focus is primarily on the accessibility of educational, health and cultural facilities, transport infrastructure and retail businesses.

Thereby empirical findings on regional disparities in Germany reveal that spatial patterns have been relatively stable since 1990; more precisely a layering of a number of patterns can be detected (see, for example, BBR, 2012):

1   A defined West–East divide (especially persistent with regard to economic indicators, very evident also in terms of subjective life satisfaction).
2   A slight South–North divide (persistent with regard to economic indicators since the 1970s but not evident in terms of subjective life satisfaction).
3   An urban–rural divide or, in the urban regions, a rural–urban divide (changing over the course of recent decades due to the weakening of suburbanization in favor of reurbanization).

The development of the indicators over the past two decades reveals an uneven picture. Several indicators suggest a general increase in regional disparities, others the contrary. Rather than a simple dichotomy, we find prosperous/growing areas as well as structurally weak/shrinking areas among both agglomerations and rural regions.

The normative principle of "equivalent living conditions" represents a central social–political task. However, the equivalence principle can today no longer be understood as it was in the 1960s and 1970s in the context of the welfare state model. Compensating for disparities was then understood first as countrywide infrastructure provision serving those regions threatened by out-migration and, secondly, as interregional resource transfer. Today, equalization policy should rather be directed to providing equal *opportunities* (instead of comprehensive services) and, with the unavoidable decline in infrastructure, the focus should be on concentrating near-household services of general interest in central places that require long-term stabilization (ARL, 2006).

The possible conflict between the growth objective and the equalizing disparities objective has long been controversially debated within regional economics and regional politics, and has in the meantime also become a topic of discussion in spatial planning. Ultimately, every society must reach a political decision as to the amount of spatial inequality it can and perhaps (in view of the trade-off with growth goals) must tolerate. In any case, the equalization task of spatial planning and regional policy in Germany continues to be highly topical.

3.2 Challenge 2: demographic change

"Germany's population is becoming fewer, older and more colorful" – this now familiar phrase is often used as a pithy summary of what "demographic change" refers to, a phenomenon that is presenting not only labor markets and social systems but also spatial planning with diverse problems. Although demographic change is actually nothing new, the processes of demographic transformation only penetrated the awareness of the German public at the end of the 1990s, and since then they have become one of the most discussed challenges facing German spatial planning.

According to an official statistical forecast of 2009, the population of Germany will shrink from 82 million in 2012 to between 65 and 70 million in 2060 (Statistisches Bundesamt, 2009). Assuming that the fertility rate of 1.4 children per woman remains at this low level in the future, as it has since about 1980, then future population development will be primarily influenced by increasing birth deficits, while in contrast demographic cohort effects and increasing life expectancies mean that the number of elderly (65+) and particularly markedly that of the very elderly (80+) is increasing. The predicted decline in population already assumes positive net migration in the range of 100,000–200,000 per year; this corresponds to the average net migration of recent decades. Migration has led to an increase in the population of non-German citizens to 7.4 million (2011), the equivalent of 9.1 percent of the total population. By far the largest group of foreigners are the Turks (1.6 million), followed by the Italians and Poles (0.5 million each). The Federal Statistical Office estimates that around 16 million people (2009) with an immigrant background (immigrants since 1950 and their descendants) live in Germany, the equivalent of 19.6 percent of the total population (Statistisches Bundesamt, 2011).

Demographic change affects many rural areas more strongly and especially with greater variability than the mostly demographically stable urban regions and metropolitan areas (BMVBS and BBSR, 2009; Reichert-Schick, 2010). Since the end of the Communist era, extremely low birth rates and sustained out-migration have led to at times dramatic declines of population in many rural areas of East Germany and to a disproportionate aging of the population due to the declining size of successive cohorts. In combination with economic structural weakness (high unemployment, low incomes), several East German regions are threatened by peripheralization despite comprehensive development measures (Barlösius and Neu, 2008; Hüttl et al., 2008). A particular challenge for spatial planning is the often unavoidable decline in services of general interest caused by decreasing viability (BMVBS, 2012; Naumann and Reichert-Schick, 2012; Winkel et al., 2010).

On the other hand, many urban and rural regions in western Germany are characterized by sustained positive net migration. As the migrants tend to be young people in particular, and thus potential parents, the balance of births and deaths is often (slightly) positive. The relocations represent the reaction of people to regionally variable employment opportunities. Not only many cities but also a number of rural regions have remarkably stable demographic and economic structures, often based on highly internationally competitive, mid-sized businesses with great export strength (Falck and Heblich, 2008; Köhler, 2007; Troeger-Weiss et al., 2008). Structurally strong rural regions are found primarily in the wider surroundings of prosperous metropolitan areas (Leber and Kötter, 2007), but there are also a number of rural regions away from the vicinity of metropolitan areas with impressive indicators for structural strength. Examples of this type of area are found, for example, in Lower Bavaria, Upper Swabia or East Westphalia.

The spatial consequences of demographic change are diverse and complex, as are thus the consequences for spatial planning. For example:

- on the one hand the overutilization and, on the other hand, the underutilization of infrastructure;
- increasingly differentiated demands on infrastructure;
- regionally very differing levels of demand for housing and building land.

The second characteristic of demographic change, the "aging" of the population, i.e. the increase in the average age and the large size of the older age cohorts, is intensely discussed with respect to pensions and the health system, but less so in terms of spatial planning. Nonetheless, most German regions are affected, rural and urban, growing and shrinking. This is not only true of rural areas experiencing out-migration, but also of suburban areas, which from the 1960s to the 1980s experienced an influx of families and are now characterized by single-family homes in which only one to two (very) elderly people live. Here, substantial adjustments of infrastructure are necessary; particularly important is that key social and cultural facilities, but also open spaces, are easily accessible without a car.

The internationalization of the population, the third characteristic of demographic change, is found particularly in the larger cities, as these are usually the first target areas for international migration. Owing to the larger number of children in immigrant households, this tends to lead to a reduced aging of the population. However, internationalization presents significant challenges for infrastructural provisions, for instance in the field of education.

In the recent past, federal spatial planning in particular has initiated an abundance of so-called "Demonstration Projects of Spatial Planning" intended to tackle the consequences of demographic change. These have tested the redevelopment of infrastructure, its flexibilization, new forms of cooperation, mixed uses, functional specializations, inter-municipal cooperations, etc. The highlight of these initiatives to date is the "Program of Action for the Regional Provision of Public Services" (BMVBS, n.d.).

3.3 Challenge 3: land policy

Spatial planning and federal policy agree on the goal of reducing the consumption of open space for settlement and transport purposes and thus reducing the increase in sealed surfaces. In line with the sustainable development principle, resource-conserving settlement development and the protection of open space are central tenets of spatial planning at all levels. The national sustainability strategy of the federal government from 2002 sets the goal of reducing the amount of open space consumed for settlement and transport purposes from the ca. 130ha a day of that time to only 30ha a day by 2020 (Bundesregierung, 2002).

Developments since then have, however, failed to conform to this objective. By 2009, the rate of land consumption had only been reduced to about 80ha a day (BBSR, 2011), and it is fairly unrealistic to think that the 30ha goal can still be achieved by 2020. It is, furthermore, uncertain whether the decrease achieved to date actually derives from political and planning strategies or primarily from weakened building activities resulting from the saturation of demand, demographic change and economic uncertainty. It can at least be said that there is a clear downwards trend in the growth of settlement areas, while the amount of land used for transport continues to increase at an almost constant rate (BBSR, 2011). Surprisingly, increases in settlement area correlates hardly at all with regional population increases: while increases in growing large cities are very moderate, they continue to be very high even in rural regions that are shrinking. Clearly, many authorities are trying to combat population decreases by creating new building land.

Why is spatial planning unable to restrict land consumption and achieve the objectives of the national sustainability strategy? It would, after all, be possible to stipulate appropriate limits in the spatial planning plans that would restrict the expansion of settlement and transport areas so that the 30ha goal could be achieved. This problem can only be understood by examining the actors who have an interest in increased land consumption. These are primarily those who want to build, thus especially private households and businesses. They regard a planned supply shortage critically, because it restricts choice and leads to price increases. Planning favors the recycling of building land, but this is also often poorly accepted in practice because brownfield sites seldom correspond to demand in terms of location, layout and potential contamination.

Building land is created by the municipalities in the course of their land-use planning and land development. This is undoubtedly the most important starting place for a resource-conserving land policy. In this context, municipalities often claim that their supply of land for housing and commercial development is "need based." But what does "need based" actually mean? Empirical investigations have shown that demand for land is only one factor among many when it comes to municipal preparation of building land. Many municipalities attempt to attract population and commerce with a supply-oriented land policy, as they regard land availability as an important factor in inter-municipal locational competition. It is only now being recognized in administrations and, with a certain time lag, in politics that space-saving settlement development not only conserves natural resources, but above all avoids the financial risks of high development expenditures and ruinous inter-municipal competition for population and commerce. There are striking regional disparities in this context (BBSR, 2011). Thus, municipalities with particularly expansion-oriented land policies are concentrated in the structurally weak rural regions. Indeed, in light of the fiscal framework conditions (the dependence of the municipal fiscal system on the inhabitants) with their counterproductive incentives, it would be naive to rely on the insight of the municipalities alone. Local land-use planning is coordinated by the *Länder* and regional planning, but nonetheless in practice the municipalities often vehemently contest spatial planning restrictions. Regional plans are usually resolved in committees made up of municipal politicians, and *Länder* planning emphasizes its "municipal friendliness" and often avoids conflicts with the municipalities, rendering expectations of a restrictive management of municipal land policy by *Länder* and regional planning largely illusionary.

Many suggestions have been developed in recent years that aim to make spatial planning management of land utilization more effective; these include those created in the framework of the research program REFINA: "Research for the Reduction of Land Consumption and for Sustainable Land Management" (Projektübergreifende Begleitung REFINA, n.d.). In particular, stringent restrictions, which are often perceived by the municipalities as inappropriately patronizing, are mostly associated with substantial conflict and political costs. Accompanying measures are thus indispensable, so as to encourage the municipalities to recognize that space-saving settlement development ultimately also benefits the municipalities themselves. Required or possible instruments are, for instance, inter-municipal cooperation when it comes to industrial estates, land monitoring and land management, realistic population and household forecasts, and, especially, improved transparency of the follow-up costs and investment risks involved in developing land for building. Neither traditional "hard" state planning management nor "soft" instruments of information, communication and cooperation are sufficient in isolation. Only when both management modes are combined and intermeshed with one another will it be possible to achieve the 30ha objective.

3.4 Challenge 4: expansion of large-scale retail

It is well known that retail is undergoing rapid structural change. Large-scale enterprises are winning market shares at the expense of smaller businesses. While the number of businesses is shrinking, total retail space is continually increasing. However, as overall turnover is stagnating, productivity per unit area is declining. Types of enterprise with car-oriented locations such as large specialist stores, shopping centers and large-scale discounters are increasing their market share, even though turnover per shop is declining here too. Classical department stores and owner-run specialist shops in inner-city locations are, in some cases, experiencing dramatic drops in turnover. Many businesses have had to close, especially on the edge of cities and in urban district centers.

The effects on spatial, settlement and service structures are diverse and are overall clearly contrary to the normative vision of sustainable spatial development. The intense competition between the highly rationalized supply forms leads to low prices and thus to welfare gains, but when overall social and ecological effects are considered, the consequences are unequivocally negative:

- The expansion of large-scale types of enterprise particularly in locations not integrated with the urban built fabric requires – also due to the large car parks – large amounts of land and causes additional motorized private transport.
- The shifts in purchasing power caused by these developments compromise the central functions of the inner cities and the urban district and local centers, leading in some cases to urban decay.
- Shops supplying the population with everyday consumer goods in close proximity to places of residence are declining, so that increasing numbers of households have to use the car to go shopping, and households without access to a car are disadvantaged. Especially in sparsely settled rural regions, the thinning out of the supply network leads to long-distance shopping trips and, furthermore, to complete dependence on motorized private transport.
- The loss of functions from historically evolved centers threatens the diversity of functions in the inner cities and urban district centers, and expansion on the edges of urban areas impacts on the urban townscape, which has grown up over time and is often of historic character. Two constitutive features of the "European City" are thus endangered.

The findings are unambiguous. Retail development controlled exclusively by the market obviously does not lead to spatial, settlement or service structures that correspond with the ecological and social requirements of the sustainability principle. However, in our liberal economic order, as protected by the constitution, planning control of retail requires precise justification and its instruments must satisfy the principle of proportionality. It would thus, for instance, be inadmissible to limit the dynamic of transformations in business forms by using spatial planning to forbid developments and thus to prevent a particular type of business from entering the market; equally inadmissible would be to place all historically evolved retail structures under protection from competition. Instead, spatial planning control can only aim to preventatively avoid negative spatial consequences (Kuschnerus, 2007).

The most important level of action for spatial planning control is undoubtedly that of the municipalities. Building legislation provides the municipalities with a differentiated catalog of management instruments, whereby key roles are played by land-use planning designations, the definition of central services areas and the treatment of large-scale retail pursuant to the Land Utilization Ordinance (BauNVO). For various reasons full use is, of course, not always made of this catalog of instruments. In some cases, the municipalities shy away from the complicated legislative implications, as designations in Local Building and Construction Plans are often contested and then rescinded by the courts due to procedural shortcomings. In some cases, municipalities believe they are better off without formal building legislation, so they can react more flexibly. Here, they fail to recognize, however, that conflicts can often only be solved through land-use planning stipulations and that a *laissez-faire* attitude, while intended to be business friendly, often creates conflicts both within the municipality and with neighboring municipalities.

Effective control of retail development thus generally requires consistent exploitation of the full potential of the land-use planning control options. The binding control tools of urban development law are generally applied when conflicts and unsatisfactory developments threaten and the problems cannot be solved in other ways using informal instruments. Two tools play key roles here: first, consultation at an early stage of development schemes and, second, municipal retail and center concepts. These are informal documents that are generally passed by municipal councils; this gives them a somewhat binding character as the municipality commits itself to the concept. They express political will to ensure ordered retail and center development.

Municipal control of retail development is important but is in no way sufficient, particularly in view of large-scale retail developments. It needs to be supplemented by regional planning control (Hager, 2010). Municipal politicians and administrators legitimately deal primarily in the interests of their own municipalities. However, this focus highlights inter-municipal competition and, with regard to retail, often means that municipalities attempt to attract external purchasing power in a largely saturated market. This inevitably impinges upon the interests of neighboring municipalities. In practice, the problem is especially virulent because the development of enterprises in the manufacturing sector has become rare, while in retail substantial investment pressure still persists. Here, effective control on the level of the "region" is called for. Also on this level, the intelligent combination and complementary implementation of informal and formal management instruments are necessary.

Many conflicts can be solved with informal types of inter-municipal cooperation. The first step is a voluntary commitment to provide information. This should be bindingly agreed among the municipalities, for example in the framework of a regional retail and center concept. Such concepts should cover not only a procedure for dealing with development schemes that impact on more than one municipality but also statements about existing and potential locations for large-scale retail enterprises. Conflicts arise repeatedly when individual municipalities opt out of these agreements, sometimes because local elections have led to changes in majorities or those responsible, sometimes because a particularly lucrative proposal has triggered a change of opinion. It is thus helpful if there is an institution of regional planning that can undertake early consultation on regionally impacting development proposals, that can initiate the drawing up of regional retail and center concepts, and that can, if necessary, chair the process. Informal instruments such as agreements to exchange information and regional retail concepts are often insufficient when it comes to serious conflicts of interests. It is therefore useful if fundamental declarations on retail development are also incorporated into regional plans as binding goals. Good examples in this context are the relevant regional planning stipulations of the Hannover and Stuttgart regions.

3.5 Challenge 5: anthropogenic climate change and energy transition

The decision to phase out nuclear energy in Germany is backed by a broad political consensus and, combined with the foreseeable shortage of oil and gas and critical appraisals of coal and lignite in view of climate protection, requires a change of energy policy that employs two complementary strategies: an increase in the efficiency of energy utilization and the extension of renewable energy production. According to the German federal government's energy concept, the proportion of renewable energy in electricity supplies should increase more than twofold from 17 percent (2011) to at least 35 percent by 2020. By 2050, 80 percent of the electricity supply and 60 percent of overall energy consumption should be covered by regenerative energy sources (Bundesregierung, 2010).

The energy transition requires substantial land consumption and has spatial planning implications on all levels from the municipalities to the national level, involving:

- locations for facilities producing renewable energy, especially wind farms;
- land for solar plants;
- locations for cogeneration plants with combined heat and power units;
- developments for storing energy, especially pumped storage plants and compressed air energy storage plants;
- land for cultivating energy crops and locations for facilities producing energy from biomass, such as biogas plants;
- locations for facilities producing energy from waterpower;
- routes for high and extra-high voltage lines to carry energy from regions with surplus production to regions of consumption.

Not all land needs are of relevance for spatial planning. However, the diverse spatial implications involved make it advisable to draw up integrated regional energy concepts that make explicit the interactions of spatial and settlement development with the extension of renewable energies. Urban development planning is particularly important in this context as many of the land requirements are only of local significance. The amendment to the BauGB in 2011 was intended to extend possibilities for municipal action in the production and utilization of renewable energies and the use of cogeneration. There are, among other things, new regulations concerning open questions about the permissibility of wind energy and solar energy facilities. Three issues in particular concern spatial policy: the spatial planning control of wind energy locations; the planning of routes for extra high voltage lines; and the planning of energy storage plants. An additional factor is the pressure for quick action created by political demands to accelerate the process.

The use of wind energy plays a key role in the extension of renewable energies as it has clear cost advantages particularly compared to solar energy, at least at present, and its extension can relatively quickly supply considerable quantities of energy. Wind energy currently produces by far the largest proportion of energy of all renewable energy sources. To date, wind energy developments have been concentrated in the northern and north-eastern *Länder*, where wind energy already covers between a quarter and half of electricity consumption. Large wind farms are being built or are planned off the coast in the North Sea and the Baltic Sea. In the meantime, increasing numbers of older facilities are being replaced by larger, high-performance wind turbines (repowering). The comparatively limited status of wind energy production in the southern German *Länder* is due to the past lack of political commitment by the *Länder* governments concerned. But the situation has changed as a consequence of the broad level of support for the energy transition.

The question here is whether the development of sites for wind energy should be controlled and, if so, using which instruments. If locational planning is left to the municipalities alone, there is the danger that a patchwork of individual developments will be strewn over the entire country, even in ill-suited locations. It would seem expedient for the various planning levels to cooperate on the basis of the mutual feedback principle. Based on national objectives and regional suitability, the federation would thus specify development goals for the *Länder* and the *Länder* would break down these goals to apply them to the regions. Regional planning would then stipulate regional Priority Areas and Suitable Areas as binding spatial planning objectives, taking into consideration relevant factors such as wind likelihood and nature and landscape conservation. As many investigations have established, there is sufficient potential land available in the interior, and not only offshore in the North and Baltic Seas, to enable the development objectives to be reached.

The second issue concerns the development of the extra high voltage grid. It is well known that the transition to decentralized energy production from renewable sources requires a substantial extension of the high and extra high voltage grid, assuming regenerative energy production is not consistently developed in consumer regions. In 2010, the German Energy Agency estimated that there was a need to extend the grid by 3,600km by 2020, involving costs of about one billion Euros a year. This will involve regional network extensions and, particularly, north–south high voltage lines, as the focus of regenerative energy production is in the north of Germany and it is anticipated that the southern German regions will have to import energy after the end of atomic energy production (dena, 2010).

The planning of an acceptable route for the extra high voltage lines seems a genuine spatial planning task. As the lines cross a large area and impact on many *Länder*, federal spatial planning could have assumed an active role and, for instance, drawn up a spatial planning plan in accordance with the Spatial Planning Act, including the associated strategic environmental impact assessment and public participation. However, with the Grid Expansion Acceleration Act (NABEG, 28 July 2011), the federal legislator has chosen a different option. It is reasonable that, based on overriding national interests, the federation has seized the initiative and drawn up a Requirements Plan and binding stipulations for the routes to be used for the high voltage lines, taking control of the planning process. A more critical view can be taken of the fact that, although the substance of these tasks is spatial planning, a federal sectoral planning department has been established to carry them out

(ARL, 2011a). Spatial planning at the federal level is obviously more urgent than ever, but it is being attended to by a new sectoral planning department.

In the meantime, there are also growing doubts about whether the massive construction of such power lines, repeatedly opposed on the local level, is actually necessary. If the extension of regenerative energy production was better coordinated at a supra-regional level and its development accelerated in the southern German *Länder* in line with requirements, then a new trans-regional power line system would actually be unnecessary.

Time-proven waterpower plants are particularly suitable for offsetting unavoidable fluctuations in wind and solar energy. Both energy storage plants with natural reservoirs (dams) and pumped storage plants are appropriate; they provide by far the greatest capacities. However, their development is only viable in areas with the appropriate relief conditions and substantial variations in altitude. Their construction furthermore involves significant intervention in the landscape and is usually greeted with fierce opposition by the populations of the affected regions. Here too it is clear that many questions concerning the ambitious German energy transition remain unresolved.

4 Dimensions and directions of change

The system of spatially related planning in Germany has been the subject of profound restructuring in recent decades. Spatial planning was implemented in the 1960s and 1970s as a multi-level system ranging from the municipality to the nation state, equipped with a differentiated set of legal management tools and inspired by the aspiration of comprehensive control, but it was never able to develop the impact intended to the expected extent. Its goals proved to be overly complicated, it suffered from the discrepancy between high aspirations and low resources, and ultimately strong sectoral policies such as regional policy and transport policy refused to submit to spatial planning coordination (Blotevogel and Schelhaas, 2011, pp. 160 ff.). Furthermore, the traditional planning system was implemented at a time of high population and economic growth rates, and had a rather reactive orientation, while at least since the 1980s proactive development planning has been called for. Spatial planning has been, however, fairly successful in the vertical coordination of *Länder* planning, regional planning and municipal land-use planning. The relationship between supra-local control and municipal planning autonomy is a source of constant conflict but, since the 1970s, the principles of subsidiarity and mutual feedback have often led to appeasement and fruitful cooperation between municipal and state planning.

In the 1990s and 2000s, this resulted in an ambivalent situation. The formal spatial planning system with its legal legitimacy, binding plans and supplementary tools for the safeguarding and implementing of spatial planning norms continued to exist and was often amended, but it actually lost some part of its control capacity. That is not to say that spatial planning had become ineffective, but it moved further from the center stage of political attention, and new problems arose for which traditional spatial planning tools were either unsuitable or were viewed by policymakers as being insufficiently suitable. This led to the development of new institutions, for example the new sectoral planning department for the planning of the high and extra high voltage lines.

Old and new challenges lead to constant pressure on the German planning system to adapt. The institutionalized planning system is dealing with the new challenges with a set of tools that was developed in the past, in part under other historical framework conditions. It can thus be asked whether the traditional planning system is able to cope with the new challenges and whether and how it is changing by a transformation of its guiding principles, legislative regulations and procedural processes.

The German planning system needs to process "inputs" from three directions – from above (1), from below (2) and from the sectoral policy departments, i.e. from the side (3).

(1) First, on the higher European level, spatial guiding visions are discursively debated and coded as principles of spatial development in documents of varying legal status and impact. Examples include the European Spatial Development Perspective (ESDP, 1999), the Leipzig Charter on Sustainable European Cities (2007) and the Territorial Agenda of the European Union (2007, 2011), and also the introduction of the territorial cohesion objective in the EU Treaty of Lisbon (2007). Also significant are the controversial debates on the goal-setting of European regional policy, which in the programming period of 2007 -2013 led to the juxtaposition of the convergence goal (inter-regional equalization objective) with the goal "regional competitiveness and employment" (growth objective).

The relationship between European and German spatial policy is characterized by considerable contingency. It is inaccurate to speak of a simple takeover at the scale of 1:1, rather the situation has been one of reciprocal impulses. German authorities have usually been actively involved in European discourses and introduced their arguments, which were often based on the experiences and traditions of the German planning system, into international debates. Moreover, the European principles are either relatively abstract, leaving Member States a great deal of scope for interpretation (regional policy), or they lack legally binding character (spatial planning). The European discourse thus rather forms a framework for spatial policy debates in Germany.

Examples of the effect of the European discourse on German spatial planning are found in the "Concepts and Strategies for Spatial Development in Germany" (BMVBS, 2006) passed by the German Ministerial Conference on Spatial Planning in 2006. This included discussion of a polycentric system of cities distributed over the entire federal territory and the composition of cultural landscapes, topics that are included in similar form in the 1999 ESDP.

(2) Second, the German planning system experiences pressure to change from bottom-up inputs. This is the case when concrete challenges on the municipal or regional scale lead to the questioning of the effectiveness of conventional planning tools, and new procedures are tested that can, in turn, lead to a change in the institutionalized planning system.

One example of this is inter-municipal cooperation in the Ruhr area (Hohn and Reimer, 2010). An initially informal cooperation network of large cities led to the wish to introduce a new formal instrument: a regional land-use plan for the six cities located at the core of the Ruhr area. A further example is the cooperative partnership in the Cologne–Bonn area that emerged within the framework of the regional structural program REGIONALE 2010 to tackle issues concerning the regional cultural landscape (Reimer, 2012). Here, informal processes of inter-municipal cooperation have revealed system incongruence through the lack of fit of existing development tools. Conventional development instruments from the various sectoral departments are often no longer able to deal with the new spatial challenges and require adaptation, which in these cases was initiated from "below," thus finding a route into valid planning law.

(3) The relationship between spatial planning on the one hand and the spatially relevant sectoral policies and sectoral planning on the other is extremely complex. It is possible to detect a growing independence of sectoral planning as a long-term trend. The increasingly "pillarized" sectoral planning departments reject the coordinating aspirations of spatial planning in its role as a supra-sectoral comprehensive planning body, so that problems of horizontal coordination continue to be unresolved (see section 2.2). The strategic potential of the supra-sectoral nature of spatial planning is but little exploited in Germany today. On the federal level and in most of the *Länder*, spatial planning is only a department in a sectoral ministry (usually in the department for the economy and/or infrastructure). Strategic concepts that aspire to coordinate sectoral planning have become rare; it is only the cities that, since the 1990s, have increasingly seized upon the notion of strategically oriented spatial planning, and this is in the form of informal strategic urban development concepts (Franke and Strauss, 2010; Hamedinger et al., 2008; Kühn and Fischer, 2010).

That is not to say that it is possible to speak of a general isolation or marginalization of spatial planning. In many sectoral planning laws, there are so-called spatial planning clauses stipulating that sectoral planning is to observe or consider the objectives and principles of spatial planning. In addition to such legislative possibilities, the influence of spatial planning is in practice primarily dependent on three factors:

- First, spatial planning can successfully influence sectoral planning when it can make qualified specialist contributions, for instance with the analysis of the spatial consequences of planned social infrastructure or with information about spatial restrictions deriving from other planning requirements of spatial planning or the planning of other departments.
- Second, spatial planning can deploy its own (very limited) political influence together with that of other policy areas, so as to achieve common objectives. One example here is creating the necessary acceptance for unavoidable reductions in infrastructure caused by declining viability due to demographic change.
- Third, spatial planning can offer its time-proven participation and communication procedures for use in the search and assessment of controversial infrastructure projects, as sectoral planning departments often have little experience with participative and cooperative planning processes.

The structural weaknesses of the traditional German spatial planning system discussed here make informal planning processes seem particularly attractive. Experience shows that they are often able to react to new challenges more quickly, more flexibly and at times more effectively. Their utilization can also maintain the functionality of formal institutionalized planning without requiring systemic restructuring processes that are associated with high transformation costs. Informal processes are particularly attractive when formal procedures of organization no longer lead to the desired successes (Hillier, 2002, pp. 126 ff.). The task for planners is then to act circumspectly and intelligently within the power-driven political processes of planning. Particularly on the local and regional levels, experimental forms of planning activity are being tested (Gualini, 2004) that can lead to a temporary bypassing of formal planning structures.

In this respect, the structural transformations of the planning system have led to scale shifting, also in Germany, actually more strongly within the practice of planning culture than within the formal institutional framework. It is well known that administrative structures tend, to a great extent, to uphold systems, so it is hardly surprising that the formal spatial planning system in Germany has changed but little since its introduction in the 1970s, with the exception of the radical transformations in the new *Länder* following German unification in 1990. Of course, the Spatial Planning Act, the planning legislation of the *Länder* and the plans and programs of spatial planning have been repeatedly amended over the decades, but this has only led to isolated adaptations. In the last two decades, relevant systemic scale shifting has occurred in three regards.

First, in the course of the reform of federalism of 2006, the federation lost its legislative authority to set frameworks for spatial planning. The Spatial Planning Act of 2008 is only legally binding for federal spatial planning, while since this time the *Länder* have had the right to deviate from the federal framework, although to date only Bavaria has made use of this right. While this reform strengthened the position of the *Länder* at the expense of the federation, the amendment of the Spatial Planning Act of 2008 also gave the federation the authority to prepare spatial planning plans for the entire federal territory. The federation has not actually used this authority yet, although the need for action on problems simultaneously affecting several *Länder* is urgent (airports, energy transition).

Second, in several *Länder* a trend to transfer authority from the *Länder* planning level to the regional planning level can be observed. This ranges from comprehensive and binding commissions being given to regional planning (e.g. in Saxony and Thuringia) to the cutting back of *Länder* spatial planning to the absolute legal minimum combined with the transfer of authority to regional planning on the basis of trust (Lower Saxony) (Münter and Schmitt, 2007).

Third, a general trend towards the municipalization of regional planning can be noted. Regional planning represents an intersection between *Länder* and municipal planning. The organization of this planning level is the responsibility of the *Länder*, which has led to the development of very varied forms of organization with greatly differing emphases being given to municipal and state components. The *Länder* have a genuine interest in their planning objectives and principles being substantiated on the regional level in accordance with the political will of the state, but how this actually occurs tends to be left to the municipalities, especially when they are willing to participate in inter-municipal coordination and consensus building. Lower Saxony has taken this "downwards" transfer of authority to the furthest extreme in that it has transferred regional planning tasks to the districts, i.e. to the municipal level.

Despite the trend to municipalization, it would be an oversimplification to speak of one-sided "downwards" scale shifting in the practice of German spatial planning. Although we can observe a tendency on the higher levels of spatial planning to reduce the "complexity" of binding stipulations in favor of informal types of control, it is nonetheless doubtful that this is connected with a general loss of control for high-level spatial planning. The combination of formal and informal types of control, which can also be collectively referred to as "regional governance," leads to a new pattern of control that is geared not towards the intentional influencing of actions (as in traditional understandings of control) but rather towards processes of coordinating the action of the actors involved. The increase in importance of this mode of control corresponds with a changed understanding of the state (Fürst, 2006, 2010).

The "downwards" transfer of authority and municipalization do not in any way mean that spatial planning is simply left to the individual municipalities. That is bound to end in disaster, if only because the municipal territorial structure in many *Länder* is much too small scale and many municipalities would be overstretched simply due to a lack of the necessary administrative personnel. Moreover, there is broad political consensus that a simple municipalization is inappropriate as a matter of principle. Most planning decisions cause external territorial effects that require the participation of neighboring municipalities. Dealing with large-scale retail is one particularly striking example of this. A further issue is that declining viability renders it impossible for many municipalities to provide a satisfactory array of infrastructure without inter-municipal cooperation. This regionalization of municipal planning corresponds to a regionalization of the action spaces of the population, who increasingly seek their places of work, shopping destinations, services and leisure-time activities not only in the municipality in which they live but in the region as a whole. The "downwards" scale shifting of spatial planning thus faces an "upwards" shifting of spatial planning issues.

In terms of municipal planning, this situation leads not to an increase in the significance of regional planning, but in a vast array of inter-municipal cooperations and new forms of governance on a small regional scale. An upwards scale shifting of spatial planning to the federal or *Länder* level has, to date, rarely been observed in Germany. Examples include the control of large-scale retail by *Länder* planning (e.g. in North Rhine-Westphalia) and the establishment of a federal sectoral planning department for the planning of the high and extra high voltage lines.

Who are the actors driving change in the German planning process? It is difficult to identify individual groups of actors as significant driving forces, as the transformation of the planning system forms part of a further reaching political–administrative system change, which has involved the introduction of new forms of governance to supplement traditional norm-bound administrative action. In some regards, the planning authorities are even pioneers of this political–administrative change, as planning activities have always been more closely tied to politics, less norm-bound and more problem-solving oriented than most administrative activities. The innovations in the German spatial planning system were without doubt primarily initiated by challenging new problems, new impulses that traditional tools could not satisfactorily manage. This includes not only the challenges discussed above, but also the change from an understanding of planning as "reactive" to one of planning as "proactive," i.e. the development from "structural planning" to "development planning." New forms of cooperative control were introduced from the 1980s onwards to accommodate this change, and were initially tested on the municipal and regional levels. The most important impulses for these initiatives came from innovative municipal and ministerial civil servants and professional planners, followed increasingly by stakeholder groups (associations, chambers of commerce, citizens' initiatives) who were drawn into preparing planning decisions as part of wider participatory processes.

The ability of a planning system to react and adapt is dependent on the historically evolved domestic institutional cultures (Börzel, 1999), i.e. the local and regional political cultures that are framed by the formal planning system but, at the same time, are objects of individual and collective processes of interpretation and action routines. The formal planning system thus only defines a framework that sets corridors of action for planning professionals (Janin

Rivolin, 2008). These findings urge caution to be taken with generalized statements about the trends and transformations of the German planning system. Germany is a federally constituted country with 16 *Länder* that enjoy far-reaching autonomy, particularly in the field of spatial planning, and with municipal planning autonomy that is anchored in the constitution. It is thus clearly questionable to speak of *one* German planning system even when only referring to the formal institutional system, and still more questionable when the focus is on planning practice. The domestic planning cultures as styles of planning practice can hardly be reduced to a single national denominator, as they differ vertically according to planning levels and horizontally according to spatially relevant policy fields, as well as – last but by no means least – territorially according to *Länder*, regions and municipalities.

5 Conclusion

German spatial planning has changed fundamentally since the 1970s. However, central tasks such as ensuring equivalent living conditions continue to be topical and the formal institutional framework has only been changed in part. But, generally speaking, spatial planning has become more strategic and, at the same time, more communicative and networked (see ARL, 2011b). Both hard and soft modes of control have become accepted standards and are combined with one another as modern territorial governance. Here the principle is: soft forms of communication and consensus building as much as possible, hard forms of binding goals and hierarchical control as much as necessary

It is difficult to assess the consequences of the current economic recession that has followed on the heels of the financial crisis. The German economy came through the 2008/2009 recession comparatively quickly and has returned to a path of moderate growth, but nonetheless the high levels of public debt and the fiscal shortages are having an obstructive effect on systems of spatially related planning. Public administrations are forced to cut personnel and the planning authorities are often disproportionally hit by such budget cuts. Simultaneously, European integration and globalization are leading to intensified locational competition, causing the cities and regions to react with increasingly aggressive locational policies in order to attract investment, qualified labor and tourists. Traditional planning systems are, however, little suited to such tasks, so that cities and regions are developing new strategies and institutions and often subordinating planning to economic policy objectives.

From the point of view of spatial planning with its commitment to the guiding principle of sustainable development, reacting to crises with this sort of priority setting is fatal. When the financial and economic crisis occupies the political limelight and neoliberal recipes are applied in an effort to combat it, then not only is the balance of the sustainability triangle threatened, but there is a danger that developments may lead to an anorexic state with marginalized spatial planning. Admittedly this dispute has not yet been concluded. The latest financial and economic crisis has shown the importance of well-functioning public institutions, including state control. In debates on the demarcation between market and state, on the role of civil society and the improvement of public spending effectiveness, spatial planning is but one piece of the jigsaw and can only fulfill its task – guaranteeing sustainable spatial development – with a functioning state and cooperative citizenship.

References

ARL – Akademie für Raumforschung und Landesplanung. (2006). *Positionspapier aus der ARL No. 69: Gleichwertige Lebensverhältnisse: eine wichtige gesellschaftspolitische Aufgabe neu interpretieren!* Hannover: ARL.

ARL – Akademie für Raumforschung und Landesplanung. (2011a). *Positionspapier aus der ARL No. 88: Raumordnerische Aspekte zu den Gesetzentwürfen für eine Energiewende.* Hannover: ARL.

ARL – Akademie für Raumforschung und Landesplanung. (2011b). *Positionspapier aus der ARL No. 84: Strategische Regionalplanung.* Hannover: ARL.

Barlösius, E. and Neu, C. (eds) (2008). *Peripherisierung: eine neue Form sozialer Ungleichheit?* Berlin: Berlin-Brandenburgische Akademie der Wissenschaften.

BauGB – Baugesetzbuch i.d.F. der Bekanntmachung vom 23 September 2004 (BGBl. I S. 2414), zuletzt geändert durch Artikel 1 des Gesetzes vom 22 Juli 2011 (BGBl. I S. 1509).

BauNVO – Verordnung über die bauliche Nutzung der Grundstücke (Baunutzungsverordnung) i.d.F. der Bekanntmachung vom 23 Januar 1990 (BGBl. I S. 132), zuletzt geändert durch Artikel 3 des Gesetzes vom 22 April 1993 (BGBl. I S. 466).

BAW Institut für regionale Wirtschaftsforschung GmbH Bremen and IW Consult GmbH Köln. (2009). *Koordinierung raumwirksamer Politiken. Möglichkeiten des Bundes, durch die Koordinierung seiner raumwirksamen Politiken regionale Wachstumsprozesse zu unterstützen.* Köln: IW Consult.

BBR – Bundesamt für Bauwesen und Raumordnung. (2012). *Raumordnungsbericht 2011.* Berlin: Deutscher Bundestag, Drucksache 17/8360.

BBSR – Bundesinstitut für Bau-, Stadt- und Raumforschung (ed.) (2011). *Auf dem Weg, aber noch nicht am Ziel: Trends der Siedlungsflächenentwicklung.* BBSR-Berichte KOMPAKT 10/2011. Bonn: BBSR.

Blotevogel, H. H. (2012). Die Regionalpolitik in Deutschland: institutioneller Aufbau und aktuelle Probleme. In H. Egli and L. Boulianne (eds) *Tagungsband: Forschungsmarkt regiosuisse and Tagung Regionalentwicklung 2011. Regionalpolitik in den Nachbarländern: Lessons Learned und Folgerungen für die Schweiz* (pp. 41–60). Luzern: Institut für Betriebs- und Regionalökonomie IBR.

Blotevogel, H. H. and Schelhaas, B. (2011). Geschichte der Raumordnung. In ARL – Akademie für Raumforschung und Landesplanung (ed.) *Grundriss der Raumordnung und Raumentwicklung* (pp. 75–201). Hannover: ARL.

BMBau – Bundesministerium für Raumordnung, Bauwesen und Städtebau (ed.) (1995). *Raumordnungspolitischer Handlungsrahmen. Beschluß der Ministerkonferenz für Raumordnung in Düsseldorf am 8 März 1995.* Bonn: BMBau.

BMVBS – Bundesministerium für Verkehr, Bau und Stadtentwicklung (ed.) (2006). *Concepts and Strategies for Spatial Development in Germany. Adopted by the Standing Conference of Ministers responsible for Spatial Planning on 30 June 2006.* Berlin: BMVBS.

BMVBS – Bundesministerium für Verkehr, Bau und Stadtentwicklung (ed.) (2012). *Region schafft Zukunft: Ländliche Infrastruktur aktiv gestalten.* Berlin: BMVBS.

BMVBS – Bundesministerium für Verkehr, Bau und Stadtentwicklung (ed.) (n.d.). *Program of Action for the Regional Provision of Public Services.* Retrieved from www.regionale-daseinsvorsorge.de/68.

BMVBS – Bundesministerium für Verkehr, Bau und Stadtentwicklung and BBSR – Bundesinstitut für Bau-, Stadt- und Raumforschung (eds) (2009). *Ländliche Räume im demografischen Wandel.* BBSR-Online-Publikation 34/09. Bonn: BBSR.

Börzel, T. A. (1999). Towards convergence in Europe? Institutional adaptation to Europeanisation in Germany and Spain. *Journal of Common Market Studies*, *37*(4), 573–596.

Bundesregierung der Bundesrepublik Deutschland (ed.) (2002). *Perspektiven für Deutschland: Unsere Strategie für eine nachhaltige Entwicklung.* Berlin: Bundesregierung.

Bundesregierung der Bundesrepublik Deutschland (ed.) (2010). *Energiekonzept für eine umweltschonende, zuverlässige und bezahlbare Energieversorgung.* Beschluss des Bundeskabinetts vom 28 September 2010. Berlin: Bundesregierung.

Danielzyk, R. and Knieling, J. (2011). Informelle Planungsansätze. In ARL – Akademie für Raumforschung und Landesplanung (ed.) *Grundriss der Raumordnung und Raumentwicklung* (pp. 473–498). Hannover: ARL.

dena – Deutsche Energie Agentur (ed.) (2010). *dena-Netzstudie II. Integration erneuerbarer Energien in die deutsche Stromversorgung im Zeitraum 2015–2020 mit Ausblick auf 2025.* Berlin: dena.

Eckey, H.-F. (2011). Wirtschaft und Raumentwicklung. In ARL – Akademie für Raumforschung und Landesplanung (ed.) *Grundriss der Raumordnung und Raumentwicklung* (pp. 637–660). Hannover: ARL.

Einig, K. (2010). Die Abgrenzung von Planungsräumen der Regionalplanung im Ländervergleich. In B. Mielke and A. Münter (eds) *Neue Regionalisierungsansätze in Nordrhein-Westfalen*. Arbeitsmaterial der ARL, No. 352 (pp. 4–31). Hannover: ARL.

ESDP. (1999). *European Spatial Development Perspective: Towards Balanced and Sustainable Development of the Territory of the European Union*. Luxembourg: Office for Official Publications of the European Communities.

Falck, O. and Heblich, S. (eds) (2008). *Wirtschaftspolitik in ländlichen Regionen*. Berlin: Duncker and Humblot.

Färber, G., Arndt, O., Dalezios, H. and Steden, P. (2009). Die regionale Inzidenz von Bundesmitteln. In H. Mäding (ed.) *Öffentliche Finanzströme und räumliche Entwicklung* (pp. 9–48). Hannover: ARL.

Franke, T. and Strauss, W.-C. (2010). Integrierte Stadtentwicklung in deutschen Kommunen: eine Standortbestimmung. *Informationen zur Raumentwicklung* (4/2010), pp. 253–262.

Fürst, D. (2006). Regional Governance: ein Überblick. In R. Kleinfeld, H. Plamper and A. Huber (eds) *Regional Governance. Steuerung, Koordination und Kommunikation in regionalen Netzwerken als neue Formen des Regierens*. Vol. 1 (pp. 37–59). Göttingen: VandR Unipress.

Fürst, D. (2010). *Raumplanung: Herausforderungen des deutschen Institutionensystems*. Detmold: Rohn.

Goppel, K. (2005). Landesplanung. In ARL – Akademie für Raumforschung und Landesplanung (ed.) *Handwörterbuch der Raumordnung* (pp. 563–571). Hannover: ARL.

Goppel, K. (2011). Programme und Pläne. In ARL – Akademie für Raumforschung und Landesplanung (ed.) *Grundriss der Raumordnung und Raumentwicklung* (pp. 435–450). Hannover: ARL.

Gualini, E. (2004). Regionalization as "experimental regionalism": the rescaling of territorial policy-making in Germany. *International Journal of Urban and Regional Research*, *28*, 329–353.

Hager, G. (ed.) (2010). *Regionalplanerische Steuerung des großflächigen Einzelhandels: Kleine Regionalplanertagung Baden-Württemberg 2009*, Arbeitsmaterial der ARL, No. 354. Hannover: ARL.

Hamedinger, A., Frey, O., Dangschat, J. S. and Breitfuss, A, (eds) (2008). *Strategieorientierte Planung im kooperativen Staat*. Wiesbaden: VS Verlag.

Hillier, J. (2002). *Shadows of Power: An Allegory of Prudence in Land-use Planning*. London: Routledge.

Hohn, U. and Reimer, M. (2010). Neue Regionen durch Kooperation in der polyzentrischen "Metropole Ruhr." In B. Mielke and A. Münter (eds) *Neue Regionalisierungsansätze in Nordrhein-Westfalen* (pp. 60–83). Arbeitsmaterial der ARL, No. 352. Hannover: ARL.

Hüttl, R. F., Bens, O. and Plieninger, T. (eds) (2008). *Zur Zukunft ländlicher Räume: Entwicklungen und Innovationen in peripheren Regionen Nordostdeutschlands*. Berlin: Akademie Verlag.

Janin Rivolin, U. (2008). Conforming and performing planning systems in Europe: an unbearable cohabitation. *Planning Practice and Research*, *23*(2), 167–186.

Köhler, S. (ed.) (2007). *Wachstumsregionen fernab der Metropolen: Chancen, Potenziale und Strategien*. Arbeitsmaterial der ARL, No. 334. Hannover: ARL.

Krautzberger, M. and Stüer, B. (2009). Das neue Raumordnungsgesetz des Bundes. *Baurecht* (2–2009), pp. 180–191.

Kühn, M. and Fischer, S. (2010). *Strategische Stadtplanung: Strategiebildung in schrumpfenden Städten aus planungs- und politikwissenschaftlicher Perspektive*. Detmold: Rohn.

Kuschnerus, U. (2007). *Der standortgerechte Einzelhandel*. Bonn: vhw-Verlag.

Langhagen-Rohrbach, C. (2011). Verkehr und Raumentwicklung. In ARL – Akademie für Raumforschung und Landesplanung (ed.) *Grundriss der Raumordnung und Raumentwicklung* (pp. 719–756). Hannover: ARL.

Leber, N. and Kötter, T. (2007). *Entwicklung ländlicher Räume und der Landnutzung im Einzugsbereich dynamischer Agglomerationen*. Bonn: Landwirtschaftliche Fakultät der Rheinischen Friedrich-Wilhelms-Universität Bonn.

Leipzig Charter on Sustainable European Cities. (2007). Retrieved from http://ec.europa.eu/regional_policy/archive/themes/urban/leipzig_charter.pdf.

Münter, A. and Schmitt, P. (2007). *Landesraumordnungspläne in Deutschland im Vergleich: Vergleichende Analyse der Pläne und Programme von 12 Bundesländern ohne NRW*. Abschlussbericht. Dortmund: ILS.

NABEG – Netzausbaubeschleunigungsgesetz Übertragungsnetz vom 28 Juli 2011 (BGBl. I S. 1690) zuletzt geändert durch Artikel 4 des Gesetzes vom 20 Dezember 2012 (BGBl. I S. 2730).

Naumann, M. and Reichert-Schick, A. (2012). Infrastrukturelle Peripherisierung: Das Beispiel Uecker-Randow (Deutschland). *disP*, *48*(1), 27–45.

Projektübergreifende Begleitung REFINA. (n.d.). *Research for the Reduction of Land Consumption and for Sustainable Land Management (REFINA)*. Retrieved from www.refina-info.de/en.

Reichert-Schick, A. (2010). Auswirkungen des demographischen Wandels in regionaler Differenzierung: Gemeinsamkeiten und Gegensätze ländlich-peripherer Entleerungsregionen in Deutschland, die Beispiele Vorpommern und Westeifel. *Raumforschung und Raumordnung*, *68*(3), 153–168.

Reimer, M. (2012). *Planungskultur im Wandel: Das Beispiel der REGIONALE 2010*. Detmold: Rohn.

ROG – Raumordnungsgesetz vom 22 Dezember 2008 (BGBl. I S. 2986), zuletzt geändert durch Artikel 9 des Gesetzes vom 31 Juli 2009 (BGBl. I S. 2585).

Schmitz, G. (2005). Regionalplanung. In ARL – Akademie für Raumforschung und Landesplanung (ed.) *Handwörterbuch der Raumordnung* (pp. 963–973). Hannover: ARL.

Scholl, B., Elgendy, H. and Nollert, M. (2007). *Raumplanung in Deutschland: Formeller Aufbau und zukünftige Aufgaben*. Karlsruhe: Universitätsverlag.

Statistisches Bundesamt (ed.) (2009). *Bevölkerung Deutschlands bis 2060. 12. koordinierte Bevölkerungsvorausberechnung*. Wiesbaden: Statistisches Bundesamt.

Statistisches Bundesamt (ed.) (2011). *Ein Fünftel der Bevölkerung in Deutschland hatte 2010 einen Migrationshintergrund*. Pressemitteilung Nr. 355 vom 26.09.2011. Wiesbaden: Statistisches Bundesamt.

Steger, C. O. and Bunzel, A. (eds) (2012). *Raumordnungsplanung quo vadis? Zwischen notwendiger Flankierung der kommunalen Bauleitplanung und unzulässigem Durchgriff*. Wiesbaden: Kommunal- u. Schul-Verlag.

Territorial Agenda of the European Union. (2007). Towards a more competitive and sustainable Europe of diverse regions. Retrieved from www.eu-territorial-agenda.eu/Reference%20Documents/Territorial-Agenda-of-the-European-Union-Agreed-on-25-May-2007.pdf.

Territorial Agenda of the European Union 2020. (2011). Towards an inclusive, smart and sustainable Europe of diverse regions. Retrieved from www.eu2011.hu/files/bveu/documents/TA2020.pdf.

Treaty of Lisbon (2007). Retrieved from: www.europa.eu/lisbon_treaty/full_text.

Troeger-Weiss, G., Domhardt, H.-J., Hemesath, A., Kaltenegger, C. and Scheck, C. (2008). *Erfolgsbedingungen von Wachstumsmotoren außerhalb der Metropolen*. Werkstatt: Praxis 56. Bonn: BBR.

Vallée, D. (2011). Zusammenwirken von Raumplanung und raumbedeutsamen Fachplanungen. In ARL – Akademie für Raumforschung und Landesplanung (ed.) *Grundriss der Raumordnung und Raumentwicklung* (pp. 567–586). Hannover: ARL.

von Haaren, C. and Jessel, B. (2011). Umwelt und Raumentwicklung. In ARL – Akademie für Raumforschung und Landesplanung (ed.) *Grundriss der Raumordnung und Raumentwicklung* (pp. 671–718). Hannover: ARL.

Winkel, R., Greiving, S., Klinge, W. and Pietschmann, H. (2010). *Sicherung der Daseinsvorsorge und Zentrale-Orte-Konzepte: Gesellschaftspolitische Ziele und räumliche Organisation in der Diskussion*. BMVBS-Online-Publikation Nr. 12/2010. Bonn: BBSR.

Zimmermann, H. (2011). Finanzsystem und Raumentwicklung. In ARL – Akademie für Raumforschung und Landesplanung (ed.) *Grundriss der Raumordnung und Raumentwicklung* (pp. 661–670). Hannover: ARL.

Further reading

ARL – Akademie für Raumforschung und Landesplanung (ed.) (2011). *Grundriss der Raumordnung und Raumentwicklung*. Hannover: ARL (in German).

BMVBS – Ministry of Transport, Building and Urban Affairs and BBR – Federal Office for Building and Regional Planning (eds) (2006). *Perspectives of Spatial Development in Germany*. Bonn/Berlin: Selbstverlag.

6

FRANCE, DRIFTING AWAY FROM THE "REGIONAL ECONOMIC" APPROACH

Anna Geppert

Chapter objectives

This chapter shows that although the French planning system has clearly drifted away from the regional economic ideal type, the evolution is neither linear, nor finished. It aims to show:

- the organization of the French planning system, which features some – but not all – of the characteristics of the comprehensive integrated ideal type;
- the shortcomings of the system when dealing with contemporary challenges, in particular difficulties linked with unclear governance patterns;
- the new disruption linked to the financial crisis, which puts spatial planning at risk of becoming the umbrella of sectoral policies designed to support economic sectors in trouble.

1 Introduction

The *EU Compendium of Spatial Planning Systems and Policies* classifies France in the "regional economic" ideal type (CEC, 1997). However, since the 1990s, the French planning system has moved towards the "comprehensive integrated" model (Farinós Dasi, 2006), an evolution that remains unfinished today. Moreover, changes are not linear. They come along with deep transformations of the institutional setting, the role of public and private actors, and concepts and theories underpinning the planning decisions. The period is characterized by an intensive sequence of large reforms: 1995, 1999, 2000, 2003, 2010 … They come with hiccups, movements back and forth, and end in successive adjustments.

This chapter aims to analyze this evolution. It is based on a review of planning policies and discourses and on case studies from the author's research activities from the past two decades. It argues that today the French planning system is hybrid, somewhere between the regional economic and comprehensive integrated approaches. The games of the stakeholders and the changes in the economic situation are key factors in these developments.

Section 2 presents the current organization of the planning system. It argues that it has today lost most of the characteristics of the "regional economic" ideal type. Section 3 shows how the system deals with key issues such as metropolitanization, urban sprawl and social

109

fragmentation. It argues that the shortcomings of the system call for further adjustments. Section 4 reflects recent trends. It argues that the ongoing financial crisis puts French spatial planning at risk of becoming the umbrella of sectoral policies designed to support economic sectors in trouble.

2 State of the art: losing the characteristics of the "regional economic" approach

The regional economic ideal type is described as follows:

> Spatial planning has a very broad meaning relating to the pursuit of wide social and economic objectives, especially in relation to disparities in wealth, employment and social conditions between different regions of the country's territory. Where this approach to planning is dominant, central government inevitably plays an important role in managing development pressures across the country, and in undertaking public sector investment.
>
> (CEC, 1997, p. 36)

The description fits well the French tradition of *aménagement du territoire*, established since the 1960s under the umbrella of DATAR.[1] At the time, France had a strongly centralized organization of powers and the central government played a dominant role. During the post-war period (1945–1975), a series of policies were implemented to counteract the imbalance between Paris and other cities and regions (Laborie et al., 1985). The main instruments were economic incentives (grants were given to firms willing to relocate outside the capital region[2]) and public investment (e.g. transportation infrastructures, communications, higher education). Specific policies supported the development of regional centers (*métropoles d'équilibre, zones d'appui*, new towns). Even at the local level, state administration played a dominant role in statutory planning, land-use management and the implementation of large urban projects.

Since the devolution reform of 1982, the picture has changed. Land-use planning and local development has become the responsibility of the municipalities (*communes*). Regional planning and economic development have been transferred to the newly created regions. The central government maintains a regulatory function, pursuing goals of national interest. It remains responsible for sectoral policies addressing the national level (e.g. infrastructures, higher education, health) and for matters of national interest such as *aménagement du territoire*. But with the shortage of public funds in the 1980s, other priorities prevailed over spatial policies. Planners entered a multi-actor system for which they were little prepared (Geppert, 1997).

Drifting away from the regional economic approach, the system acquired characteristics of the comprehensive integrated model. Issues of vertical and horizontal cooperation and policy integration became top of the agenda. In terms of regulatory and strategic planning, the hierarchy of planning documents was improved to achieve better coherence. In terms of policy-making and public investment, multi-actor and multi-level cooperation increased.

Planning documents are elaborated at different scales by different tiers of public authorities: central government (DATAR), regions, municipalities and groups of municipalities. However, it is only at the local level that the hierarchy is actually complete (Figure 6.1).

110

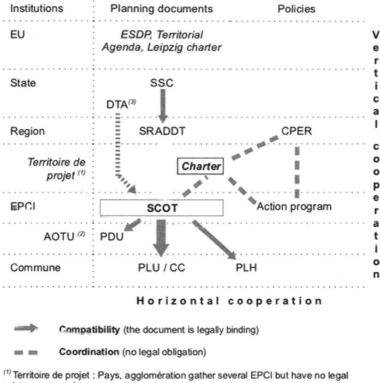

Figure 6.1 Coordination and cooperation in the French planning system

At the national level, France has no national spatial development perspective, but only sectoral guidelines. In 1995,[3] a reform of the French planning system instituted such a document at the top of the hierarchy, the *Schéma National d'Aménagement et de Développement du Territoire* (SNADT). It was intended to ensure coherence between planning documents and policies of different levels, as well as to improve the coordination of state policies. The SNADT was to be voted on by Parliament and, in 1996, DATAR proposed a first draft. It contained spatial principles, for instance that no place should be more than 45 minutes from high-speed transportation (highway, high-speed train, airport). However, in a context of tension, maps were withdrawn from the document, just as happened at the same time with the European Spatial Development Perspective (Faludi and Waterhout, 2002). Despite this, due to many tensions, the government never put the SNADT on Parliament's agenda. In 1999, the next reform[4] suppressed the would-be SNADT, returning to ruling national policies with a series of sectoral guidelines: the *Schémas de Services Collectifs* (Geppert, 2001).

At the regional level, a sustainable spatial development perspective is elaborated and regularly updated. Although named *Schéma Régional d'Aménagement et de Développement Durable du*

Development Councils. However, implementation has revealed certain limits to the system. In the face of contemporary problems and challenges, its efficiency is questionable.

3 Problems and challenges

This section addresses contemporary problems and challenges starting from their spatial dimension and "zooming in" on three scales. At the national level, metropolitanization affects large city regions adjusting to global territorial competition. At the scale of urban areas, urban sprawl modifies the distribution of human settlements and activities in response to the evolution of the socio-economic context. Within cities, socio-spatial fragmentation increases disparities between rich and deprived neighborhoods.

Globalization results in the emergence of an *archipelago economy* to which few places belong (Veltz, 1996). A major issue is then the competitiveness of French metropolitan areas. National decision-makers agree that in France, "apart from Paris and Lyon, big cities are only metropolises in the offing" (Conseil Économique et Social, 2003). DATAR has ordered surveys investigating the place of French cities in a European context (Cicille and Rozenblat, 2003, updating Brunet, 1989; DATAR, 2003; Beliot and Fouchier, 2004).

The French system lacks institutional settings as well as a collaborative culture for addressing challenges at this scale. As a result, major cities pursue their own objectives, competing rather than collaborating with their neighbors. Other parts of metropolitan areas are overlooked and are tempted to develop free-rider strategies, trying to make the best of any development opportunity without taking into consideration the broader picture.

In 2004, to address this issue, the central government launched a call for "metropolitan collaborations" (DATAR, 2004a). It met with great success – nearly all eligible cities volunteered. However, the "metropolitan projects" did not focus on international functions, but rather on local issues (Geppert, 2006; Motte, 2007). Places below the sea level of the *archipelago economy*, in particular small- and medium-sized cities in rural areas, lack territorial attractiveness (Geppert, 2009). After strong lobbying by the association of the mayors of medium-sized cities (*Fédération des Maires des Villes Moyennes*, FMVM), the French government launched a policy enhancing their territorial capital (FMVM, 2005; DIACT, 2007). Yet, as a result of the economic crisis, the grants promised by central government have very severely diminished and the process has slowed down.

Within city regions, processes of urban sprawl create major challenges, both environmental and social. When endorsing the Kyoto Protocol, French authorities were very confident in the capacity of the nation to fulfill its requirements, as France has a rather modern industry and the benefits of nuclear energy production which, leaving aside other risks, does not generate greenhouse gases. A decade later, it appeared that all indicators were red. The reason is urban sprawl, generating a dramatic increase in car mobility. It comes along with other environmental risks (e.g. excessive land artificialization, increasing flood hazards).

It also leads to social questions. From the mid-1990s to the mid-2000s, land and real-estate prices rocketed. In the countryside, differentiated spaces appeared. Areas with specific assets became privileged enclaves. Less-attractive peripheries developed small family house developments. Home to a homogeneous lower-middle-class population, they appear fragile in times of economic downturn. This occurred in the 1980s, when the combination of growing unemployment with low inflation led many households into trouble with their mortgages. It has been happening again since the 2008 crisis, and some municipalities are struggling to cope with too many debts. Such processes are often worsened by the homogeneity of age structures of these areas. Planning reforms have brought new answers to the issue of urban sprawl, in particular the "15 km rule" (see section 4.2). However, these are so far not sufficient to counteract the vigorous process, in particular due to the games of the actors.

Inside cities, riots such as that in the suburbs of Paris in fall 2005 have attracted public attention, and social diversity (*mixité sociale*) has become a national goal. Since the 2000 reform, planners have diversity high on their agenda, and municipalities are obliged to include at least 20 percent social housing. In deprived neighborhoods, addressed by the *politique de la ville*, the emphasis is put on social and employment issues (e.g. tax-free zones). Since 2006, a program of large-scale physical interventions has started, supported by specific funds delivered by two national agencies. The *Agence Nationale pour la Rénovation Urbaine* (ANRU) deals with physical interventions and the *Agence pour la Cohésion Sociale et l'Égalité des chances* (ACSÉ) deals with social aspects. A massive national investment policy supporting the reconstruction and transformation of whole urban areas is based on the idea that only large-scale intervention can really produce effects, changing realities and the image of an area. Nevertheless, in spite of decades of public intervention, the same deprived areas "benefit" from successive regeneration programs, showing that the problems remain unsolved.

Cutting across these issues, governance has become a major concern. As urban and metropolitan areas continue to enlarge, the discrepancy between administrative perimeters and spatial issues that require solutions is growing. Functional urban areas (in the French statistical nomenclature *aires urbaines*) are much broader than municipalities, EPCI and even the SCoTs; institutional settings and planning documents do not reach the appropriate dimension. Public participation, rather low in French culture, appears challenging as well. Another set of questions is related to issues of the transparency of public decisions and the use of public funds. Are the endeavors of the various public actors redundant, competing or complementary? How can public–private collaborations be developed? This issue has been shown to be crucial at different scales, metropolitan (Geppert, 1997; Jouve and Lefèvre, 2002; Le Galès and Lorrain, 2003) as well as local (Goze, 2002; Geppert, 2008). It also has been invoked by the public reports of major national institutions, and in particular by the high chamber of Parliament, the Senate, which is especially concerned by local matters (Sénat, 2003).

In this struggle with major spatial challenges, the planning system still calls for further adjustments. Dimensions and directions of change are not linear and show multiple trajectories.

4 Dimensions and directions of change

First, we examine the progressive adjustment of the different actors to this new environment. Second, we discuss how the renovated tools and planning modes resulting from the previously described evolution have worked, for better and for worse. Third, we turn to a summary of the evolution of planning concepts. Finally, we consider the impacts of the contemporary economic crisis on the policy agenda.

4.1 Actors experiencing the new rules of the game

No longer the dominant actor, central government is trying to define its role in a *modern state, modest state* (Crozier, 1991). In the context of the 1990s to the 2010s, it has to prove the legitimacy and choose the nature of its interventions, not least in spatial planning. Throughout the entire period, central governments have tried to improve the institutional framework for planning decisions by numerous reforms. Sometimes the state has also tried to regain control over local decisions, without success.

One example is the implementation of the 1999 reform of municipality groupings (EPCI).[10] Groupings were fragmented and lacked financial and political integration. For instance, planning documents for urban areas were elaborated by specific groupings created for this purpose only, because the EPCI ensuring territorial management of urban agglomerations were too narrow. The reform was intended to overcome these handicaps. In the course of implementation, the representatives of the state (*préfets*) were able to reject groupings that appeared spatially inappropriate, for instance covering only part of an urban agglomeration. At the end of the day, the *préfets* made little use of this possibility and the reform appears unaccomplished (Cour des comptes, 2005). One reason for this was lobbying by certain local representatives with national functions (ministries, members of parliament). Another reason was that the *préfets* did not feel that it was legitimate to interfere directly with local governments, considering that their role was rather a facilitating one.

Another example was the *Directive Territoriale d'Aménagement* (DTA). The 1995 reform created the possibility for central government to elaborate such a document for broader areas when issues of national interest are at stake. This concerns large natural areas subject to high environmental pressure (e.g. Alpes Maritimes, Bouches du Rhône, Seine estuary, Loire estuary) but also highly populated areas with strong social disparities (Lyon metropolitan area, North Lorraine mining belt). The DTA had a double role. On the one hand, they were binding, so that where a DTA existed, the central government would recover control over local planning documents. On the other hand, they would improve policy coordination through the association of local stakeholders. The elaboration of these documents proved very slow (only nine DTA had been approved by 2010). Local actors see this as being due to the reluctance of the state to commit to spatial planning. In contrast, the *préfets* blamed the duration of consultations with local stakeholders. Whatever the explanation, coordination has prevailed over control: since the 2010 reform[11] DTA have been replaced by *Directives Territoriales d'Aménagement et de Développement Durable* (DTADD), which have no regulatory effect.

The central government is withdrawing from direct planning responsibilities in favor of collaborative processes. This is coherent with the continuation of the devolution reform initiated in 1982. In 2003, the French constitution was amended, indicating that "the organization of the French republic is decentralized." Giving more power to local governments, the state tries to promote new policies by delivering financial incentives, often modest, monitored by calls for proposals. These calls are a somewhat recent phenomenon in French culture. In the 1990s, the first calls were minimally directive; more recently selection criteria have become more precise. While strategic choices are left to local actors, emphasis is put on working methodology and on governance issues. Application guidelines are becoming more comprehensive. In parallel, DATAR has developed a constellation of consultancy providers to offer methodological support. From being a policy initiator, the state has come to a position as a "critical friend" of local endeavors.

In spite of these experiences, the number of tiers of local government and the unclear distribution of competences hamper the necessary multi-level coordination. Regional planning and economic development are the competence of the region, a new tier of local government created by the 1982 devolution. Although many regions were given names referring to historical provinces or counties, their limits are not consistent with history, or with geography. They have little budget and little experience. They have quite efficiently accomplished the management of responsibilities they inherited in 1982, such as regional railway transportation or secondary schools. This leaves little room for a comprehensive approach to regional territorial issues, and the regional plans (SRADDT) tend to focus on economic issues – e.g. the development of promising sectors. Spatial strategies are rarely evident.

In the field, regions face the competition of the *départements*. These have existed since the French Revolution and have substantial budgets and experienced staff. Also, although formally they had no competence in spatial planning, they develop proper strategies. They appear as strong players, sometimes redundant and/or rivals of the regions. In spite of coordination negotiated through the CPER, competing strategies lead to a lack of coherence between planning policies and to fits and starts in common projects. To most observers, these two levels represent one too many. In 2010, this issue was addressed by a reform.[12] The rather unsatisfactory compromise was to reduce the number of elected representatives through a single election, but to keep both levels of local government with the representatives sitting in both assemblies. The implementation of the decision was due in 2014, but in 2012 this reform was withdrawn.

At the local level, tension remains between municipalities and groupings. The 1999 reform aimed to strengthen the EPCI. It instituted three categories of groupings: *communauté urbaine* for cities above 500,000 inhabitants, *communauté d'agglomération* for cities above 50,000 inhabitants and *communauté de communes* for smaller groupings. The higher the category, the stronger the financial and political integration of the municipalities – but also the higher the funding provided by the state. The implementation of the reform has confirmed the strong reluctance of mayors to transfer their power to the upper level (Assemblée Nationale, 2005; Cour des comptes, 2005; Sénat, 2006). Many municipalities accepted losing some of their regular funding in order to avoid a transfer of too many competences to the EPCI. For instance, Nice (900,000 inhabitants) remained a *communauté d'agglomération* for ten years. Reims (200,000 inhabitants) opted for the *communauté de communes*, a status for rural groupings. In the longer term, funding remains an argument and the groupings tend to upgrade to the "right" category. Given the persisting fragmentation of the EPCI, the 2010 reform relaunched the process, with completion scheduled for 2014. So far, the process is late due to problematic negotiations.

The involvement of non-institutional actors, the private sector, NGOs and citizens is not a strong feature of French planning culture. Mandatory public consultations are held in the process of establishing planning documents or realizing major investments, such as transportation infrastructures. However, the procedure (*enquête publique*) is usually performed as the very last step before implementation and has little influence on the final outcomes.

Progressively, the emphasis on public participation is growing. For instance, neighborhood councils flourish. This leads to the question of democratic legitimacy as these participatory endeavors mobilize a small number of people so "active minorities," as part of all possible negotiation arenas, appear. The boundary between participation and lobbying is often fuzzy.

The picture given here is much oriented towards the institutional setting. This reflects the French realities of the last decade. Much time and energy has been dedicated to the institutional issues, without achieving a clear picture. However, meanwhile, planning modes and tools have changed.

4.2 Planning modes and tools

The evolution of planning modes and tools may be the most important change of the past decade. First, new requirements were addressed to planners. Second, traditional planning tools became more strategic and soft spatial planning entered planning practice.

The reform of 2000 introduced new requirements for local stakeholders and for planning documents. Their implementation met with some difficulties, likely to influence the evolution of the legislation. To improve social diversity, French municipalities must have at least 20 percent social housing; if they do not reach this threshold, they are fined. On average, 20 percent is not a very high level as "social housing" designates public housing for middle classes, which is historically well developed. Most larger cities have levels exceeding the limit and the legislation primarily affects well-off, small suburban municipalities. But the main methodological shortcoming of the approach is that, in the cities, exclusion and fragmentation occur at the much more detailed scale of neighborhoods. The municipal indicators may therefore be good, while the actual situation is extremely contrasted. The effects of the 20 percent rule remain moderate and it is also likely that the new threshold of 25 percent established in 2012 will make no dramatic change.

Another legal requirement instituted in 2000 is known as the "15 km rule," which aims to counteract urban sprawl. Elaborating a SCoT is compulsory for cities with over 10,000 inhabitants. But smaller municipalities may be ruled by a municipal land-use plan only. Also, before the reform, many small municipalities close to cities were tempted not to participate in the common document, in order to keep full control over their urbanization choices. During the 1980s and 1990s, these free-riders contributed to a large extent to urban sprawl. Since 2000, municipalities located within a distance of 15 km from the outer limit of an urban agglomeration have lost the right to elaborate a land-use plan and deliver building permits if they are not covered by a SCoT. The intention was to impose, if not an authoritarian limitation of construction in suburban areas, at least a coherent strategy cooperatively defined through the drawing up of the SCoT.

In the process of implementation, some shortcomings appeared. First, the distance stipulated proved too short. A counterproductive effect of the legislation was that the efforts undertaken to contain sprawl in core cities generated a spillover that benefited a second ring of villages, located at a distance of 15–30 km from the city – at the end of the day, this was simply a further dilution of the urban area. After the 2010 reform,[13] the "15 km rule" is to be extended to include more municipalities. In 2013, it will affect municipalities located around cities of 15,000 inhabitants. In 2017, all French municipalities are required to be covered by a SCoT or freeze urbanization.

Second, in many areas suburban municipalities developed alternative strategies. Creating "unions of peripheries," they elaborated "defensive" SCoTs to avoid negotiating with central cities (Figure 6.2). These SCoTs are usually much more permissive, although perfectly in line with legislation. To improve the quality of the overarching planning document, the 2010 reform obliges the SCoT to define precise objectives in terms of reducing land consumption, and to justify choices made. However, no national indicators are set by the legislation. It is thus quite difficult to foresee the effects of this new requirement.

The second major evolution is the introduction of a strategic dimension in statutory planning documents, in particular the SCoT (Motte, 2006; Geppert, 2008). In the 1990s, the equivalent document (*schéma directeur*) faced several criticisms. One was of being over-prescriptive, using a zoning technique more appropriate for an actual land-use plan. Another was of being rigid, in particular due to the very long procedures involved in the elaboration and revision of the plan. Finally, it was considered too static and not dynamic enough, due to a gap between land-use regulations and development strategies.

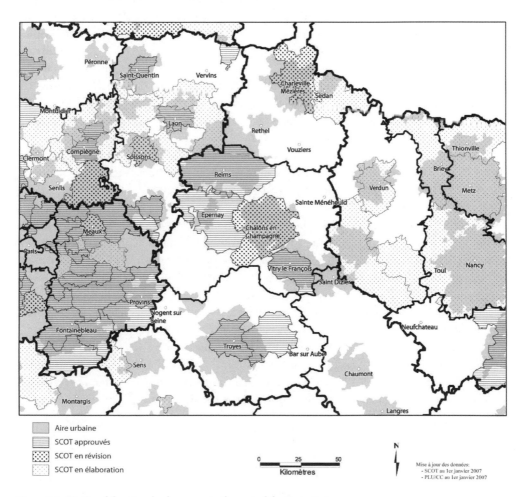

Figure 6.2 SCoT and functional urban areas in the east of the Paris Basin

Since 2000, both the SCoT and PLU feature a sustainable development perspective, the *Projet d'Aménagement et de Développement Durable* (PADD). This "political" part of the document is not binding, but is supposed to inspire the compulsory measures gathered in the regulatory section. The difference between the documents is also more visible. The PLU remain mainly regulatory, while the SCoT contain a clearer expression of development strategies and more flexible prescriptions. For instance, it is now possible to subordinate the urbanization of new areas to the creation of means of public transportation (Figure 6.3).[14]

Multi-actor and multi-sector cooperation is enhanced in the process of developing planning documents. More stakeholders are invited to participate in the elaboration of the document, albeit always in a consultative role. Public participation is also promoted, for instance public consultations must be held from the beginning of the process of drawing up the documents. Furthermore, the implementation of the document must be monitored at least every six years.

While statutory planning was becoming more strategic, the tools for soft spatial planning were refined. In particular, they were used to experiment with more participatory processes, through their development councils, including civil society. In 1999, it was discussed whether development councils should have elected representatives at all – finally the choice was left in the hands of municipal representatives, as long as civil society represents the majority. Indeed, some *territoires de projet* have decided to turn the council into a non-political body. This opening up to civil society meets a real demand. The author has been involved in such development councils: meetings were attended, questions and proposals brought by the audience. Today, many *territoires de projet* have developed new means of communication oriented towards the wider population (newsletters, websites).

The intention of the reform was that a coherent system should spontaneously appear. "Soft spaces" would serve as incubators of spatial visions and territorial strategies. Naturally, the stakeholders would then mature to broaden institutional perimeters, overcome sectoral gaps, etc. So far, this has not happened. Planning perimeters remain narrow; one out of three SCoT hardly covers more than the physical agglomeration. At the same time, the charters of the soft *territoires de projet* tend to avoid topics related to statutory planning and focus on more consensual approaches such as territorial marketing and territorial identities. With the exception of rural areas that had no planning documentation before 2000, regulatory documents and soft spatial planning have not really met.

Nevertheless, the *territoires de projet* introduced a three-fold governance model to the French planning system. The political decision rests with the elected representatives from the different municipalities and EPCI. The development council, mirroring the civil society, has a real influence and a role as an incubator for new ideas. Technical management is ensured by the usual civil servants, but more networking occurs between staff from different sectors and different places. This three-fold model is now being extended by many local governments to include other matters.

The 1992 document (above) uses zoning, trying to make it more flexible by defining "mixed" areas. The 2008 (below) uses more symbolic representations but includes "strategic" decisions such as the subordination to future urbanisation to public transportation.

Schéma de cohérence entre l'urbanisation et la création de dessertes en TC

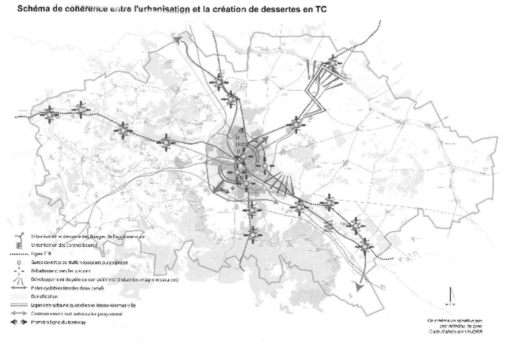

Figure 6.3 Two generations of plans for the urban area of Reims
Source: AUDRR, 1992; 2008

121

4.3 Planning ideas, doctrines, concepts

The "failure of planning" in the 1980s resulted in a distrust of the planning ideas and concepts that were traditional to the French model. Starting from the 1990s, planners have had to rebuild their legitimacy on new ground, creating a non-linear path of evolution.

On the one hand, since the 1980s a quest for economic development has been supported by pragmatic, flexible approaches grounded in neoliberal doctrines fostering territorial competitiveness. In 2006, DATAR became DIACT, standing for *Délégation Interministérielle à l'Aménagement et à la Compétitivité des Territoires*. Functionally, it integrated the *Agence Française pour les Investissements Internationaux* (AFII), the French international investment agency. The plural "territories" replacing the singular "territory" is emblematic and was accompanied by a change of paradigm in French spatial planning. The aim is no longer to bring republican equality to all places, but to make the best of territorial diversity and to help every place optimize its assets (Geppert, 2009). The concept of equity (fair treatment) has replaced equality (equal, not to say similar, treatment). Concepts such as territorial capital are now emphasized. In December 2009, after persistent lobbying by its staff, DATAR recovered its historical acronym. However, it now stands for *Délégation Interministérielle à l'Aménagement du Territoire et à l'Attractivité Régionale*.

On the other hand, since the late 1990s sustainability (*développement durable*) has become prominent. Its double-d is now present in most planning acronyms (e.g. PADD, DTADD, LOADDT). The concept, though, remains somewhat fuzzy. Of its three "pillars," the environmental is the most developed, and sustainability appears to a certain extent to be the nickname given to the strengthening of environmental requirements (e.g. environmental impact assessments, eco-buildings). The social pillar is often reduced to consideration of deprived neighborhoods and the economic element is frequently left out of the equation. The integration of these pillars in a systematic approach is yet to be achieved.

Finally, an emphasis is put on the development of the knowledge economy imported from European discourse. One part is related to the metropolitanization issue; another main endeavor has been supporting a cluster policy (*pôles de compétitivité*) inspired by the works of Porter, which have been translated into French (Porter, 1999). The policy aims to support French industries (DATAR, 2004b). The "French cluster model" is considered rooted in space, as the central pillar of the territory–industry–research triangle. For this reason, DATAR is in charge of the policy (Darmon and Jacquet, 2005). However, some authors argue that this is not so much spatial planning as a sectoral policy under a territorial disguise.

4.4 Policy agenda: spatial planning in a time of crisis

The 2008 economic crisis affected national and local policy agendas. The shortage of public funds has hit the type of long-term endeavors characteristic of spatial planning. The feeling of emergency has led to the favoring of selected projects that are tightly linked to supporting chosen economic sectors. In this situation, the evolutionary path of spatial planning may change trajectories.

The evolution of the Grand Paris project illustrates the impact of the crisis on public policies. In 2007, an international competition invited ten international teams to produce a "new, global planning project for the broader Paris" (wording from the speech given by the French President at the opening of the competition, 17 September 2007). In 2009, the ten projects were exhibited for half a year. Widely supported by computer imaging, they were circulated worldwide. In 2010, a permanent structure, the Atelier International du Grand Paris (AIGP), was established to "keep alive reflections and debates about the future of the capital."

However, when it came to implementation, the Grand Paris project changed course and focused on major public transportation investment. The infrastructure as such is ambitious and much needed. The future Grand Paris Express is an automatic metro of 205 km that will circle around the capital region, stopping at 72 stations (57 of which are new). A state-owned company, the *Société du Grand Paris* (SGP), has been created specifically to handle this project. It is expected to cost over 30 billion Euros, and is promoted as being highly innovative, both technologically and environmentally. For the moment, the project is at the stage of environmental impact assessments. The final infrastructure should comprise four segments, opening from 2018 to 2025.

At the same time, 17 suburban areas around future train stations were selected for regeneration and redevelopment as clusters focused on different specializations. These spaces should benefit from a specific procedure called *Contrat de Développement Territorial* (CDT), organizing the multi-actor collaborations. However, the shortage of funding has already hit the implementation timetable. In 2012, the first deadlines had to be postponed. The Paris example is specific because of its size; however, similar situations occur in many cities. In the late 2000s, a number of interesting competitions, public debates and consultations took place but, after 2008, implementation has mostly been put on hold.

A similar evolution from spatial to sectoral has occurred in terms of sustainability. Ever since its first version in 2003, the French National Strategy for Sustainable Development (NSSD) has claimed a "holistic" approach. However, "holistic" does not mean spatial. The subtitle of the 2010–2013 strategy is "Towards a green and fair economy." The content addresses economic issues (sustainable consumption and production, knowledge society, governance), environmental and social thematic issues (energy and climate, transport, resources management, risks and health, social cohesion) and international matters (sustainable development, global poverty). In contrast to certain European countries (Denmark, Finland, Ireland, Latvia, Lithuania, Slovenia, Switzerland, United Kingdom), the strategy does not refer to city planning and housing. The question is whether "sustainability," in a series of very sectoral approaches, is a new competitor for spatial planning.

In 2007, then President Nicolas Sarkozy launched a wide public consultation called *Grenelle de l'Environnement*, in reference to the historical Grenelle agreement that settled the conflict of May 1968 and established a new basis for French society. Planning was part of the debate, which resulted in the new requirements being addressed by statutory plans. However, as the construction sector was suffering, supporting energy-saving construction appeared to be an appealing way of associating environmental concern with economic help. Construction labels, such as *Haute Qualité Environnementale* (HQE), *Bâtiment Basse Consommation* (BBC) and passive houses, flourish. *Eco-quartiers* (ecologically friendly neighborhoods) are also being developed, although their quality is sometimes questionable. The quick economic return and the visibility of such policies draw attention towards the scale of the construction, mostly in small district units, which leaves little political space for spatial planning.

DATAR – Délégation à l'Aménagement du Territoire et à l'Action Régionale. (2004a). Pour un rayonnement européen des métropoles françaises – Appel à cooperation. Paris: DATAR.

DATAR – Délégation à l'Aménagement du Territoire et à l'Action Régionale. (2004b). La France, puissance industrielle – une nouvelle politique industrielle par les territoires. Paris: DATAR.

DIACT – Délégation Interministérielle à l'Aménagement et à la compétitivité des Territoires. (2007). 20 Villes moyennes témoins – Appel à experimentation. Paris: DIACT.

Faludi, A. and Waterhout, B. (2002). *The Making of the European Spatial Development Perspective.* London: Routledge.

Farinós Dasi, J. (ed.) (2006). *Governance of Territorial and Urban Policies from EU to Local Level, ESPON Project 2.3.2.* Luxembourg: ESPON Coordination Unit.

FMVM – Fédération des Maires des Villes Moyennes. (2005). 22 mesures pour les villes moyennes et leurs agglomérations. Paris: FMVM.

Geppert, A. (1997). The renewal of the French system of planning: sharing the planning decisions between the state and the local governments. Communication au Congrès d'AESOP. Nijmegen: Working paper.

Geppert, A. (2001). Schémas de services collectifs: objectif coherence. *Pouvoirs locaux*, No.50 (III/2001), 22–24.

Geppert, A. (2006). Les coopérations métropolitaines: un décryptage. *Urbanisme*, No.18 (Spécial congrès de la FNAU), 44–46.

Geppert, A. (2008). Vers l'émergence d'une planification stratégique spatialisée. Mémoire en vue de l'habilitation à diriger les recherches. Université de Reims-Champagne-Ardenne, Reims. Vol. 1. Retrieved from www.aesop-planning.eu.

Geppert, A. (2009). Attractivité en absence de métropolisation: le problème des villes moyennes. In P. Ingallina, J.-P. Blais and N. Rousier (eds) *L'attractivité des territoires: regards croisés* (pp. 121–124). Paris: PUCA – Plan urbanisme construction architecture.

Goze, M. (2002). La stratégie territoriale de la loi SRU. *Revue d'Economie Régionale et Urbaine*, 5, 761–777.

Haughton, G., Allmendinger, P., Counsell, D. and Vigar, G. (2010). *The New Spatial Planning: Territorial management with soft spaces and fuzzy boundaries.* London: Routledge.

Jouve, B. and Lefèvre, C. (2002). *Métropoles ingouvernables: Les villes européennes entre globalisation et decentralization.* Paris: Elsevier.

Laborie, J.-P., Langumier, J.-F. and de Roo, P. (1985). *La politique française d'aménagement du territoire de 1950 à 1985.* Paris: La Documentation française.

Le Galès, P. and Lorrain, D. (eds) (2003). *Revue Française d'administration publique*, No.107. Paris: La Documentation Française.

Motte, A. (2006). *La notion de planification stratégique spatialisée en Europe (1995–2005).* Paris: PUCA – Plan urbanisme construction architecture.

Motte, A. (ed.) (2007). *Les agglomérations françaises face aux défis métropolitains.* Paris: Economica.

Porter, M. (1999). *La concurrence selon Porter.* Paris: Village mondial.

Sénat. (2003). Rapport d'information n°252 sur l'état du territoire, Rapport n°252 annexé à la séance du 3 avril 2003. Rapport du Sénateur J.-F. Poncet.

Sénat. (2006). Rapport d'information sur l'intercommunalité à fiscalité propore, Rapport n°193 annexé à la séance du 1er février 2006. Rapport du Sénateur P. Dallier.

Veltz, P. (1996). *Mondialisation, villes et territoires: une économie d'archipel.* Paris: PUF.

Further reading

Booth, P., Breuillard, M., Fraser, C. and Paris, D. (eds) (2007). *Spatial Planning Systems of Britain and France: A comparative analysis.* London/New York: Routledge.

Geppert, A. (2009). Polycentricity: can we make it happen? From a concept to its implementation. *Urban Practice and Research*, 2(3), 251–268.

Guet, J. F. (2008). *City and Regional Planning in France: From the European spatial development perspective to local urban plans.* Lyon: CERTU.

Waterhout, B., Othengrafen, F. and Sykes, O. (2012). Neo-liberalization processes and spatial planning in France, Germany, and the Netherlands: an exploration. *Planning Practice and Research*, 6, 1–19.

7

THE MODERNIZATION OF THE ITALIAN PLANNING SYSTEM[1]

Valeria Lingua and Loris Servillo

Chapter objectives

This chapter depicts the attempts of innovation of recent Italian planning activity, from the second half of the last century up to now. The main purpose is to reflect on the issues, targets and trajectories of innovation, at different scales of planning, in order to highlight the strengths and limitations of the current trend toward a reform of the planning system. Particularly, the chapter aims to:

- identify the three main aspects that can be considered structural features of the planning system;
- define challenges and attempts of modernization, the role of different reformist seasons;
- look at the reasons of the constraint of programming capacity at national and local levels and the recurrence to the "state of emergency" as an occasion of change;
- understand the function of the administrative reform, enshrined in the Constitutional Changes of 2001, and of the consequent regionalization of planning competences;
- list the principal instruments and institutional procedures introduced by the administrative reform;
- identify the main actors of change at different scales of planning: the urban areas and the regions;
- define the cultural debate and the attempts of reforming the Italian statutory planning system at the regional level; and
- look at the last national attempt to reorganize the institutional levels and the consequences for the Italian planning system at national, regional and sub-regional levels.

1 Introduction

A series of innovative efforts to modernize Italian spatial planning has taken place in the past two decades. Their experimental phases have concluded, allowing for a better evaluation of provided benefits, missed opportunities and misleading directions.

The chapter focuses on this process of modernization, analyzing issues, targets and trajectories, in order to highlight the strengths and limitations of the current trend toward a reform of the planning system. Section 2 describes the structural features of the spatial planning system. Four storylines provide a focus on the crucial problems and challenges (section 3), while in section 4 an examination of the dimensions and direction of changes of the past 20 years permits identification of the actors involved, the modes and planning tools and their adaptation in various regional planning styles.

In the conclusion, the authors emphasize that the current situation is still characterized by the lack of a coherent reorganization of the entire framework system, paying the consequences of the absence of a structural reform at the national level, although there have been various interesting legislative innovation processes at the regional level and a wide range of attempts at operative innovations at the local level.

2 The Italian planning system: structural characteristics

The Italian planning system is characterized by a relatively stable structure inspired by the traditional "urbanistic" typology (CEC, 2000; ESPON, 2007), which is based on the centrality of the master plan at the municipal level and on a legislative framework that is still defined by the original National Spatial Planning Law n. 1150 dated 1942.

Three main aspects can be considered to be structural features of the planning system: a strong predominance of the master plan at the local level, despite the growth of supra-local planning capacities; the architectural roots of the discipline, supporting a combination of urban design strategies, land-use prescriptions and territorial governance in a complex legislative framework; and the persistence of conformative prescriptions in spite of a largely absent programming capacity.

Concerning the first aspect, the crucial role of the local level (municipality) is rooted in the traditionally strong autonomous political structure of the Italian territory. Since the planning system was formalized in its own technical devices by Law n. 1150/1942, the municipal level, through different experimental forms of land-use planning, has been the fundamental actor in managing urban growth and territorial changes. All the reforms and the growing complexity of the planning system only slightly affected the primacy of municipalities as the main planning actors, despite a growing capacity to tackle territorial dynamics from supra-local levels. Nevertheless, the reform of the Constitution in 2001 changed the denomination of the field of planning competences from "Urbanistica" to "Governo del territorio" (territorial government), which indicates a wider approach being taken to the spatial dynamics and dismisses an expression related to a mainly urban focus. At the same time, the reform of the constitution in 2001, in line with the principle of subsidiarity affirmed at EU and national levels, confirmed the centrality of the local level in managing spatial planning issues.

A second structural aspect of the Italian planning tradition and its cognitive framework is the interaction, both in theoretical debates and in practice, between the world of architecture and urban design, in which Italian planning education is rooted, and planning as politics and policy domain.

On the one hand, the architectural background of most of the well-known masters and their experience of the relationship between planning and urban design traditions in the twentieth century (Palermo and Ponzini, 2010) to some extent strengthens the identification of the Italian system as urbanistic type oriented. The figure of the "architetto–urbanista" (architect–urbanist), as defined by Quaroni (1967), despite a deep understanding of the cognitive, normative and managerial dimensions of urban planning (Astengo, 1971), had the essential function of designing the physical transformations of the city and the region (Samonà, 1959; De Carlo, 1964; Secchi, 1989; Gregotti, 2002). For more than 30 years, in the second half of the century, a strong debate focused on the way that historical–geographical and morphological–environmental perspectives, together with a sociological–anthropological understanding of the local context, could interpret spatial forms and sense of places in order to critically identify possibilities for change, and thus integrate strong elements of urban design strategy into the master plan.

On the other hand, the large debate on the polity of spatial planning and studies on decision-making processes and governance introduced to the core of the disciplinary debate issues such as the social construction of the decision-making process (Bellaviti, 1995), planning management (Campos Venuti, 1967) and the role of scientific knowledge in supporting planning decisions (Astengo, 1966). The concept of planning as a public function of local administration was at the heart of the mainstream of a vast reformist period at the beginning of the second half of the century, revealing the ongoing interpretation of the discipline. Moreover, in the last three decades innovations have been seen with the introduction of more flexible instruments and of shared decision-making processes based on the direct involvement of private stakeholders (Campos Venuti, 1967, 1987, 1991; Indovina, 1991; Campos Venuti and Oliva, 1993), albeit not without some difficulties. However, the ideological position of the mainstream disciplinary debate supporting a strong public role in the management of planning processes has the drawback of a certain rigidity in the acceptance of innovations. In the 1980s, when the reformist aspiration declined, accompanied by a lack of expectation in the spatial planning discipline, some ideological estoppels also came to an end, making possible changes that the specialized debate now continues to address as a tendency either to deregulation (Salzano, 1998) or to modernization (Campos Venuti, 1991).

Moreover, it is worth mentioning that at the crossing point of these two streams of the debate, strong attention to social needs and the role of planning in reforming society and providing an emancipatory trajectory for the local community was at stake. This perspective is at the basis of important examples of participatory planning processes during the 1960s and 1970s, as well as behind the theorizations of ways to express local society's self-organization in planning and urban design. This culture and its milestone experiences re-emerged in the new phase of participatory processes in the 1990s and 2000s, despite being framed by a different cultural and institutional context.

The third important feature of the Italian planning system is the conformative interpretation of planning practices, with great attention being paid to both quantitative parameters and the legal status of the landowner's right to build. The strong role of parametrical coefficients for the quantitative determination of public spaces and services (the so-called *standards*, introduced in 1967) is still the effect of measurements elaborated in the second half of the twentieth century in answer to the growing threat of speculative processes and urban transformation without planning management. Strongly connected to this, the history of the discipline has been characterized by a long-term attempt to reform the legal framework of the zoning-based distribution of building rights (Campos Venuti, 1967; Astengo, 1971), in order to introduce principles of equality in economic gains and to reduce backstage pressures in the decision-making process concerning the elaboration of land-use plans with close relations between land-use choices and changes in land value. Despite several attempts to introduce more equitable practices in the distribution of building rights, either through radical legislative reforms in the 1970s (Campos Venuti and Oliva, 1993) or through articulated legal-economical procedures called *processi perequativi* (equalizing processes), this still remains a controversial issue (Urbani, 2011), although several pieces of legislation (in particular at regional level) have tried to define legal operative frameworks.

In general, however, the use of the strength of the juridical status (of landownership, of zoning prescription, etc.) and the debate on the legal legitimacy of the policy choices are typical of a context where politics has unstable authority and a historical weakness in implementing its decisions. This is a context in which the main changes are determined by urgency due to emergency conditions in cases of big crises or tragic events, and, most of all, on the wave of a collective shock. In these conditions, partial reforming laws or emergency laws have been passed,[2] determining incremental reforms of the planning system, even including specific measures that have brought about significant modifications, but always tackling specific aspects rather than the entire framework. The result is a step-by-step process of change, characterized by the coexistence of mainstream features and innovative elements of planning styles, by path dependency and inertia to changes, and by the coexistence of different regional styles.

3 Problems, challenges and attempts at modernization

Despite having faced several long-term modernization attempts with changing agendas, different discourses and spatial challenges in time, the Italian planning system has always been characterized by strong inertia. It is worth mentioning, thus, that the changes that have been taking place in the past two decades are part of several long-term storylines, which fostered the various reform attempts. Problems, challenges and reforms have followed strict path-dependent evolutions that can be traced from the post-war period until now.

The rise of various spatial challenges, for instance growing environmental sensibility and the issue of the requalification of existing urban areas, in particular in the 1980s, as well as the emergence of extensive territorial phenomena beyond the local administrative dimension (e.g. costal development, metropolitan areas, urban sprawl phenomena), contributed to important reforms of the discipline. At the same time, the technical debates concerning its modernization have tried to tackle chronic deficits, for instance the need for more competences at supra-local levels, in particular related to environment protection and the coordination of large-scale dynamics, and for more programming capacity to enable the combination of spatial planning policies with territorial development strategies.

Thus, different modernization processes have been initiated by different institutional actors, but not always in a coherent framework. In the following sub-sections, four storylines are mentioned, combining problems and challenges in different reform attempts. Discussion first considers how extensive aspects of change have been added through the years, not always in a coherent fashion, and not always by adopting the same perspective, but often using the expression "the reformist season." Second, it addresses how some challenges have emerged in the past two decades, both from the EU and from domestic sources. This need for modernization and the advancements matured in the institutional and cultural debate have affected different levels and actors in various ways, but principally the regions. Third, the chronic lack of a programmatic approach, in particular at national level, is cyclically highlighted. However, despite some important episodes and the growing role of the regions, a coherent reform is still missing. Finally, despite the insufficient role of the state in spatial planning terms, exceptional emergencies have become a structural way of promoting change through a sort of "state of emergency" approach.

3.1 The reformist seasons

"Reformist season" is an expression that has been cyclically used to identify those periods characterized by intense attempts to modernize the planning system. In addition to the first reformist season of the post-war period, which occurred in the 1960s and 1970s, at least two different periods had been labeled with this expression in the past 30 years.

The reformist season of the 1980s marked a significant rupture with the rigidity of the master plan and its exclusive public domain, introducing forms of negotiations and involving private stakeholders in the decision-making process (Campos Venuti, 1991). It has therefore been termed *urbanistica contrattata* (contractual spatial planning; Salzano, 1998), referring to the contracting phases involved in the making of the master plan and other planning instruments. This position raised strong criticism from the part of the planning culture that was still an expression of the first cultural season. In particular, the conceptualization of the planning discipline as a public function of local administrations and a tool against speculative forces was deeply embedded in some professionals and scholars of the planning schools, characterized by a strong ideological interpretation of the public administration and of public primacy in planning choices.

Seen from a wider perspective, the planning system was facing the inadequacy of its measures and mechanisms characterized by excessive red tape and very slow procedures. Moreover, new spatial issues were challenging its classic modus operandi: the presence of large derelict brownfield areas, and urban decay and social disintegration in outlying neighborhoods, were two of the main new urban phenomena and revealed an increasing fragmentation of interests in spatial transformations of internal parts of the city. On the one hand, old manufacturing sites, contended for by real estate agents and entrepreneurial forces, were intended as key areas for a general urban renewal wave and for a re-branding of the city's image, through new functions and new interventions in modern architectural styles. On the other hand, due to their strategic position in the city center, these areas were considered to provide an opportunity to solve some chronic problems and the lack of public services, offering space for social housing and green areas. For the first time, public authorities faced extensive problems related to the renewal of city districts/urban sectors that land-use plans and traditional planning instruments were unable to manage, while the urban demands for planning had shifted from urban expansion management to reorganizational and restructuring capacity. Thus, the conformative criterion based on the parametric evaluation of *standards* had shown its limits, together with the synoptic, rational, exclusive and inflexible government system (Bobbio, 1996; Mazza, 1997), while the planning issues required articulated approaches based on integrated socio-economic policies and qualitative performances in terms of policy contents and design capacity.

At the same time, as a consequence of these spatial changes and planning inadequacy, the 1980s was characterized by a strong de-legitimation of the traditional planning system, which was considered unable to face current problems and provide effective and rapid answers. In a cultural context that supported free market orientation, the first amnesty law for the extensive illegal building phenomenon was approved in 1985, in support of discourses that pointed at the rigidity of the planning system as one of the causes of illegal construction activities. This was the framework that the reform attempts tried to tackle, providing answers to the new needs by abandoning a rigid vision of planning as a primarily public domain and supporting the opening up of decision-making and spatial implementing processes to allow more substantial involvement of private actors.

With the epochal political crisis at the beginning of the 1990s, in which the extensively corrupted political system collapsed (the so-called episode of *Tangentopoli*), a cultural break could be witnessed. From this period onward, a new reformist season can be identified, not completely disjointed from the previous one, but acting in a completely different political and cultural context. As the dawn of a new political regime structured on a bipolar system based on left- and right-wing coalitions emerged, the following years were again characterized by reformist actions (mainly during the left-wing-oriented coalitions led by R. Prodi), with much innovation and experimentation in new forms of programs focused on the new territorial emergencies. In favor of this general shift, the European Union played an important role, spreading different modus operandi through structural fund allocation procedures, direct programs, discourses and best practices (Janin Rivolin, 2003a, 2003b). These aspects affected in particular local administrations (with the rise of strategic programming capacity) and the national level with a new direct coordinative role (as will be discussed in section 3.4).

3.2 The administrative reform and the regionalization of planning competences

The new allocation processes of European Structural Funds that were adopted after the reform of the Single Act in 1987 led to a stronger relationship between the EU and the regions, which were considered the proper level to deal with and connect with local and supra-local demands. In Italy, in line with the new political context after the epochal political crisis, this process had the fundamental consequence of increasing the need for a structural reform that adapted the administrative system to the principles of subsidiarity and devolution throughout the whole decade of the 1990s.

The most coherent subsidiarity-oriented administrative reform (known as "Bassanini" from the name of the minister in charge of the process), via a series of legislative measures between 1997 and 1999,[3] achieved the adoption of local governance issues that arose from the wider European context. This reform was conceived to activate a process of progressive devolution or transfer of powers and competences to the pertinent institutional level, according to the complexity and territorial dimension of the questions faced. It was envisaged as a substantial reform, because it aimed to replace hierarchical and conformative-oriented government by establishing new governance-oriented relationships both among institutions and between institutions and the involved stakeholders. Moreover, the process of renovation of the hierarchical levels and competences of public administrations, concluded in 1999, led to the reform of the fifth title of the 1948 Italian constitution in 2001 (constitutional laws n. 1/1999 and n. 3/2001).

The structural subsidiarity-oriented reorganization of powers and competences had a significant impact on territorial planning. The modification to article 117 of the constitution conferred upon the state and the regions concurrent powers in matters of urban planning and territorial government. In these areas, the regions started to have legislative authority, while the state was asked to promulgate laws that provided general principles, to define the general lines of national territorial development and to finance special interventions for specific municipalities, provinces, metropolitan cities and regions. Consequently, the regions obtained ample powers and discretion in defining the objectives, procedures and instruments of territorial government, while the reform of the national framework law was seen as a law providing principles and directives of a general character.

However, if the reform confirmed the role of regions as the principal contexts for elaborate innovative processes and legislative frameworks, it then, de facto, represented a withdrawal of the hopes for a reform at the national level.

3.3 The lack of spatial programming capacity

Already in the 1960s, in a period of booming economy, a shared perception developed that the management and the coordination of economic dynamics with a spatial perspective could be possible, in order to reduce the growing disparities in Italy (e.g. between the North and the South or between urban and rural areas). In this context, the national level tried to define what would later appear as the unique attempt at a spatial development program at the national level.[4] In the same way, in the 1970s, the introduction of the regions as an operative administrative level tried to provide this level with spatial programming and coordinating capacities. However, in both cases the attempt to set spatial development capacities failed, with the consequential cultural acceptance of the sectoral distinction between economic development and spatial management, the former mainly focused on the national and regional levels, the latter mainly focused on the urban level.

From the last decade of the twentieth century until the present day, some national programming capacities have arisen once more. On the one hand, the reformist period and the reform of the public administration introduced innovative procedures in planning activities, including some local spatial development programs based on negotiation and public–private partnerships (e.g. the *Patti Territoriali*). On the other hand, in order to provide a national framework for the most recent program of EU Structural Funds (2007–2013), a new attempt at defining a vision of the national territory took place at the beginning of this decade. Based on different cross-border areas, the so-called *Piattaforme Territoriali* (territorial platforms), through which territorial cooperation strategies beyond regional administrative units were to be implemented, can be considered an attempt to formalize the innovative experiences that matured through the reformist period and to implement spatial development capacities.

However, the changes of national government, the economic crises and other structural factors rendered the reform ineffective in its coordinative and innovative aspects. Indeed, in general terms, these factors continue to impede the definition of a real spatial development programming capacity. Despite these integrative premises and intentions in the national

with special (often deviating) laws. In particular, it was under the auspices of a department under the Ministero delle Infrastrutture e Trasporti (although it has changed name several times) and the activities of architect G. Fontana, a civil servant who coordinated the different arenas in which the discussions took place, that several integrated programs were put in place, with the high point occurring during the left-wing national coalition led by R. Prodi, with P. Costa as minister. The new operative framework defined by the ministerial department, which managed to maintain coherence despite the different political coalitions in power over the 20 years, provided the instruments for new urban interventions, with the support of the planners' associations, as the *Istituto nazionale di urbanistica* (INU – National Town Planning Institute) and *Società Italiana Urbanisti* (SUI – Italian Society of Urban planners), the academia and the municipalities represented by the activism of the *Associazione Nazionale Comuni Italiani* – ANCI (National Association of Italian Municipalities).

Moreover, from a disciplinary perspective, the main structural changes took place during the first Prodi government with the so-called Riforma Bassanini (from the name of F. Bassanini, at that time Minister of Public Administration) and the constitutional changes in 2001 still under the left-wing national coalition, albeit no longer represented by R. Prodi as prime minister. In a political context in which the populist party "Lega Nord" was riding the need for reforms of the centralized public administration, the left-wing coalition approved a historical reform of the constitution in which the competences of spatial planning were delegated to the regional level, together with other important functions. These changes consolidated the process of neo-regionalism in spatial planning, redefining the institutional regions' role and giving them concurrent legislative responsibilities and competences in territorial governance and spatial planning fields.

These institutional changes, together with supra-local dynamics, brought new conditions to the relationships between different administrative levels and the forming of supportive coalitions of spatial planning practices (Servillo and Van den Broeck, 2012). In particular, during the early years of the 1990s, a new configuration started to emerge, with a sort of new "alliance" between the state (in particular the department in charge of the definition of the Integrated Programs and the Department's use of co-funding systems through calls for programs) and municipalities (ANCI and specific municipalities), parallel to the evermore autonomous role of the regions (mainly the central-north regions), which was increasingly becoming the preferential administrative level for use as interlocutor with the EU structures.

On the one hand, the combination of the direct election of the mayors and the new programming role of the state provided the conditions for the development of a series of urban renewal programs throughout the decade, with the state as promoter and coordinator and the cities as local laboratories for the elaboration of strategic interventions through innovative governance processes and the involvement of private stakeholders in decision-making. On the other hand, the programming of the EU Structural Funds raised the necessity to develop the capacity to elaborate spatial development strategies in the regional authorities, for which several governance tools were developed as part of the overall reform of the state.

The new operative framework determined and increased the capacity to involve different public stakeholders (inter-institutional coordination, with co-funding processes) and to activate public–public and public–private partnerships for strategic spatial planning processes, in which for the first time the local administrations improved their crucial role as network administrators and managers with a variety of actor constellations: NGOs, real estate agents, enterprises, regional stakeholders, etc.

The Europeanization of the planning system affected in particular these relationships and the role of the different institutional actors, with several repercussions for all planning practices, although there continued to be no national reform to provide a coherent framework and stability in the oncoming years. For instance, the necessity to define the strategic national framework for the 2006–2013 structural funds program, as already mentioned, represented an important challenge at the national level in the middle of the 2000s. The strategic national framework, which involved the role of the Ministry of Economy and the Ministry of Infrastructure and Transport, together with the wide participation of public stakeholders (regions and municipalities) and various scholars as consultants at round tables and in spatial analyses, constituted a national vision for the first time in Italy. It indicated specific areas of intervention using the evocative image of interregional, national and international "territorial platforms" where the cooperation between different regions was to be stressed. Moreover, the introduction of new projects for urban areas (Servillo, 2008) and the definition of strategic contexts using the concept of "territorial platforms" placed urban areas at the center of a national strategy.

Moreover, important achievements were made, in particular during the 1990s, in the development of institutional procedures that guaranteed horizontal and vertical coordination in multi-dimensional and multi-sectoral governance processes, using the EU and its indications as a source of inspiration. The above-mentioned reform of the state on the occasion of the Bassanini mandate provided new instruments for facilitating public–public and public–private procedures. The main innovation in terms of public–public partnerships was the institutionalization of two main instruments, aimed to achieve more flexibility in decision-making and introduced in 1990 by laws n. 142 and 241, as a first step for the administrative reform that occurred during the 1990s: the *accordo di programma* and the *conferenza dei servizi*. The former is a "contractual agreement" among public actors interested in program implementation based on a collaborative, horizontal and non-hierarchical, decision-making process, in which time, cost and responsibilities are shared among participants. The latter is a sort of "call for a meeting," organized by the administration in order to gather together all the contributions of different administrations and institutions on the same topic.

In the context of public–private partnerships, moreover, an important expansion of contractual practices was launched in 1996 by law n. 662, which provided for the institutionalization of local development agreements in the framework of "negotiated programming" (Salone, 1999; Ancona, 2001; Governa and Salone, 2005). This act represented an effort to apply the criterion of transparent public–private partnership methodology in different contexts and through various instruments,[6] but with a territorial perspective. The "contractual approach" (Urbani, 2000) developed through these instruments constituted a significant extension of the recourse to contractual relationships, reinforcing dialog among public institutions and the decentralization of powers, and represented one of the most significant processes in the transformation of political administrative activities in Italy from authoritarian planning procedures to decision-based models, centered on collaborative and negotiated planning processes (Bobbio, 2000).

In this context, different levels of innovation are occurring. In some contexts, cities have already formed strong coalitions, thereby developing their multi-level and multi-sectoral governance framework, in some isolated cases for the process of forming a strategic spatial plan, and in several cases in Emilia Romagna and Veneto where regional authorities strongly sustain the union of municipalities for developing spatial planning activities. In other cases, mostly in southern Italy, a certain inertia to innovation and continued central financial management have preserved the tendency towards top-down decision-making processes.

Moreover, these differences are the expression of the lack of national reform and delegation to the regional autonomies of new planning laws. In some cases, there has been only a scattered follow-up of these trends, but in others the proposals of the public domain and the relationship with private actors and the market have produced substantial changes in regional approaches. Traditional political orientations and specific cognitive elements carried by different academic actors provided the cultural background to the regional debates that determined different paths of evolution. In particular, different positions emerged when considering the private sector's contribution and the forms of expression of the public administrations' power.

On the one hand, administrations have implemented the partnership between public and private sectors, maintaining a strong role for the public domain. The use of "invitations" and "notices to tender" as practices to involve private stakeholders in the definition of territorial and urban targets are subject to the leadership capacities of the regional administration. Agreements should be reached about the feasibility of actions and the achievement of public works.

The second approach advocates a more liberal perspective. The most advanced practices took place in Lombardia (regional law n. 12 of 11 March 2005), which has limited the definition of a priori vision to broad territorial strategic lines. However, the agenda of public works should be based on free consultation with the private agencies, according to market needs and in the context of a service plan[7] (Palermo and Pasqui, 2008).

In spite of the different positions on this issue (De Luca, 2008), it is important to highlight the new interpretation of the public administration's role as an enabling institute for inclusive processes for decision-making (Bobbio, 2004).

4.2 Planning modes and tools, from local to interregional innovation

In the early years of the 1990s, three thematic bunches of experiments deeply changed planning practices through experimentation and the innovation of new instruments: "complex programs," strategic urban planning and interregional cooperation for spatial planning. In the first and second cases, the local level was the focus of the experimentation and also the primary institutional actor, although a new configuration of horizontal and vertical cooperation was activated. Moreover, all the innovations were based on the wide involvement of private and non-governmental stakeholders, and civil society participation in the decision-making processes, as mentioned above.

Concerning the first group, the scene of Italian planning practices was influenced by urban renewal programs that originated at the European level, such as URBAN or Urban Pilot Projects, and acquired a series of innovative operative instruments during the last decade of the century. Aimed at remedying the urban transformation issues, they were labeled as "complex urban programs" because of the different and multifaceted issues they targeted. From a governance perspective, several innovations concerning procedures, organization and partnerships took place (Lingua, 2005, 2007). The term program stems from the articulation of policies and intervention in a flexible short-to-medium-term timeframe, with defined resources and responsibilities, and shared modalities of intervention.

These instruments brought about very important processes of change from an institutional point of view, with reference to ordinary practices and administrative models. Moreover, the modalities of competitive allocation of European funds were experimentally adapted at the national level for the managing of the funds dedicated to these programs, inducing local administrations to partake in transparent competitions based on defined criteria. Among the most important achievements, moreover, has been the increased capacity to involve different public stakeholders (inter-institutional coordination, with co-funding processes) and to activate public–private partnerships for strategic spatial planning processes, in which for the first time local administrations improved their crucial role as network administrator and manager.

Nevertheless, the propulsive energy dropped in the following decade, together with a change in political context, although further heterogeneous developments were seen in different areas. Some regions framed the renewing program methodology in their legislative framework (e.g. Emilia Romagna) or started experimenting with their own programs; and at the national level some new programs were developed, but without presenting real forms of innovation.

The second key element is strongly in line with the previous group of programs. It concerns the diffusion, mainly at the local level, of experimental applications of strategic planning methodology (Curti and Gibelli, 1996; Pugliese and Spaziante, 2003). On the one hand, the growing awareness of the importance of building up a shared strategy for local development, and on the other hand the impossibility of achieving a general reform of the planning system and tackling the rigidity of the master plan, provoked the widespread diffusion of voluntary forms of strategic plans in many metropolitan areas (Turin, Florence, Verona, Venice, Milan, Trieste) and medium-sized cities (La Spezia, Novara, Pesaro, Trento). In general terms, these episodes show a paradoxical situation: the structural inability to modernize the system with adequate tools (for instance, the unachieved introduction of spatial planning tools for the management of metropolitan regions) provided the conditions to experiment with the most innovative and advanced governance practices related to urban strategic planning, with all the richness and, at the same time, the risks of an unframed experimentation phase.

Both the above-mentioned complex programs and strategic planning practices were made possible by the basis provided by the new way of facilitating horizontal cooperation among public stakeholders (the *accordo di programma* and the *conferenza dei servizi*) and the contractual instruments for public–private partnerships ("negotiated programming" contracts and pacts).

In addition to this context, another experience has a significant potential both in relation to the framework of Italian regional planning practices, and in the wider European panorama of European territorial cohesion: the so-called *Interregional Table of the Padano-Alpine-Maritime Macro-Area* among the regions of Veneto, Emilia Romagna, Friuli Venetia Giulia, Piedmont, Lombardy, Liguria and Valle d'Aosta, and the provinces of Trento and

contractual procedures with the other institutions and stakeholders involved (e.g. Tuscany) and with strong interaction with private stakeholders (e.g. Lombardy).

Due to the new issues raised by the cultural debate and by legislative changes, regional territorial plans show different forms and speeds of adaptation[8] in this updating process, but they are united by the common need to overcome the traditional approach to territorial planning, through a plan of a strategic rather than a structural nature: the *PTR* must provide an idea of the future, a common objective, a shared vision among all different actors. Local and provincial authorities are required to share and to specify this scenario, also by coordinating lower-level and sectoral planning in terms of consistency and compliance with the regional guidelines.

Even in terms of treatment of public–public and public–private relationships (section 4.1), different types of planning systems can be identified, within which territorial interests are regulated and governed (Belli and Mesolella, 2009; De Luca and Lingua, 2012a):

- planning that maintains the primacy of public power in the field of urban and territorial transformations, with a collaborative approach among institutions;
- negotiation-based planning, open to flexible management of territorial governance, and based also on consultation with the private sector;
- updated, semi-classic planning, based on a robust hierarchy among the institutions.

The experience of the region of Tuscany belongs to the first type: it has directly influenced many regional experiences (first Liguria, Umbria and Emilia Romagna). This type of planning seems to move in the direction of spatial policies based on strategic factors, with the aim of reaching shared goals – regardless of the linguistic formulation of the instrument used – through conferences, planning agreements and more or less solid forms of cooperation and consultation, and also through the participation of diverse actors, not only from the institutions, moving along a subtle line between government and processes of governance.

The Lombardy experience belongs substantially to the second type; it is based on a premise of maximum public decision-making flexibility. The concept here is that territorial governance cannot be associated with one single procedure or an univocally determined planning instrument, but it must be understood as the design of the decision-making process and of the subsequent and consequent actions. The underlying idea is that, in dense urban systems with high-density infrastructures, it is not useful to give planning contents a normative value – with the exception of particular safeguards – but urban transformation programs and projects must be decided on in compliance with the administration's negotiating strategies and follow an evaluation of the expected results.

Less clear-cut experiences belong to the third type, such as that of Apulia or Veneto, where the themes of subsidiarity, consultation, joint planning and also of participation are grafted onto the traditional model, though not departing excessively from conformity between the plans. Thus, innovations in connection with the system of evaluation or participation in public decisions are "adapted" to and "modeled" on the classic planning system. Regional planning systems have shown different paths of reform since the constitutional reform and have aquired legislative competences in the spatial planning domain. They have implemented the traditional hierarchical spatial planning system as defined by the obsolete national law in different forms and intensities, introducing elements of strategic planning and negotiating capacities into their spatial planning instruments in a diversified way according to the regional context.

However, the lack of a coherent national legal framework and the delegation of new planning laws to the regional authorities have diffused the follow-up of these reforming trends and the innovative potential of this period. Today, in a time of spending review due to the international financial crisis and its severe effects at the national level, the L. 214/2011 – approved by Monti's government – anticipates a planned constitutional reform which aims to reorganize the traditional institutional levels by merging provinces and small municipalities.

The subsequent provisions (Law n. 135, 8 July 2012) provide for the reorganization of the institutional levels in three directions:

- unification of the provinces on the basis of minimum requirements: population of more than 350,000 residents and area of not less than 2,500 km^2, in addition to the aspect of territorial continuity;[9]
- establishment of the "metropolitan city" as an institutional level within a general reorganization of administrative boundaries, in which provinces are abolished and municipalities merged;
- merging of competences among small municipalities, toward the *unioni di comuni* (union of municipalities).[10]

This reform of the institutional system concerns the Italian planning system and its regional variations and interpretations, as it configures two robust levels of regional intervention that, in addition to providing guidance for regional planning, are also asked to provide guidelines for identifying and managing sub-regional planning areas. The latter can range from establishing a simple legal framework for cooperation to the specific geographical identification of areas for inter-communal planning (De Luca and Lingua, 2012b).

5 Conclusion

A long-term, step-by-step reforming process has characterized the Italian planning system over the past 20 years, due first to the emerging role of the EU, influencing the relationship between the national and the regional level in a multi-level (supra-national) governance framework and, second, to the needs of structural reforms concerning the functioning of the state and the planning system and its technical instruments. Moreover, internal changes in society, due to the fragmentation of interests and actors, and also external changes, linked to increased requests for competitiveness and cooperation within a system that has progressively become detached from administrative borders and unable to tackle larger strategic questions, have led to important changes.

A new attitude towards the planning discipline arose during the 1990s, aimed at setting conditions for local development and shifting attention from regulative mechanisms to urban and territorial strategic interventions. A progressive attitude characterized public administration action, aimed at abandoning bureaucratic and top-down approaches in order to establish management capabilities concerning plans and, thus, the management of territorial dynamics. The new approach to multi-level governance and spatial planning issues assumed a double nature. On the one hand, it implied a relevant modification of the character of public action, induced by various driving forces – primarily EU modus operandi – in decisional processes, which changed the roles in the multi-level government *filiere* (sort of institutional chains between planning levels), in particular at the national and regional levels. On the other hand, public activities engaged in the development of new intervening instruments, characterized by both public–public and public–private partnership issues, and by an attempt to integrate actions related to different sectors. This situation involved the growth of an inclusive, participative and negotiable dimension in the planning process, with the involvement of public and private subjects, which favored widespread forms of governance characterized by contractual and negotiated approaches.

New socio-economic demands at the end of the twentieth century and the emergence of the EU permitted a significant evolution of the discipline through important innovations both in the administrative system and in different and transverse areas of spatial planning (e.g. urban renewal and strategic planning), which was increasingly based on a performance-oriented approach. More generally, the evolution of traditional urbanism to a territorial government orientation, and the integration of territorial development policies based on contractual approaches and socio-economic feasibility, showed attempts to bridge spatial planning and spatial development strategies. Territorial governance came to be no longer considered as compliance-oriented land regulation or city shaping, but embedded strategic spatial planning methodologies for local development aims. Several programs and practices narrowed the gap between spatial planning as urban and physical land-use planning and economic development planning; these were, however, mainly restricted to debate at this time, rather than being effective in legislation practice.

These changes took place most of all through innovative programs that enlarged the fields of Italian spatial planning, weakening to a certain extent the "centrality" of the land-use plan, with interesting peculiarities. First, the reform concerned especially the municipalities, with the experimentation of a series of practices involving local authorities or groups of them, and in some cases with supra-local authorities playing a coordinative role. Second, they were mostly defined at the national level, where a new role in coordinating the development policies and elaborating the new programs had already been defined. Third, however, the necessary national-level legislative reform failed to take place, whilst the regional level became the center of innovation due to decentralizing processes affecting the location of the most important planning functions.

In this sense, the institutional reform that characterized the whole of the 1990s represented a significant effort to decentralize administrative competences from the central state to local authorities. However, the gradual devolution of power to the regions relating to urban development and territorial governance collided with a trend towards concentration and central intervention on some projects and specific issues, causing new conflicts between the central and local levels.

A clear case is the issue of the new institutional reorganization by Monti's government: the impasse of the long advocated but never achieved reform of institutional levels, that should have instituted Metropolitan Areas and "Unions of Municipalities" as administrative areas for territorial governance processes beyond the strict municipal boundaries (Dematteis, 2011), were bypassed by these "informal" practices of strategic planning, which managed to tailor processes for strategic metropolitan plans and policies (Salet and Gualini, 2007). It is only with the recent Monti government that it has been possible to reach a legislative solution for supra-local administrative cooperation, within a general reorganization of administrative boundaries in which some provinces and small municipalities were merged. After 30 years of propositions and discussions, the achievement has once again been reached through an emergency (the deep economic crisis and the necessity for public administration to be simplified and made more efficient), and not through a well-thought-out reform based on disciplinary debate.

In conclusion, in Italy there have been considerable changes to the original conformative model, bringing in performance-oriented practices and strategic planning approaches. The actual situation is characterized by the coexistence of the "urbanist" tradition of planning with new innovative elements in different paths of change. Moreover, the institutionalization of these trends and the federalist reform in process have determined a picture made up of regions with different speeds of reform. In this framework, regions are the main actors of the reform, with significant divergences in terms of forms of structural and policy innovations and subsequently in their competitive capacity in the European context. Since the modernization processes have not tackled the national framework, the actual situation is characterized by a regional reforming patchwork and a step-by-step process, with different intensities of innovation and still with a strong predominance of local-level planning features.

Notes

1 This chapter is partially based on a previous publication, which has been used as a basis for further detailed identification of the direction of changes in the Italian planning field: L. Servillo and V. Lingua (2012). The innovation of the Italian planning system: actors, path dependencies, cultural contradictions and a missing epilogue. *European Planning Studies*, *1*, 1–18.

2 As an example, in 1967, under the emotion of the drama caused by the flood in Florence and Agrigento's earthquake, the so-called "Legge ponte" ("Bridge Law" n. 765/1967) was adopted, which sped up the plan elaboration process but, most of all, it limited the building capacity of areas without planning rules and instruments, and introduced parametrical limits to constructions (among them the "urbanistic standards"). However, this did not happen without an Italian trick: the postponement of one year before the law took full effect, which led to a peak of submissions of building permissions, while within a couple of years the legitimacy of zoning areas for public interests was weakened by juridical verdicts.

3 Law n. 59/1997, law n. 127/1997, Legislative Decree n. 112/1998 and Legislative Decree n. 300/1999.

4 Called *Progetto 80*, it was a vision forecasting spatial development for 20 years, still based on a rationalist and functionalist approach, using the most advanced experiences in Europe as references, with the clear intent of combining for the first time spatial and economic planning approaches. However, it remained a sophisticated exercise without real consequences and, as a matter of fact, the programming approach combining spatial policies and economic development strategies has always been neglected at the national level.

5 In the case of L'Aquila, regional capital of Abruzzo, the conditions of a significant historical, architectural and monumental site with elevated costs of reconstruction legitimized the abandonment of a coherent strategy of reconstruction in favor of a faster and easier strategy of reconstruction outside the city center, in a safer zone, which also hid speculative and illegal processes. In this regard, see the position of the Istituto Nazionale di Urbanistica (National Town Planning Institute) on the website www.inu.it/blog/terremoto_abruzzo.

6 Several instruments were defined: *Intesa istituzionale di programma* (Institutional Program Agreement), *Accordo di programma quadro* (Framework Program Agreement), *Patto territoriale* (Territorial Pact), *Contratto di programma* (Program Contract) and *Contratto d'area* (Area Contract). Despite the fact that these instruments may be redundant (Gualini, 2004), they all allow important references to the territorial dimension and to

specific elements of territorial identity. Moreover, some of these instruments, i.e. *Patti territoriali* and *Accordi di programma*, were already used in specific domains, such as waste management, sanitary policies, etc. For an overview see Bobbio (2000).

7 On the basis of this law and of the experience of Milan's master document, a broad debate began on the necessity of opening up the planning system to forms of self-organization in the spirit of an active liberalism (Moroni, 2007), through a strict definition of the public authority's competences and the liberalization of land-uses, which became a subject for negotiation with the public administration.

8 For an examination and comparison of regional planning instruments, refer to De Luca and Lingua (2012a).

9 This approach has been strongly criticized by local administrations and academics because it is not *place-based*, as it does not take into account the experiences of integration and territorial cooperation already in place, going beyond purely quantitative parameters to refer to project-related forms of cooperation, aimed to develop strategic issues of spatial management and socio-economic development. See, for instance, the debate on the National Town Planning Institute's website (www.inu.it) and on the website of the Union of Italian Provinces (www.upinet.it).

10 This form is midway between inter-municipal cooperation and inter-municipal consolidation; member municipalities keep their legal identity but all functions are managed by the Union which is a sort of consortium; these unions are voluntary, but they are strongly solicited by the provincial level or by the territorial Prefect.

References

Ancona, G. (2001). *Programmazione negoziata e sviluppo locale*. Bari: Cacucci.

Astengo, G. (1966). Urbanistica. *Enciclopedia Universale dell'Arte*, Vol. XIV (pp. 542–643). Venezia: Sansoni.

Astengo, G. (1971). L'Urbanistica. *Le scienze umane in Italia, oggi* (pp. 199–216). Bologna: Il Mulino.

Bellaviti, P. (1995). La costruzione sociale del piano. *Urbanistica*, *103*, 92–104.

Belli, A. and Mesolella, A. (eds) (2009). *Forme Plurime della Pianificazione Regionale*. Firenze: Alinea.

Bobbio, L. (1996). *La democrazia non abita a Gordio*. Milano: FrancoAngeli.

Bobbio, L. (2000). Produzione di politiche a mezzo di contratti nella pubblica amministrazione italiana. *Archivio di Studi Urbani e Regionali*, *58*, 111–142.

Bobbio, L. (2004). *A cura di, A più voci. Amministrazioni pubbliche, imprese, associazioni e cittadini nei processi decisionali inclusivi*. Roma: Edizioni Scientifiche Italiane.

Campos Venuti, G. (1967). *Amministrare l'urbanistica*. Torino: Einaudi.

Campos Venuti, G. (1987). *La terza generazione dell'urbanistica*. Milano: FrancoAngeli.

Campos Venuti, G. (1991). *L'urbanistica riformista*. Milano: Etas.

Campos Venuti, G. and Oliva, F. (1993). *Cinquant'anni di urbanistica in Italia*. Bari: Laterza.

CEC – Commission of the European Communities. (2000). *The EU Compendium of Spatial Planning Systems and Policies: Italy*. Luxembourg: European Communities.

Curti, F. and Gibelli, M. C. (1996). *Pianificazione strategica e gestione dello sviluppo urbano*. Milano: Feltrinelli.

De Carlo, G. (1964). *Questioni di architettura e urbanistica*. Urbino: Argalia.

De Luca, G. (2008). Quale natura cooperativa per la pianificazione regionale. In A. Belli and A. Mesolella (eds) *Forme plurime della Pianificazione Regionale*. Firenze: Alinea.

De Luca, G. and Lingua, V. (2010, July). Cooperative regional planning: a tool to strengthen competitiveness: the Italian case, proceedings of the XIV AESOP Annual Conference *Space is Luxury*. Helsinki.

De Luca, G. and Lingua, V. (2012a). *Pianificazione Regionale Cooperativa*. Firenze: Alinea.

De Luca, G. and Lingua, V. (2012b, September). Cooperative regional planning: the Italian approach to macro-regional issues, proceedings of the IX Towns and Town Planners of Europe, *Smart Planning for Europe's Gateway Cities: Connecting Peoples, Economies and Places*. Roma: INU Edizioni.

Dematteis, G. (ed.) (2011). *Le grandi città italiane: società e territori da ricomporre*. Venezia: Marsilio.

ESPON – European Spatial Planning Observation Network. (2007). *Governance of territorial and urban policies from EU to local level*. ESPON Project 2.3.2, final report. Retrieved from www.espon.eu/export/sites/default/Documents/Projects/ESPON2006Projects/PolicyImpactProjects/Governance/fr-2.3.2_final_feb2007.pdf.

Governa, F. and Salone, C. (2005). Italy and European Spatial Policies: Polycentrism, Urban Networks and Local Innovation Practices. *European Planning Studies*, *13*(2), 265–283.

Gregotti, V. (2002). *Architettura, tecnica, finalità*. Bari: Laterza.

Gualini, E. (2004). *Multi-Level Governance and Institutional Change: The Europeanization of Regional Policy in Italy*. Aldershot: Ashgate.

Indovina, F. (1991). *La ragione del piano: Giovanni Astengo e l'urbanistica italiana*. Milano: FrancoAngeli.

Janin Rivolin, U. (2003a). Nuovi soggetti o nuove responsabilità? L'intervento territoriale comunitario come campo di interpretazione. In G. D. Moccia and D. De Leo (eds) *I nuovi soggetti della pianificazione*. Atti della VI Conferenza Nazionale SIU. Milano: FrancoAngeli.

Janin Rivolin, U. (2003b). Shaping European spatial planning: how Italy's experience can contribute. *Town Planning Review*, *74*(1), 51–76.

Janin Rivolin, U. (2008). Conforming and performing planning systems in Europe: an unbearable cohabitation. *Planning Practice and Research*, *23*(2), 167–186.

Lingua, V. (2005). I Programmi complessi, strumenti innovativi in via di estinzione? *Archivio di Studi Urbani e Regionali*, *83*, 87–104.

Lingua, V. (2007). *Riqualificazione urbana alla prova*. Firenze: Alinea.

Mazza, L. (1997). *Trasformazioni del piano*. Milano: FrancoAngeli.

Moroni, S. (2007). *La città del liberalismo attivo. Diritto, piano, mercato*. Torino: CittàStudi.

Palermo, P. C. and Pasqui, G. (2008). *Ripensando sviluppo e governo del territorio: critiche e proposte*. Santarcangelo di Romagna (RN): Maggioli.

Palermo, P. C. and Ponzini, D. (2010). *Spatial Planning and Urban Development: Critical Perspectives*. Dordrecht: Springer.

Properzi, P. L. (2003). Sistemi di pianificazione regionale e legislazioni regionali. *Urbanistica*, *121*, 60–64.

Pugliese, T. and Spaziante, A. (eds). (2003). *Pianificazione strategica per le città: riflessioni dalle pratiche*. Milano: FrancoAngeli.

Quaroni, L. (1967). *La Torre di Babele*. Padova: Marsilio.

Salet, W. and Gualini, E. (eds) (2007). *Framing Strategic Urban Projects: Learning from Current Experience in European Urban Regions*. London/New York: Routledge.

Salone, C. (1999). *Il territorio negoziato: strategie, coalizioni e "patti" nelle nuove politiche territoriali*. Firenze: Alinea.

Salzano, E. (1998). *Fondamenti di urbanistica*. Bari: Laterza.

Salzano, E. (2008). *Sull'articolazione dei piani urbanistici in due componenti: come la volevamo, com'è diventata, come sarebbe stata utile*. Bologna: Archivio Osvaldo Piacentini.

Samonà, G. (1959). *L'urbanistica e l'avvenire della città negli stati europei*. Bari: Laterza.

Secchi, B. (1989). *Un progetto per l'urbanistica*. Torino: Einaudi.

Servillo, L. (2008). Urban areas and EU territorial cohesion objective: present strategies and future challenges in Italian spatial policies. In R. Atkinson and C. Rossignolo (eds) *Spatial and Urban Planning in Europe*. Amsterdam: Techne Press.

Servillo, L. A. and Van den Broeck, P. (2012). The social construction of planning systems: a strategic-relational institutionalist approach. *Planning Practice and Research*, *27*(1), 41–61.

Urbani, P. (2000). *Urbanistica consensuale*. Torino: Bollati e Boringhieri.

Urbani, P. (2011). *Urbanistica solidale: alla ricerca della giustizia perequativa tra proprietà e interessi pubblici*. Torino: Bollati e Boringhieri.

Further reading

Colavitti, A. M., Usai, N. and Bonfiglioli, S. (2013). Urban planning in Italy: the future of urban general plan and governance. *European Planning Studies*, *21*(2), 167–186.

Servillo, L. and Lingua, V. (2012). The innovation of the Italian planning system: actors, path dependencies, cultural contradictions and a missing epilogue. *European Planning Studies*, *1*, 1–18.

Vettoretto, L. (2009). Planning cultures in Italy: reformism, laissez-faire and contemporary trends. In J. Knieling and F. Othengrafen (eds) *Planning Cultures in Europe* (pp. 189–204). Farnham: Ashgate.

Zanon, B. (2013). Infrastructure network development, re-territorialization processes and multilevel territorial governance: a case study in Northern Italy. *Planning Practice and Research*, *26*(3), 325–347.

Zanon, B. (2013). Scaling down and scaling up processes of territorial governance: cities and regions facing institutional reform and planning challenges. *Urban Planning and Research*, *6*(1), 19–39.

8

THE EVOLUTION OF SPATIAL PLANNING IN GREECE AFTER THE 1990s

Drivers, directions and agents of change

Panagiotis Getimis and Georgia Giannakourou

Chapter objectives

The primary purpose of this chapter is to provide readers with an inclusive explanation and understanding of the evolution of the spatial planning system and policies in Greece during the period 1990–2012.

The objectives of the chapter are:

- to analyze the main problems, demands and challenges that led to major changes in the Greek planning system during that period;
- to explain the dimensions and the directions of change, i.e. the kind and the content of changes observed in the Greek planning system after the 1990s;
- to stress the role of various actors and actor constellations in producing change and institutional innovation; and
- to highlight the impact of the current economic crisis on Greek spatial planning policy and institutions.

1 Introduction

The aim of this chapter is to examine the evolution of the spatial planning system and policy in Greece over the period 1990–2012. The focus is, in particular, on analyzing the main problems and challenges that led to major changes in the Greek planning system, explaining the dimensions and the directions of change, and highlighting the role of various actors and actor constellations in producing change and institutional innovation.

The chapter consists of five sections and the conclusion. Section 2 presents the position of the Greek spatial planning system within different taxonomies developed in European comparative studies over the past two decades. Additionally, it sets out the critical features of the mainstream spatial planning system through a literature review. Section 3 focuses on the framing agenda of Greek spatial planning in the 1990s and 2000s. Its ambition is to identify the main problems, demands and challenges that have served as driving forces of change during this same period. In section 4, the directions of change are analyzed; that is, the kind and the content of changes observed in the Greek planning system after the 1990s. Section 5 focuses on the role of actors and actor constellations that have functioned as "change agents" in planning debates and practices. Section 6 discusses the impact of the recent economic crisis on Greek planning. The chapter concludes by summarizing the current status of the Greek planning system and by expressing some preliminary thoughts on its future development.

2 Setting the scene

2.1 The Greek planning system within existing spatial planning taxonomies

The Greek spatial planning system belongs to the "Napoleonic family" or to the "urbanism" ideal type, according to the different typologies of spatial planning systems (Nadin and Stead, 2008). These typologies either follow classifications (or families) of the legal and administrative systems within which planning operates, or they apply a wider set of criteria but nevertheless produce a similar set of ideal types.

In the taxonomy of national planning systems by Newman and Thornley (1996), Greece is classified under the Napoleonic family of planning. The Napoleonic legal style "has a tendency to use abstract legal norms," aims "to think about matters in advance" and "prepare[s] a complete system of rules based upon the codification of the abstract principles" (Newman and Thornley, 1996, p. 31). The authors highlight the high degree of centrality of the Greek planning system, which is in a constant state of flux.

> Laws and policies undergo regular change as there is no political consensus over planning and each change of government brings shifts in approach and laws. The legal context that has built up over time is therefore piecemeal and complex, involving a labyrinth of amendments, exemptions and special laws, and has not been properly codified.
>
> (Newman and Thornley, 1996, p. 57)

However, the authors note, this legal rigidity goes in parallel with the problem of enforcing spatial planning, while the reality of development does not necessarily relate to the legal framework (e.g. uncontrolled urban sprawl, illegal parceling of land, illegal housing, inefficient implementation of ex-post spatial planning regulations).

In the *EU Compendium of Spatial Planning Systems and Policies* (CEC, 1997) Greece is classified under the "urbanism tradition," which has "a strong architectural flavour and concern with urban design, townscape and building control" (CEC, 1997, p. 37). Furthermore, it is characterized as a "regulatory" spatial planning system, based on hierarchical structures, command and control mechanisms and a strong legalistic tradition. The spatial planning system focuses on the control of building permissions, land-use regulations and statutory plans. However, the problems of implementation of ex-post mainstream statutory planning regulations leave the existing problems unresolved.

The recent ESPON 2.3.2 study (2007), highlighting issues of territorial governance, also classifies the Greek spatial planning system under the "urbanism tradition." Indeed, as the final report notes, the Greek planning system is actually in a "state of turbulence, still dominated by a traditional 'urbanism' and land-use planning model, but full of pockets of innovation, resistance and occasional breakthroughs" (ESPON, 2007, p. 259).

Finally, from a government perspective, Greece, along with the other Mediterranean countries (Spain, Portugal and Italy), has been said to represent a "Mediterranean syndrome" of government (La Spina and Sciortino, 1993) associated with a rigid, legalistic and formal model of planning regulation.

Although the aforementioned comparative studies and typologies highlight crucial features of the Greek spatial planning system, it should be noted that they do not analyze the institutional changes that have occurred during the past two decades. Furthermore, these taxonomies are synchronic, not diachronic. Thus, they cannot capture the dynamics and the contradictions of the ongoing planning agendas, the directions of change, the main driving forces and the new challenges in spatial planning discourses and practices as well. Moreover, by focusing solely on the legal framework and the different legal traditions, these taxonomies fail to explain the implementation processes of spatial planning while at the same time neglecting the different "equi-functional" mechanisms (e.g. between spatial and sector planning or between regional development and spatial planning at different scales) (Fürst, 2009, p. 28).

2.2 Primary features of the mainstream spatial planning system in the early 1990s

The Greek planning system has been traditionally dominated by issues of physical planning. Its main concerns were, on the one hand, "the interface between private and public land ownership and, on the other, the development rights of landowners" (CEC, 2000, p. 15). However, as post-war urbanization took place at a very fast rate, planning authorities proved unable to plan ahead of urban development and provide agglomerations with the necessary urban infrastructure. Hence, spatial planning in Greece did not lead development but rather responded to change with a considerable time lag (CEC, 2000, p. 29).

Under these conditions, planning policies were usually developed as an ex-post regulatory and corrective mechanism aimed at legitimizing pre-existing unauthorized, privately owned structures, developed without planning (Getimis, 1992, p. 244). This is especially true for urban planning, which functioned as a mechanism of political expediency and electoral patronage (e.g. legalization and inclusion of squatter zones within town plans, especially before elections) (Getimis, 1989, p. 71). For the majority of politicians, spatial planning was seen "as a means to serve their voters' private interests. Hence, technical infrastructure projects and integration of unauthorized land development into the statutory plans are the most popular spatial interventions and those most likely to be given political priority" (Wassenhoven et al., 2005).

Ex-post planning only led to minor modifications in the pre-existing urban structures, while the introduction of higher rates for land exploitation created new possibilities for the capitalization of real estate, satisfying the different interests of small landowners. The changes that were foreseen (the provision of the minimum prerequisite infrastructure) were necessary "constitutive" conditions for a more or less rational valorization of private land property. This "constitutive" character of Greek planning policies (Getimis, 1992, p. 245) was derived from the major problem posed by the indeterminate and vague character of land ownership rights in Greece. The latter has remained unclear until today and is a matter of controversy and conflict between various public and private landowners (individuals, the state, the church, etc.). Furthermore, the lack of a cadastre engenders long-term legal proceedings over territorial claims.

3.2 The shift of environmental issues: from EU influence to citizen movements

Of equal importance was the need to integrate the principles and requirements stemming from the European Community Environment Law into planning legislation and processes. In fact, European environmental policy intervened directly in Greek spatial planning by changing the conceptual basis of spatial planning and/or planning procedures themselves (Giannakourou, 2011). As a result of the interplay between EU environmental policy and Greek planning policy, in the late 1990s the principle of sustainability was incorporated in new legislation for urban and regional planning (L. 2508/1997 and L. 2742/1999). The fact that the new statutes addressed the principle of sustainable development as a target of urban and regional development and planning was seen by some scholars as a sign of the European Spatial Development Perspective's (ESDP) influence on domestic planning agendas (Sapountzaki and Karka, 2001). However, the influence of the ESDP has not been the only factor of change. Besides the ESDP, "political action from the side of NGOs, domestic and international, as well as the sort of development targets enjoying financial assistance by the EU" (Sapountzaki and Karka, 2001, p. 424) are considered as important facilitators for this development.

Changes in planning objectives in response to EU discourse were followed by important changes in the licensing process of public and private development projects due to the European Impact Assessment (EIA) directive. The latter was transposed into Greek law in 1990 and was applied systematically thereafter, leading to a large amount of environmental consents being granted for both large- and small-scale projects throughout the 1990s and 2000s. The wide use of this directive changed the procedural standards of most installation processes for both public and private development projects. Moreover, the provisions of the EIA directive for public involvement strengthened the voice and the influence of environmental NGOs and grassroots groups, thereby providing new institutional access points for direct action (Giannakourou, 2011, p. 37). Overall, reliance on the EIA directive has strengthened the role of individuals and NGOs both in monitoring public and private development projects and in bringing critical development projects in front of the Greek administrative courts, the Council of State in particular (Giannakourou, 2011).

Besides EU pressure, a parallel shift involving environmental issues took place from below. From the mid-1990s, various citizen movements began to bring a number of environmental considerations into central and local planning agendas, along with demands for more openness and participation in planning decisions. These pressures brought governance objectives to the central stage of planning dialog (Wassenhoven et al., 2005).

3.3 The need for effectiveness: towards more flexible and less time-consuming planning procedures

Complex and time-consuming planning procedures, along with the number of public authorities involved in various environmental permits and installation licenses, are considered to have been among the main legal and administrative barriers for public infrastructure works and private development projects in the 1990s. Under these conditions, many would-be investors, whose applications stalled in bureaucracy, finally abandoned the proposed developments. At the same time, conflicts about planning decisions were increasing, with many appeals having to be decided by the courts, especially the Council of State.[1] This situation called once again for clear and unambiguous legal procedures in the planning process.

Against this background, the winning of the bid for the Olympic Games in 2004 by the city of Athens in 1997 was seen by the government as a call for planning effectiveness. The challenge to comply with Olympic timetables and to speed up the relevant planning processes rendered the idea of special planning statutes for the Olympic venues increasingly necessary. The main idea was that Olympic legislation should allow "fast track" and *ad hoc* solutions in order to "bypass" obstacles of mainstream spatial planning. To this end, large-scale deviations from urban plans should be allowed, along with the shift of regulatory powers for granting permits and licenses to the central state (Giannakourou, 2010).

3.4 The rise of territorial governance concerns

The concept of governance was introduced to the Greek spatial planning agenda mainly through EU-financed programs and EU-generated legislation. In this regard, European Community Initiatives (Urban, Interreg, Leader, etc.) have functioned as a vehicle for the introduction of new principles of governance in planning practices (e.g. participation, coherence, accountability), especially at the regional and local levels of territorial administration (Giannakourou, 2005). At the same time, vertical and horizontal coordination became necessary vis-à-vis EU structural funds and in particular during the process of preparation and implementation of the CSFs (Wassenhoven et al., 2005). Finally, as analyzed above, civil society has been empowered through community environmental legislation, especially the Information and the EIA directives.

The rise of territorial governance issues became more perceptible in the case of the Athens Olympic Games of 2004. The preparation of this mega-event in the city of Athens functioned as a catalyst for consensus building throughout the country's political and judiciary system. Due to the "Olympic pressure," several issue-based and project-based mechanisms of coordination were established, in most cases including social and private organizations as partners. Involving several actors and stakeholders created trust and social capital and provided legitimacy to the whole effort. The mega-event of the Games seemed thus to function as a "school of governance" (Getimis and Hlepas, 2007), facilitating "experiments" of strategic steering, stakeholder consultation and multi-actor coordination in the metropolitan area of Athens.

4 Dimensions and directions of change in the 1990s and 2000s

The basic movements observed in the Greek spatial planning system and policy in the 1990s and 2000s can be grouped, according to the kind and the content of changes, into four major directions: first, changes in the agenda and the objectives of planning; second, changes in planning instruments and institutions; third, changes in planning style; and finally, changes in planning practices.

4.1 Changes in planning objectives

Greece's planning agenda in the 1980s was dominated by issues of urban planning. The basic policy objectives in this period included the modernization of urban planning legislation, the establishment (for the first time) of a new environmental law, the search for effective land management especially in the suburban, coastal and other sensitive areas, the renewal of city centers, especially in historic towns, and the effective management of unauthorized use and development (CEC, 2000). To this end, in 1982 the Ministry of Spatial Planning, Settlement and the Environment launched a large-scale operation for the country's urban restructuring, under the acronym EPA,[2] aiming in particular to deal with long-term problems and pathologies of Greek towns and cities, like the uncompleted urban plans, the illegal settlements and constructions and the lack of adequate urban infrastructure.

While the EPA operation was still running in the early 1990s, in 1994 the ministry launched a new operation for the country's regional restructuring focusing on the modernization of national and regional planning legislation. The new planning agenda of the 1990s and 2000s emphasized the role of strategic spatial planning in promoting economic growth, social cohesion and sustainability, along with the need to accelerate major infrastructure projects, such as the new Athens airport, the Rion bridge, the north–south and the west–east (*Egnatia*) motorways, and achieving greater flexibility in formulating policy responses towards large- and medium-scale private developments in the areas of industry, services and tourism. Overall, one may observe a shift from the previous dominant type of physical planning towards a more strategic and development-oriented spatial approach that could be able to increase the country's attractiveness and competitiveness in the context of European integration and globalization. This goal was first announced in the first draft of the General Spatial Planning Framework elaborated upon in the late 1990s. It has since been further pursued through the active promotion of Trans-European Networks connecting the north–south and west–east of the country and of several secondary development axes in western Greece, northern Crete and other parts of the country. The attraction of major events such as the Athens Olympic Games of 2004 must be seen as a complementary development goal in this perspective aimed at reinforcing the international role of Athens and its position in interurban competition on the EU scale (Economou et al., 2001; Beriatos and Gospodini, 2004; Wassenhoven et al., 2005).

In practice, this shift has been illustrated through a range of mechanisms comprising the establishment of special spatial planning frameworks at the national level for facilitating private developments in tourism, industry and energy, the centralization of policy direction for major public infrastructure projects and the introduction of special Olympic spatial plans that bypass the obstacles generated by the established land-use regulations and building conditions in Attica.

4.2 Changes in planning instruments and institutions

Changes in planning objectives were accompanied by changes in planning instruments and institutions. Both urban and regional planning legislation were amended in the late 1990s in order to incorporate new concepts and principles, and new tools and organs as well, capable of promoting sustainable territorial development at several levels of government (national, regional, local) and better coordination between various types of plans and territorial policies. Urban planning legislation was the first to be amended in 1997. L. 2508/1997 on sustainable urban development updated and enriched the pre-existing legal framework for physical planning. The new law emphasized, among other things, the need to establish master plans for all large urban centers, apart from Athens and Thessaloniki, integrated urban plans for all cities and smaller settlements and special plans for second and vacation home development. It also introduced special provisions for urban regeneration projects.

This legislative reform was followed two years later by the replacement of the fundamental law on spatial planning (360/1976) with a new framework Act (L. 2742/1999). The new Act provided for a series of strategic-level plans (frameworks) at the national and regional levels. The provisions of the new Act provide evidence of the direct influence of the ESDP on the Greek national spatial planning agenda (Giannakourou, 2005). Indeed, both the preamble of the bill and the Act itself make direct reference to the basic policy options of the ESDP, such as "polycentric and balanced spatial development," "parity of access to infrastructure and knowledge" and a "new urban–rural partnership" (Giannakourou, 2005). The main planning instruments under L. 2742/1999 are the General and the Special (sectoral) Spatial Planning Frameworks at the national level and the Regional Spatial Planning Frameworks (RSPFs) at the regional level. Twelve of the 13 RSPFs were approved in 2003, with the exception of the Region of Attica, the greater part of which is covered by a special Master Plan of metropolitan character (Master Plan of Athens). Besides the RSPFs, the first national spatial plan, known as the "General Framework for Spatial Planning and Sustainable Development," along with three Special Spatial Planning Frameworks concerning, respectively, Renewable Energy Sources (RES), tourism and industrial developments, were approved in 2008 and 2009, after a long period of discussions and negotiations. Their approval was in part a response to the case law of the Council of State which, in interpreting article 24 of the Greek Constitution,[3] considered national and regional planning guidance as a prerequisite for the location of productive activities and public infrastructure projects at specific sites (Giannakourou, 2007). In this respect, the institutionalization of national and regional spatial planning was seen both by the government and by major stakeholders as a step towards promoting legal certainty for major public and private developments.

Besides new planning instruments, planning legislation enacted in the late 1990s tried further to promote a broader devolution of planning powers to regional and local levels of government, along with creating new coordinative and steering institutions at the national level. To this end and in line with more general modifications in the country's administrative map,[4] L. 2508/1997 delegated important powers to regional administrations and local tiers of government concerning the elaboration, approval, amendment and revision of town plans[5] and the monitoring and control of different types of urban plans. Changes in the allocation of planning powers between different levels of government were followed by the creation of an inter-ministerial committee of planning at the state level aimed at improving coordination between different policies with planning impact (Coordination Committee of Governmental Policy for Spatial Planning and Sustainable Development). At the same time, attempts to foster more systematic consultation with key stakeholders were made through the creation of a National Council for Spatial Planning and Sustainable Development, consisting of representatives from major stakeholders of the public and private sector (e.g. experts, scientists, representatives from professional associations, Chambers, etc.). The opinion of the Council is required for the approval of the General and Special Frameworks for Spatial Planning and Sustainable Development.

However, some of these efforts failed, while others were gradually undermined:

1   The devolution of planning powers to regions and elected local authorities met with serious legal objections from the Council of State. In fact, the Court has recognized urban and regional planning as a state function that, under the Constitution, pertains only to central government. Hence, planning powers delegated in the 1990s to local authorities and regions were transferred back to the central state. Apart from the legal disputes (e.g. whether a function is considered to be a local affair or not, decisive for whether it is a municipal responsibility or not), the spatial planning system remained highly centralized, hierarchical and susceptible to *ad hoc* pressures and demands (Getimis, 2010; Getimis and Hlepas, 2010).

2   The Coordination Committee of Governmental Policy for Spatial Planning and Sustainable Development never functioned between 1999 and 2009. It is only recently (2010) that this body was activated as a coordinative mechanism between those sections of the government concerned with the economy and those responsible for the environment and the territory.

3   Although consultation and participation of key stakeholders in national and regional planning took place, rather systematically, between 2000 and 2004, these processes were weakened in the following period (2005–2009), leading to the National Council for Spatial Planning and Sustainable Development assuming a more formal role. The debate on the draft Special Planning Frameworks for tourism, industry and RES that followed in this body proved highly controversial, creating large tensions between the government and key stakeholders (e.g. Technical Chamber of Greece, Tourist Chamber of Greece, etc.).

Overall, one could hardly talk of a real shift in the governance patterns of Greek spatial planning in the 1990s and 2000s. However, despite legal and institutional impediments, "governance has made its way into several contexts of the Greek public sphere over the last decade, although not necessarily with explicit recognition in official pronouncements" (Wassenhoven et al., 2005). Several public fora for dialog and debate have been created outside the formal government system, either in the form of academic networks, professional and civil society groups and NGOs or through specialized conferences and the press (Wassenhoven et al., 2005). Further, new governance schemes have been developed "in the shadow of official structures," as in the case of the Athens Olympic Games.

4.3 Changes in planning style

Although spatial planning in Greece during the 1990s and 2000s remained predominantly focused on land-use regulation, a parallel shift towards strategic spatial planning took place in the late 1990s. This shift was expressed both in L. 2742/1999 for national and regional planning and in the content of spatial planning documents formulated following the adoption of this Act. Under the new strategic approach, spatial planning is considered as a tool for identifying long- and medium-term objectives and strategies for national and regional territories and reconciling competing policy goals, especially in the areas of economic development, the environment and social cohesion policies. In this regard, L. 2742/1999 set out three basic goals of national territorial policy, based on the principles of the ESDP, namely balanced polycentric development and a closer relationship between town and country, equal access to basic services of general interest and wise management of natural resources and cultural heritage. Spatial planning documents formulated under the new law's provisions, including the General and the Special Planning Frameworks and the RSPFs as well, tried to specify and apply these general objectives on the national and regional scales by providing guidance for the spatial distribution of development and investment, coordinating infrastructure projects and productive activities (e.g. tourism, agriculture, industry) with the maintenance of environmental assets, and serving as a general framework for land-use planning.

Besides the turn towards strategic planning, shifts in the style of Greek planning during the period also comprised organizational changes, e.g. changes in management and decision-making processes. In this regard, there were institutional developments that indicated that policymakers were searching for more participative, involved modes of planning. Indeed, at both the national and regional scales, planning schemes provided by L. 2742/1999 were subject to a broader consultation process at the national and regional levels, within either statutory (National Council for Spatial Planning and Sustainable Development and Regional Councils) or voluntary (e.g. informal regional conferences and seminars) fora of debate and dialog. Moreover, the Special Planning Frameworks, elaborated after the SEA (Strategic Environmental Assessment) Directive came into force, were additionally subjected to strategic environmental assessment at the national scale. Although consultation processes during 2007–2009 were rather controversial, as explained earlier, it should be admitted that it was the first time since the launching of the EPA operation in the early 1980s that Greece engaged in major public debate about the country's future spatial development, a debate that involved many levels of government, key stakeholders, major NGOs, the academic community and the Greek parliament itself. In this sense, we could argue that new elements of consensus-oriented planning, based on participation and consultation, were introduced into the existing framework of the previously dominant command and control planning ("paternalistic") style.

Finally, in order to become effective, spatial planning under the new legal framework was designed as an evidence-based process. To this end, L. 2742/1999 provided for the creation of a national spatial information network under the auspices of the Ministry of Spatial Planning. The network was designed to collect, integrate and make use of spatial data created by the Ministry of Spatial Planning, other ministries and public organizations, among them the universities and the country's research centers. The information produced within the network should be able to assist in territorial policy formulation and in the appraisal and review of statutory spatial planning documents. However, despite mandatory provisions, the network still remains ineffective. This shows that, despite good intentions, strategic spatial planning has not yet been fully implemented on the ground. The inherent reluctance of the Greek public authorities to develop horizontal ties must be seen as the main cause of this deficit. Nevertheless, recent developments show that something is changing in this area. The transposition of the Inspire Directive into Greek law has served as an opportunity to establish a National Geo-information Committee (NGC) answerable to the prime minister and chaired by the minister responsible for planning and environmental policy. The members of the Committee include the General Secretaries of the most pertinent ministries regarding the implementation of the Inspire Directive. The NGC will assume the role of a high-level, decision-making body which will be responsible for the establishment, monitoring and evaluation of a national policy and framework with regard to spatial data collection, management, availability, sharing and exploitation throughout the public sector. However, whether this new committee will be able to overcome administrative reluctance and blockades still remains to be seen.

4.4 Changes in planning practices

Strategic planning, along with voluntary partnerships and informal networking arrangements, was also practiced in the case of the Olympic Games of 2004. The Games functioned as a platform for "experimental governance" (Giannakourou and Trova, 2001) and as a "catalyst of problem-solving" (Getimis and Hlepas, 2007). Central guidance and coordination along with effective monitoring and evaluation processes were some of the main techniques used here. The first critical step for the management of the whole Olympic project was the creation in 1998 of the organizing committee of the Athens Olympic Games (Athens 2004 S.A.), in the form of a public limited company. The new entity took on administration and management responsibilities that had previously been dispersed between several other public authorities, while it directly referred to and had the active political support of the head of the government, the prime minister. "Athens 2004" functioned as a kind of junction point or nexus for the development of horizontal and vertical networks. In this regard, new vertical and horizontal linkages were shaped against a background of effectiveness due to the urgent pressure of achieving concrete results. The traditional command and control techniques of the Greek legalistic administration were abandoned and new cooperative strategies formed on a win–win basis, especially through the signing of Memoranda of Understanding (MoUs) between Athens 2004 on the one hand and local authorities affected by the Games or key stakeholders on the other (e.g. the Athens Hotels Association). The signing of MoUs was used during the period of Olympic preparation as a broader instrument with which to create strategic alliances and increase the legitimacy and the performance of the Olympic project.

"Athens 2004" also coped with a major problem that could delay or even foil the construction of the Olympic works, namely the lack of strategic spatial planning. So, in 1999, strategic spatial and environmental impact assessments were prepared for key Olympic sites, thus preventing long-lasting and costly litigation that could have jeopardized construction activities. In parallel, an attempt was made to broadly "rescale" the Olympic projects to the level of the Athens Master Plan through the passing of L. 2730/1999. This incorporated the Olympic projects "in special urban planning guidelines for the Olympic poles system that was going to be established in Attica," and, at the same time, introduced "special plans of integrated development in the areas of key Olympic installations, which allowed for derogations from general and specific urban regulations in force in each area" (Giannakourou, 2010, p. 105). Furthermore, public dialog with important actors was initiated in a way that reduced local reactions. The start of construction activities thus had to be postponed in many cases, but an acceleration of efforts during the closing period led to the accomplishment of the projects within the time limits. In a few cases, where objections from environmental NGOs and activists had led to litigation, the "Olympic vision" that influenced perceptions throughout the political and the judiciary system ("national duty/benefit") functioned as a catalyst for problem solving.

Besides the case of the Athens Olympic Games, new governance practices also appeared during the implementation process of EU programs and initiatives (e.g. Urban, Interreg, Leader, etc.). These programs were mainly managed by local development agencies. The latter built a wide network of partnerships around them and employed *ad hoc* governance practices in order to achieve coordination across multiple jurisdictions and multiple plans (Wassenhoven et al., 2005). Although some scholars describe this process as an "external institutional shock" for Greek local and regional institutions (Paraskevopoulos, 2001), empirical evidence shows that transformative dynamics have been unequal, influenced by pre-existing institutional traditions (Paraskevopoulos, 2001) and politics and economic geography as well (Chorianopoulos, 2008).

5 Main actors triggering changes in the Greek planning system

Several actors have been involved in the process of planning change in Greece in the 1990s and 2000s. Most initiatives for planning reforms stemmed from the central government, in particular the Ministry of the Environment, Spatial Planning and Public Works (YPECHODE). The latter was responsible for the enactment of new legislation and for the elaboration of most planning documents and the financing of planning operations as well. The initiatives taken by YPECHODE must be seen as a response to both domestic and European pressures and impulses.

Regarding EU influence on the Greek spatial planning system and policy, one should distinguish between two major pathways of Europeanization. First, legal and political compliance, which includes changes in planning objectives, instruments and structures in order to comply with EU rules and/or political and economic pressures (Giannakourou, 2011). In this regard, one may refer for instance to the significant changes brought about by the EIA and the Information Directives in planning procedures in Greece that were analyzed earlier (see also Giannakourou, 2011, pp. 37–38). Second, voluntary policy transfer, which concerns the voluntary adoption of EU-generated discourse, concepts and principles in order to legitimize changes and reforms in the domestic arenas of planning (Giannakourou, 2011). This was, for instance, the case with the direct incorporation of the main ESDP policy aims and options in the country's new law on strategic spatial planning that was passed in September 1999 (L. 2742/1999). The use of the European spatial development discourse strengthened the hands of Greek policymakers to enable them to better position and justify the reform of national and regional planning legislation that had already been announced at the time of the ESDP approval (Giannakourou, 2005, 2011). Given this conjuncture, reference to the ESDP and to the broader European discourse offered domestic politicians additional arguments supporting a strategic turn in Greek spatial planning while, at the same time, increasing the political capacity of the Greek Ministry of Planning in the inter-ministerial negotiations that preceded the deposit of the bill in the Greek Parliament (Coccossis et al., 2005).

The efforts undertaken by YPECHODE in the 1990s towards the modernization of the Greek planning agenda and legislation were supported by a small, albeit dynamic, community of planners, comprising academics and private consultants as well. The members of this community, emanating from the country's main academic planning departments[6] and other institutions, such as the scientific journal *TOPOS* and the Association of Greek Planners (SEPOX), shared common perceptions about spatial development problems and common concerns about the type of planning policies to be applied. Their participation in the high-level groups formed by YPECHODE in the mid-1990s "gave them the opportunity to construct a coordinative discourse on spatial planning priorities and strategies that functioned as a frame of reference for the Ministry's envisaged reforms" (Giannakourou, 2011, p. 36). The discussions held within these high-level groups, along with the publications and the conferences organized in the academic planning circles, provided the basic set of ideas and discourses that were finally incorporated in the new law for spatial planning passed in 1999 (L. 2742/1999).

The replacement of the Minister and of the Secretary General of Spatial Planning in 2001 led to the dismantling of the high-level groups that were created under their auspices during the previous period (Giannakourou, 2011, p. 36). So the role of the aforementioned planning community was consequently weakened. The decline of expert knowledge coincided after 2004 with the appearance of strong sector interests seeking to influence planning decisions in their favor. The approval of the Special Planning Frameworks for Renewable Energy Sources, Industry and Tourism in the late 2000s is representative of this movement as it shifted spatial planning priorities at the national level in more sectoral directions. Decisive steps here came from the pressure brought to bear by large business associations including the Hellenic Federation of Enterprises (SEB), the Association of Greek Tourism Enterprises (SETE) and the Greek Association of Renewable Energy Sources RES Electricity Producers (ESEAPE). These actors asked for special planning policies on a national scale that could set out clear guidelines for the site allocation of relative projects in specific geographical areas and facilitate interested investors by settling competitive and contradictory land-uses.

Besides sector interests, spatial planning developments in the 2000s must also be attributed to the pressure exercised by the case law of the Council of State. This functioned as a facilitator for the re-centralization of planning policies and for the search of effectiveness and legal security through a planning-led development approach. Starting in the late 1990s, local opposition to commercial and industrial developments as well as to wind parks led to a barrage of legal appeals to the Council of State contesting planning consents and/or development licenses for the above activities. The court's decisions focused on the lack of official land planning that could define, countrywide, land-uses and activity zones. The need to respond to this case law led in the mid-2000s to the elaboration and approval of the three Special Frameworks for tourism, industry and RES development. Their approval was seen as a necessary condition for providing legal certainty for public and private development projects and putting an end to the everlasting legal conflicts brought before the Council of State regarding economic development investments (Giannakourou, 2010).

Apart from the above-mentioned agents, several other actors have been involved in different stages of the planning process, albeit in a more reactive than proactive way. Among them, reference should be made to some of the country's major professional organizations, such as the Technical Chamber of Greece and the Athens Bar Association, and to national-scale environmental NGOs, such as the WWF-Hellas and the Hellenic Society for the Protection of the Environment and of Cultural Heritage. Most of these actors were practically absent from the debates taking place in the planning fora during the 1990s, and at the same time appeared to feel rather uncomfortable vis-à-vis the new strategic spatial planning discourse launched by the Ministry of Spatial Planning in the late 1990s. However, despite their initial "silence," these actors gained ground in the mid-2000s, due mainly to their opposition to the planning agenda adopted by the conservative Minister of Planning, George Souflias. What brought these actors together during that period was their shared belief that environmental and landscape protection should be prioritized over economic interests and land development investments. Under this discourse, in the late 2000s this constellation of actors formed a strong advocacy coalition opposing the proposals included in the drafts of the Special Planning Frameworks for tourism and RES development. This coalition resisted, in particular, planning changes that would make it easier to build holiday houses on the islands and coastal areas on the one hand and install wind parks on small islands and protected areas on the other. Regarding especially the Special Spatial Planning Framework for Tourism, this coalition was supported by the tourist industry (National Hoteliers Association), which saw the danger of prioritizing certain areas and types of development while neglecting others in terms of investment. Public reactions continued even after the approval of the schemes. So, both the planning schemes for RES development and for tourism have been subjected to applications for annulment with the Council of State, applications that are still pending. This development confirms that, despite formal provisions contained in L. 2742/1999, planning practices in the 2000s remained largely controversial, unable to generate trust between the state, society and the market and to guide planning procedures in a more consensual direction.

6 Greek spatial planning after the economic crisis: 2010–2012

The financial and economic crisis Greece has been facing since early 2010 is also impacting, among other policy fields, on Greek spatial planning. In this respect, two major directions of change in Greek spatial planning policy and legislation can be distinguished.

The first direction of change is related to a more general wind of "privatization" that has been experienced in Greece over the past two years. Indeed, the financial and economic crisis and the consequent government downsizing have acted as a stimulus for private sector involvement in areas of public policies that were previously the public sector's responsibility. In this regard, various spatial planning functions and activities that were traditionally the responsibility of public services and public agencies have been recently transferred to private entities. Among them are the outsourcing of planning assessments and controls to private consultants and practitioners and the management of public spaces and of entire urban areas by private entities as well (Giannakourou and Balla, 2012). Regarding, on the one hand, the outsourcing of planning powers to private consultants, one should refer to two important Acts that passed through Greek Parliament in late 2011: L. 4014/2011 and L. 4030/2011. The former provides for the outsourcing of the assessment of Environmental

Impact Assessments (EIAs) to private consultants (Certified Environmental Assessors), while the latter provides for the delegation of building inspection functions to independent certified private inspectors operating under the supervision of the Ministry of Environment. Certified Environmental Assessors are entitled, whenever so requested by the responsible government authority, to proceed with a thorough examination of the EIAs submitted to public services, to make any necessary contacts with authorities designated to be consulted on the environmental report and to draft the environmental terms to be included in the environmental license. Building inspectors, for their part, may proceed with the control of all constructions for which a building permit has been issued so as to ensure that the technical criteria under which the permit has been granted are properly implemented and enforced. Regarding, on the other hand, the private management of public spaces and entire urban areas, one should refer to L. 4062/2012 establishing the general legal framework for the development and exploitation of the former Hellinikon International Airport area and to L. 3986/2011 (Art 12, par. 7), as amended by L. 4092/2012, establishing the legal framework for the development and sale of the remaining public assets. Both laws ensure that not only the drafting but also the implementation of the urban plans to be approved for the development of the public estates under privatization fall under the exclusive initiative and responsibility of the investor – to be selected through the sale process. So, according to the aforementioned laws, the maintenance, cleaning and renewal of public technical equipment, as well as the maintenance of infrastructure works, the traffic network and green spaces, is carried out at the expense and under the diligence and responsibility of the private developer, by way of derogation from any relevant provision.

The privatization of planning powers and services is not the only implication of the current financial and economic crisis for Greek planning. Growing private sector involvement in urban development goes along with the search, on the part of the government, for more flexible and market-oriented types of planning. The emergence of a pro-growth planning agenda is the second direction of change currently being tried out in Greece. The purpose of pro-growth planning is to facilitate and support private initiatives and spatial investments instead of only regulating and controlling private development. In this respect, pro-growth planning is called to overcome delays and weaknesses perceived in traditional land-use planning processes. The latter have often been accused of "dampening" private development initiatives because of, among other things, excessive regulation and/or the lack of appropriate regulation and legal certainty (Giannakourou, 2010; OECD, 2011). Efforts towards a pro-growth planning approach have been manifested in two important Acts passed by the Greek Parliament in 2010 and 2011: first, L. 3894/2010 establishing special "fast track" licensing for strategic investments; second, L. 3986/2011 (Arts 10–16) introducing a special and simplified planning regime for the privatization of public land. The former concerns strategic investments, i.e. large-scale investments, deriving either from the private sector or from public–private investment partnerships, that may generate quantitative (e.g. budget, employment positions) and qualitative (e.g. the promotion of innovation, protection of the environment) results of major significance for the national economy overall, and which may consequently facilitate the country's exit from the economic crisis. The latter, known as the first Implementation Law, was voted on in June 2011 and includes the emergency measures for the implementation of Greece's Medium-Term Fiscal Strategy Framework 2011–2015, among them measures concerned with the development of public properties in view of their privatization. Both laws, despite their different scope and the legal instruments used, share the same perception vis-à-vis spatial planning. It is regarded as a tool for enabling development and responding to the search for private investments. To this end, the aforementioned Acts introduce special planning rules and processes that replace the conventional land-use plans with alternative zoning mechanisms. Those zoning mechanisms, if they are considered compatible with national planning directives, can then "bypass" regional and local spatial and land-use plans. Such special regimes thus do not involve the wholesale transformation of the existing conventional planning system. This remains in principle intact and is only subject to selective "bypasses" that enable *ad hoc* departures from existing plans and processes.

7 Conclusion

Summing up, one may argue that Greek spatial planning has undergone significant changes in the past 20 years both as to its structures and tools and as to its objectives, discourses and practices. The new planning agenda focused upon the role of strategic spatial planning in promoting economic growth, social cohesion and sustainability, along with the need to accelerate major public infrastructure projects and achieve greater flexibility in formulating policy responses towards large- and medium-scale private developments. This shift was driven both by EU pressures and impulses and by domestic needs and problems. However, the turn towards strategic- and development-oriented spatial planning referred mainly to the regional and national levels, while urban planning, despite legislative amendments, remained focused on land-use regulation. In this sense, divergent planning objectives coexisted during this period, making the planning landscape more complex and fussy. Changes in planning scope were accompanied by changes in planning instruments and institutions and in planning practices as well, with the case of the Athens Olympic Games being the most important example of experimental governance during the period 1999–2004. However, once again, these changes coexisted with traditional features of Greek planning, namely command and control policy instruments, hierarchical governance and adversarial planning practices.

A multiplicity of actors played a decisive role in the formulation and implementation of planning policies during this period, engendering different kinds of change. First, the central state along with the planning community functioned as the main drivers for modernizing the planning agenda and introducing EU-generated concepts and ideas in the domestic planning discourse. Moreover, private sector stakeholders (e.g. investors in the tourism, industrial and energy sectors) latched strongly onto "fast track" solutions and simplification of planning regulations, in order to overcome complex burdens and delays. Furthermore, various citizen movements and environmental NGOs brought various environmental considerations into central and local planning agendas, along with demands for more openness and participation in planning decisions. In this regard, it has to be noted that both EU environmental legislation and the new consultative structures for strategic planning established in the 1990s (National Council for Spatial Planning and Sustainable Development) gave voice to a wide range of actors, until then "silenced" or underrepresented in the public fora of planning. However, although consultation and participation of key agents in national and regional planning broadened in the 2000s, traditional features of the hierarchical and adversarial policymaking still persisted, giving rise to new tensions between the state, society and the market and leading to a new cycle of judicial litigation.

Overall, one can hardly speak of a radical shift in the policy style of Greek spatial planning in the 1990s and 2000s. Instead, a mixture of different patterns of institutional persistence and innovation arose during that period, indicating a complex process of continuity and change. Recent developments show that the government, under the pressure of the current economic crisis, is being directed towards institutional alternatives to traditional land-use planning in order to facilitate pending decisions for major private investments and "bypass" existing "obstacles, created by established regulatory planning tools and the licensing procedures based on them" (Giannakourou, 2010, p. 105). Yet, these alternative planning regimes (privatization of planning powers and services, outsourcing, pro-growth planning) do not address the root of the planning problem in Greece. They leave mainstream planning features intact while at the same time ignoring the potential offered by strategic planning and governance to produce vision, prospect and consensus for the country's future spatial development. Under these conditions, the future of the existing multiple trajectories of continuity and change in the Greek planning system is unpredictable. The transition phase characterized by the coexistence of planning practices of differing scopes, planning modes and tools, actor constellations and policy styles is still ongoing. The question is therefore not if the "urbanism tradition" of the Greek planning model is still dominant 15 years after the *EU Compendium*, but in which direction the analyzed tensions between changes and continuities will lead. And this is a matter that will be decided not only at the national level but also in a multi-scale European and global context.

Notes

1 The Council of State (*Symvoulio tis Epikrateias*) is the supreme administrative court in Greece. Its competences are basically determined by the Constitution and include the annulment of administrative acts for the exceeding of power or the violation of law, the cassation, on final appeal, of final decisions of the lower administrative courts and the hearing of substantive administrative disputes. Besides these judicial competences, the Council of State is also responsible for the legal control of all decrees with a regulatory character.
2 Epixeirisi Poleodomiki Anasygrotissi (EPA).
3 Article 24 of the Greek Constitution contains specific clauses concerning the obligation of the State to plan the structure of the national territory and the settlements and to protect the physical and cultural environment.
4 Broader institutional changes in the 1990s included the creation of second-tier local authorities in 1994, the amalgamation of small communities into larger municipal units (Kapodistrias program of 1994) and the transfer of powers to regional authorities in 1997.
5 Apart from planning competences, local authorities were given important delegated powers, transferred from several ministries other than the Ministry of Environment (e.g. the licensing of industrial development, the compulsory acquisition of land for agricultural land improvement projects, the designation of land in seaport zones to be used for public purposes, etc.).
6 Departments of Urban and Regional Planning of the National Technical University of Athens and the Aristotle University of Thessaloniki, and the new Department of Planning and Regional Development of the University of Thessaly.

References

Beriatos, E. and Gospodini, A. (2004). "Glocalising" urban landscapes: Athens and the 2004 Olympics. *Cities*, *21*, 187–202.

CEC – Commission of the European Communities. (1997). *The EU Compendium of Spatial Planning Systems and Policies*. Luxembourg: Office for Official Publications of the European Communities.

CEC – Commission of the European Communities. (2000). *The EU Compendium of Spatial Planning Systems and Policies: Greece*. Luxembourg: Office for Official Publications of the European Communities.

Chorianopoulos, I. (2008). Institutional responses to EU challenges: attempting to articulate a local regulatory scale in Greece. *International Journal of Urban and Regional Research*, *32*(2), 324–343.

Coccossis, H., Economou, D. and Petrakos, G. (2005). The ESDP relevance to a distant partner: Greece. *European Planning Studies*, *13*(2), 253–264.

Economou, D. (2002). The institutional framework of spatial planning and its adventures. *Aeihoros*, *1*(1), 116–127.

Economou, D., Getimis, P., Demathas, Z., Petrakos, G. and Pyrgiotis, Y. (2001). *The International Role of Athens*. Volos: University of Thessaly Press.

ESPON. (2007). *Governance of Territorial and Urban Policies from EU to Local Level, ESPON Project 2.3.2, Final Report*. Esch-sur-Alzette: ESPON Coordination Unit. Retrieved from www.espon.eu.

Fürst, D. (1999). Humanvermögen und regionale Steuerungsstile: Bedeutung für das Regionalmanagement? *Staatswissenschaften und Staatspraxis*, *6*, 187–204.

Fürst, D. (2009). Planning cultures en route to a better comprehension of planning processes. In J. Knieling and F. Othengrafen (eds) *Planning Cultures in Europe: Decoding Cultural Phenomena in Urban and Regional Planning* (pp. 23–48). Aldershot: Ashgate.

Getimis, P. (1989). *Urban Policy in Greece: The Limits of Reform*. Athens: Odysseas.

Getimis, P. (1992). Social conflicts and the limits of urban policies in Greece. In M. Dunford and G. Kafkalas (eds) *Cities and Regions in the New Europe* (pp. 239–254). London: Belhaven Press.

Getimis, P. (2010). Strategic planning and urban governance: effectiveness and legitimacy. In M. Cerreta, G. Concilio and V. Monno (eds) *Making Strategies in Spatial Planning: Knowledge and Values* (pp. 123–146). Heidelberg: Springer.

Getimis, P. and Hlepas, N. (2005). The emergence of metropolitan governance in Athens. In H. Heinelt and D. Kuebler (eds) *Metropolitan Governance: Capacity, Democracy and the Dynamics of Place* (pp. 63–80). London/ New York: Routledge.

Getimis, P. and Hlepas, N. (2007). From fragmentation and sectoralisation to integration through metropolitan governance? The Athens Olympics as a catalytic mega-event. In J. Erling Klausen and P. Swianiewicz (eds) *Cities in City Regions: Governing the Diversity* (pp. 127–173). Warsaw: European Urban Research Association.

Getimis, P. and Hlepas, N. (2010). Efficiency imperatives in a fragmented polity: reinventing local government in Greece. In H. Baldersheim and L. E. Rose (eds) *Territorial Choice: The Politics of Boundaries and Borders* (pp. 198–213). Basingstoke: Palgrave Macmillan.

Getimis, P. and Kafkalas, G. (1992). Local development and forms of regulation: fragmentation and hierarchy of spatial policies in Greece. *Geoforum*, *23*(1), 73–83.

Getimis, P. and Kafkalas, G. (2002). Comparative analysis of policy-making and empirical evidence in the pursuit of innovation and sustainability. In H. Heinelt, P. Getimis, G. Kafkalas and R. Smith (eds) *Participatory Governance in a Multi-Level Context: Concepts and Experience* (pp. 155–171). Opladen: Leske + Budrich.

Giannakourou, G. (1992). Private interests' legitimization methods in the Greek urban administration. *TOPOS*, *4*, 113–133.

Giannakourou, G. (2005). Transforming spatial planning policy in Mediterranean countries: Europeanization and domestic change. *European Planning Studies*, *13*(2), 319–331.

Giannakourou, G. (2007). Urban and regional planning and zoning. In K. Kerameus and P. Kozyris (eds) *Introduction to Greek Law. Third Revised Edition* (pp. 167–177). Athens: Kluwer Law International, Ant. Sakkoulas Publishers.

Giannakourou, G. (2010). Investment land-planning in Greece: problems and solutions. *The Greek Economy*, *4*(62), 103–110. Retrieved from www.iobe.gr/docs/economy/en/ECO_Q4_10_REP_ENG.pdf.

Giannakourou, G. (2011). Europeanization, actor constellations and spatial policy change in Greece. In D. Stead and G. Cotella (eds) Differential Europe: domestic actors and their role in shaping spatial planning systems. *disP*, *47*(3), 33–42.

Giannakourou, G. and Balla, E. (2012, October). Privatization of planning powers and planning processes in Greece: current trends, future prospects. Paper presented at the 6th Conference of the Platform of Experts in Planning Law, *Privatization of Planning Powers and Urban Infrastructure*, Lisbon. Retrieved from www.internationalplanninglaw.com/files_content/Greece_Privatization%20of%20planning%20powers%20and%20processes.pdf.

Giannakourou, G. and Trova, E. (2001). *The Olympic Games and the Law: The Legal Framework of the Olympic Games 2004*. Athens-Komotini: Ant. N. Sakkoulas Publishers.

La Spina, A. and Sciortino, G. (1993). Common agenda, southern rules: European integration and environmental change in the Mediterranean states. In J. D. Liefferink, P. H. Lowe and A. P. J. Mol (eds) *European Integration and Environmental Policy* (pp. 217–236). London/New York: Belhaven Press.

Nadin, V. and Stead, D. (2008). European spatial planning systems: social models and learning. *disP*, *44*(1), 35–47.

Newman, P. and Thornley, A. (1996). *Urban Planning in Europe: International Competition, National Systems and Planning Projects*. London: Routledge.

OECD – Organisation of Economic Co-operation and Development. (2011). *Economic Surveys: Greece 2011*. Paris: OECD Publishing.

Paraskevopoulos, C. J. (2001). Social capital, learning and EU regional policy networks: evidence from Greece. *Government and Opposition*, *36*(2), 251–275.

Sapountzaki, K. and Karka, H. (2001). The element of sustainability in the Greek statutory spatial planning system: a real operational concept or a political declaration? *European Planning Studies*, *9*(3), 407–426.

Spanou, C. (1996). On the regulatory capacity of the Hellenic state: a tentative approach based on a case study. *International Review of Administrative Sciences*, *62*, 219–237.

Wassenhoven, L., Asprogerakas, V., Gianniris, E., Pagonis, T., Petropoulou, C. and Sapountzaki, P. (2005). National overview: Greece, ESPON 2.3.2 Project (Governance of Territorial and Urban Policies. From EU to local level – European Commission – Lead Partner: University of Valencia), National Technical University of Athens, Laboratory for Spatial Planning and Urban Development (Project Coordinator for Greece: L. Wassenhoven).

Further reading

Dimitrakopoulos, D. and Passas, A. (eds) (2003). *Greece in the European Union*. London/New York: Routledge.

Heinelt, H., Sweeting, D. and Getimis, P. (eds) (2006). *Legitimacy and Urban Governance: A Cross-national Comparative Study*. London/New York: Routledge.

ISOCARP – International Society of City and Regional Planners. (2002). *Planning in Greece, Special Bulletin 2002, 38th International Planning Congress*. Athens: GND – ISOCARP.

Lyrintzis, C. (2011). Greek politics in the era of economic crisis: reassessing causes and effects. *The Hellenic Observatory Papers on Greece and Southeast Europe*. London School of Economics and Political Science. Retrieved from www2.lse.ac.uk/europeanInstitute/research/hellenicObservatory/pdf/GreeSE/GreeSE45.pdf.

Monastiriotis, V. (ed.) (2011). The Greek crisis in focus: austerity, recession and paths to recovery. *Hellenic Observatory Papers on Greece and Southeast Europe, Special Issue*. London School of Economics and Political Science. Retrieved from www2.lse.ac.uk/europeanInstitute/research/hellenicObservatory/pdf/GreeSE/GreeSE%20Special%20Issue.pdf.

Van den Berg, L., Braun, E. and Van der Meer, J. (eds) (2007). *National Policy Responses to Urban Challenges in Europe*. London: Ashgate.

9

SPATIAL PLANNING IN FLANDERS

Serving a bypassed capitalism?

Pieter Van den Broeck, Frank Moulaert, Annette Kuhk, Els Lievois
and Jan Schreurs

Chapter objectives

The chapter:

- gives a brief overview of the technical features of spatial planning in Flanders;
- analyzes the social forces that have nourished or hampered the particular approaches to spatial planning;
- illustrates how a strategic-relational institutionalist theoretical framework can be mobilized to analyze planning systems, in this case the Flemish planning system;
- shows how different groups have (re)produced different (sometimes competing) planning systems (e.g. the planning permit system, spatial structure planning, land-use planning, infrastructure planning, project planning, environmental planning) and how different selectivities were and are embedded in these systems;
- shows one general struggle over Flemish planning, between actors representing property ownership and actors arguing for collective action in space; and
- claims that, since 1999, Flemish structure planning and land-use planning have been reoriented towards the protection of private property.

1 Introduction

This chapter explains how spatial structure planning in Flanders is under transformation. It examines the roots of the existing system of spatial planning in Flanders, which has been an autonomous planning system since the 1980 devolution of the Belgian planning system to the three regions (Flanders, Wallonia, Brussels). The chapter tries to assess why the present Flemish government holds an unclear view of how spatial planning should develop in the future. Should it maintain existing systems of planning permits, land-use bookkeeping and bureaucratized structure plans, which embody the defensive strategies of most land-use sectors? Or should it move forward to other more strategic and bottom-up democratic planning approaches in which the concept of spaces of transformation stands central? The authors analyze the social forces that have until recently nourished or hampered particular approaches to spatial planning. The conclusions of this analysis are used as a springboard to assess the future orientations of spatial planning in Flanders.

In section 2, the chapter gives a brief overview of the technical features of spatial planning in Flanders. It sketches how there has been an evolution towards a mixed system of land-use planning and spatial structure planning, and how the structural aspects of spatial planning in Flanders have been hollowed out since the beginning of the 2000s. Section 3 focuses on the social forces that have, over the past 50 years, supported spatial planning transformations through time. A strategic-relational institutionalist theoretical framework is used, which dialectically relates the practices of individual and collective actors in relevant social groups to planning instruments and systems in their institutional frames. The analysis focuses on how different groups – structured by different institutional backgrounds – have (re)produced different (sometimes competing) planning systems and how different selectivities were and are embedded in these systems. In section 4, the chapter gives an overview of the challenges for the present government in the domain of spatial planning and environmental policy and examines how these are connected to each other. In conclusion, the chapter highlights some recurrent issues and characteristics of the Flemish planning (sub)system(s) and assesses these according to their socio-political characteristics and position(s) in society.

The chapter is based on research in the project Spatial Planning To Strategic Projects (SP2SP) which was funded by the Institute for Scientific Research and Technology Development of the Flemish government (IWT) and in the Policy Centre Space and Society funded by the Flemish government.

2 A technical history of spatial planning in Flanders: from land-use planning to spatial structure planning and back

We first look at a brief history of spatial planning in Flanders. This is approached in a rather technical way, indicating the different milestones in law making and regulation building. This exercise will be clarified later by looking at the historical dynamics and especially the social forces that are behind this legal framework, its regulations and policy instruments.

Preceded by a long pre-war history of making draft proposals (Janssens, 1985), the Belgian parliament voted on a first law on town planning in 1962 (*Wet van 29 maart 1962 houdende de organisatie van de ruimtelijke ordening en van de stedebouw*). This law has dominated land-use regulations in Belgium and in Flanders for more than 30 years (Albrechts, 1999, 2001a). First, it formalized and centralized the system of planning permits that had existed since the beginning of the nineteenth century. From then on, every intervention in the built environment needed a planning permit delivered on the basis of building plans and had to be judged by newly created administrations on different levels of government. Also different levels of appeal and a system of control of the implementation of given permits were introduced. Second, the law enabled property owners and developers to apply for allotment permits on the basis of allotment plans. And third, the law introduced a system of hierarchical plans to be developed by the national government (national plan, regional plans, sub-regional plans) and the municipalities (local plan, sub-local plan).

After having prepared drafts of 48 sub-regional plans in the second half of the 1960s, and to stop the rapid increase in the number of allotment permits that were granted to property owners, in 1972 the Belgian government passed a royal decree to formalize and standardize the sub-regional plans (*K.B. van 28 december 1972*). Between 1974 and 1983, the draft plans were all transformed into legally binding land-use plans for the whole of the Belgian territory on a scale (1/25,000) that permitted the positioning of individual plots and their designated land-use on the sub-regional land-use plan (Figure 9.1). Neither a national plan nor regional plans as foreseen in the 1962 law were ever made. After 1972 (and already before that), the 1962 Town Planning Law was amended several times, specifically in the 1980s, giving more opportunities for landowners to build on plots outside areas designated as building land. Especially, the so-called "mini" decree in 1984 (*Decreet van 28 juni 1984 houdende aanvulling van de wet van 29 maart 1962 houdende de organisatie van de ruimtelijke ordening en van de stedebouw*) stimulated this evolution. In the meantime, some municipalities successfully created their own local and sub-local land-use plans, thus giving more detailed guidelines for local land-uses (approximately 1/1,000) (European Commission, 2000).

At the same time, a strong orientation away from land-use and zoning planning towards more structural planning had been going on. During the 1970s, the planning community reacted against the reduction of the sub-regional plans to land-use plans which assigned one of the legally possible land-uses to every plot in the country, encouraged landowners to develop their land and stimulated *ad hoc* changes of the existing land-use plans to the benefit of specific real estate developments. Consequently, in the beginning at the local level and later on at the regional scale, the planning community started arguing for and experimenting with alternative, more flexible planning instruments (see also Albrechts, 1982; De Jong and De Vries, 2002; Van den Broeck, 1987; Vermeersch, 1975). In the 1980s, this reaction became widespread when different sectors realized that the demands made by the different users of land were no longer compatible, and that the country had ended up with a patchy kind of spatial planning and land-use allocation that was not sustainable in the long run and that had in practice become an *ad hoc* "first come first served" approach. Although the land-use planning system was rather centralized, the land was reallocated and the land-use plans were changed according to the demands of major stakeholders.

After 30 years of experimenting with local structure planning – accelerated after 1970 by the ongoing federalization of Belgium (see below) – in 1996 the Flemish parliament voted on the so-called Spatial Planning Decree (*Decreet houdende de ruimtelijke planning van 24 juli 1996*), which laid out the legal basis for structure planning in Flanders. With the decree, a three-tier subsidiary system of spatial plans was created. First, the Flemish government, all five provinces and all 308 Flemish municipalities were obliged to make structure plans including a vision, strategies and actions for the spatial future of their territory. Second, these structure plans were supposed to be complemented with so-called spatial implementation

Figure 9.1 Excerpt from the sub-regional plan for the sub-region of Antwerp
Source: Agentschap voor Geografische Informatie Vlaanderen (2006)

plans (RUPs), which would gradually replace the existing hierarchical land-use plans based on the 1962 Town Planning Law. These RUPs can still be seen as land-use plans, but leave more flexibility for governments in designating and regulating land-uses. As a first application of the 1996 planning decree, in 1997 the first spatial structure plan for Flanders became operational (see also Albrechts, 1999, 2001a, 2001b; Benelux Economic Union et al., 2007).

Also in 1996, the 1962 law and its later changes were integrated in one decree (*Decreet betreffende de ruimtelijke ordening, gecoördineerd op 22 oktober 1996*). This decree would exist in parallel with the 1996 spatial planning decree, the 1999 decree following it and later changes of the latter.

In 1999, parts of the (Belgian) 1962 Town Planning Law and the 1996 (Flemish) planning decree were integrated in the Flemish 1999 Decree on Spatial Planning (*Decreet van 18 mei 1999 houdende de organisatie van de ruimtelijke ordening*). The 1999 decree integrated (1) the 1999 subsidiary system of structure plans for all Flemish levels of government; (2) the 1999 subsidiary system of legally binding but flexible RUPs for all levels of government; and (3) a planning permit system based on the system of 1962 but more restrictive towards development possibilities in non-housing areas. The 1999 system initiated the production of structure plans for all five provinces, structure plans for 250 municipalities (80 percent in 2010) and RUPs on every level of government, the latter replacing parts of the still valid sub-regional land-use plans.

However, from a few months after it was passed, the 1999 Decree on Spatial Planning underwent continuous changes, more or less preserving the system of structure plans, RUPs and planning permits, but decreasing the flexibility of the RUPs, re-increasing development possibilities in non-housing areas and limiting possibilities to mobilize both structure plans and RUPs. In 2009, these numerous changes were integrated into a new decree – the Flemish "Planning Codex" (Vlaamse regering, 2009), which now regulates spatial planning in Flanders. Also, the Flemish government changed the spatial structure plan for Flanders in 2003 and 2010 in order to increase local economic development possibilities. At the same time, preparatory activities, negotiations and consultations are being conducted to work towards a new spatial structural plan for Flanders, referred to as a spatial policy plan by the Flemish government that was elected in 2009.

3 Institutional dynamics of Flemish spatial planning since 1962

3.1 An institutionalist approach

The previous section gives us a technical overview of the types of legal sources that have been established for spatial planning in Flanders and how these legal sources have been translated into decrees, regulations, policy instruments and so on. In this section, we look at the evolution of the social forces that have driven the history of Belgian/Flemish spatial planning. We look at the history of spatial planning by identifying the key actors, institutional dynamics and design of spatial planning instruments that have played a role in the making of spatial planning in Flanders from 1960 until today.

To do this, we adopt a perspective that enables us to understand and evaluate planning instruments and systems in their institutional dynamics. This perspective is institutionalist and builds on expertise that we developed in previous research, using a framework based on institutionalist planning theory, non-rationalist sociological/critical institutionalism, the strategic-relational approach and studies of science, technology and society (Moulaert, 2000; Moulaert and Mehmood, 2009; Moulaert et al., 2007; Servillo and Van den Broeck, 2012; Van den Broeck, 2008, 2010, 2011a). We analyze planning instruments and planning systems as social practices in an "institutional field," rather than as technical means for predefined ends. We see an institutional field as constituted of actors belonging to relevant social groups and instrument groups (i.e. planning systems) in institutional frames, expressed and analyzed in terms of each other. We claim that different relevant social groups reproducing different planning systems are active in Flanders at the same time. Our approach thus reaches beyond instrumentalist analyses that focus on the efficiency and effectiveness of planning systems. Starting from a social political interest we ask ourselves: how do Belgian/Flemish planning systems change in the societal context, why do planning systems change, who benefits from which planning system and its changes, and who tries to have an impact on which planning system and how, for what reasons and with what consequences for its socio-political content and meaning? We thus analyze how regional, national and international societal changes influence Belgian/Flemish planning and how these changes are mediated by the dialectics of actors and institutions of Belgian/Flemish planning.

The interaction between actors, institutional dynamics and planning instruments design can be sub-divided into different episodes.[1] These episodes could be related to the legal milestones we mentioned above. But, in fact, they refer much more to the transformation and reconfiguration of the coalitions and antagonisms between the different actors that have played a role in the making of spatial policy and planning in Flanders. To understand these reconfigurations, a historical analysis should take transformations in the Belgium/Flemish Keynesian welfare state into account.

3.2 General socio-economic dynamics in Flanders after 1945 as a background

The social economic transformation in the second half of the twentieth century has been analyzed as a transformation from manufacturing in an economy based on mass production and mass consumption to a service economy based on flexible production, differentiation of consumption and a replacement of production by services (Moulaert and Swyngedouw, 1989; Moulaert et al., 1988; Van den Broeck, 2008). Following the crisis of Keynesianism in the 1970s, a more or less new regime of accumulation emerged internationally but also in Belgium, after 20 years of economic restructuring and the introduction of a number of neo-liberal policies in the 1980s and 1990s. This was based on a shift from social to economic policy, a permanent monitoring of wages and competitiveness in comparison to Belgium's neighboring countries, high-end, demand-based production of highly differentiated products, production without stocks, flexible work organization, etc. This is production no longer oriented towards employee demand but towards capital demand (Witte and Meynen, 2006).

At the same time, we have seen a social political transformation of the so-called "pillar society" which was organized in socio-political families according to religious, ideological and cultural dividing lines. Within these families, different movements, corporatist organizations and service organizations have played a significant role, and have contributed to the reproduction of the socio-ideological dividing lines within Belgian/Flemish society. Over the past three decades, however, the socio-political families and corresponding corporatist decision-making mechanisms have been challenged by new socio-political issues (e.g. ecological crisis, migration), new political actors, the federalization of Belgium, the introduction of market-oriented policies, decreasing power of the unions, etc., thus fragmenting and pluralizing society.

One should not underestimate the role of the cultural ideological transformations in the remaking of spatial planning within Belgian/Flemish society. We should mention here the transition from Christian Democracy and solidarity to ideological liberalism, which is probably the most important cultural ideological transformation. But we should also refer to the growing influence of market fundamentalism always privileging the market to satisfy human needs. This also affects the personal spheres of life and feeds into a growing individualism and the rise of one-issue interest communities today. Since the latter have their specific land-use claims, their coordination becomes very difficult.

The socio-economic and socio-political dynamics of the transformation of the welfare state provide us with a general background for an analysis of the development of planning in Belgium/Flanders. Since these macro-structural transformations are mediated by more concrete institutional dynamics related to spatial policy, we need to focus on specific dialectics of actors in relevant social groups and planning instruments within their institutional frames. We organize this analysis according to five episodes in which we see more or less coherent planning instrument groups (planning systems) and concomitant relevant social groups (re)producing these instrument groups.

3.3 Episode 1 (1962–1972): proliferation of housing allotments and socio-economic regional surveys

In 1962, the Law on Town Planning (see above) added a hierarchical and multi-level system of land-use planning to the 150-year-old system of planning permits. This system embodied a compromise between the stakes of the Belgian pre-war planning community (planning as a collective interference in spatial organization), property owner corporations and the development sector (protection of property rights), and the economic sector (planning as an economic project towards regional development and the construction of the welfare state) (Albrechts et al., 1989; Janssens, 1985; Ryckewaert and Theunis, 2006; Saey, 1988). However, rather than the land-use plans, it was the instrument of the allotment permit introduced by the 1962 law that was mobilized first. Massive numbers of landowners and the development sector supported by law firms applied for allotment permits to secure the development rights of their land (Figure 9.2) (Anselin et al., 1967).

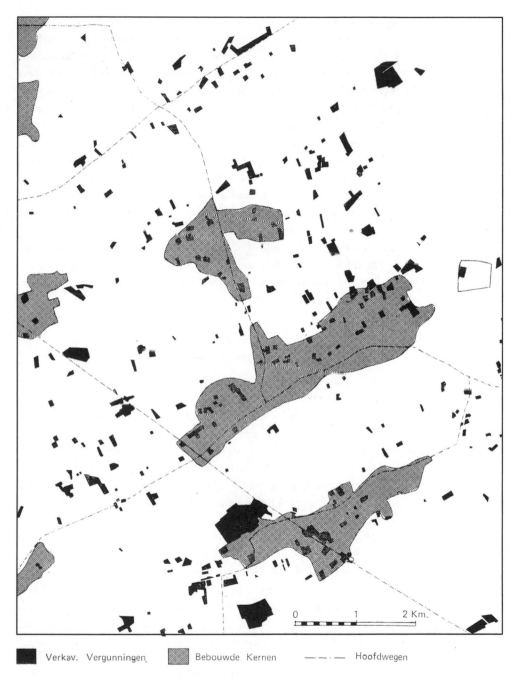

Verkav. Vergunningen   Bebouwde Kernen   —⸱—⸱— Hoofdwegen

Figure 9.2 Allotment permits in a rural community

Source: Van Havre, D. (1967)

The land-use planning system complemented a system of (Fordist) social economic planning, supported by agents representing the manufacturing sector who feared that there would not be enough land available to support economic expansion. A very strong interest in sectoral economic policy was imbued in the so-called economic expansion laws (see for example the analysis by Willekens and Moulaert, 1987). At the same time, there was strong support in favor of making land available that would host the different economic enterprise zones, industrial activity zones, etc. Following a number of regional surveys in the 1950s and 1960s, in 1965 the (Christian Democrat) Belgian Minister of Public Works and Town Planning thus commissioned his administration and several planning consultants to draft sub-regional plans, as foreseen in the 1962 Town Planning Law. The bridge between the economic expansion initiatives on the one hand and land-use provisions on the other was materialized in the so-called infrastructure planning that supported the coordinated planning and implementation of infrastructure, enterprise zones, housing areas and landscaping. Infrastructure planning was meant to equip the enterprise zones with the appropriate infrastructure to make sure that productivity would be optimized. At the same time, infrastructure planning had to guarantee different enterprise zones were properly networked through highway systems, railway systems, water transportation routes and so on.

3.4 Episode 2 (1972–1983): land-use planning versus structure planning as an offspring of socio-economic planning

Following the 1972 decree on the form and content of sub-regional plans (as foreseen in the 1962 law), in 1974 the Belgian (Christian Democrat) Secretary of State for Housing, Spatial Planning and Regional Economy commissioned the transformation of the drafts of sub-regional plans into legally binding plans. This was a reaction to the aforementioned peaking number of granted allotment permits and the ensuing pressure on the institutional system to create more order in the coordination of the different land-use claims. Indeed, there had been an increase in claims on scarce land and conflicts between the biased demands from the economic and the construction sector and public efforts for the preservation of nature and green zones in Flanders.

The detailed form and the legally binding and regulatory character of the sub-regional land-use plans made them part and parcel of the planning permit system, as formalized in the 1962 Town Planning Law. Indeed, the planning permit system regulated the right to use and develop land on the basis of belonging to the proper functioning zone. For example, construction of houses was only permitted in housing zones and construction of factories in zones reserved for manufacturing activities, etc. As in the previous episode, the social forces reproducing and operating within the planning permit system included property owner corporations, the building and development sector and the associated legal world of law firms and law schools. But to maintain the planning permit system, the Belgian government installed a new extensive administration for spatial planning which operated on the national, provincial and municipal levels, thus expanding the relevant social group.

The dialectics of the planning permit system also included protesting voices against the exaggerated use of land and the granting of land permits for purely economic functions and against the (successful) demand of landowners to designate an excess of land for housing and economic development. The environmental movement, the community of spatial planners, community developers, colleges for community education and the union-based left wing of the Christian Democrat party protested against the consumerism of the welfare state and the favoritism of the corporatist and "pillared" decision-making. As part of their role in habitats structured by institutional dynamics surrounding former socio-economic planning, these groups made a plea in favor of structure planning, of which bits and pieces were already present in the former regional surveys and the draft sub-regional plans referred to above. The plea for more structure planning was meant to integrate social and environmental planning with spatial structure planning. In more general terms, spatial structure planning was intended to integrate the different functions in society and the economy into a more dynamic spatial plan in which the various interests and social actors would be present, both as claimants and as actors in the coordination of the planning system. After experiments with local structure planning in different Flemish municipalities (see e.g. Figure 9.3 showing a structural scheme for the development of the Rupelstreek south of the city of Antwerp; see also Van den Broeck, 1987), the now Flemish Christian Democrat Minister for Spatial Planning laid the grounds for spatial structure planning on the Flemish level by commissioning a group of planning academics and consultants to make a draft spatial structure plan for Flanders. The group produced two documents for discussion in 1983–1984 but without immediate practical effect.

To conclude this episode we should point out that, besides the crisis of the Fordist welfare state which initiated protest and the rise of a group arguing for spatial structure planning, the federalization of Belgium was an important factor in the rise of spatial structure planning. The state reforms of 1970 and 1980, the former establishing three cultural entities (Flemish, French and German communities) and three territorial entities (Flemish, Walloon and Brussels regions), and the latter establishing regional governments and devolving competences such as

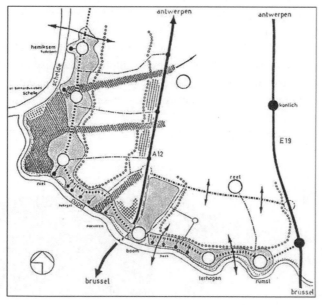

Figure 9.3 Experiments with local structure planning

Source: Van den Broeck, J. and Wuillaume, P. (1986)

spatial planning to the regions, were a precondition for the creation of a new Flemish ministry and administration of spatial planning. This necessitated creating a vision on Flemish planning policy, supporting experiments with new planning instruments and permitting direct contacts between the planning community – as embedded in the progressive movement – and the ministry, and thus put Flemish spatial structure planning on the political agenda.

3.5 Episode 3 (1983–1991): predominance of the planning permit system and the rise of urban design

In this episode, the planning permit system, including its property development and legal logic, regained its position as the most important system in the spatial organization of Flanders. Accordingly, the impact of actors and ideas referring to spatial structure planning on the Flemish level decreased drastically. This is shown in the growing influence of agents acting in favor of a permissive planning permit system and supporting particular land-use claims. In fact, the Flemish "mini" decree of 1984 increased opportunities for property owners and developers to build on land designated as non-housing areas in the sub-regional land-use plans (Figure 9.4) (Grietens, 1995; Renard, 1995). Also – stimulated by the international breakthrough of market-oriented approaches reacting to the crisis of the welfare state in the 1970s (Witte and Meynen, 2006) – a new Flemish government of liberal and right-wing Christian Democrats (and three consecutive liberal Flemish Ministers of Spatial Planning) entered the political arena in 1985 and particularly focused on economic development. In 1987, this government also abandoned the social urban renewal policy that had been launched at the end of the 1970s and was related to the actors, ideas and instruments of spatial structure planning (Knops et al., 1992).

Taken together, relaxing the planning permit system and abandoning the social urban renewal policy meant the disappearance of the instruments for and a weakening of institutions defending spatial structure planning and social urban planning, and this before it was ever established at the regional level. In fact, the first spatial structure plan for Flanders was only voted on in 1997 (see below). At the local level, however, different municipalities continued experimenting with spatial structure planning and neighborhood development (Van den Broeck, 1987) and thus maintained an expanding network of actors favoring spatial structure planning.

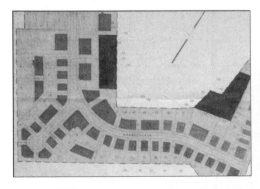 

Figure 9.4 Effects on open space of a permissive planning permit system

Source: Vloebergh, G. (2010)

178

At the same time, local authorities took on board new instruments of urban design that focused on envisioning new futures for so-called strategic spaces in cities. This was stimulated by economic restructuring and the corresponding emergence of brownfields on former industrial sites that needed redevelopment. Also, the disciplines of architecture and urbanism recovered from a crisis they had gone through in the 1960s, and southern European urbanism inspired Flemish architects, urbanists and planners (Loeckx and De Meulder, 2007). Another factor supporting the spread of urban design was the rise of a "new urban policy" and the corresponding project mode of development (Moulaert et al., 2003). The instruments of urban design favored urban designers, planners, Flemish cities and parts of the development sector in their strategies to work on Flanders' spatial organization and further deteriorate its land-use balance.

3.6 Episode 4 (1991–1999): spatial structure planning, environmental policies, regional development, community development and mobility planning in a common framework

In 1991, a new center-left Flemish government of Social Democrats, Christian Democrats and Flemish nationalists was elected. This was one of the factors that opened up new opportunities for the proponents of spatial structure planning who had lost their influence on the Flemish level in the previous episode. The development of environmental planning – increasingly related to spatial planning – into an ever more important policy field in the previous episode was another factor. Similarly, scandals concerning spatial planning, caused by the permissive planning permit system, and successes in the adjacent policy fields of mobility planning, nature development and community development, increasingly put spatial structure planning on the political agenda. In the background, new stages in the federalization process in 1988 and 1993 also played a role (Albrechts, 2001a; Van den Broeck, 2008; Witte and Meynen, 2006). Consequently, the progressive network that had been developing since the 1970s gained power. This group included city planning departments, some municipalities, academics, consultancy firms, inter-municipal corporations, an enlarged Flemish administration for spatial planning, the environmental movement, proponents of sustainable traffic and public transport, community developers, two successive center-left Flemish governments and their respective party-networks, two proactive ministers for spatial planning (of whom one had been the Minister of Environmental Policy in the 1980s), people from different cabinets, etc. It succeeded in establishing the new planning decree in 1996 which outlined the new subsidiary system of spatial structure plans (see Figure 9.5) and a new generation of land-use plans (RUPs) on all three levels of government (see above), a spatial structure plan for Flanders in 1997 and the integrative decree on spatial planning in 1999 (Albrechts, 1999; Merckaert, 2008). Also, the planning permit system was made more restrictive towards development outside of housing areas and more open to the discretionary power of administrations judging planning applications (see various chapters in Hubeau and Vandevyvere, 2010).

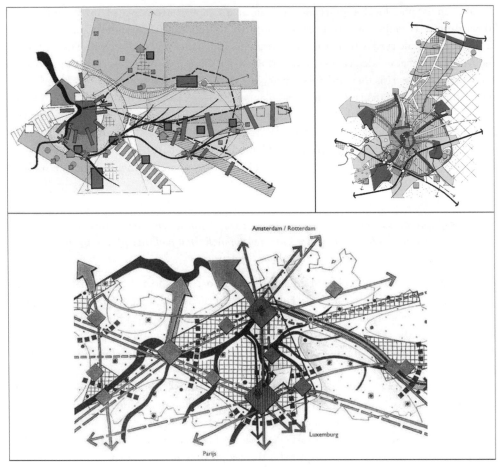

Figure 9.5 Schemes for the desired spatial structure in the structure plans for the province of Antwerp, the city of Ghent and the Flemish region

Sources: Provincie Antwerpen (2003); Stad Gent (2003), Vlaamse regering (1997)

At the same time, spatial structure planning intensified previously existing relationships with other planning systems affecting Flanders' spatial organization. Reacting against consumption-driven suburbanization and following opportunities offered by urban restructuring and urban brownfields, instruments of project-oriented urban design were developed in a few emblematic urban projects, in which proponents of structure planning were also involved. In addition, instruments originated in regional development (e.g. strategic plans, regional economic platforms) that were somewhat familiar to structure planning. These operated in areas of economic restructuring and were often funded by European development funds (Tubex et al., 2005). They evidently focused on economic development but – influenced by EU criteria for integrated area development – sometimes received a broader territorial focus and stimulated cooperation between economic actors, Flemish public administrations, municipalities, unions and development agencies. In such cases, spatial structural planners were often involved. The same relationships existed with actors promoting alternative transport modes such as public transport, functional cycling and transport by inland waterways, and with community and neighborhood development in cities as well as in rural areas (De Decker et al., 1996; Koning Boudewijnstichting, 1996).

3.7 Episode 5 (1999–2009): fragmentation of structure planning, return of the planning permit system and project planning

Following the approval in 1997 of the Spatial Structure Plan for Flanders and the 1999 Decree on Spatial Planning, the Flemish administration started implementing these on the one hand through planning processes for urban areas, Flemish harbors, rural areas and infrastructure, and on the other by transforming these processes into old and new generation land-use plans (Vlaamse overheid Departement Ruimtelijke Ordening, 2009). All five Flemish provinces and 80 percent of the municipalities developed their own structure plans after intensive planning processes (Muyters, 2009). However, their quality and impact differ significantly.

Pressure by legal actors and organizations and landowners against the increased interference of government in space, discussions between sectors on the division of space as foreseen in the spatial structure plan for Flanders and bureaucratization of the system of structure planning led to structure planning becoming increasingly static and detached from social and economic planning processes. Moreover, the center-right governments that were elected in 1999 (liberal – Social Democrat) and in 2004 (liberal – Christian Democrat) introduced a parallel circuit of planning initiatives for the benefit of specific interest groups such as landowners, the economic sector, specific recreational activities, etc., thus undermining the compromises that had been embedded in the spatial structure plan for Flanders. At the same time, these governments – driven by property owners and their lawyers – once more relaxed the planning permit system and reversed the 1999 changes in land-use planning, both in favor of easier property development in non-housing areas. These shifts were in tune with the international neo-liberal shift towards more market- and property-oriented policies, the ongoing restructuring of the Belgian/Flemish corporatist and "pillared" welfare state, and policies favoring individual accountability and rights (Blommaert, 2007; Van den Broeck, 2008; Witte and Meynen, 2006). After ten years of changes to the 1999 mixed system of structure planning and land-use planning, the Flemish government approved the new "Codex of spatial planning" in 2009 (Vlaamse regering, 2009), which integrated all the previous changes, favoring a liberal planning permit system, restricting structure planning and enabling "short-tracking" of strategic projects.

The changes in the 2000s also favored the further development of the gentrification and project-oriented urbanistic approach (Boudry et al., 2006; Loeckx, 2009), which had originated in previous episodes and was based on instruments such as master plans, public–private partnerships, design competitions, management tools, project subsidies, research by design, city-marketing, etc. This approach was connected to Flemish urban policy (Loopmans et al., 2007; Van den Broeck, 2011b, 2012) and was also supported by proponents of the increasingly restricted structure planning system. But other policy fields interfering in Flanders' spatial organization also developed their own instruments, operated autonomously and lost the connections with spatial structure planning that had been installed in the previous episode. Examples include environmental planning, regional rural development, infrastructure and transportation planning, housing planning, etc. This was also supported by the 2003–2006 reform of the Flemish administration according to the "good governance" principles of new public management (Van den Broeck et al., 2009).

The internal weakening of spatial structure planning, the loss of societal support, the return of the permissive planning permit system, the shift in focus of structural planners towards the implementation of urban projects and the reduced coherence between different sets of planning instruments weakened the coalitions that had been supportive to the making of structure planning. At the beginning of the 2000s, Flanders thus entered a period of fragmentation of planning instruments and started moving towards a system with one set of instruments per planning domain.

4 Challenges for spatial structure planning in Flanders

Having looked at its history and identified the various cohesive, transformative and fragmenting forces, we are now in a position to identify the challenges for spatial structure planning in Flanders.

On the one hand, we could say that spatial structure planning in Flanders has led to an impressive list of planning achievements, partly coordinated by the Flemish administration for spatial planning and partly implemented in adjacent policy domains. It has led to the establishment of planning departments and structure planning tools at the levels of the Flemish government, provinces and municipalities. It has fostered the building of successful coalitions of actors for the construction of useful structure planning instruments. It has contributed to transformations in land-use, to the preservation of open space and to a return of interest in the city with an increasing number of investments, not only in the economy, but in housing, public space, social infrastructure and so on. And it has produced a relatively new equilibrium between economic activity and environmental sustainability in the peripheral areas of the city. It has also led to better planning of the use of space by economic sectors.

On the other hand, we see substantial challenges. First, there is a returning and growing interest in private property rights. The supremacy of private property rights and its embeddedness in a range of Belgian and Flemish institutions,[2] the institutional stability of the planning permit system and tensions between public and private interests have obscured the policy debate. Time and again, property rights as embedded in the planning permit system and numerous other institutions have restricted planning instruments. Examples include: the transformation of the local land-use plans, as foreseen by the 1962 Town Planning Law, from action-oriented plans to tools for controlling planning applications and for guaranteeing opportunities for development; the formalization of sub-regional land-use plans (also foreseen in the 1962 law) for the whole of the Belgian territory, which took control of development rights away from the government; the freezing of the public sector's discretionary power by pushing the new generation of land-use plans (foreseen in the 1999 Law on Spatial Planning) back into the format of the old land-use plans; and the integration of structure plans into the planning permit system by using them to judge planning applications. The struggle over the role of the planning permit system has thus overtaken the future of the spatial structure plan, as well as the coordination between the different spatial claims and the way in which new challenges (e.g. climate change, migration, demographic change, financial and economic crisis) are addressed.

Second, we have seen an autonomization of spatial planning policy. This is due to cutbacks in socio-economic planning after the crisis of Fordism, the detachment of spatial planning from socio-economic planning after the federalization of Belgium and the devolution of spatial planning competences towards the regions, and the dynamics of spatial planning in the second half of the 1990s and the beginning of the 2000s. In line with these developments, we noticed an impoverishment of strategic spatial planning. Despite the importance of the strategic aspect in its philosophy and basic documents, spatial structure planning in Flanders today has again become much more oriented towards the implementation of land-use plans and respect for the different zoning agreements that have been negotiated between different actors constituting Flanders' socio-political field.

Third, the autonomization of spatial planning policy is related to a strengthening of different policy domains, the stronger profiling of the different skills and professions defending their own business and their own domains, and the political power game of the various ministers and departments involved in spatial planning policies. Environmental specialists such as bio-engineers aim to protect nature, urbanists and urban architects defend design, spatial planners defend the rational organization of space, etc., each following their own path. This relates to the ongoing restructuring of the Belgian/Flemish public domain and the introduction of a new spatial societal project by the governments elected in 1999, 2004 and 2009, which broke up the networks between the actors that had produced spatial structure planning and stimulated the autonomous development of the policy domains that had been momentarily connected in the 1990s.

Our claim that planning policy domains have become more autonomous, that sets of instruments have become more policy domain oriented and that the strategic character of spatial planning has been watered down, should not necessarily lead us to pessimism or fatalism. In fact, we have in Flanders, at the present time, a wide and rich diversity of spatial societal projects. We could call this phenomenon a kind of policy in instrumentalism in which all domains seem to have their own spatial policy and their spatial plans. This by itself could be an opportunity for a renewed interest in spatial planning and a new coherent spatial societal project. However, ambiguities in recent policy documents (Muyters, 2009; Vlaamse regering, 2008) seem to contradict these opportunities. For example, these documents apparently favor economic demands for more space, hardly refer to social values such as equity, solidarity, prevention of exclusion or enhancing democracy, make a plea for taking away supposed institutional barriers to economic and property development, and hollow out concepts on spatial quality and sustainability (Moulaert et al., 2012). At this moment, it is unclear whether or how these tendencies will again be redirected by the ongoing process of preparing for a new spatial policy plan for Flanders (Vlaamse regering, 2012), the 2008–2009 financial crisis, the concomitant rise of public debt and the growing influence of the Flemish nationalist party.

5 Conclusion

In this chapter, we have analyzed Flemish spatial planning instruments since 1962 as organized in different systems, (re)produced and transformed by different individual and collective actors and shaped by a range of institutional dynamics. We based this analysis on our institutionalist approach developed in previous and current research. This approach argues in favor of a dynamic analysis, showing how changes in actors in relevant social groups and their positions and practices, institutional changes and macro-structural changes are potential drivers of non-linear, path-dependent and path-shaping institutional and agency changes. Moreover, it enables a deeper understanding and evaluation of the socio-political content and meaning of a planning system and of who is privileged or discriminated by the interests and values inscribed in planning systems and institutional frames.

Analyzing Belgian/Flemish planning instruments and systems in this way showed how, in the context of a developing welfare state, pre-war planners, property owners and economic players imbued a compromise between their respective interests in the 1962 Town Planning Law, thus creating a system of planning permits on the one hand and of hierarchical plans on the other. While the law initiated the preparation of draft sub-regional plans, it was especially mobilized by property owners to secure the development rights of their land. This triggered the then Minister of Spatial Planning to commission the conversion of the draft sub-regional plans into legally binding sub-regional land-use plans for the whole Belgian territory, meant to restrict uncontrolled development and degradation of open spaces. At the same time – in a context of protesting Keynesian consumerism and the crisis of the welfare state – environmentalist, community-oriented and planning-minded actors experimented with spatial structure planning. In the 1980s, however, property owners, economic actors and legal actors and organizations expanded opportunities for land development. This was done by loosening up the planning permit system (now including the sub-regional land-use plans) and by countering the upcoming structure planning. A new Flemish government, in the context of the international shift towards market-oriented policies, supported this evolution. In the 1990s, the proponents of environmental planning, spatial planning and community development benefited, among others, from progress in the environmental movement, scandals caused by an overly permissive planning permit system, the election of two successive center-left Flemish governments and the ongoing federalization of Belgium. These actors gained momentum and succeeded in preparing the first structure plan for Flanders and laws supporting a planning system of more restrictive planning permits, spatial structure plans and a new generation of land-use plans. In the 2000s, Belgium followed the international shift towards ideological neo-liberalism stressing market-oriented policies and individualism. Two successive governments thus transformed the 1999 planning system once more into a predominantly flexible planning permit system in which structure planning became restricted.

Our analysis shows how, in the past 50 years, planning has been embedded into different planning (sub)systems, each reproduced by different actor groups which, in their turn, were structured by these systems. Examples include the planning permit system, spatial structure planning, land-use planning, infrastructure planning, project planning, environmental planning, etc., all of which changed content and meaning several times. Consequently, spatial structure planning as well as land-use planning (the planning permit system) are but part of the dynamics of several planning (sub)systems that continuously interact. At the end of the 2000s, the coherence between these interacting planning (sub) systems, each expressing different stakes, values and societal projects, decreased considerably. Recent debates show both the necessity and the potential of realizing new (partial) coherence between these differing projects, although new public initiatives still seem to be moving in the opposite direction.

Within these complex dynamics, one general struggle between actors representing property ownership and actors arguing for collective action in space became especially apparent. In this struggle, land and real estate ownership expressed through a permissive planning permit system has been shown to be predominant, especially in the 1960s, 1980s and 2000s. This is due to the embeddedness of property rights in several Belgian/Flemish institutions, as analyzed above. The changes in the planning system realized in the 1990s partly and temporarily challenged this logic of individual property. The system was more open to changes in the planning context, differing opinions on appropriate action, the gradual interactive definition of planning goals, interaction between different users of space, and participation of deprived actors and functions (e.g. open space and nature, low-income groups, ethnic minorities). The 1990s system, however, changed only a small part of the institutional frame that structures the predominant planning permit practice, and left the logic of individual property largely untouched. Today, Flemish structure planning and land-use planning have been reoriented towards the protection of private property, which hampers the capacity of government to implement a coherent spatial policy and collective spatial projects. Hopefully, recent debates can initiate new trajectories towards a new more or less coherent spatial societal project and new concomitant planning instruments.

Notes

1 A more extensive elaboration of this research can be found in the research reports by Van den Broeck et al. (2010, 2011) and Van den Broeck (2012).
2 Examples of these include: the housing policy in the twentieth century stimulating individual ownership, resulting in nearly 75 percent of the Flemish population owning their houses; the small-scale structure of the sector of building and development; the embeddedness of private ownership in the ideology of the Christian Democrat party, which dominated the political landscape during more than half of the twentieth century; the Fordist socio-economic structure oriented towards even development of the different Flemish regions; the historic dispersed spatial structure of Flanders; the legally binding sub-regional land-use plans created in the 1970s, which de facto meant that development rights in Belgium were individualized; principles of "static" legal certainty as embedded in parts of the legal sector, which consider development rights as definitively "given"; and the characteristics and predominance of the property market (Van den Broeck et al., 2011).

References

Agentschap voor Geografische Informatie Vlaanderen. (2006). Gewestplan. Toestand 01/01/02. Retrieved from http://geo-vlaanderen.agiv.be/geo-vlaanderen/gwp/#

Albrechts, L. (1982). Van voorbereiding naar actie: een verruiming van het planningsbegrip. *Ruimtelijke planning*, 1–24.

Albrechts, L. (1999). Planners as catalysts and initiators of change: the new structure plan for Flanders. *European Planning Studies*, 7, 587–603.

Albrechts, L. (2001a). Devolution, regional governance and planning systems in Belgium. *International Planning Studies*, 6, 167–182.

Albrechts, L. (2001b). From traditional land use planning to strategic spatial planning: the case of Flanders. In L. Albrechts, J. Alden and A. Da Rosa Pires (eds) *The Changing Institutional Landscape of Planning* (pp. 83–103). Aldershot: Ashgate.

Albrechts, L., Moulaert, F., Jones, P. and Swyngedouw, E. (1989). *Regional Policy at the Crossroads: European Perspectives*. London: Kingsley.

Anselin, M., Blanquart, G., Demeyere, C., Lauwereys, J., Mortelmans, J., Vanden Borre, P. and Van Havre, D. (1967). Themanummer over verkavelingen. *Stero, publicatie voor stedebouw en ruimtelijke ordening*, 1.

Benelux Economic Union, Chambre des Urbanistes Belges and Brussels Capital Region (AATL/BROH). (2007). Planning systems in Belgium: Flemish region, Walloon region, Brussels capital region. In J. Van den Broeck (ed.) *ISOCARP World Congress Special Bulletin* (pp. 23–90). Antwerpen: City of Antwerp in association with ISOCARP.

Blommaert, J. (2007). *De crisis van de democratie: Commentaren op de actuele politiek*. Berchem: EPO.

Boudry, L., Loeckx, A., Van den Broeck, J., Coppens, T., Patteeuw, V. and Schreurs, J. (2006). *Inzet, opzet, voorzet: stadsprojecten in Vlaanderen*. Antwerpen: Garant.

De Decker, P., Hubeau, B. and Nieuwinckel, S. (1996). *In de ban van stad en wijk*. Berchem: EPO.

De Jong, M. and De Vries, J. (2002). The merits of keeping cool while hearing the siren calls: an account of the preparation and establishment of the Flemish spatial planning system. In M. De Jong, K. Lalenis and V. Mamadouch (eds) *The Theory and Practice of Institutional Transplantation: Experiences with the Transfer of Policy Institutions* (pp. 231–246). Dordrecht: Kluwer.

European Commission. (2000). *The EU Compendium of Spatial Planning Systems and Policies*. Luxembourg: Office for Official Publications of the European Communities.

Grietens, E. (ed.) (1995). *Ruimtelijke wanorde in Vlaanderen: het zwartboek van de stedebouwwacht*. Brussel: Forum Ruimtelijke Ordening (Samenwerkingsverband tussen BBL, BIRO, Natuurreservaten vzw, VFP).

Hubeau, B. and Vandevyvere, W. (2010). *Handboek ruimtelijke ordening en stedenbouw* (2nd edn). Brugge: Die Keure.

Janssens, P. (1985). De ontwikkeling van de ruimtelijke ordening in België. *Ruimtelijke planning*, 14, 1–36.

Knops, G., Baelus, J., Van den Broeck, J., Vermeulen, A., Hendrickx, D. and Allaert, G. (eds) (1992). *Stadsvernieuwing in beweging*. Koning Boudewijnstichting in opdracht van de Vlaamse Gemeenschapsminister voor Ruimtelijke Ordening en Huisvesting. Brugge: Van de Wiele.

Koning Boudewijnstichting. (1996). *Handleiding voor buurt- en wijkontwikkeling*. Brussel: Koning Boudewijnstichting.

Loeckx, A. (2009). *Stadsvernieuwingsprojecten in Vlaanderen: Ontwerpend onderzoek en capacity building*. Amsterdam: SUN.

Loeckx, A. and De Meulder, B. (2007). Stadsprojecten tussen globalisering en stadsvernieuwing. In P. Stouthuysen and J. Pille (eds) *The State of the City: The City is the State* (pp. 175–202). Brussel: VUB Press.

Loopmans, M., Luyten, S. and Kesteloot, C. (2007). Urban policies in Belgium: a puff-pastry with a bittersweet aftertaste? In L. van den Berg, E. Braun and J. Van der Meer (eds) *National Policy Responses to Urban Challenges in Europe* (pp. 79–103). Aldershot: Ashgate.

Merckaert, A. (2008). *De sociale constructie van een ruimtelijk structuurplan voor Vlaanderen*. Antwerpen: Artesis Hogeschool Antwerpen, Departement Ontwerpwetenschappen, Opleiding Master in de Stedenbouw en Ruimtelijke Planning.

Moulaert, F. (2000). *Globalization and Integrated Area Development in European Cities*. Oxford: Oxford University Press.

Moulaert, F. and Mehmood, A. (2009). Spatial planning and institutional design: what can we expect from transaction cost economics? In H. Geyer (ed.) *International Handbook of Urban Policy*, Vol 2 (pp. 199–211). Cheltenham: Elgar.

Moulaert, F. and Swyngedouw, E. (1989). Survey 15: a regulation approach to the geography of the flexible production system. *Society and Space*, 7, 327–345.

Moulaert, F., Martinelli, F., Gonzalez, S. and Swyngedouw, E. (2007). Introduction: social innovation and governance in European cities. Urban development between path dependency and radical innovation. *European Urban and Regional Studies*, 14, 195–209.

Moulaert, F., Rodriguez, A. and Swyngedouw, E. (2003). *The Globalized City: Economic Restructuring and Social Polarization in European Cities*. Oxford: Oxford University Press.

Moulaert, F., Swyngedouw, E. and Wilson, P. (1988). Spatial responses to Fordist and post-Fordist accumulation and regulation. *Papers of the Regional Science Association*, 64, 11–23.

Moulaert, F., Van den Broeck, P. and Van Dyck, B. (2012). *Een groen ruimtelijk beleid: Reflectienota voor de Vlaamse Groenen*. Heerenveen: Groen.

186

Muyters, P. (2009). *Beleidsnota ruimteljke ordening 2009–2014. Een ruimtelijk beleid voor en op het ritme van de maatschappij*. Brussel: Vlaamse overheid.

Provincie Antwerpen. (2003). *Ruimtelijk structuurplan provincie Antwerpen*. Antwerpen: Provincie Antwerpen.

Renard, P. (1995). *Wat kan ik voor u doen? Ruimtelijke wanorde in België: een hypotheek op onze toekomst*. Antwerpen: Icarus.

Ryckewaert, M. and Theunis, K. (2006). Het lelijkste land, de mythe voorbij. Stedenbouw en verstedelijking in België sinds 1945. *Stadsgeschiedenis*, *1*, 148–168.

Saey, P. (1988). *De eerste generatie projecten van ruimtelijke ordening op macro-niveau in Vlaanderen*. Gent: Seminarie voor Menselijke en Ekonomische Aardrijkskunde.

Servillo, L. and Van den Broeck, P. (2012). The social construction of planning systems: a strategic-relational approach. *Planning Practice and Research*, *27*, 41–61.

Stad Gent. (2003). *Ruimtelijk structuurplan Gent*. Gent: Stadt Gent, Dienst Stedenbouw en Ruimtelijke Planning.

Tubex, S., Voets, J. and De Rynck, F. (2005). *Een beschrijvende analyse van ruimtelijk-ecologische en socio-economische arrangementen in Vlaanderen (Rep. No. Rapport van het Steunpunt Beleidsrelevant Onderzoek Vlaanderen – Bestuurlijke Organisatie Vlaanderen)* Gent: SBOV – Steunpunt Bestuurlijke Organisatie Vlaanderen.

Van den Broeck, J. (1987). Structuurplanning in de praktijk· werken op drie sporen. *Ruimtelijke planning*, *19*, 53–119.

Van den Broeck, J. and Wuillaume, P. (1986). De Rupelstreek, een streek in de kering. In A.Verbruggen (ed.) *Liber Amicorum Prof. Dr. Pierre-Henri Virenque* (pp. 245–284). Antwerpen: Universiteit Antwerpen, Studiecentrum voor Economisch en Sociaal Onderzoek.

Van den Broeck, P. (2008). The changing position of strategic spatial planning in Flanders: a socio-political and instrument based perspective. *International Planning Studies*, *13*, 261–283.

Van den Broeck, P. (2010). *De sociale constructie van plannings- en projectinstrumenten. Onderzoek naar de socio-technische evolutie van het "Eerste Kwartier" in Antwerpen* Leuven: K.U. Leuven, Departement Architectuur, Stedenbouw en Ruimtelijke Ordening.

Van den Broeck, P. (2011a). Analysing social innovation through planning instruments: a strategic-relational approach. In S. Oosterlynck, J. Van den Broeck, L. Albrechts, F. Moulaert and A. Verhetsel (eds) *Strategic Spatial Projects: Catalysts for Change* (pp. 52–78). London/New York: Routledge.

Van den Broeck, P. (2011b). Limits to social innovation: shifts in Flemish strategic projects to market oriented approaches. *Belgeo, Belgisch Tijdschrift voor Geografie*, *1–2*, 75–88.

Van den Broeck, P. (2012). Analyse van het Vlaams planningsinstrumentarium. Projectplanning. Voortgangsverslag 5 van werkpakket 10 voor het Steunpunt Ruimte en Wonen.

Van den Broeck, P., Kuhk, A. and Verachtert, K. (2010). Analyse van het Vlaams planninginstrumentarium. Structuurplanning. Voortgangsverslag 1 van werkpakket 10 voor het Steunpunt Ruimte en Wonen.

Van den Broeck, P., Verachtert, K. and Kuhk, A. (2011). Analyse van het Vlaams planninginstrumentarium. Vergunningensysteem. Voortgangsverslag 4 van werkpakket 10 voor het Steunpunt Ruimte en Wonen.

Van den Broeck, P., Vloebergh, G., De Smet, L., Wuillaume, P., Wouters, E. and De Greef, J. (2009). De sociale constructie van instrumenten. Toepassing op Vlaamse planningsinstrumenten Eindrapport van werkpakket 5 voor het IWT onderzoeksproject SP2SP.

Van Havre, D. (1967). *Verkavelingen en bodembeleid. Stero, publicatie voor stedebouw en ruimtelijke ordening, 1*. Gent: RUG – Hoger Institut voor stedebouw, ruintelijke ordening en ontwikkling.

Vermeersch, C. (1975). De structuurplanning als type ruimtelijke planning, een geldig alternatief? *Stero, tijdschrift voor stedebouw en ruimtelijke ordening*, *10*, 24–34.

Vlaamse overheid Departement Ruimtelijke Ordening. (2009). Introductienota voor de Vlaamse Minister bevoegd voor Ruimtelijke Ordening en Onroerend Erfgoed.

Vlaamse regering. (1997). *Ruimtelijk structuurplan Vlaanderen*. Brussel: Vlaamse regering.

Vlaamse regering. (2008). *Pact 2020: een nieuw toekomstpact voor Vlaanderen, 20 doelstellingen Vlaanderen in actie*. Brussel: Vlaamse regering.

Vlaamse regering. (2009). *Vlaamse Codex Ruimtelijke Ordening*. Brussel: Department Ruinte Vlaanderen.

Vlaamse regering. (2012). *Advies over Vlaanderen in 2050: Mensenmaat in een metropool? Groenboek Beleidsplan Ruimte Vlaanderen*. Brussel: VLOR – Vlaamse Onderwijsraad.

Vloebergh, G. (2010, March). Presentation on Flemish planning in the final SP2SP conference, Leuven.

Willekens, F. and Moulaert, F. (1987). Decentralization in industrial policy in Belgium. In H. Muegge, W. Stöhr, B. Stuckey, and P. Hesp (eds) *International Economic Restructuring and the Territorial Community* (pp. 314–336). Aldershot: Avebury.

Witte, E. and Meynen, A. (2006). *De geschiedenis van België na 1945*. Antwerpen: Standaard Uitgeverij.

10

SPATIAL PLANNING IN THE UNITED KINGDOM, 1990–2013

Vincent Nadin and Dominic Stead

Chapter objectives

The objectives of this chapter are:

- to explain how spatial planning in the United Kingdom has been shaped by its constitution as a union state, the underlying social model and legal tradition;
- to highlight the challenge of spatial socio-economic disparities for planning – between north and south, between urban and rural and between rich and poor neighbourhoods in cities;
- to describe three waves of change from the early 1990s, including the attempt to change the culture of planning from primarily land-use regulation to embrace a more strategic approach;
- to show that spatial development outcomes are shaped by a deeply rooted underlying doctrine and wide competition over the control of planning systems where 'no-one is in complete control', which results in more incremental and fewer strategic decisions.

1 Introduction

Town and country spatial planning is deeply embedded in the operation of central and local government in the UK and, indeed, in the psyche of the nation. From its origins in public health and housing policy, its scope has widened to encompass and interact with almost all government policy. Planning processes are open and participatory, and decisions are universally respected. Planning is praised by those whose interests and quality of life it protects and condemned by those whose objectives are frustrated. It can facilitate great wealth creation and obstruct investment in equal measure.

It is not surprising, therefore, that there is perpetual competition over who controls its policies, its operation and interests served. The result has been an endless and accelerating process of review and reform. Consequently, planning in the UK has changed significantly since 1990, though arguably the fundamental characteristics remain the same. Modifications to the underlying 'planning doctrine' have had a lasting effect, but some principles are beyond review. Notions such as urban containment and heritage conservation have become fixed as conventional wisdom. The key turning points in change have tended to correspond to changes in government, but all administrations tend to be schizophrenic about planning, since it can both help and hinder the objectives of sector departments. One consistent objective of successive administrations has been to simplify and streamline planning, mostly without success.

In this chapter, we begin with an explanation of the key characteristics of town and country planning (and spatial planning) in the UK, and a summary of the main challenges facing government and planning authorities from the 1990s. We then identify and review three broad periods of change: the introduction of a plan-led approach in the 1990s; the emergence of spatial planning in the 2000s; and the accent on localism from 2010.

2 The UK spatial planning systems

2.1 The United Kingdom: government and social model

The United Kingdom of Great Britain and Northern Ireland (to give the full name of the country) is a 'multinational' or 'union state'. This distinguishes it from unitary states that have one 'central government' and federal states that have a formal allocation of competences between federal and state governments. As a union state, the UK has 'a compound form, in which different units have been added on, keeping some of their old institutions and practices, but without a formal federal division of powers' (Keating, 2006, p. 23).[1] There is a common UK government and also separate governing institutions for Northern Ireland, Scotland and Wales (formally known as 'devolved administrations'). These constitutional arrangements are asymmetrical; the autonomy and competences of the nations vary.

A detailed explanation of change in all four nations of the UK is not within the scope of this book. So while we give an overview of the trajectory of planning for the whole of the UK, the accent of parts of the chapter is on England. It can be assumed that planning is devolved and that there is separate legislation and planning policy in each of the four countries.[2]

Another characteristic of the UK that is fundamental to understanding the operation of spatial planning is the underlying 'social model'. By social model we mean the collection of shared values in a society, particularly in terms of the rights and responsibilities of the individual and the state, the role of the market and relations between them (Nadin and Stead, 2008). The social model of the UK is often described as liberal Anglo-Saxon and contrasted with social democratic and conservative (or corporatist) models evident in continental Europe (Esping-Andersen, 1990; Alber, 2006; Nadin and Stead, 2008; Stead and Nadin, 2009).

The liberal stream in British society is certainly of long standing, and so with it is a strong emphasis on individual responsibility, a flexible labour market and acceptance of relatively high levels of inequality. But since the mid-twentieth century, liberal ways have been mixed with more social democratic values. World War II dramatically shifted attitudes towards more agreement on the need for state intervention and less tolerance for social and economic inequalities (Ward, 2004; Cullingworth and Nadin, 2006). This paved the way for the creation of the modern planning system and regional policy in the UK (along with other state enterprises such as the National Health Service), with extensive powers to regulate the market in land-use in the interests of social and economic renewal. More liberal principles re-emerged quickly with the accent on the individual rather than collectivist approaches, private sector investment and minimum regulation of markets, all consolidated by the Thatcher government from 1979.

During the 1990s, there was a re-injection of social democratic values in the UK, and what has been described as a turn to an 'Anglo-social model' (Stanley and Lawton, 2007; Finlayson, 2009). In particular, the Blair government from 1997 espoused a 'third way' that combined continued adherence to competition, private entrepreneurialism and 'loose regulation' with more state intervention in the social democratic mode, seeking a more even distribution of income and welfare (Pearce and Paxton, 2005). This continuing interaction between collectivist social welfare and individualist liberal principles explains the seeming inconsistencies in the systems of British town planning.

Although there has been less deregulation in the planning field than elsewhere, especially where vested interests are protected by the system, privatization, deregulation and a reliance on market and civil society solutions have had a strong impact. Also, the overlaying of reforms arising from a liberal individualist perspective onto a planning system conceived in a collectivist spirit has produced a strong planning system but with development led by the private sector (or public sector agencies acting like the private sector) in a context of fragmented governance. Planning authorities directly implement very little, but seek to regulate and influence the actions of other actors and agencies with varying levels of autonomy. One result is a very long history of public and private sectors working in partnership (Shapely, 2012). Power has become very dispersed with no one agency 'in control'.

2.2 Town and country planning in the UK

The 1947 Town and Country Planning Act set down the modern planning system in Britain. It was a monumental achievement made possible by the impact of war on physical conditions, on political will and on social attitudes. It nationalized all rights to develop land (including building, engineering, mining and other operations in, on, over or under land or any material change in the use of a building). It created the discretionary system of regulation based on indicative plans that is the hallmark of British planning, and it established the principle that those who were prevented from realizing the potential value of land because of planning regulation were not entitled to any compensation (Cullingworth and Nadin, 2006). Moreover, it introduced a system for the recovery of betterment, the difference between the market value with permission to develop and existing use value. The 1947 Act and its successors have given the UK strong and 'mature' systems of spatial planning.

In theory, planning powers in the UK belong to central government, which makes law that permits certain competences to the devolved administrations and local government. Thus, competences are divided between national government (one of the four nations' governments) and local authorities. There was a regional tier of planning bodies in England from 1997 but they were abolished in 2011. Local authorities are large by continental European standards with an average size in England of about 140,000 people. Nevertheless, their competences are relatively limited and there is no constitutional safeguard for their powers. They can and are overruled by the centre. A critical point for urban development is that there is very little local taxation and local authorities rely on central government rather than their local taxpayers for the bulk of their income, thus reducing the incentive to support physical development. Local authorities regulate development and formulate local policy instruments, while national government (across the four nations) plays a supervisory and strategic role via planning law, policy and guidelines; by 'calling-in' or retrieving decisions on certain cases for their own decision; and by dealing with appeals. From time to time, central government has played a more direct role in urban development through national agencies, for example in the development corporations that developed the new towns. Large-scale national interventions such as slum clearance, mass housing projects and urban motorways are now much less important (Grant, 2001) but, by 2010, they were on the increase again, with plans for major new energy and transport infrastructure projects, and in marine planning.

The general characteristics of planning in the UK set out in the *EU Compendium of Spatial Planning Systems and Policies* (CEC, 1997) still generally stand and are shared by the planning systems in England, Northern Ireland, Scotland and Wales.

- There is comprehensive regulation of land-use and development (the main exceptions being in agriculture and forestry), but it is largely separated from controls on building, pollution and transport. There is a general presumption in favour of sustainable development; that is, it is up to the planning authority to explain why a development should not be approved.
- National planning policies together with local development plans are the primary consideration in making decisions about development, and the means for wider participation in policymaking. Local development plans must be in conformity with national policies. Plans are not legally binding (they are not law) nor are they detailed in the form of zoning plans, but use more performance criteria.
- Decisions on development proposals are made at the time the proposal comes forward. The 'decision moment' is therefore near the end of the process, whereas in systems employing legally binding zoning plans, decisions are effectively made at the time the plan is adopted.
- Applicants for approval to develop have some discretion in how they meet the terms of the policies. Decision-makers also have some discretion, in for example requiring certain outcomes or 'conditions' in relation to a particular development. Decisions contrary to policy, or 'departures', may be permitted if they can be fully justified. However, the system is intended to be 'plan-led'.
- Decisions are made by local government politicians on the recommendation of professional officers, and this is the same body that makes the local policies. Most decisions are made by officers making use of 'delegated powers'. There is relatively little involvement of the courts, although this has been increasing. Instead, appeals are heard by a representative of the national minister (or equivalent).
- There have been few automatic value capture duties associated with approvals to develop, but instead locally negotiated agreements have been widely used for recouping betterment. Since 2010, it has been possible for local authorities to levy a standard charge on development to fund infrastructure.
- There is a very well-established separate planning profession in the UK, encouraged by the need for much negotiation with the system, and with strong influence over the education of planners.

The *EU Compendium of Spatial Planning Systems and Policies* (CEC, 1997; Nadin and Stead, 2013) refers to four ideal types or 'traditions' of spatial planning and suggests that the planning systems of the UK are most closely characterized by the 'land-use management tradition'. The land-use management tradition or model of planning is concerned with 'managing and regulating physical development to meet general planning principles and wider societal goals such as housing provision and protecting environmental heritage' (Dühr *et al.*, 2010, p. 182). It deals with the classic externality effects of land-use change and provides a basis for recouping betterment. Land-use regulation is a feature of most other planning systems, but in the case of the UK it has been dominant. The urbanism tradition including zoning to control urban form is not well developed in the UK. The quality of the public realm has come to the fore from time to time, particularly where urban spatial qualities are associated with economic development, as in the reports of an *Urban Task Force* chaired by the architect Lord Richard Rogers of Riverside (1999). Zoning and binding regulation plans have been advocated but have made little practical inroads beyond experimental schemes.

The regional economic planning tradition was important in the UK for three decades after World War II, but apart from European cohesion policy investment it is now unimportant.[3] Instead, central government effectively subsidizes the poorer regions through welfare payments while investment continues to be concentrated in the rich regions as explained below. Regional economic development agencies still exist, but they have been poorly funded and have limited impact. Although planning in the UK could in no way be described as 'comprehensive integrated' or strategic, there has been coordination often through voluntary arrangements of local governments especially in the metropolitan areas. They have had mixed success. During the 2000s, there was a concerted effort to move more comprehensively in this direction. Repeated calls for some kind of national strategic planning and consideration of regional policy investments for the whole of the UK or England go unheeded, while there is 'national planning' in Northern Ireland, Scotland and Wales, as explained below.

Studies of European comparative planning law invariably distinguish the discretionary approaches to planning in the UK and Ireland from the dominant zoning approaches in continental Europe (Booth, 1996, 1999). Zweigert and Kötz (2004) provide the underpinning explanation for this distinction. The continental legal systems share a similar 'legal style' that relies on the adoption of abstract rules and principles in advance of the nature of particular decisions being known, and that applies irrespective of the details of the case. In contrast, the English common law system offers far fewer rules. Law has been built up on a case-by-case basis as the decisions of the courts are recorded. According to Zweigert and Kötz (2004, p. 71), the English 'never make a decision until it has to be made' and 'are not given to abstract rules and hold no trust in best laid plans'. It should be acknowledged here that zoning plans do not by definition lead to greater accordance between plans and development, or to less flexibility (Moroni, 2007; Buitelaar and Sorel, 2010). Some aspects of planning in the UK are very rigid, not least policies on urban containment and strong resistance to development in the countryside. Nevertheless, the underlying ethos of spatial planning in the UK is more discretionary, which means more attention to negotiated solutions when development proposals are made.

It should be apparent by now that competences for planning in the UK are relatively centralized – in terms of the four nations. The four variants of national policy are closely followed and widely quoted in disputes. The operation of local authorities and other agencies in bringing about development is closely controlled and monitored at the national level. In England, it could be argued that the national minister makes all the very important or controversial decisions. The minister's inspectors (or recorders in Scotland) hold public inquiries (hearings) of draft development plans and test their 'soundness'. Their findings are binding on the local authority. The system is also generally administrative rather than judicial in nature. The role of the courts is to determine the meaning of the law where it is disputed – though this can have consequences for policy. There are rights to appeal to central government where permission to develop is refused, but the final decision by the minister is not open to challenge, unless the powers given by law are exceeded. For most appeals, the minister's power to decide the appeal is delegated to an inspector, who acts as an independent tribunal. There are no third-party rights of appeal.

Not surprisingly, public engagement in plan-making and development regulation is central to planning in the UK. There are very many large and small NGOs that have a very great influence on planning policy and decisions. They provide a force for continuity in the system largely in respect of conservation and environmental sustainability objectives, although there are also many organizations that represent business and development interests. The largest NGO, the National Trust, has more than five million paid members in England and Wales alone. NGOs participate extensively through the formal plan-making procedure which allows for periods of publicity, consultation, final formal objection and a public hearing. There is no right of legal challenge to plans except where the procedures have not been followed properly.

3 Problems and challenges

The UK, like other rich European countries, faces great challenges, not least tackling global economic competition and the risks associated with climate change, and particularly so in the aftermath of the 2007 banking crisis. The emphasis in this section is on the problems that are most relevant for spatial planning, and those that are more specific to the UK. The dominant concern with climate change at both national and local levels is considered in the discussion of recent changes.

Figure 10.1 illustrates the distribution of urban land-use and main transport infrastructure in the UK. England is very urbanized and densely populated with 401 persons/km. The concentrations of population are in the south-east region (in and around London) and conurbations of the Midlands and north-west. This broad pattern has changed very little for over a century; 'many places are populated because they were populated in the distant past ... [and] Other land is sparsely populated because it was sparsely populated in the past, and the past is being preserved' (Dorling, 2005, p. 176). The spatial development pattern at the national scale has little to do with demand (which would have produced much more development in the countryside), but is a product of public policies, especially planning policies.[4]

The continued 'preservation' of development patterns and particularly the clear separation of town and country is coming under great strain, especially in the south. After a period of stability, the population of the UK has grown relatively quickly since 2000 and there is increasing demand for homes and services associated with falling household size and increasing prosperity (Breheny and Hall, 1999). Projections estimate that the 2012 UK population of about 62 million will grow to 73 million by 2035 (ONS, 2012). Recent and projected growth is concentrated in the south-east, the south-west and the east of England.

Figure 10.1 Urban land-use and main infrastructure networks in the UK

These regions have experienced steady population and household growth since 1971, almost entirely because of immigration mostly from central and eastern Europe. So there has been urban growth but generally in the form of dispersal of population in a process of 'counter urbanization' to city fringes and then to accessible small towns in rural areas near metropolitan centres (Champion, 1989). A 'Golden Arc' has been described defining the outer extent of metropolitan London 'as far as Exeter and Dover' (TCPA, 2011, p. 12). In contrast, the north of England and Scotland have experienced overall population decline together with the same counterurbanization trends resulting in high vacancy in the cities, or 'shrinkage'.

Containing urban growth is a clear achievement of government planning in the UK, but it comes with severe 'unintended consequences'. Change of use 'from agricultural to residential use can increase the price of land by as much as 600–700 times' (Foresight Land Use Futures Project, 2010, p. 182). House prices have risen faster than incomes or general price inflation. Some rural areas have become very exclusive, especially those with reasonable access to the main urban centres. Planning restrictions on development in the countryside have led to gentrification of the countryside, a general failure to meet local demands, increased prices and a reduction in quality of new homes (Evans and Hartwich, 2005; Satsangi et al., 2010). The main tool available to provide affordable housing has been planning gain or value capture, which has been described as an 'ad hoc and uncertain tax on residential developers through the planning system' (Oxley, 2004, p. 169).

Economic development follows a similar pattern as shown in Figure 10.2. The area of each region is drawn to reflect its total GDP, demonstrating very clearly the concentration of economic power in London and the south-east, with a few 'pockets' elsewhere. The result is a 'north–south divide', the enduring pattern of economic and social geography of Britain. The divide is not just about wealth. A league table of the performance of English cities based on poverty, unemployment, education, health and other measures puts only one northern city (York) in the top 12 (Dorling, 2010). Trends show widened disparities in the UK between regions and within cities since the 1980s (Massey and Allen, 1988; Dorling, 2005, 2010).

Coe and Jones (2010, p. 5) explain the overlapping sets of processes 'that have shaped this UK space economy'. At root, globalization alongside aggressive financialization of the UK economy driven by neoliberal policy has made London the pre-eminent global financial market but with fragmented effects on the UK as a whole. Allied to this, while the UK still has a significant manufacturing sector, tertiarization of the economy or the relative growth of the service sector continues. The favourable areas for service sector growth are mostly in and around London. These more recent trends have reinforced the very 'uneven social and economic geography' of the UK, and the concentration of extreme pressures on land-use in the south of England. Other problems arise from this concentration, including increasing demands for fresh water where it is most difficult to provide; demand for more land release in areas in the south-east that are mostly flood plain; and increasing costs of infrastructure in a congested region.

Similar disparities are evident at the city scale, with large pockets of high deprivation juxtaposed with better-off neighbourhoods. The long history of urban renewal in UK cities has improved conditions dramatically in some places, but deeply entrenched poverty and exclusion remains (Tallon, 2010). Of the 21 million homes in England, 35 per cent were 'non-decent' meaning they needed repair, modern facilities and/or thermal insulation (DCLG, 2009). Cities in 'the north' tend to be heavily dependent on public subsidy with a disproportionately high number of public sector jobs. Consequently, northern cities generally did not benefit from sustained growth in the UK economy from 1993 to 2007. Conversely, they suffered badly from the recession and public spending cuts following the banking crisis of 2007, while the effects in London have been negligible (Martin, 2010; Hall, 2011). Disparities between the north and south have been reinforced (Ertürk et al., 2011) and despite a policy commitment to reduce the gap, government spending is 'disproportionately weighted towards the Greater South East' (Burch et al., 2009, p. 588). London

> receives more than twice as much per capita funding than any other English region on transport ... more than 50 per cent more for policing and public safety ... [and] more per capita funding for education, training and economic development than any other part of the UK.
>
> (Muson, 2010, p. 85)

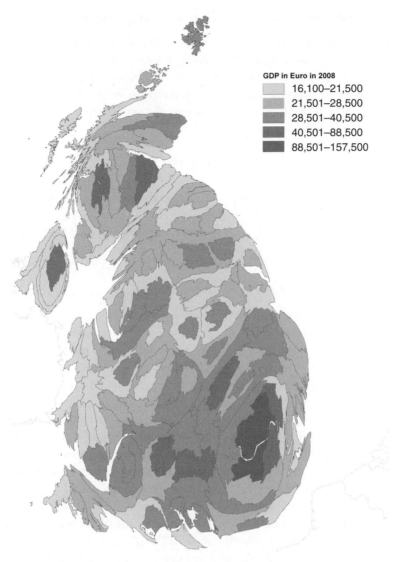

GDP in Euro in 2008

- 16,100–21,500
- 21,501–28,500
- 28,501–40,500
- 40,501–88,500
- 88,501–157,500

Figure 10.2 Distribution of GDP in the UK: cartogram of NUTS 3 regions in 2008

In sum, spatial development in the UK is dominated by London and its immediate hinterland (Amin *et al.*, 2003) and increasingly so. London's global city status as a pre-eminent node for advanced business services (Pain, 2009) brings great advantages but also great imbalance in the country. Until the 2000s, no other city in the UK appeared in the top 100 global connected cities (Taylor *et al.*, 2010). While there are signs of improvement, the metropolitan regions and provincial cities elsewhere in the UK lag far behind, and what progress there is depends in part on connections with London (Taylor, 2010).

4 Dimensions and directions of change: three waves

This section reviews the main turning points since 1990 presented as three waves of reform, together with explanations in relation to the main driving forces, prior to considering the general trends in terms of changing power relations among actors; planning tools; and planning doctrine.

Figure 10.3 shows in diagrammatic form the main trends in spatial planning that followed in the UK after 1990. It is selective, only including the major reforms so as to highlight in particular the three main 'waves' of change:

- from the early 1990s, the promotion of a 'plan-led system' and the incorporation of sustainability objectives;
- from the late 1990s, the introduction of the 'spatial planning approach' alongside extensive devolution of competences;
- from 2010, the strengthening of neighbourhood planning and a fresh emphasis on infrastructure.

4.1 1990s: the plan-led approach

Prior to 1990, the most significant reform to planning was made in 1968 when strategic decisions about the form of development in structure plans were separated from detailed policies in local plans; a principle that has survived, though in different forms. Otherwise, the most important changes were to strengthen enforcement and conservation of the environment and heritage (Moore, 2012), and in the collection of betterment or value capture, a particularly contentious issue (Cullingworth, 1980; Blundell, 1993).

The Conservative administration of Margaret Thatcher came to power in 1979 with a promise to 'release enterprise' in the face of the catastrophic decline of British industry in the context of global competition. Deregulation was a hallmark of this administration including the rolling back of local government planning regulation and the wholesale abolition of strategic planning authorities in the metropolitan areas; the introduction of centrally controlled development corporations and simplified planning zones; and the downgrading of plans in favour of market decisions. Thus, planning at the start of the 1990s was in a parlous state, characterized by *ad hoc* and reactive decision-making by tight and exclusive policy communities working in separate silos, with development interests wielding considerable power and little incentive for local planning authorities to prepare plans. However, the Conservative Party relies for support on two key branches of society – a mix of business interests, who do not always agree and 'compete for space'; and voters in countryside areas and small towns who jealously guard their exclusivity. For that reason, there was no 'free for all'. The system remained in place for governments from the early 1990s to try to employ in more positive ways. The struggles over control of the system remained.

Although the 'neoliberal' tag applies to all governments of whatever persuasion since the 1980s, the fiercely neoliberal approach to public services has receded. A new planning Act in 1991 brought a big change in direction to a 'plan-led system' where each local planning authority was required to have an up-to-date plan for its whole area (and still is) with decisions based on the plan. The hallmark discretion in decision-making remained, but decisions

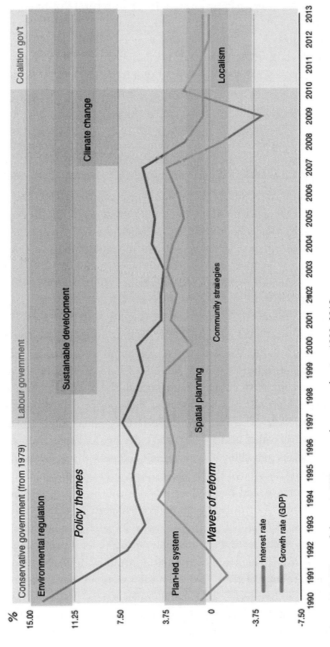

Figure 10.3 Waves of change in UK town and country planning 1990–2013

have since required explicit reasoning with reference to 'the development plan'. At the same time, central government strengthened its own position in decision-making through clearer statements of planning policy. Scotland introduced a system of planning policy statements from the 1970s (Raemakers *et al.*, 1994), and this approach was also in place by the beginning of the 1990s in the other nations. The number of separate planning policy documents on issues as diverse as town centres, noise and archaeology steadily increased but became cumbersome, and has been reduced now to one or two documents in each nation (except Northern Ireland which has 22 separate statements).

National planning policy has been a powerful tool to ensure a more consistent approach to decision-making (Land Use Consultants, 1995) and for ministers (or equivalents) to exercise strong control over local planning decisions. Policy is non-binding but commanding. Decisions will often be informed by competing interpretations of policy statements. Local development plans have to be in conformity with national policies. Non-conformity of plans or decisions may be a reason for the minister to override local wishes. Ministers often 'call-in' controversial or nationally significant developments for their own decision and then weigh various national and local government policies in coming to a decision. For example, the Scottish Minister found in favour of a major golf complex promoted by the international financier Donald Trump. The development included 500 new houses to cross-subsidize the development and the loss of a site of special scientific interest, which was contrary to the council's own planning policies. The minister invoked 'the national interest' because of the economic and social advantages despite damage to assets protected for their 'national importance' (DPEA, 2008).[5]

Central interference in local decisions in England was not difficult given the dire performance of local planning authorities in producing plans. By 2002, 13 per cent of local planning authorities had a statutory development plan in place – some 11 years after the mandatory requirement and 34 years after they were given competences to prepare such plans. A messy reorganization of local government in England did not help with a mixture of single and two-tier local authority structures established. Scotland and Wales found a much clearer resolution with each agreeing a single tier of large unitary authorities providing more distinct planning responsibilities at the local level. But the critical factors explaining performance were local opposition and controversy that made good use of extensive and open plan-making procedures to force delay, politicians' unwillingness to commit and poor management (Steel *et al.*, 1995; RTPI, 2000; Nadin, 2007). Above all, there was little attention in government as to how the new 'model' of planning would be put into practice and how professional practices would adapt. It was instead imposed from above in the style of new public management with associated targets and indicators (Clifford, 2013). The idea of spatial planning, despite 'a plethora of advice', was for many uncertain and ambiguous, and 'many local planners became dependent on guidance "from above"' (Gunn and Hillier, 2014). Authorities facing strong but unpopular demand for housing around the south-east of England were often more successful in adopting a plan that could be used to reject development. And a general point that has stood the test of time is that all planning authorities should be making planning decisions on the basis of a coherent set of planning policies and land allocations that cover its whole area.

During the 1990s, planning policies of government at all levels became heavily influenced by the notion of environmental sustainability and then later broader notions of sustainable development. The UK approach to environmental problems was at first fragmented and seldom ambitious in addressing the strong definition of sustainability, but much more concerned with dealing with 'measurable impacts'. Only from the 2000s did it become more actively engaged with the precautionary principle, which is now well established, at least in policy (Cullingworth and Nadin, 2006, p. 252). The first *UK Sustainable Development Strategy* was adopted in 1994, the first of any nation following the 1992 Rio Earth Summit. The second version in 1999 revealed the shifting influences over such policy statements through the inclusion of a commitment to maintain 'high and stable levels of economic growth'. Many policy statements have followed together with more demanding legislation on such matters as strengthening pollution control, flood management and setting up new environment agencies. Much of this activity, as in the rest of Europe, was related to EU legislation, including the 1985 Environmental Assessment and 1992 Habitats Directives (Commission Directive 85/337/EEC and Commission Directive 92/43/EEC).

The environmental sustainability agenda drew new actors into the planning arena in the 1990s, demanding more rigorous testing of development proposals against environmental protection criteria. These actors sought to insert a technocratic approach to decision-making in a system that by then was firmly embedded in interest mediation and negotiated outcomes, informed by, but not driven by, scientific evidence. This has created difficulties for planning, not least in adding to the need for impact statements of all kinds to inform decision-making. Professional appreciation of the notion of sustainability also has to confront a consistent theme in central government interpretations from the 1990s to the 2010s that even sustainability means economic growth.

4.2 2000s: devolution and the spatial planning approach

From 1997, a left-of-centre government led by Blair moved quickly to devolve government, in terms of more autonomy for the constituent nations of the UK and in terms of more local and civil society influence on decision-making. The UK government comprehensively devolved competences to the three nations (known formally as the 'devolved administrations'), with the creation of Assemblies in Northern Ireland and Wales, and the re-establishment of the Scottish Parliament that had been dissolved in 1707.[6] This had the effect of creating more diversity in the way planning is practised in the countries of the UK (Allmendinger *et al.*, 2005). The Scottish Parliament quickly consulted on ideas for a distinctive approach to planning in Scotland (Scottish Parliament, 1999). But the effects of devolution should not be exaggerated; there have always been differences in the actual practice of planning in the four countries, and the basic principles remain the same throughout the UK. Variation in planning practice is probably as wide within England as it is within the UK because of the great variation in economic and social conditions in this one nation (Allmendinger, 2006).

Since then, many changes have been made, but the differences with England are largely at the surface. Allmendinger (2001) predicted that, despite devolution, the trajectory of planning reform was likely to remain the same in Scotland and England, and so it has proved to be in the main, despite the Scottish Nationalist Party taking control from 2007. Reform proposals for 2013 parallel closely an emphasis on 'simplification and streamlining' in England (Scottish Government, 2013). During the 2000s, there was a similar alignment in attempts to bring forward 'the spatial planning approach'. Despite periodic attempts at regional planning, the UK has a generally weak record of making spatial strategy (Nadin and Stead, 2011), preferring instead to 'muddle through'. Attention to strategy has been dependent on 'the attitude taken by government to strategic intervention through the planning system to redress market failure: in terms of its ideological acceptance, its perceived effectiveness in responding quickly to changing circumstances, and the attendant costs of regional bureaucracy' (Swain et al., 2013, p. 2). In general, right-of-centre governments have been against and left-of-centre more accepting.

The 1997 Blair government was intent on breaking down the insulation of government departments, improving coordination, strengthening local government, engaging communities in decision-making and focusing more on outcomes rather than outputs (DTLR, 1998). This meant, for example, asking how the housing quality of families could be improved rather than just how the number of houses could be increased. Outcomes are the result of the interaction of policies in particular areas, so the accent on coordination was accompanied by emphasis on 'place-based strategies'. Devolution of competences to local authorities was intended to improve local community leadership and coordination across services. From 2000, local authorities were given a duty to create a 'local strategic partnership' involving government, civil society and business interests, with responsibility for the making of 'community strategies'. The objective was to fundamentally improve local leadership and the engagement of local people in decisions that affected them (Doak and Parker, 2005; Morphet, 2011). The formal planning instruments had to coordinate with the community strategies.

By the early 1990s, the Conservative government was encouraging more voluntary cooperation among local planning authorities on 'regional planning guidance' (a very basic form of agreement about regional strategic priorities) in order to address problems of housing land allocation and conflicts between the urban and rural authorities. From the late 1990s, regional strategic planning was strengthened under an incoming Labour government, and from 2004 comprehensive 'regional spatial strategies' became a legal requirement in England. The ambitious goals of government were 'to put planning at the centre of the spatial development process, not just as a regulator of land and property uses, but as a proactive and strategic coordinator of all policy and actions that influence spatial development' (Nadin, 2007, p. 43). This was the culmination of a far-reaching review of the strengths and weaknesses of the planning system in England in recognition that it had not adjusted adequately to great changes in conditions and societal ambitions (Cullingworth, 1997). Instead, planning was entangled in 'a bureaucratic regulatory routine, largely preoccupied with procedural rather than substantive issues' (Davoudi, 2006, p. 21). A long list of contemporary criticisms could be added, including the poor evidence base for policy, dissatisfaction with the quality of outcomes, ritualistic community engagement and failure to prepare up-to-date plans. There was little recognition of the impact of other sector policies on spatial development (Stead and Meijers, 2004) and 'a multiplicity of often overlapping and sometimes conflicting plans and strategies' (RCEP, 2002, p. 1).[7]

A wide consensus was formed supporting 'a culture change in planning' towards a 'spatial planning approach'. The explanation from government was that 'spatial planning goes beyond traditional land use planning to bring together and integrate policies for the development and use of land with other policies and programmes which influence the nature of places and how they can function' (ODPM, 2004a, p. 30). These ideas were heavily influenced by the European planning discourse at the time, in particular the debates around the European Spatial Development Perspective (CSD, 1999), and the priorities of the incoming Labour government seeking to modernize and 'join up' government to deliver democratic renewal and progressive outcomes (Allmendinger and Tewdwr-Jones, 2000; Morphet, 2004). In practice, the government encouraged using planning to assist other sectors to achieve their goals (e.g. education, health, economic development); to inject a spatial dimension into thinking about sectoral policies; and to create new planning policy communities that cooperated in a collaborative policymaking process.

The use of the term 'spatial planning' here may be confusing. For clarity, in the UK the term is used to denote a more integrating role for planning (joining up the spatial impacts of sectoral policies) in contrast to its role in the regulation of land-use change. Although this reform is sometimes portrayed as a shift from one system to another, land-use regulation prevails, albeit with a revised remit. The use of the term 'spatial planning' is important; 'it represented a break with the immediate past. It moved planning back into a delivery role and a corporate role' (Morphet, 2011, p. 13).

A whole suite of new planning tools was provided to promote a culture shift, including regional spatial strategy and local development frameworks for local planning authorities incorporating a 'core strategy'. Aside from the instruments, the change to a spatial planning approach needed a period of adjustment and learning in the profession. In the event, early experiences were poor, with widespread uncertainty about what was needed often resulting in relatively minor, and unsuccessful, adjustments to former practices, rather than wholesale change. It was always going to require a longer-term view to 'change the culture', but progress was reined in when a new Coalition government of Conservatives and Liberals came into office in 2010.

For the devolved administrations, one feature of the reorientation of planning towards more sectoral coordination that is very distinctive from England has been the creation of spatially explicit 'national plans'. The first 'national plan' in the UK was formulated in Northern Ireland in the late 1990s in a climate of optimism following the Belfast Agreement of 1998 on power sharing among the religious and political parties. The Agreement included a specific commitment to a regional plan to tackle planning issues in a 'divided society' (Murray, 2009, p. 130). The 2001 *Regional Development Strategy for Northern Ireland 2025* (DRDNI, 2001) was 'very much in the mould of EU developments in spatial planning, placing Northern Ireland in its European and global context and seeking to integrate concerns about the physical development of its territory with social, economic and environmental objectives' (Cullingworth and Nadin, 2006, p. 96). The Strategy was amended in 2008 and replaced in 2012 with the *Regional Development Strategy 2035*, which among other things continues with 'encouraging compact urban forms' in the context of great spatial dispersal of housing in Northern Ireland (DRDNI, 2012, p. 41). Progress has also been made on a *Framework for Collaboration* on the island of Ireland.

The first National Planning Framework for Scotland was published in 2004 (Scottish Government, 2004) and provided 'an audit of where Scotland was at that time with respect to social, economic and environmental conditions … a template against which policies in train could be assessed, resources identified … and an integration of strategic thinking secured across different sectors, protagonists and policies' (Lloyd and Purves, 2009, p. 88).

A revised *National Planning Framework 2* was published by the Scottish Government in 2009, this time with statutory status – that is, required by law. It looks forward to 2030 with an emphasis on 'the improvement of infrastructure to support long-term development' (Scottish Government, 2009, p. 1). It identifies 14 'national developments' or strategic projects, including road, rail and airport improvements that 'make a significant contribution to Scotland's sustainable economic development ... improvements in internal connectivity ... and the achievement of climate change, renewable energy or waste management targets' (Scottish Government, 2009, p. 39). An 'Action Plan' deals with more detailed implementation, though many policies remain rather general, if not vague, such as the intention to create sustainable communities (Nadin and Stead, 2011). The Scottish Government is firmly committed to this national-level approach to planning and, in 2013, work was well under way on version 3.

In a similar fashion to Scotland, planning law in Wales states that 'there must be a spatial plan for Wales' and that the National Assembly should approve it. The *Wales Spatial Plan: People, Places, Futures* was published by the Welsh Government in 2004 (Welsh Government, 2004) with a 20-year horizon. A 2008 update maintains the same broad strategy of 'making sure that decisions are taken with regard to their impact beyond the immediate sectoral or administrative boundaries and that the core values of sustainable development govern everything we do' (Welsh Government, 2008, p. 3).

Despite numerous calls for a similar 'national plan' for England (or the UK as a whole) (RTPI, 2006; TCPA, 2011), there is no spatial strategy covering England. A *Communities Plan* of 2004 (ODPM, 2004b) broke with tradition by identifying at the national level locations for four areas of major growth, although only in very general terms. As in the other nations, there are many other sectoral strategies operating at the national level that have strong influence on spatial development, such as the *UK Sustainability Strategy* (2005) and the *UK Low Carbon Transition Plan* (2009), and on transport, biodiversity and other subjects, but again rarely with any spatial content. A *National Infrastructure Plan* for the whole of the UK was published by the Treasury in 2011 (HM Treasury, 2011), though with references to the devolution of decisions on most infrastructure to the nations.

During the 2000s, HM Treasury, under the previous government, undertook two deep reviews of the relationship between the planning system and economic health of the country, known as the Barker Reviews after the author (2004, 2006). The first investigated the chronic (under)supply of new housing in England in relation to demand – and among other reasons found lack of availability of land through the planning system to be a major barrier. The second Barker Review, on *Land Use Planning* (Barker, 2006), found it to be 'a vital support to productivity and economic growth', called for more simplification of complex procedures and proposed incentives for planning authorities to be more market responsive. All of the many recommendations had been voiced before in different forms, but these reports were commissioned by the powerful Treasury and therefore influential.

4.3 Climate change

We should also mention here the impact on planning policy and procedures of the risks associated with climate change, or more specifically the *Stern Review of the Economics of Climate*

Change (2006). Stern likened the potential effects of climate change to 'the great wars and the economic depression of the first half of the twentieth century' (p. vi), and described the planning system as a key tool in avoiding such risks, noting that alternative ways of managing flood risk, for example, would be more costly. The review recommended that 'action should be integrated into development policy and planning at every level' (p. xxii). Again, the main actor here is the Treasury, although climate change and planning were responsibilities of other ministries. But this gave impetus to change and, in 2008, a *Climate Change Act* put emissions targets on a statutory footing and created a new Department of Energy and Climate Change.

For planning, the impacts have been felt in the increasing complexity of criteria for policy and decision-making, including assessments of impact. Again, the policy community around many planning issues has been widened with more involvement of scientists and specialists. In a similar vein, the EU's Water Framework Directive and its requirement for the preparation of river basin and flood risk management plans has emphasized a more technocratic approach in the planning process as it engages with environmental management regimes. The expectations of environmental professionals about how scientific evidence is used, about policy formulation and about implementation of policy does not necessarily accord with the politics-laden negotiative or deliberative style of policymaking in planning. At the same time, the climate change agenda, and growing awareness of sustainable development objectives before it, have prompted 'many communities to generate their own plans and strategies similar to the Local Agenda 21 initiatives of the 1990s' (Wilson and Piper, 2010, p. 13), thus directing attention to more local approaches to planning.

4.4 2010s: localism

A third phase of reform in England began with the election of a Coalition government in 2010. Its principal reforms may seem at first to have reversed previous initiatives with the abolition of the regional spatial strategies (with the exception of London), a strong accent on 'localism' in decision-making and a new centralized planning procedure to help deliver major infrastructure in energy and transport. But, aside from the wholesale clearance of the regional planning machinery (a repeat of what a Conservative government did in 1951), much of this is a continuation of previous trends. Even strategic planning is given attention, but in new groupings of city regions. And the new administration took forward many of the points raised in the Barker Reviews. The difference is in the subtle but significant changes that have been made to give more advantage to development businesses. This is couched in an argument against 'the complexity' of a system in which planning authorities struggled to produce plans and deliver housing (in the south of England); as a call for more varied local planning policies reflecting the concerns of local communities; and to some degree hidden by claims that the reforms are meant to achieve 'the greatest possible degree of local control' (Conservative Party, 2009, p. 1). The Conservative half of the Coalition government has taken the lead, but its Liberal Democrat partners had also offered to return 'decision making, including housing targets, to local people' in its manifesto (Liberal Democrats, 2010, p. 81).

After taking office, the government produced a new system of 'neighbourhood planning'; greatly reduced national planning policies into a single 'national planning framework'; and made a 'presumption in favour of sustainable development' – whilst 'seeking to reduce or contain the environmental role of planning ... to privilege economic growth' (Cowell, 2012, p. 14). The onus on planning authorities continues to deal quickly with development proposals and explain why they should not be accepted.[8] On the one hand, the reforms apparently offered something to local (often Conservative) interests opposed to the imposition of large-scale housing development, but who may be prepared to create and implement their own local policies; and on the other, offered something to business and industry interests who seek a relaxation in regulation and more certainty. On the latter, the Coalition government was quick to reintroduce old instruments from the 1980s such as 'enterprise zones' that to some extent bypass the planning system. Although presented as a radical departure, the notion of neighbourhood planning is not new either. The practice of (informal) parish or community planning was well established, at least in tight-knit communities (Owen, 2002), and the 1997 Labour administration had put much effort into engaging communities in local authority strategies. Neighbourhood planning may suffer the same criticism as its predecessors, which concentrated on providing opportunities for collaboration, but 'lacked any clear view of how conflicting interests might be realigned' (Gallent and Robinson, 2012, p. 192). While setting up neighbourhood planning mechanisms, the general thrust of policy is meant to advantage business interests.

A *2011 Localism Act* and *National Planning Policy Framework* (NPPF) (DCLG, 2012) has implemented many proposals. It achieved something of a sleight of hand in gaining a ringing endorsement from the Major Developers' Group for the apparent government commitment 'to liberalize the planning system'; but also from the National Association of Local Councils because of its intention to give local people more power over planning in their neighbourhood. But they also faced fierce opposition from professional and conservation interests which, unusually, propelled planning into the media spotlight. The main point of opposition was the presumption in favour of sustainable development, a phrase explained by government as 'a need for positive planning ... to encourage and not act as an impediment to sustainable growth' (DCLG, 2012, p. 6). Many observers interpret this as giving a bias in planning policy to business and development interests, and it would be difficult to argue differently given the rather crude assemblage of rhetoric extolling the virtue of environmental protection and neighbourhood decision-making, whilst also asserting the priority of economic growth. NGOs led opposition to the *Framework*, particularly the National Trust and Campaign to Protect Rural England, with sometimes equally crude rhetoric. A picture of Los Angeles urban sprawl was used early in the debate, but with some justifiable argument that, aside from specially designated areas, 'the proposals are overwhelmingly geared to delivering the needs of business and short-term growth rather than long-term needs of communities and the environment' (*The Times*, 2011). One of the consultant authors of the *Framework* was quoted giving a frank assessment: 'It's not meant to be the opportunity for communities to resist development. It's meant to be part of a strategy which encourages greater development' (quoted in Kirkup and Hope, 2011). The opposition position was put most strongly by George Monbiot as a fight between corporate power and democracy where the wullies (build whatever you like wherever you like) 'have their hands in the glove of government' (Monbiot, 2011).

5 Conclusion

With these waves of reform in mind, we now turn to conclude on the general implications for the role of actors and interests in planning; the approaches to planning and tools used; and the underpinning principles of planning in the UK.

5.1 Actors

The lasting effect of the neoliberal social model in the UK is that the planning system exerts influence in spatial development by working with a great many actors representing a wide range of interests. Government reforms have created a complex web of governance with public services and regulation provided by many public agencies, quasi-public sector bodies and private companies. Their roles are not always clear; for example, public goods may be delivered by the private sector. Alongside government initiatives, and encouraged by them, NGOs have grown and developed high-level research and lobbying capacity so that they play a central role in the policy process. Though the difficulties of policymaking in this 'congested policy environment' and questions about accountability have been widely recognized, the process has continued under successive administrations. The dispersal of power among many interests tends to slow down the development process and prevent many radical departures from policy, which can be seen as both positive and negative. Either way, it is certain that the process of planning – and its lack of mechanisms to agree and implement broad strategic directions for urban development have led to planning muddling through and, in parts of the country, amorphous urban sprawl (Phelps, 2012). In a context of great pressure for urban growth in the south of England and competition between many 'private interests' (whether for or against development), both decision-making and urban development have been fragmented.

But as numerous authors have pointed out, while no one may be 'in charge', power inequalities remain, and among the many actors, some have disproportionate influence. In this regard, the role of the Treasury in reviewing planning practice and leading policy development in England from the mid-2000s is instructive. Business and industry interests have sought influence via this channel as well as through the much less business-oriented 'planning ministry', the Department for Communities and Local Government. However, despite having a powerful position, the Treasury has been no more successful in addressing the main challenges, partly because it has not adapted to the complex interaction of many sector policies in particular places. Its influential role does illustrate the re-centralization of power. In contrast to the rhetoric of localism, spatial planning is still 'strongly steered by central priorities and narratives' (Allmendinger and Haughton, 2012, p. 97). Devolution to the nations has also tended to focus competences in new central administrations. Yet in the 'deliberative process', the powerful ministries of government have been set against increasingly powerful civil society actors who have led the argument against weakening planning control over growth, and who have won a number of high-profile battles. In broad policymaking, civil society has become an equally significant player alongside the state and market.

5.2 Planning modes and tools

At risk of oversimplification, the trajectories of modes of planning in the UK were: in the 1990s away from *ad hoc* 'muddling through' to more plan-based decision-making; in the 2000s to introduce more indicative planning and strategy making; and so far in the 2010s to more centrally directed strategic decisions and less strategy making. Underlying these changes, we would highlight four consistent but to some extent incompatible trends. First, much decision-making is increasingly plan-led. This effectively moves the 'decision moment' to an earlier stage in the planning process. Planning authorities have great difficulty reconciling local conflicts when preparing plans (there are numerous 'communities' with competing objectives) and of meeting both local and national/regional objectives. This is leading to more national government intervention in local policymaking.

Second, policy and decision-making are also increasingly informed by more scientific analysis, especially regarding environmental impacts, and this may be leading to a more technocratic planning style, which has not been seen in the UK since the 1970s. The need for more evidence collection and analysis rather flies in the face of successive governments' failed attempts to streamline and speed up procedures. It may even harbour a more imperative style of planning, where more decisions are made 'in advance' in fixed plans, or made solely on their technical merits based on impact assessments.

Third, and on quite a different tack, planning processes have involved more negotiation among an increasingly wide range of actors. The role of the plan has not been to communicate an end-state but to provide a focus for shaping attention to key issues and collaborative policy formulation (Healey, 1997). In this context, Shucksmith (2009, p. 12) argues that the state 'exercises generative power to stimulate action, innovation, struggle and resistance, to release potentialities, to generate new struggles and to transform governance itself ... in such a context of confused power where nobody is in charge'. Shucksmith is referring to the rural development process, but his arguments apply equally well in other 'territorial management' settings with the consequence that any rigid plans become redundant. As explained, the UK is well placed to move towards a more deliberative style of planning as plans have been less fixed in the UK, and progress on strategic spatial planning at both national and local levels exemplifies this shift. But there is a critical tension with an emerging technocratic and centralized style. Also, the collaborative and deliberative styles may 'foreclose all but narrow debate and contestation around a neoliberal growth agenda' (Allmendinger and Haughton, 2012, p. 91). Certainly, the respective roles of the state and market are barely discussed in mainstream planning, but there is certainly great overt political conflict about the policies and outcomes that result from a neoliberal agenda. As indicated at the beginning of this chapter, the UK cannot be understood as a neoliberal model. In regard to its land or territory, there remains a very strong social democratic ethos.

Fourth, planning bodies are addressing cross-boundary issues, and in a limited way creating new cross-boundary institutions for functional regions, for example the river basin management plans. Haughton *et al.* (2010) refer to this as planning in soft spaces with fuzzy boundaries. But mainstream planning has remained strongly embedded in administrative jurisdictions; for example, the regional spatial strategies of the 2000s were based on government administrative regions, which in some cases had little functional planning logic.

Similarly, local plan strategies often omit any connection with neighbouring areas. The lack of strategic approaches across planning boundaries, especially between rural and urban areas, remains a real impediment to effective strategic planning. Since 2011, the abolition of the regional spatial strategies is opening up opportunities for more experimentation and innovation as planning authorities collaborate voluntarily to address 'the key economic layer' of sub-regions and city-regions (TCPA, 2011, p. 43; Morphet and Pemberton, 2013).

5.3 Planning ideas, doctrines, concepts

By definition, doctrines are slow to change, which is one explanation why changing the culture of planning to a more strategic approach had relatively poor purchase in practice, though it was popular among the 'elites' of planning (Dühr *et al.*, 2010). So despite the introduction and reintroduction of tools, there is some consistency in the underlying values that shape planning in the UK. For planners, the public interest and public service ethic are still central (despite their ambiguity), and good planning requires bringing together sound technical knowledge with an understanding of what local communities value. There are continuing assumptions that the public interest is best served through applying concepts such as urban containment, the compact city and heritage conservation. Ideas from environmental sustainability and to some extent adaptation to climate change are now well established, including, for example, the protection of critical natural capital, ecosystems services and local energy generation. There is also more reflection on rather blunt concepts such as 'green belts' and their possible negative effects, but public attitudes are even slower to change and entrenched interests hold back any radical reformulations. And planners are well aware that the planning system and its concepts can be, and are, manipulated by powerful interests, whether in business or politics.

For central government, the dominant policy imperative for planning since the 1990s has been economic growth, and this has not varied with changes of government. The involvement of HM Treasury in planning policy has ensured that this continues, but other parts of government promote other agendas, not least in relation to environmental and heritage protection, renewable energy provision, security and many other concerns. There is an abundance of alternative ideas and concepts circulating for planners to consider, with the potential of planning for health as a front-runner (Barton *et al.*, 2012). If this idea were to achieve the prominence it deserves, then the planning system would have come full circle from its early roots in dealing with public health problems, but today developing such policies in a much more collaborative way.

Acknowledgement

We are grateful to Alex Wandl of TU Delft for his help with Figures 10.1 and 10.2.

Notes

1 The term 'Great Britain' refers to England, Scotland and Wales only, and the 'British Isles' refers to the geographical area which also includes the Republic of Ireland, the Isle of Man and the Channel Islands.
2 The UK Parliament and government ministers make planning-related law and policy only for England (with a few exceptions). The Scottish Parliament legislates for Scotland and policy is made by Scottish government

ministers and their departments based in Edinburgh. Wales has an Assembly based in Cardiff whose law-making powers at the time of writing are being extended, whilst it is already autonomous in making planning policy for Wales. Northern Ireland has its own Assembly that makes planning law and policy.

3 An explanation of the *EU Compendium*'s traditions and the British systems of town and country planning is given in the ESPON report 2.3.2 on Governance of Territorial Policies and Urban Policies (Farinos Dasí, 2006). Note that its suggestion that the UK is moving towards a more regional economic approach is incorrect and reflects a misunderstanding of either the *EU Compendium* traditions or the UK planning systems, or both (see Nadin and Stead, 2013).

4 An exception to the rule of urban containment is Northern Ireland where a long history of conflict has influenced the approach to land-use planning, and where there has been extensive development of new homes in open countryside.

5 For a full review of the decision-making procedure for this development which provides a detailed insight into the intricacies of the operation of the discretionary system in the UK and the role of the Scottish Minister, see the 5th Report 2008 (session 3) of the Scottish Parliament Local Government and Communities Committee, available at http://archive.scottish.parliament.uk.

6 Devolution to Northern Ireland was more difficult because of the history of 'direct rule' from 1972 in the context of the conflicts. Powers were devolved to a Northern Ireland Assembly in 1998 but the Assembly was dissolved on numerous occasions because of further conflicts until 2007 (Knox, 2009).

7 For a full review of the critique of planning in the early 2000s, with a list of sources, see Nadin (2007).

8 In addition, the 2010 government introduced a system of tariffs to compensate communities for loss of amenity and necessary infrastructure – which had been proposed by the former government. The coalition has not, at the time of writing, acted in any significant way on other proposals, notably limiting appeals in planning, introducing third party appeal rights, freeing up changes of use with a form of 'flexible zoning' and substantially limiting the power of inspectors to matters of process, leaving all substantive decisions to 'local people'.

References

Alber, J. (2006). The European social model and the United States. *European Union Politics*, 7(3), 393–419.

Allmendinger, P. (2001). The future of planning under a Scottish Parliament. *Town Planning Review*, 72(2), 121–148.

Allmendinger, P. (2006). Escaping policy gravity: the scope for distinctiveness in Scottish spatial planning. In M. Tewdwr-Jones and P. Allmendinger (eds) *Territory, Identity and Spatial Planning* (pp. 153–166). London: Routledge.

Allmendinger, P. and Haughton, G. (2012). Post-political spatial planning in England: a crisis of consensus? *Transactions of the Institute of British Geographers*, 37, 89–103.

Allmendinger, P. and Tewdwr-Jones, M. (2000). New Labour, new planning: the trajectory of planning in Blair's Britain. *Urban Studies*, 37(8), 1379–1402.

Allmendinger, P., Morphet, J. and Tewdwr-Jones, M. (2005). Devolution and the modernization of local government: prospects for spatial planning. *European Planning Studies*, 13(3), 350–370.

Amin, A., Massey, D. and Thrift, N. (2003). *Decentring the Nation: A Radical Approach to Regional Inequality*. London: Catalyst.

Barker, K. (2004). *The Barker Review of Housing Supply*. London: HM Treasury.

Barker, K. (2006). *The Barker Review of Land Use Planning: Final Report*. London: HM Treasury.

Barton, H., Horswell, M. and Millar, P. (2012). Neighbourhood accessibility and active travel. *Planning Practice and Research*, 27(2), 177–201.

Blundell, V. H. (1993). *Labour's Flawed Land Acts 1947–1976*. London: Economic and Social Science Research Association.

Booth, P. (1996). *Controlling Development: Certainty and Discretion in Europe, the USA and Hong Kong*. London: UCL Press.

Booth, P. (1999). Discretion in planning versus zoning. In J. B. Cullingworth (ed.) *British Planning: 50 Years of Urban and Regional Policy* (pp. 31–44). London: Athlone.

Breheny, M. and Hall, P. (1999). *The People: Where Will They Live?* London: TCPA.

Buitelaar, E. and Sorel, N. (2010). Between the rule of law and the quest for control: legal certainty in the Dutch planning system. *Land Use Policy*, 27(3), 983–989.

CEC – Commission of the European Communities. (1997). *The EU Compendium of Spatial Planning Systems and Policies*. Luxembourg: Office for Official Publications of the European Communities.

Champion, A. G. (1989). Counterurbanization in Britain. *Geographical Journal*, *155*(1), 52–80.

Clifford, B. P. (2013). Reform on the front line: reflections on implementing spatial planning in England, 2004–2008. *Planning Practice and Research*, *28*(4), 361–383.

Coe, N. M. and Jones, A. (2010). Introduction: the shifting geographies of the UK economy? In N. M. Coe and A. Jones (eds) *The Economic Geography of the UK* (pp. 3–11). London: Sage.

Commission Directive 85/337/EEC on the Assessment of the Effects of Certain Public and Private Projects on the Environment, Official Journal No. L 175, 05/07/1985, 40–48.

Commission Directive 92/43/EEC on the Conservation of Natural Habitats and of Wild Fauna and Flora, Official Journal No. L 206, 22/07/1992, 7–50.

Conservative Party. (2009). *Open Source Planning, Policy Green Paper No. 14*. London: The Conservative Party.

Cowell, R. (2012). The greenest government ever? Planning and sustainability in England after the May 2010 elections. *Planning Practice and Research*, *28*(1), 27–44.

CSD – Committee on Spatial Development. (1999). *The European Spatial Development Perspective*. Luxembourg: Office for Official Publications of the European Communities.

Cullingworth, B. and Nadin, V. (2006). *Town and Country Planning in the UK*. London: Routledge.

Cullingworth, J. B. (1980). *Land Values, Compensation and Betterment: Environmental Planning 1939–1969, Volume 4*. London: HMSO.

Cullingworth, J. B. (1997). British land-use planning: a failure to cope with change? *Urban Studies*, *34*, 945–960.

Davoudi, S. (2006). Evidence-based planning. *disP*, *42*(2), 14–24.

DCLG – Department for Communities and Local Government. (2012). *National Planning Policy Framework*. London: DCLG.

Doak, J. and Parker, G. (2005). Meaningful space? The challenge and meaning of participation and new spatial planning in England. *Planning Practice and Research*, *20*(1), 23–40.

Dorling, D. (2005). *Human Geography of the UK*. London: Sage.

Dorling, D. (2010). Persistent north–south divides. In N. M. Coe and A. Jones (eds) *The Economic Geography of the UK* (pp. 12–28). London: Sage.

DPEA – Department for Planning and Environmental Appeals, Scotland. (2008). *Report by Reporters Appointed by the Scottish Ministers, Case Reference: CIN/ABS/001*. Falkirk: DPEA.

DRDNI – Department for Regional Development, Northern Ireland. (2001). *Regional Development Strategy for Northern Ireland 2025*. Belfast: DRDNI.

DRDNI – Department for Regional Development, Northern Ireland. (2012). *Regional Development Strategy 2035: Building a Better Future*. Belfast: DRDNI.

DTLR – Department for Transport, Local Government and the Regions. (1998). *Modern Local Government: In Touch with the People*. London: HMSO.

Dühr, S., Colomb, C. and Nadin, V. (2010). *European Spatial Planning and Territorial Cooperation*. London: Routledge.

Esping-Andersen, G. (1990). *The Three Worlds of Welfare Capitalism*. Cambridge: Polity Press.

Evans, A. W. and Hartwich, O. (2005). *Unaffordable Housing: Fables and Myths*. London: The Policy Exchange.

Farinos Dasí, J. (2006). ESPON Project 2.3.2, Governance of Territorial and Urban Policies from EU to local level, final report. Esh-sur-Alzette: ESPON Coordination Unit.

Finlayson, A. (2009). Planning people: the ideology and rationality of New Labour. *Planning Practice and Research*, *25*(1), 11–22.

Foresight Land Use Futures Project. (2010). *Final Project Report*. London: Government Office for Science.

Gallent, N. and Robinson, S. (2012). *Neighbourhood Planning: Communities, Networks and Governance*. Bristol: Polity Press.

Grant, M. (2001). National-level institutions and decision-making processes of spatial planning in the United Kingdom. In R. Alterman (ed.) *National-level Planning in Democratic Countries: An International Comparison of City and Regional Policy-making* (pp. 105–126). Liverpool: Liverpool University Press.

Gunn, S. and Hillier, J. (in print). When uncertainty is interpreted as risk: an analysis of tensions relating to spatial planning reform in England. *Planning Practice and Research*.

Haughton, G., Allmendinger, P., Counsell, D. and Vigar, G. (2010). *The New Spatial Planning: Territorial Management with Soft Spaces and Fuzzy Boundaries*. London: Routledge.

Healey, P. (1997). *Collaborative Planning*. London: Macmillan.

HM Treasury. (2011). *National Infrastructure Plan 2011*. London: The Stationery Office.

Keating, M. (2006). Nationality, devolution and policy development in the United Kingdom. In M. Tewdwr-Jones and P. Allmendinger (eds) *Territory, Identity and Spatial Planning* (pp. 22–34). London: Routledge.

Kirkup, J. and Hope, C. (2011). Planning reforms: stop locals resisting developers. *The Telegraph*, 12 September.

Knox, C. (2009). The politics of local government reform in Northern Ireland. *Local Government Studies*, *35*(4), 435–455.

Land Use Consultants. (1995). *Effectiveness of Planning Policy Guidance Notes*. London: HMSO.

Liberal Democrats. (2010). *Liberal Democrat Manifesto 2010*. London: Liberal Democratic Party.

Lloyd, G. and Purves, G. (2009). Identity and territory: the creation of a national planning framework for Scotland. In S. Davoudi and I. Strange (eds) *Conceptions of Space and Place in Strategic Spatial Planning* (pp. 71–94). London: Routledge.

Massey, D. and Allen, J. (1988). *Uneven Re-development: Cities and Regions in Transition. A Reader*. Milton Keynes: Open University Press.

Monbiot, G. (2011). War with the Wullies. *The Guardian*, 26 September.

Moore, V. (2012). *A Practical Approach to Planning Law*. Oxford: Oxford University Press.

Moroni, S. (2007). Planning, liberty and the rule of law. *Planning Theory*, *6*(2), 146–163.

Morphet, J. (2004). *RTPI Scoping Paper on Integrated Planning*. Unpublished RTPI paper. London: Royal Town Planning Institute.

Morphet, J. (2011). *Effective Practice in Spatial Planning*. London: Routledge.

Morphet, J. and Pemberton, S. (2013). Regions out – sub-regions in. Can sub-regional planning break the mould? The view from England. *Planning Practice and Research*, *28*(4), 384–399.

Murray, M. (2009). Building consensus in contested spaces and places? The Regional Development Strategy for Northern Ireland. In S. Davoudi and I. Strange (eds) *Conceptions of Space and Place in Strategic Spatial Planning* (pp. 125–146). London: Routledge.

Muson, S. (2010). The geography of UK government finances: tax, spend and what lies in between. In N. M. Coe and A. Jones (eds) *The Economic Geography of the UK* (pp. 79–90). London: Sage.

Nadin, V. (2007). The emergence of spatial planning in England. *Planning Practice and Research*, *22*(1), 43–62.

Nadin, V. and Stead, D. (2008). European spatial planning systems, social models and learning. *disP*, *44*(1), 35–47.

Nadin, V. and Stead, D. (2011). Nationale ruimtelijke ordening in het Verenigd Koninkrijk [National spatial planning in the United Kingdom]. *Ruimte & Maatschappij [Space and Society]*, *3*, 49–72.

Nadin, V. and Stead, D. (2012). Opening up the compendium: an evaluation of international comparative planning research methodologies. *European Planning Studies*, *21*(10), 1542–1561.

ODPM – Office of the Deputy Prime Minister. (2004a). *Planning Policy Statement 11: Regional Spatial Strategies*. London: The Stationery Office.

ODPM – Office of the Deputy Prime Minister. (2004b). *Sustainable Communities: Building for the Future*. London: ODPM.

ONS – Office of National Statistics. (2012). *2011 Census: Population Estimates for the United Kingdom, 27 March 2011*. Newport: ONS.

Owen, S. (2002). From village design statements to parish plans: some pointers towards community decision making in the planning system in England. *Planning Practice and Research*, *17*(1), 81–89.

Oxley, M. (2004). *Economics, Planning and Housing*. Basingstoke: Palgrave Macmillan.

Pain, K. (2009). London: the pre-eminent global city. *Sciences Humaines, Les Grands Dossiers*, *17*, 30–32.

Pearce, N. and Paxton, W. (2005). *Social Justice: Building a Fairer Britain*. London: IPPR.

Phelps, N. (2012). *An Anatomy of Sprawl: Planning and Politics in Britain*. London: Routledge.

Raemakers, J., Prior, A. and Boyack, S. (1994). *Planning Guidance for Scotland: A Review of the Emerging New Scottish National Planning Policy Guidelines*. Edinburgh: Royal Town Planning Institute in Scotland.

RCEP – Royal Commission on Environmental Pollution. (2002). *Environmental Planning*. London: The Stationery Office.

Rogers, Lord R. (1999). *Towards an Urban Renaissance: Final Report of the Urban Task Force Chaired by Lord Rogers of Riverside*. London: Spon.

RTPI – Royal Town Planning Institute. (2000). *Fitness for Purpose: Quality in Development Plans*. London: RTPI.

RTPI – Royal Town Planning Institute. (2006). *Uniting Britain: The Evidence Base, Spatial Structure and Key Drivers*. London: RTPI.

Satsangi, M., Gallent, N. and Bevan, M. (2010). *The Rural Housing Question*. Bristol: Policy Press.

Scottish Government. (2004). *National Planning Framework for Scotland*. Edinburgh: The Scottish Government.

Scottish Government. (2009). *National Planning Framework for Scotland 2*. Edinburgh: The Scottish Government.

Scottish Government. (2013). *Planning Reform: Next Steps. The Scottish Government's Key Actions on Planning Reform*. Edinburgh: The Scottish Government.

Scottish Parliament. (1999). *Land Use Planning Under a Scottish Parliament*. Edinburgh: The Scottish Parliament.

Shapely, P. (2012). Governance in the post-war city: historical reflections on public–private partnerships in the UK. *International Journal of Urban and Regional Research*, 37(4), 1288–1304.

Shucksmith, M. (2009). Disintegrated rural development? Neo-endogenous rural development, planning and place-shaping in diffused power contexts. *Sociologia Ruralis*, 50(1), 1–14.

Stanley, K. and Lawton, K. (2007). *The Anglo-social Model: Space for Subsidiarity, Responsibility and Freedom*. Paper for IReR Seminar Governance: The Lombardy Way. London: Institute for Public Policy Research.

Stead, D. and Meijers, E. (2004). *Policy Integration in Practice: Some Experiences of Integrating Transport, Land-use Planning and Environmental Policies in Local Government*. Paper presented at the conference on the Human Dimensions of Global Environmental Change: Greening of Policies – Interlinkages and Policy Integration, Berlin.

Stead, D. and Nadin, V. (2009). Planning cultures between models of society and planning systems. In J. Knieling and F. Othengrafen (eds) *Planning Cultures in Europe: Decoding Cultural Phenomena in Urban and Regional Planning* (pp. 283–300). Aldershot: Ashgate.

Steel, J., Nadin, V., Daniels, R. and Westlake, T. (1995). *The Efficiency and Effectiveness of Local Plan Inquiries*. London: HMSO.

Stern, N. (2006). *The Economics of Climate Change: The Stern Review*. Cambridge: Cambridge University Press.

Swain, C., Marshall, T. and Baden, T. (eds) (2013). *English Regional Planning 2000–2010: Lessons for the Future*. London: Routledge.

Taylor, P. J. (2010). *UK Cities in Globalization, GaWC Research Bulletin 357*. Retrieved from www.lboro.ac.uk/gawc.

Taylor, P. J., Hoyler, M., Evans, D. M. and Harrison, J. (2010). Balancing London? A preliminary investigation of the 'core cities' and 'northern way' spatial policy initiatives using multi-city corporate and commercial law firms. *European Planning Studies*, 18, 1285–1299.

TCPA – Town and Country Planning Association. (2011). *England 2050? A Practical Vision for a National Spatial Strategy*. London: TCPA.

The Times (2011). Planning revolt fuels fears over economy. 1 September 2011.

Ward, S. V. (2004). *Planning and Urban Change* (2nd edn). London: Spon.

Welsh Government. (2004). *The Wales Spatial Plan: People, Places, Futures*. Cardiff: Welsh Government.

Welsh Government. (2008). *People, Places, Futures: The Wales Spatial Plan 2008 Update*. Cardiff: Welsh Government.

Wilson, E. and Piper, J. (2010). *Spatial Planning and Climate Change*. London: Routledge.

Zweigert, K. and Kötz, H. (translated by T. Weir) (2004). *An Introduction to Comparative Law* (3rd edn). Oxford: Oxford University Press.

Further reading

Allmendinger, P. and Haughton, G. (2013). The evolution and trajectories of English spatial governance: 'neoliberal' episodes in planning. *Planning Practice and Research*, *28*(1) 6–26.

Baker, M. and Wong, C. (2013). The delusion of strategic spatial planning: what's left after the Labour government's English regional experiment? *Planning Practice and Research*, *28*(1) 83–103.

11

CHANGING PLANNING IN THE CZECH REPUBLIC

Karel Maier

Chapter objectives

This chapter explains the following facts:

- Czech spatial planning was, in the past decades, exposed to both global and specific local pressures shared with other countries of the former Soviet domain. The combined effects of political and economic change coincided with an increased impact of delayed and, therefore, hurried international integration and globalization.
- The mission and priorities of planning have changed in the past two decades as a result of the political transformation. From a one-sided promotion of development nowadays, the official national priorities of planning follow the EU sustainability and competitiveness debate. The planning practice is more conservative: it remains based on a "value-free" role of a planner who executes the orders of those in power. Plans are expected to serve the interests of the state as well as the increasingly powerful developers lobbied by local politicians.
- The shift of planning concepts in the inertia of the practice widens the gap between the formal position of statutory "territorial" planning in terms of its maturity and legal powers on one side, and its actual effectiveness on the other. The recently emerged and looming issues of territorial disparities, sprawling suburbanization and spatial fragmentation are only slowly reflected by planning practice.

1 Introduction

A centralized hierarchy of planning that encompassed all societal and economic activities was embedded in the political doctrine of communist states. Spatial planning, however, was restricted to physical matters and as such was institutionalized as territorial planning (*územní plánování*). Separately, regional planning (*oblastní plánování*) served as the spatial outlet of national economic planning. As the term territorial planning is still in use, this will also be used in the following text.

During the two decades that have elapsed since the break-up of communist rule, Czech planning has had to adjust to essential changes in economy, society and also technology. The transformation of planning was constrained by an unfavorable political environment which often confused spatial (urban, regional, countryside) planning with the totalitarian control of the economy, and consequently society, characteristic of the past.

This chapter will provide a brief overview of the changing scene that has influenced planning since 1990; it will describe the actual state of the art in terms of traditions, legal frameworks, mission, maturity and role of planning; it will characterize major changes, problems and challenges; and it will describe the dimensions and directions of current changes in terms of public interest as a cornerstone of modern planning, actors and driving forces and the planners' role in the changing environment of planning. Planning ideas, doctrines and concepts along with the way in which they have been reflected in political agendas will be analyzed against this background.

The chapter is an outcome of the research project WD-07-07-4, "The conception of spatial planning and territorial disparities," supported by the Ministry for Regional Development of the Czech Republic and elaborated at the Czech Technical University in Prague.

2 Description of the system

2.1 Evolution of the planning environment

The two decades from the 1989 break-up can be divided into three periods: (1) transition, when basic strategic decisions were made; (2) transformation, in which reforms towards a market economy were in progress and democratic institutions were built; and (3) consolidation of new power elites and institutions connected with EU integration (cf. Wasilewski, 2001).

(1) The post-1989 transition was driven by the effort to release from the straightjacket of the "planned society." However, the vision of an alternative was not clear. It ranged from a mixed economy with a remarkable share of the communal sector, and the laissez-faire liberalism of the nineteenth century. In the end, the resulting "post-planned society" is based on a market economy and formal plural democracy but it has retained some fragments of both the initial extremes as well as the preceding communist system.

In this heterogeneous environment, the role and position of spatial planning was difficult to identify: the only shared view was that this would be acceptable and useful only if it were radically different from what had gone before. National economic planning and regional planning as its spatial tool, which had been responsible for the allocation of investments under a command economy, were abolished in 1990. However, formal continuity of territorial planning was retained as the 1976 Planning and Building Act and its planning instruments remained in force.

The reforms of the 1990s emphasized the strong position of communities, the total number of which exceeds 6,000 in a country with a total population of 10 million. They were charged with all local self-government responsibilities including planning. The consequent fragmentation of territorial planning into numerous, mostly small units resulted in its weak capacity to cope with pressure from private/privatized investors. Small municipalities did not have the capacity to establish and enforce policies to manage development activities. Instead of actively coordinating spatial activities, planning just reacted to particular projects in order to avoid the most obvious territorial conflicts.

(2) During the transformation and pre-accession period before 2004, the country introduced numerous institutions, instruments and procedures that made it compatible with EU

standards. A regional tier of governance was re-established at NUTS 3 level in 2001, with both elected councils and administration branches of the state. As the small village communities/municipalities were unable to manage the administration, new administrative units of Municipalities with Extended Powers were introduced and, in 2003, most administrative tasks including planning were transferred to them.

(3) The period of consolidation is closely connected to the EU accession and integration. As the country was not a member of the EU before 2004, it did not participate in the discussions that resulted in fundamental EU documents relevant to the spatial development of the EU, namely the European Spatial Development Perspective (ESDP) and the Lisbon and Gothenburg Agenda. Nevertheless, the regional and spatial policies of the EU were already part of the adjustment to EU standards of the pre-accession period, as was the introduction of certain EU-wide procedures (Strategic Environmental Assessment (SEA), following the EC Directive 2001/42/EC; CEC, 2001) and initiatives (European Common Indicators (ECI); CEC, 2002). These adjustments were mostly introduced in a top-down manner (Stead and Nadin, 2010, p. 157) using legal amendments; they were generally accepted as a prerequisite for EU accession. The state represented by national government acted as the gateway for the new, EU-born rules and procedures, while regions and municipalities received the EU standards via the national government. The horizontal flows of Europeanization (Stead and Nadin, 2010, p. 159) between the Czech Republic and other EU members were marginal, and circular flows from Czech planning back to the EU cannot be identified at all.

2.2 The nature of planning and the planning profession

The *EU Compendium of Spatial Planning Systems and Policies* (CEC, 1997) distinguished four major traditions of spatial planning in Europe: regional–economic; comprehensive/integrated planning; land-use planning; and urbanism (CEC, 1997, pp. 36–37). The *Compendium* did not cover the countries outside the EU at the time of the elaboration. Following the *Compendium* classification, the tradition of Czech, Slovak and the other planning systems of former parts of the Habsburg Monarchy is anchored in the urbanism (*Städtebau*) group, despite Austria being classified as comprehensive in the *Compendium*. The urbanism tradition was a base for blueprint designs of towns and villages typical for planning under communist rule.

This urbanism-based planning has been modified in the past two decades by influences from various sources. Visiting experts introduced strategic planning early in the 1990s (e.g. the Strategic Plan for Prague was elaborated under British guidance). Later, the land-use approach inspired some features of the 1990 amendments to the Planning and Building Law. More recently, comprehensive planning elements were introduced with the 2006/2008 national Spatial Planning Policy, namely the instruments of development areas and development axes.

Currently, the Czech planning system is a conglomeration of different approaches; there is a certain tension between the urbanism orientation prevailing among practicing planners, the law with land-use management elements in local planning, and comprehensive planning at the regional and national levels. While Stead and Nadin (2010, pp. 165–166) suggest that "the countries of Central and Eastern Europe are pressing forward in the creation of more

217

'comprehensive integrated' forms of spatial planning and to a lesser extent the 'regional economics' approach," it should be noted that Czech regional policy took inspiration from regional economics.

Planners professionally recruit from various academic backgrounds: there is no independent master's degree program in planning at Czech universities. Most spatial ("territorial") planners were trained as civil engineers or architects. Regional managers are often recruited from economists, and regional analysts are mostly geographers. The diverse professional background of planners and the fragmentation of planning in territorial management branches contribute to the weak identity of the profession.

2.3 Legal instruments for planning

Czech spatial management runs under the institutional duality of regional (economic) cohesion policy and territorial planning. The regional policy was introduced by the national government in 1998 but, until 2001, it had to deal with a lack of institutional environment, namely the non-existent regional tier of administration for spatial development (Figure 11.1). The Regional Development Act was enacted in 2000 with later amendments that adjusted it to the EU *acquis communataire* rules. Since EU accession, Czech regional policy has, in 2002, 2006, 2007 and 2009, been integrated in EU cohesion policy.

The Act requires that the national Strategy of Regional Development should be elaborated and updated regularly. The Strategy should use the outcomes of territorial planning and coordinate sectoral policies. In practice, sectoral policies frequently do not take spatial effects into account (Sýkora, 2006, pp. 114, 132).

State regional assistance is channeled to the Regions of the Concentrated Assistance of the State, as delimited in 1998 and since reviewed on the basis of multiple criteria among which unemployment rate plays a dominant role. The shifts in this delimitation reflect the changing nature of the problem: while rural peripheries were assisted in the 1990s, nowadays the old industrial regions of north-western Bohemia and the Moravian-Silesian (Ostrava) region receive assistance.

Since the accession to the EU in 2004, "cohesion regions" (NUTS 2) have been introduced as spatial units for the purposes of EU regional structural funds and programs. The NUTS 2 regions typically merge two or more administration regions (NUTS 3) of the country. Due to their size, the NUTS 2 regions often combine both territories with reasonably high prosperity and structurally weak territories.

The Planning and Building Act 2006 deals with territorial planning. Following more than a decade of patchwork amendments, it replaced the previous 1976 Act. The official aims of the new legislation were to streamline the process of development and to promote sustainable development as the ultimate aim of planned development. Following the requirement of the European Landscape Convention "to integrate landscape into its regional and town planning policies" (CEC, 1990, Art. 5b), landscape receives the same importance as the built environment in the 2006 Act. The hierarchical principle of planning has been strengthened, with the "higher" territorial level being binding for the "lower" ones, although regions can intervene in local development only in matters of regional importance.

To ensure improved and more effective information flows, the Act requires that a permanent database with all territory-relevant data on the levels of micro-regions and regions be developed, maintained and displayed on the internet. Particular investors and offices are to provide their relevant data to planning offices. The permanent database enables monitoring to become an integral part of planning: the reviewed analyses of the territorial data serve the periodic reviews of each local or regional plan, and the evaluation of sustainable development on local and regional levels.

The national Spatial Development Policy was introduced by the 2006 Act (Figure 11.2). The Policy sets national priorities for sustainable development as frameworks for regional and local planning and for the management of sustainable development. It identifies development areas, development axes and specific areas where the balance between environmental quality, social cohesion and the economy is corrupted, with requirements for planning and decision-making in these areas and on these axes. A set of area-specific requirements is another part of the policy, which mostly deals with the territorial impact of large projects for new motorways, roads and other infrastructures.

Apart from the planning legislation, the legal protection of resources and values in the public interest is provided by numerous specific laws, state agencies and mechanisms that represent specific public interests: nature protection, pollution control, monument conservation and protection of cultural heritage, protection of mineral resources, protection of forests and agricultural land, water management and protection of water resources, transport and energy infrastructures, etc. Each of these laws nominates a state agency that is entitled to raise comments in the planning process, and sets special rules and regulations for the delineated territories/areas of the specific public interest, such as national parks, protected landscape areas, territorial systems of ecologic stability, nature parks, water protection areas, conservation areas/zones, protected areas of mineral resources, etc.

2.4 Position of planning

The *EU Compendium of Spatial Planning Systems and Policies* defines maturity of planning by the provision of up-to-date policy instruments, vertical integration and cooperation between levels of administration, transparent and productive consultation and public acceptance of the need for planning and regulation (CEC, 1997, pp. 35 ff.). Following these criteria, the Czech planning system can be classified as mature. Planning instruments are clearly defined, they are regularly updated, and they are unified and coordinated, the upper tiers being binding for the lower tiers of plans. Specific public interests are represented in the planning process by the legally defined partners and the protected areas.

The legal power of territorial planning did not basically change during and after the transformation period, maintaining its binding/statutory character: any decision on a change of use of any piece of land within the area of a plan is obliged to follow the plan regulations. On the other hand, the official mission of planning as expressed in the law experienced several fundamental changes. The 1976 Act on Planning and Building insisted that "territorial planning is a component of societal controls. It solves systematically and comprehensively the functional use of land, provides the principles of its organization and coordinates in contents and time construction and other activities influencing the development of the area" (Act on Planning and Building 1976, §1(1)). The 1992 amendment deleted the first sentence about societal controls, leaving the mission unexpressed (Act on Planning and Building 1992,

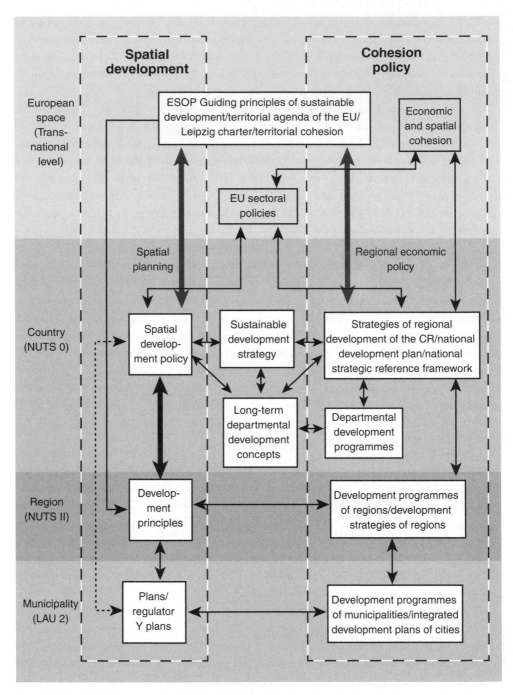

Figure 11.1 Institutional environment of Czech spatial management

Source: Spatial Development Policy (MMR, 2008)

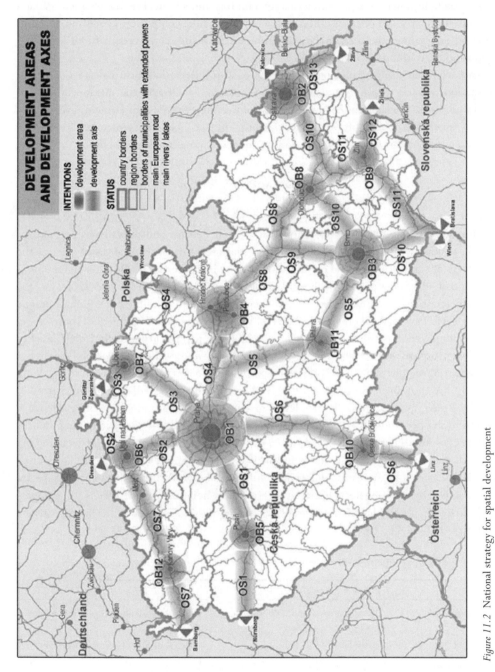

Figure 11.2 National strategy for spatial development

Source: Spatial Development Policy (MMR, 2008)

§1(1)). The current Act (2006) defines the mission of sustainable development for territorial planning as: "[to] constitute preconditions for building and sustainable development of land that consists in balanced relations of favorable environmental conditions, economic development and cohesion of the community, which meets contemporary needs without impeding living conditions in future generations" (§18(1)).

Apart from the changing mission, unspoken actual priorities that form the practice of and expectations related to planning also changed (Table 11.1). Despite the mission of sustainable development declared in the law, in terms of everyday practical application planning has evolved rather as a tool to promote development, often to the detriment of environmental protection and heritage conservation as well as other constituents of sustainability.

3 Problems and challenges

3.1 Recent and upcoming issues

(1) The economy has become the prime issue for all debates and prevailing criterion for decision-making related to spatial planning and management. Territorial disparities, as the side effects of transformation and privatization, loomed large in the 1990s, after the previous state control of the economy through regional planning had been abolished in 1990; later, the gap between prosperous and lagging regions stabilized. While the GDP per capita in Prague exceeds the EU average, all other regions (NUTS 3) show less than 75 percent of the average. Most regional centers still maintain their societal status and quality jobs, but their level of economic prosperity can hardly compete with regional centers in more developed countries. Old industrial regions and peripheral rural regions are affected by social downgrading. With relatively low housing costs, they are targeted by socially deprived, unemployed people, typically Roma, as a most mobile population group, while young and educated people leave for better job opportunities. This further strengthens the already existing gap in the potential of human resources between the booming capital metropolitan regions and the declining old industrial and peripheral rural regions. In this way, the economic disparities are aggravated by social polarization. Increasing differences in income between particular social groups are not welcomed by traditionally egalitarian Czechs even when the poverty share is still comparatively low: 9 percent compared to the EU 27 average of 16.5 percent after social transfers in 2008 (EUROSTAT, 2009).

Table 11.1 Changing environment and position of spatial/territorial planning

Period	Proclaimed mission of planning	Actual priorities
Before 1989	Support for social and economic development	Control spatial allocation of investment
1990–1998	Laissez-faire – enable the market to work	Survival of planning as an activity and profession Enable development
1998–2006	Coordinate and regulate development	Enforce public projects (infrastructure)
2006–	Sustainable development	Make development happen

(2) The environment, particularly environmental pollution, was one of the triggers for citizen protests that in the end contributed to the political break-up in 1989. Strong legal environmental protection was institutionalized in the first half of the 1990s, and the decline of heavy industry as a major pollution producer resulted in a remarkable decrease in pollution by industrial activities. Consequently, the environmental issues lost their priority in public opinion and disappeared from governmental agendas during the following transformation, which was focused on the economy. The pre-accession arrangements formally enforced environmental concerns in legal acts and procedures but they could hardly challenge the priority of economic growth in the agendas. Nowadays, environmental issues are returning to the public scene with more general scope, spanning from habitat protection to the quality of the living environment, public spaces and landscape.

(3) Demographic change results from the concurrence of increased life expectancy, delayed marriages and births, and low birth rates. The impact is currently moderated by the baby boomers born in the 1970s coming to reproductive age; but severe population decline with ageing is forecast for the following decade. Czech cities and towns have not suffered from shrinkage yet but, in the future, this may develop as a problem, especially for rural peripheries and some old industrial regions with a shortage of jobs.

An ageing population in general is considered a major social and economic problem for the future but its spatial dimensions have not been fully reflected. The issue has not been addressed either by territorial planning (which does not deal with non-physical phenomena) or by regional policies. The concept of cohesion is envisaged socially and territorially but not demographically. While rural areas far from major centers have traditionally been demographically "the oldest," the recent ageing affects housing estates in cities where the original residents are reaching retirement age. In this way, demographic segregation results from the previous housing policy (Musil, 1987, 2004). This may coincide with increasing social segregation because, for many, getting old means becoming poor. Seniors need easily accessible services and facilities while their purchasing power is weak.

(4) Opening the border proved to be a process rather than an act. The initial expectations of borderless connectedness and integration after the withdrawal of the Iron Curtain were only fragmentarily fulfilled. In most cases, the natural divides that mostly coincide with the national borders, as well as the absence of historical links between the communities living on the opposite sides of the border, proved to be strong factors.

During the transformation, the revitalization of the borderlands at the (West) German and Austrian borders was fueled by the disparity between the neighboring economies resulting in various gray economy activities. It was only gradually that cross-border businesses started to be based on more sustainable kinds of cooperation, and cross-border access to jobs and public services is still restricted. Planning endeavored to coordinate development and/ or improvement of transportation infrastructures between the neighboring areas, but the service of the new or improved links does not always fulfill expectations (e.g. some rail services with Poland were recently cancelled).

(5) Patterns of migration have also been changing. Unlike the previously prevailing movement from rural areas to cities and industrial regions, intra-national migration flows are more balanced now, but international in-migration is increasingly gaining importance. Migrants from Slovakia and from outside the EU (mostly from Vietnam, Ukraine and Russia)

help to compensate for the existing natural population decline. The number of foreign-born residents in the country increased from 266,000 in 2005 to 435,000 in 2010 (ČSÚ, 2010), which accounts for more than 4 percent of the total population nationally, but 12 percent of the population in Prague. Intra-nationally, the Roma population, which records a very high birth ratio, is extremely mobile. Romas seeking a job may in the future migrate from the old industrial regions where they mostly live now (enjoying the affordability of housing there) to flats in the cities vacated by the suburbanites.

Apart from the quantitative changes of population, the "qualitative" migration change in terms of the concentration of educated, well-paid populations in certain cities/city regions and localities within them may be significant. On a regional and national scale, it can be assumed (but not proved, owing to the continued lack of official data from the 2011 census) that the movement of young, educated people is from the eastern part of the country and from peripheral, rural and old industrial regions to Prague and, to a lesser degree, to other large centers, especially in the currently more prosperous western and southern parts of the country.

3.2 Problems of spatial development

Since the transformation, spatial trends have been similar to those in Western European cities and regions since the 1970s and 1980s. However, there are several features that may make the changes worthy of deeper consideration. The speed and relative scope of the changes expose the affected areas and communities to various challenges and pressures. Some aspects of the privatization process were further reaching than in most EU 15 countries, whereas private businesses did not exist and the market was attributed rather to the gray economy in pre-1989 Czechoslovakia.

(1) The territorial disparities are the central agenda of regional economic policy (see Figure 11.1). The actual shape and scope of the assistance of regional policy are, however, politically determined. The state started to intervene in the regional economy after 1998 with the policy of stimulating new jobs in industry to replace those that were lost from collapsing factories during the economic transformation. Potential investors, who initially preferred Prague and its immediate hinterlands, were offered new development sites in old industrial regions, with the state funding infrastructures in these areas. In this way, non-metropolitan regions were re-industrialized, keeping the unemployment rate reasonably low (under 5 percent before the current economic crisis). This policy helped to make use of the local skilled labor force and, in this way, prevented migration. The dark side of this policy was its insensitivity to the quality of the newly developed industry. In the new industrial investment, energy-demanding assembly plants prevailed, mostly the car industry, which appreciated booming East European markets and the low local wages of that time. The unstructured stimulation of new industrial site development also resulted in the excessive consumption of suburban land, while inside the same cities and townships, industrial brownfields were emerging at the same time.

On a smaller territorial scale, disparities have grown within cities and urban regions. As a most extreme indication of spatial social segregation, exclusion enclaves have emerged, especially in old working-class districts and housing estates in the declining old industrial regions

(MPSV, 2006; Sýkora, 2007; Sýkora et al., 2007; Toušek, 2011). In contrast, gentrification is changing certain attractive historical cores as well as selected fashionable inner-city districts, and gated communities have emerged in the last decade. While the regional disparities have been mitigated by regional policy and are thus nowadays in general stabilized, there has not yet been an adequate policy response to disparities on the local level, despite the proclaimed objective to deal with them in the Policy of Spatial Development.

(2) Suburbanization and urban sprawl are other outcomes of the shift from a planned society to liberalism. It was triggered in the 1990s by the boom of logistic, shopping and leisure centers on the urban fringe of major cities. The suburban housing boom followed at the end of the 1990s. Later, suburbanization also affected smaller cities and their hinterlands. Local mayors of small rural municipalities welcome prospects of growth for their villages, and they compete with each other by offering development sites in local plans. The new developments are not appropriately served by facilities, public services or infrastructures. Suburbanization has contributed to the dramatic increase of car traffic, and most suburban residential satellites have turned into bedroom communities for the core cities. Residential suburbanization also contributes to social polarization on the local level, as new developments are usually targeted at buyers with certain income levels. Although the economic crisis has slowed down the suburban boom recently, the sites earmarked for development remain available in local plans, often with buried investments in utilities, and both developers and local councils hope for recovery.

The planning response to sprawl was delayed and inadequate due to the absence of a regional tier in the 1990s, and the general mood of the "post-planned" society. It was only the Spatial Development Policy that stated the priority to "prevent [green zones] from development within the development areas and development axes in specific areas, where the landscape is adversely impacted by human activities; the goal is to preserve continuous zones of undeveloped spaces within the proximity of cities" (MMR, 2006, 2008). Obviously, this quite general statement cannot erase the vast tracts of developable land already approved in existing local plans or prevent developers and individual builders from building on the subdivided plots. Even with landscape protection and accessibility of facilities and infrastructure becoming an issue, the turn towards regional coordination and regulation of suburbanization and urban sprawl will be difficult and is already lagging behind the actual course of events.

(3) Fragmentation of the landscape as a side effect of the accelerated refurbishing of national infrastructure with new motorways and, to a lesser extent, improved waterways and railways receives less attention. So far, the only planning remedy consists of making artificial motorway crossings for animals. It has been estimated that the grade of fragmentation of the Czech landscape will catch up with that of Germany by 2020 (Anděl and Petržílka, 2009); the current economic crisis may cause delay, but it obviously cannot stop the trend.

Also, the planning response exists on a national level but it has had little practical effect. The Spatial Development Policy (MMR, 2006, 2008) states the requirement to "[p]reserve landscape penetrability and minimize landscape fragmentation when locating transport and technical infrastructure; if it is reasonable, locate these infrastructure into common corridors."

3.3 Priorities of planning

Fully in accordance with the implementation part of the Policy of Spatial Development, infrastructure and, in particular, transportation development are the priority of most plans. From the national scale to regional and local plans, all instruments of planning are required to create legal and technical preconditions for the development of new infrastructures. On the international scale, the Czech Republic initiated the coordination of national spatial strategies and cross-border infrastructure projects among the Visegrád states, Romania and Bulgaria (MMR, 2010).

With increasing competition for jobs and for residents as taxpayers among municipalities, local councils use plans to supply potential investors with developable sites, complementing the effort for infrastructure development. In practice, this supply-oriented planning policy often results in an exorbitant total amount of land being designed for development in certain regions, and in economically unsustainable spatial patterns, especially when the narrowly defined physical planning lacks an appropriate counterpart in adequate economic management and appraisal. Thus, the hopes of many have proved to be illusionary for small communities to increase their prosperity through planning new industrial sites. Also, social impacts from oversized growth are often underestimated or even ignored.

In contrast to development-oriented planning, there are several sectoral systems aimed at the protection of values (e.g. nature, cultural heritage, water and mineral resources). These protective systems entered planning from outside the system, to defend specific public interests. The 2006 Planning and Building Act attempted to soften this dividing line between development-oriented planning and "regressive" value protection by introducing a category of values for planning, especially architectural and urban ones. The planning values are identified by in-situ analyses and they are required to be considered in local plans.

Flood protection emerged as another major planning concern in the aftermath of the disastrous floods in 1997 and 2002 that affected large parts of the country. Planning efforts concentrate on protecting built-up areas from flooding and preventing development in areas at risk of flooding. Additionally, plans are made to improve the hydrologic conditions of the landscape, but they often remain unexecuted due to ownership and financial problems, and also owing to their long-term rather than immediate effects.

4 Dimensions and direction of change

4.1 Driving forces

(1) Privatization of nationalized state property including the restitution of the former private housing stock triggered a shift from public to private ownership in the first half of the 1990s. The housing restitutions were followed by the privatization of the original public housing stock from the second half of the twentieth century. Nowadays, most of the land and housing property is privately owned, including development sites indicated by plans. In the case of privatized multi-family housing, particular dwelling units were usually sold to "sitting" tenants. In this way, a block of flats may be co-owned by hundreds of individuals. Also former factory precincts, after their production had collapsed, were sometimes subdivided and leased or sold to different individuals for various uses. The fragmented pattern of property ownership often constrains any coordinated improvement action.

Planning activities were also privatized. In the post-1989 transition, the formerly state-controlled designing and planning institutes were privatized, and the Chief Architect Offices that had been responsible for planning in major cities were abolished. Since then, privately practicing planners, authorized by the Czech Chamber of Architects, offer their services to municipalities and regions on a market basis.

Since 1998, the administration and procuring of plans may be outsourced to private persons authorized for this activity. Since 2007, detailed local plans can be outsourced to private persons, and private, authorized "building inspectors" may replace Building Offices in the process of issuing a building permit. While the procedures performed by state agencies such as the Planning or Building Office fall fully under the scrutiny of appeal (and as such they have been criticized for bureaucracy and red tape), the new, outsourced institutions act swiftly and are outside external review as well as public control.

In general, all the above-mentioned aspects of privatization deeply affected the planning system as well as planning practice. In some respects, the privatization of planning went further than in "traditional" democracies of Western Europe.

(2) The impact of deregulation and the rule of law in planning has been less straightforward. Czech planning has definitely made a long journey from the pre-1990 blueprint plans towards current regulations based on legally defined public interests. The fragmented state of ownership, with often conflicting interests in the use of a territory, leads to emphasis on the formal legality of planning and the decision-making processes. Sometimes this happens on account of problems with content: legally difficult transformations are left out and the present unsatisfactory state is petrified instead. A "good plan" may then no longer be one with a strong concept that helps to improve quality of life, but one that successfully faces all objections and court appeals. This makes the scene of Czech planning "gray" as "form wins over contents, tool over objective, technology over creativity" (Černý, 2010, p. 13).

(3) An increasing influence of globalization resulting from the opening of the Czech economy in the 2000s followed the preceding 1990s wave of property privatization and deregulation. Now the Czech economy is heavily export oriented, with a small domestic market. Owing to weak domestic capital during the transformation, almost all large enterprises are now under the control of international capital (Brynda, 2011). Also, most of the investments in new industries and businesses has come from abroad. The global economy and multinational companies also increasingly influence the development strategies of regions and municipalities. The limited capacity, weak professional identity of planning and its "value free" doctrine (see below) make principal planning decisions subordinate to the interests of global capital.

The economic crisis and the consequent need for fundamental changes of the economy have not yet affected the new EU member states as deeply as in the case of, e.g., the Mediterranean. The 1990 economic transformation followed by the boom connected with EU accession made people in East-Central Europe believe that the current crisis will not require another basic transformation. Rather, the debate revolves around the financial sustainability of public budgets, leaving aside the "western" concerns of sustainable consumption of natural resources such as energy and land. Thus, the link between the debates on the economic crisis and on planning is not well pronounced.

4.2 Functions of planning

(1) The blueprint master planning from the pre-1989 era was abandoned, but the urbanism tradition of planning persists, especially at the local level. Many planners try to design cities and villages: they focus on the shape and network of spaces but also on the shape of buildings. The 2006 Planning and Building Act makes this possible on the grounds of landscape character as a legitimate public interest, especially at the fringe of built-up areas or in other visually sensitive places, but no general mechanism for the evaluation of design quality exists. Apart from the design function, the transformation of planning has brought new planning functions of relevance to a market economy with a plural society, multiple interests and a specific role for the public sector.

(2) The regulative function has replaced the former directive control. Local plans are required to specify and allocate permitted, conditioned and prohibited uses for each land-use zone. They also determine the intensity of urban use and the pattern of development in development areas. Detailed regulations for building shape are provided by detailed zoning plans. On the national and regional levels, regulation is restricted to enforcement of national/specific interests.

(3) The strategic function of planning was also introduced in the transformation period. Strategic plans were imported and introduced as being separate from territorial planning, but they have no legal basis and no statutory power. Nowadays, both territorial and strategic plans exist at all territorial levels. While territorial planning strives to be comprehensive, strategic plans are selective in terms of topics and issues. The original variety in methodology of developing strategic plans is currently tending to converge; but there are differences in their elaboration ranging from relying entirely on expert work to a participatory approach (Maier, 2000). The value of strategic planning, if evaluated by the frequency of references made to such plans (Faludi, 2000), is doubtful, as they often do not survive the election period of the council that procured the plan.

The strategic aspect of territorial planning was strengthened on the national and regional levels by the 2006 legislation. The law also tried to cope with the duality between strategic and territorial plans by requiring local (territorial) planning briefs to reflect existing strategic documents for the relevant region and/or municipality.

(4) With land, property and development having regained their market value, the information function of plans is becoming an important complement to the legal power of statutory planning documents as well as the indicative importance of strategies. Ideally, the plans should guarantee environmental quality and a certain standard accessibility of facilities and public services for residents, and they should also provide information about future development by indicating development opportunities. The value of such information is unfortunately impaired by numerous cases of tailor-made amendments to statutory plans for the benefit of powerful individuals; moreover, often conflicting with sustainability and the overall concept of the amended plan.

The entire territorial planning system remains deeply anchored in managing growth, rather than making better use of the existing resources. This makes the position of planning vis-à-vis the current economic crisis difficult.

4.3 Flexibility and certainty in planning and decision-making

The *EU Compendium* uses the criteria of flexibility and certainty for decision-making built into the national planning systems to distinguish between indicative and discretionary groups in European planning systems (CEC, 1997, p. 45). The indicative systems expect that decisions be clearly delineated by a binding detailed land-use plan; the discretionary systems expect guidance from plans through administrative and political discretion, rather than immediate decision-making.

Czech planning belongs to the indicative group, like other Central European planning systems. Decisions on any land-use change have to comply with the binding regulations of a plan. However, the plans allow a certain amount of discretion within the regulations: provision exists for individual consideration by a Building Office but only in the issues and within the discretionary limits indicated in the plan concerned.

If the intention of a property owner or a developer conflicts with the existing regulations relevant to the site, the owner/developer can apply for a change to the local plan. The process of negotiation and approval of such a change requires similar procedures to that of a new plan. The numbers of such applications for site regulation changes reach into the tens or even hundreds annually in larger cities. The law does not make any distinction between the procedures for minor changes and changes that would impact the entire district or a city (e.g. a new shopping center instead of a green area).

The discussion about flexibility versus certainty of plans is still ongoing. While political debate supports more flexibility in plans, the practice of making local land-use plans, which is under the jurisdiction of municipalities (e.g. self-governments of elected councilors), still prefers detailed regulations that are binding for the issuing of planning permissions and building permits by Building Offices (local branches of the central government). The move towards discretionary local plans, as often advocated by planners, may expose the planning authorities concerned to increased pressure from various interest groups, often backed by local politicians.

4.4 Planning culture and planning profession

Despite the changing planning environment and newly emerging problems and challenges, the very discipline and approaches of planning are strongly predetermined by "planning culture" (CULTPLAN, 2007, p. 11; Gullestrup, 2001). The planning culture is affected by the societal environment in which planning functions. It is determined by the conditions for and expectations of the planning activities and by the background of planning professionals. As a "soft" factor based on human attitudes, expectations and capacity, planning culture is characterized by deep path dependency. It is therefore useful to look as far back as pre-1989 history. Territorial and regional planning, which was fully subordinated to national economic planning, were reduced to a mere technique, without their own values. This "value-free" position persisted in the culture of planning even after the omnipresent state control had disappeared. Planners simply changed their "master" from the command-and-control state to the business interests of investors, developers and local politicians as the immediate clients of plan-making. Planners are expected to serve their clients, who make orders and pay for their fulfillment. Even the professional Ethical Code of the Czech Chamber of Architects (ČKA, 2008), as an umbrella institute that should guarantee quality and professionalism in architecture and spatial planning, has recently reduced responsibility to society to the mere prevention of conflicts of interest. In this way, the concept of service to the public has disappeared from the obligations of architects and planners altogether.

Within "value-free" planning, planners do not create visions for future development or future landscape changes. Rather, they are expected to push through the pretensions of developers and potential investors so that the requirements of the authorities and laws are met. Under these circumstances, the stated objective of sustainable development may easily be impinged upon in favor of the particular interests of local landowners, developers and councilors. Planners may use their professional skills to find explanations that stand up to the surveillance of regional authorities.

4.5 Planning concepts

The "value-free" (anti-)doctrine of current Czech planning eclectically mixes the concepts and ideas imported from the EU and adjusts them to the local interests represented by their clients. Since the ESDP (CEC, 1999), polycentric development has been considered a tool for more balanced territorial development leading to cohesion on a European scale. The Territorial Agenda of the EU makes the polycentric development of metropolitan regions, cities and urban areas one of the priorities of EU policy. The concept of polycentricity was incorporated in the 2006/2008 national Spatial Development Policy (MMR, 2006, 2008).

The theme of polycentric development is not new for Czech planning. Pre-1989, Czechoslovak regional planning sought a balance between jobs and housing within microregions. Christaller's central place theory was applied to develop a spatial pattern of evenly dispersed regional and sub-regional centers, each with its own serviced area. This pattern was exposed to an unregulated market in the 1990s, which led to soaring spatial disparities, common in all transforming countries of East-Central Europe at that time (Petrakos et al., 2005; REPUS, 2007). Recent development has strengthened the monocentricity (Sýkora, 2006).

The early post-1989 attempt to enhance regional centers was made by establishing new regional universities in the 1990s. The control and administrative position of regional centers was emphasized in 2001 when regional self-government and administration was (re-)introduced. Presently, the actual prosperity and attractiveness of the regional centers varies. The strengthening of some regional cities as "counterweight" centers can be expected only in certain cases, and within the national hierarchy they will continue as second rank centers. The REPUS (2007) project identified Brno as the undisputed second major center in the country, while Ostrava is affected by its past history of heavy industry. More recent studies (Maier et al., 2010) suggest that European integration might have a different impact on different parts of the country. Moravia and Czech Silesia may be exposed to the attraction of major centers in neighboring countries (Vienna and the Upper Silesian conurbation with Cracow), while Bohemia is likely to remain fully within the domain of Prague.

Sustainability was difficult to accomplish during the transformation when immediate challenges and problems prevailed over long-term considerations. Urgency made economic recovery and growth the overall priority, as has remained the case in planning until now.

The Strategy of Sustainable Development (MŽP, 2010 – amendment to the first Strategy from 2004) was developed with the time horizon of 2030. It identified the following priorities with respect to territorial development: (1) strengthening of territorial cohesion as a means for increasing economic and environmental potential, competitiveness and social level of regions. Cities should accelerate regional growth and harmonize relations between urban and rural parts; (2) improved quality of life by improved accessibility of services and culture, as well as better housing, another group of objectives; (3) more effective and strategic territorial planning, which helps land-use to be more efficient and protects unbuilt land from development; and (4) an efficient state with stabilized public finance, e-government and an institutionalized, non-profit sector collaborating with the public administration.

The Planning and Building Act (2006) makes the sustainable development of territory a central mission of planning. The ecological concern is treated as a "specific public interest," entering planning from the outside. Issues of social cohesion and economic durability, the other segments of sustainable development, remain conceptually weak in the considerations of planners and politicians, despite economic interests being the omnipresent priority.

Risks and threats are gaining increased importance vis-à-vis recent experiences of disastrous floods, news about terrorist attacks (as yet not in the country), concerns about energy safety and the vulnerability of major infrastructures. The traditional concept of town planning as a means to accomplish a "good city" (Lynch, 1981, pp. 111–239) is exposed to emerging new issues that planning has to cope with. This deflects the idea of planning from "making a good city" to "mitigating threats," and it directs the concern of planning towards resistance to undesirable events rather than reaching an optimum for all. Unlike the concept of sustainability that deals with society, the environment and the economy as a whole, the notion of resistance is often selective and even exclusionary: it encompasses rather limited issues, segments of population and/or areas of territory. It is in tune with decreasing social cohesion as a general trend shared with most developed countries.

4.6 Actors and powers of decision-making

(1) The state remains a prime actor in both territorial planning and regional policy. The hierarchical structure of planning with the state government and relevant ministries at the top is expected to define national priorities and enforce the public interest in spatial development from the national level to all lower levels of planning and decision-making.

Horizontally, specific public interests have their own legally defined powers and responsibilities, mostly with a territorial expression. The protection of a particular specific interest is almost absolute within the territorial and/or legal domain. The authorities can veto plan proposals if they interfere with their domain, but their powers may be weak when it comes to enforcing a specific interest outside of it. The fragmented system of protection of the specific public interests often results in conflicts in the territories where the domains of contrasting special interests overlap. To interpret public interest in any one particular planning case involves a complex intergovernmental play among the authorities, e.g. within planning but without public participation. The basic decisions take place behind the scenes – in negotiations and deals among councilors, planning offices, special interest authorities and developers. While the legal power of the state and its agencies is central in planning, their actual influence on what occurs is constrained by global actors on the economic side.

(2) Municipalities including small communities are another actor on the public side that has received ample rights and responsibilities in the context of local development. Neither state nor regional governments have the right to constrain local plans and consequent decisions as long as they do not interfere with national or regional policies, specific public interests and/or projects.

The power of the market challenges the legal power of the state and municipalities. Multinational companies are a prime investor and government officials listen carefully to these big players and make the development sites ready for them. On the local level, a coalition between the town hall and local business groups or developers is frequently an additional feature. The regional level of territorial planning and regional economic policy act as a policy pipeline from the national to the local level.

The interconnectedness between business and politicians and political clientelism are currently hot issues of public debate. During the transitional and transformation periods, business actors often tried to ignore or overrule planning; now they have found ways to drive planning "from the rear seat" through their connections to councilors and top officials. In this way, planning is shifting from its traditional mission of promoting and enforcing the public interest towards addressing particular economic interests.

(3) The position of civic society in planning procedures is legally clearly defined: citizens and citizen group representatives can raise their comments at all stages of the plan-making process. All the comments and positions must be considered and studied. The practice fulfills the legal minimum, but rarely goes beyond it, inviting citizens to be active participants of planning. Especially in large cities and with large projects, where the positions of citizens and potential investors are often contradictory, officers and developers often try to keep civic opponents away from relevant information. Citizens are sometimes portrayed as NIMBYists. Stead and Nadin (2010, p. 167) commented that the lack of progress on establishing more effective and democratic planning processes in some parts of Central and Eastern Europe is concerning.

Examples of the way civic society is treated were the recent cases of major road construction projects in Prague (the inner-city ring road tunnel where citizens were not fully informed about all the nuisances connected with the construction; the north-western section of the express ring road connecting the airport area and the motorway leading to Dresden that infringes on the protected nature area) and in Brno (the western motorway bypass of the city that cuts through a valuable natural environment). In all these cases, there was no consideration of public opponents who defended natural and cultural values against the "road concrete lobby" supported by councilors; while in the case of the north-western section of the motorway in Prague, the project became for a certain period a matter of controversy between the regions of Prague and Central Bohemia.

Civic society engagement declined following the wave of civic movements in 1989, but since around 2000 it has been steadily increasing. Citizen groups learned to seek professional help and in this way to improve their chances of reaching their objectives. As in many other cases, external help and input from more established democracies represented, e.g., by the EU is still crucial for the sustainability of this trend.

(4) The power of planners as an expert profession is ambiguous. Legal representation of planners is provided by the Czech Chamber of Architects with the prerequisite of membership

of an independent planning business. However, this professional representation covers only a segment of the fragmented profession, not encompassing administrators and regional managers. Informally, planning professionals are considered as the executive arms for the planning process, rather than experts who should be listened to.

All in all, the whole planning process is far from being communicative in the sense of Habermas (1987, pp. 297–298) or collaborative following Healey (1997, pp. 284–315); it is rather characterized by power conflicts with fighting and power coalitions behind the scenes, as described by Flyvbjerg (1998). From the command and control style of the state, it shifted to a similar style that encompasses state and municipal interests driven from behind by developers and major investors. The role of citizen groups has seldom reached a level where involvement has been more than taking a protesting stance in large cities and with large projects. It is only in smaller municipalities where citizens' voices are sometimes listened to when developing strategies.

5 Conclusion

The actual transformation of planning occurred with the introduction of EU standards, procedures and concepts, and with the multiplying of planning functions. The institutional continuity of the planning system in the post-1989 transition proved an asset, as did the empowerment of the municipalities that received ample rights and responsibilities for decisions on local development. The legal instruments of planning reflected deep societal and economic changes, as the planning profession was affected by privatization and outsourcing. On the other hand, the societal environment as well as the path dependency and inertia of "value-free" planning suppressed deeper conceptual changes in planning culture.

"Value-free" planning is still conceived as a technique rather than a conceptual effort. The inherent doctrine of planning is missing. Consequently, planning culture remains somewhere back in the 1970s and 1980s when planners were requested to just execute the commands of governmental economic plans. However, unlike the pre-1989 era, there is no central directive "master" for planning, which makes it difficult for planners lacking their own doctrine to resist pressures from various power and business groups. Consequently, the shared European concepts of polycentric development, sustainability and risk management/ mitigation of threats are conceived as being external to the planning agenda, while planning practice is exposed to the problems of spatial disparities, pollution, natural disasters and the risk of infrastructural collapse. Organizationally, the separation of regional policy and strategic planning from territorial planning limits the scope of intervention by particular planning institutions and contributes to its weakened effectiveness.

Planning is a tool, and people use it for accomplishing their aims. The current model of spatial planning serves the state and municipal politicians, and through them the powerful actors, namely investors and developers. In a polarized society that has difficulties in communication and that, instead of win–win solutions, believes in the necessity of win–lose results, planning serves the winning side of the power game. Consequently, the officially proclaimed planning goals of sustainable development and the mission of public wealth traditionally embedded in the institutions of spatial planning are compromised by compliance with the interests of major players.

References

Anděl, P. and Petržílka, L. (2009). Vývoj fragmentace krajiny dopravou v ČR v letech 1980–2040 [The development of landscape fragmentation in the Czech Republic in 1980–2040]. *Proceedings of the 18th Conference ESRI*, 50–56.

Brynda, R. (2011). Umíst'ování výrobních závodů a průmyslových zón v Ústeckém kraji. *Urbanismus a územní rozvoj XIV*, 1, 44–51.

CEC – Commission of the European Communities. (1990). *European Landscape Convention*. Retrieved from http://conventions.coe.int/Treaty

CEC – Commission of the European Communities. (1997). *The EU Compendium of Spatial Planning Systems and Policies*. Luxembourg: Office for Official Publications of the European Communities.

CEC – Commission of the European Communities. (1999). *European Spatial Development Perspective (ESDP)*. Luxembourg: Office for Official Publications of the European Communities.

CEC – Commission of the European Communities. (2001). *Directive 2001/42/EC of the European Parliament and of the Council, on the Assessment of the Effects of Certain Plans and Programmes on the Environment*. Luxembourg: Office for Official Publications of the European Communities.

CEC – Commission of the European Communities. (2002). *Towards a Local Sustainability: European Common Indicators*. Retrieved from http://ec.europa.eu/environment/urban/common_indicators.htm.

Černý, Z. (2010). GIS: dobrý sluha, ale špatný pán [GIS: a good servant but evil master]. *Aktuality AUÚP, 81*, 10–13.

ČKA – Česká komora architektů [Czech Chamber of Architects]. (2008). *Profesní a etický r̆ád* [*Professional and Ethical Code*]. Czech Chamber of Architects. Retrieved from www.cka.cc.

ČSÚ – Český statistický úřad [Czech Statistical Office]. (2010). Statistical data on population. Retrieved from www.czso.cz/csu/cizinci.nsf/kapitola/ciz_pocet_cizincu.

CULTPLAN. (2007). *Cultural Differences in European Cooperation: Learning from INTERREG Practice*. Retrieved from www.cultplan.org.

EUROSTAT. (2009). At-risk-of-poverty rate after social transfers by gender. Retrieved from http://epp.eurostat.ec.europa.eu/portal/page/portal.

Faludi, A. (2000). The performance of spatial planning. *Planning Practice and Research, 15*(4), 299–318.

Flyvbjerg, B. (1998). Rationality and power: democracy in practice. In S. Campbell and S. S. Fainstein (eds) *Readings in Planning Theory* (2nd edn) (pp. 318–329). Oxford: Blackwell.

Gullestrup, H. (2001). The complexity of intercultural communication in cross-cultural management. In J. Allwood and B. Dorriots (eds) *Anthropological Linguistics 27 – Intercultural Communication – Business and the Internet*, 5th NIC Symposium. Gothenburg.

Habermas, J. (1987). *The Philosophical Discourse of Modernity: Twelve Lectures*. Cambridge, MA: MIT Press.

Healey, P. (1997). *Collaborative Planning*. London: Macmillan Press.

Lynch, K. (1981). *Good City Form*. Cambridge, MA: Massachusetts Institute of Technology.

Maier, K. (2000). The role of strategic planning in the development of Czech towns and regions. *Planning Practice and Research, 15*(3), 247–255.

Maier, K., Mulíček, O. and Franke, D. (2010). Vývoj regionalizace a vliv infrastruktur na atraktivitu území České republiky [Development of regionalization and the influence of infrastructures on the attractiveness of the territory of the Czech Republic]. *Urbanismus a územní rozvoj XIII*, 5, 71–82.

MMR – Ministry for Regional Development. (2006). Spatial Development Policy 2006. Retrieved from www.mmr.cz/getmedia/23ca2d77-697f-4db4-b2c8-7de17fbfed3d/PUR_eng.

MMR – Ministry for Regional Development. (2008). Spatial Development Policy 2008. Retrieved from www.mmr.cz/getdoc/ef497e10-bb4f-4c7e-9253-b6ba24f41751/Politika-uzemniho-rozvoje-CR-2008----v-anglickem-j.

MMR – Ministry for Regional Development. (2010). *Společný dokument územního rozvoje států V4+2* [*Common Document of the V4+2 States*]. Praha: MMR.

MPSV – Ministry of Labour and Social Issues. (2006). *Analýza sociálně vyloučených romských lokalit a komunit a absorpční kapacity subjektů působících v této oblasti* [*Analysis of Socially Excluded Roma Localities and Communities, and Absorbing Capacity of Subjects in this Area*]. Retrieved from www.esfcr.cz/mapa/souhrn_info.html.

Musil, J. (1987). Housing policy and the sociospatial structure of cities in a socialist country: the example of Prague. *International Journal of Urban and Regional Research, 1*, 27–36.

Musil, J. (2004). *Srovnání vývoje struktury obyvatelstva v C̆R a v jiných státech v Evrope̮* [*Comparison of the Development of Population Structure in the Czech Republic and Other European States*]. Proceedings of the ForArch Conference. Prague: ABF.

MŽP (Ministry of Environment). (2010). *Strategický rámec udržitelného rozvoje ČR* [*Strategic Framework of Sustainable Development*]. Retrieved from www.mzp.cz/C1257458002F0DC7/cz/strategie_udrzitelneho_rozvoje/$FILE/KM-SRUR_CZ-20100602.pdf.

Petrakos, G., Psychari, Y. and Kallioras, D. (2005). Regional disparities in EU enlargement countries. In D. Felsenstein and B. Portnov (eds) *Regional Disparities in Small Countries* (pp. 233–250). Berlin/Heidelberg/New York: Springer.

REPUS. (2007). INTERREG IIIB CADSES Project, *Strategy for a Regional Polycentric Urban System in Central Eastern Europe – Final Report: Regional Polycentric Urban System*. Budapest: VÁTI.

Stead, D. and Nadin, V. (2010). Shifts in territorial governance and the Europeanization of spatial planning in Central and Eastern Europe. *Territorial Development, Cohesion and Spatial Planning* (pp. 154–177). London: Routledge.

Sýkora, I. (2006). Urban development, policy and planning in the Czech Republic and Prague. In U. Altrock, S. Günter, S. Huning and D. Peters (eds) *Spatial Planning and Urban Development in the New EU Member States: From Adjustment to Reinvention* (pp. 113–140). Aldershot: Ashgate.

Sýkora, L. (2007). Social inequalities in urban areas and their relationships with competitiveness in the Czech Republic. *Social Inequalities in Urban Areas and Globalization: The Case of Central Europe*. Pécs: Centre for Regional Studies of Hungarian Academy of Science.

Sýkora, L., Maier, K., Drbohlav, D., Ouředníček, M., Temelová, J., Janská, E., Čermáková, D., Posová, D. and Novák, J. (2007). *Segregace v České republice* [*Segregation in the Czech Republic*]. Prague: Charles University.

Toušek, L. (2011). *Sociální vyloučení a prostorová segregace*. Plzeň: Centrum aplikované antropologie a terénního výzkumu, Katedra antropologických a historických věd FF ZČU. Retrieved from http://antropologie.zcu.cz/socialni-vylouceni-a-prostorova-segregace.

Wasilewski, J. (2001). Three elites of the Central-East European democratization. In R. Markowski and E. Wnuk-Lipiński (eds) *Transformative Paths in Central and Eastern Europe* (pp. 133–142). Warszawa: Instytut Studiów Politycznych Polskiej Akademii Nauk.

Further reading

Kostelecký, T. and Čermák, D. (2004). *Metropolitan Areas in the Czech Republic: Definitions, Basic Characteristics, Patterns of Suburbanisation and Their Impact on Political Behaviour*. Prague: Sociological Institute.

Maier, K. (2011a). The pursuit of balanced territorial development: the realities and complexities of the cohesion agenda. In N. Adams, G. Cotella and R. Nunes (eds) *Territorial Development, Cohesion and Spatial Planning* (pp. 266–290). London: Routledge.

Maier, K. (2011b). Changing spatial pattern of East-Central Europe. In L. Mierzejewska and M. Wdowricka (eds) *Contemporary Problems of Urban and Regional Development* (pp. 113–131). Poznań: Boguck.

Maier, K. (2012). Europeanization and changing planning in East-Central Europe: an easterner's view. *Planning Practice and Research*, 27(1), 137–154.

Pichler-Milanovič, N., Gutry-Korycka, M. and Rink, D. (2007). Sprawl in the post-socialist city: the changing economic and institutional context of central and eastern European cities. In C. Couch, L. Leontidou and G. Petchel-Held (eds) *Urban Sprawl in Europe Landscapes: Land-Use Change and Policy* (pp. 102–135). Oxford: Blackwell.

Sýkora, L. (2007). The Czech case study: social inequalities in urban areas and their relationships with competitiveness in the Czech Republic. In V. Szirmai (ed.) *Social Inequalities in Urban Areas and Globalization: The Case of Central Europe* (pp. 77–104). Pécs: Centre for Regional Studies of Hungarian Academy of Science.

12

SPATIAL AND STRATEGIC PLANNING IN TURKEY

Institutional change and new challenges

Gülden Erkut and Ervin Sezgin

Chapter objectives

The chapter aims to describe:

- the Turkish planning system in a national–historical context;
- the introduction of strategic planning, legal obstacles and political challenges in Turkey;
- the administrative reforms and the effects of central government on the planning system;
- central governments' big projects and the deterioration of the municipal plan (the case of Istanbul), referring to the emergence of new actors in the Turkish planning system;
- the role of Regional Development Agencies in the Turkish planning system; and
- the shift of state power, from central to local and back again.

1 Introduction

The aim of this chapter is to introduce the Turkish planning system and its institutional background from a historical perspective, delineate key changes that have taken place in the last decade and indicate conflicts and pitfalls within the planning system through reference to some current experiences in Turkey. The chapter focuses on the following questions and issues:

- What have been the major changes in the planning system at national, regional and local levels in Turkey, especially in the past two decades? Which new institutions have been introduced?
- What are the dimensions and directions of change concerning legislative and institutional reforms, central–local relations, public–private partnerships and scales?
- Which key actors have emerged as powerful factors influencing major planning decisions and urban/regional change?
- What are the challenges to the fostering of regional and urban development in the near future?

This chapter is structured as follows: after briefly describing the current position of the planning system in Turkey, which has developed from the 1920s, the basic problems and challenges of the existing situation are presented in section 2. In section 3, attention then turns to the dimensions and direction of change, before section 4 examines the emerging actors and their influence on planning practices, with reference to strategic planning in Istanbul. Based on concrete spatial planning practices in the metropolitan area of Istanbul and Thrace, section 5 analyzes new perspectives and challenges that may prove to be obstacles to the fostering of regional and urban development in the near future. The chapter ends with concluding remarks regarding the planning system in Turkey.

2 Features, problems and challenges of the spatial planning system in Turkey

Based on a short description of the main historical periods, the socio-economic and legislative changes affecting spatial planning in Turkey are presented in this section. Furthermore, the main driving forces influencing planning changes, both internal (administrative reforms, neoliberal political agenda) and external (EU accession process, globalization), are analyzed, providing information about legislative and institutional change and the raison d'être.

In Turkey, urban policy and urban planning processes are affected by major social, economic, political, demographic and technological transformations. Five distinctive periods separated by socio-political and socio-economic breaking points can be defined within the time of the Turkish Republic. First was the nation-state building period, starting from the establishment of the republic and lasting until World War II. This period was characterized by a strong centralization tendency in accordance with the nation building process. An important aspect of this process was the citizen exchange between the Greek community living in Turkey and the Turkish community living in Greece. This resulted in Turkey, especially Istanbul, losing important skilled labor. In terms of spatial planning, the invitations extended to French and German experts to plan, respectively, Istanbul and the newly established capital Ankara were the key events of the period. These first experiments shaped planning tradition and education in Turkey.

The second period is between World War II and the "Planned Development Period" (1945–1960). Characteristic of this period were relatively high rates of industrialization and mobilization that were dependent on American Marshall Aid and were followed by massive rural–urban migration. The first illegal housing neighborhoods were established in big cities such as Istanbul at this time in order to accommodate the cheap labor necessary for the growing industrial sector. With foreign experts continuing to be invited to Turkey, several cities in Anatolia were planned in a second wave after Istanbul and Ankara. Planning education also took place in faculties of architecture, although not in independent departments but rather as part of urbanism courses.

The third period is called the "Planned Development Period" (1960–1980), referring to the establishment of the State Planning Organization (SPO) in 1960 and the introduction of the first five-year national development plan in 1963, prepared by the SPO. From this time until its recent transformation into the Ministry of Development in 2012, the SPO was responsible for preparing the five-year[1] development plans, which were primarily oriented towards economic development, lacked detailed spatial decisions, and were not considered as the basis for spatial plans at the regional and provincial levels, except in terms of their role in the allocation of public investments. They were, and still continue to be, the highest level of the Turkish planning hierarchy. These plans were prepared by selected experts from related fields, including spatial planning. The first regional development plans for the Zonguldak and Çukurova regions were also developed in this period by the SPO. The establishment of the first City and Regional Planning department at the Middle East Technical University, Ankara, also corresponds with the beginning of the period.

The fourth phase covers the time between 1980 and 2000. It is considered to start with the so-called "24 January Decisions" made on 24 January 1980 that devalued the Turkish lira, initiated a large privatization program and opened up the Turkish economy for foreign investment. In other words, a neo-liberal agenda was introduced in Turkey, which later in that year, on 12 September, was fortified by a military coup (Boratav, 2007, p. 145). Although a radical change in the planning context was not observed, the high migration rate and continuing informal housing development process settled down in the urban context of Turkey. The end of the period is marked by two important incidents, namely the 1999 Marmara earthquake and the 1999 Helsinki Summit of the EU that opened possibilities for the Turkish candidacy to the EU. The impacts of these two events have strongly shaped planning practices and the urban transformation of Turkey in the last decade. The Marmara earthquake caused the deaths of more than 18,000 people. The number of buildings demolished or seriously damaged exceeded 100,000, 90 percent of which were housing units. Afterwards, this situation was used as the justification for many urban renewal projects all around Turkey. Even the extension of the duties and rights of the Mass Housing Authority (TOKI) was legalized by the Law on Transformation of Areas with Disaster Risks 6306, 15 May 2012. Meanwhile, the EU candidacy brought with it the necessity of harmonizing Turkish laws and legislation with the *acquis communautaire*, including areas of public administration and spatial planning.

The fifth period covers the last decade and, together with the two incidents mentioned above, signifies a social and economic transformation of the country in terms of legal and institutional structure, urbanization process and planning practices. Indeed, the evaluation of this period will be the aim of the following discussion.

The main characteristics of these periods, and their impact on space, planning activities and specific legislative developments, are summarized in Table 12.1, which highlights the ways that the planning institution responded to major socio-economic changes.

Within the past two decades, changes in spatial planning in Turkey were anchored by the trend towards strategic spatial planning and multi-level governance, as was also the case in recent decades in Europe. Reforms in the public administration laws, amendments of existing laws, privatization and related project-based planning activities characterize this period.

Turkey is a unitary state with a strong centralist tradition. The central state dominates all levels of sub-national government by hierarchical decision-making and executes control over local government. Local administration consists of three main administrative tiers, namely Special Provincial Administrations, Municipalities or Greater Municipalities and Village Administrations. Municipalities are administrative units governed by directly elected mayors and primarily represent the urban areas of the related provinces and districts. They are responsible for producing the development (1/5,000 scaled) and implementation plans (1/1,000 scaled) in their jurisdictions. This duty was transferred from central government in

Table 12.1 Social, spatial and legislative change in Turkey

Periods	Main characteristics and developments	Impact on space and planning	Legislative development, institutions, actors
1923–1945	• After the Republic, nation-state building period • Developing a national economy • Population exchange caused loss of skilled labor and population loss in Istanbul	• Ankara is the new capital city • Foreign experts are invited for planning competitions • H. Jansen, Ankara Master Plan (1927); H. Prost, Istanbul Plan (1936); Ernst Reuter (advisor of Ataturk, founder of Urban and Regional Planning Chair in Ankara University) • Population increase in Ankara	• Municipality Law 1580/1930–1936 • General Health Law 1953
1945–1960	• Starting from World War II up to the Planned Development Period • Mechanization in agriculture by Marshall Aid	• Migration from rural to urban areas • Housing need increased • First generation of unauthorized/squatter housing • Dual housing market: formal/informal	• In 1954 the Turkish Chamber of Architects and Engineers established • After 1955, Istanbul Technical University, Political Science Faculty in Ankara and Fine Art Academy in Istanbul became influential in planning • Ministry of Housing and Resettlement established in 1958
1960–1980	• Planned Development Period • Five-year development plans starting from 1963	• Zonguldak Regional Plan in 1961 and Çukurova Plan in 1962 • SPO responsible for regional economic development plans	• State Planning Organization (SPO) established in 1960 • Undergraduate education in city planning started in 1961 at the Middle East Technical University in Ankara • Squatter Law 3191/1966 • Chamber of City Planners established in 1968
1980–2000	• Following 1999 Helsinki Summit, EU accession period • Neo-liberal economic policies and globalization • Europeanization	• Marmara region earthquake in 1999, Earthquake Master Plan for Istanbul	• Development Law 3194/1985

Continued

Table 12.1 Social, spatial and legislative change in Turkey, *continued*

Periods	Main characteristics and developments	Impact on space and planning	Legislative development, institutions, actors
2000+	• Public administration reform, devolution • Privatization	• 26 NUTS 2 (Nomenclature of Territorial Units for Statistics) regions and 12 NUTS 1 regions defined • Corporate Strategic Plans of public bodies required and prepared • Metropolitan Plan of Istanbul by IMP (Istanbul Metropolitan Planning Office) • OECD Territorial Review of Istanbul • Environmental Plans of NUTS 2 regions • Regional Plans of NUTS 2 regions	• Public Procurement Law 4734/4 January 2002 • New public administration Laws of Municipality 5215/9 July 2004 and Metropolitan Municipality 5216/10 July 2004 • Provincial Special Administration Law 5302/22 February 2005 • Union of Local Administrations Law 5355/26 May2005 • Urban Regeneration Law 5366/16 June 2005 • Development Agency Law 5449/25 January 2006 • Ministerial reorganization in 2011 by decree law • Newly formed Ministry of Development, Decree Law KHK/641 – 3 June 2011; Ministry of Environment and Urbanism, Decree Law KHK/644 – 29 June 2011 • Law on Transformation of Areas with Disaster Risks 6306/16 May 2012 • Law on establishing 13 new greater city municipalities, 6360/12 November 2012

Source: Prepared by the authors after Eraydın (2011) and Tekeli (1994)

1985 through the Development Law 3194/1985. Greater municipalities can be considered as metropolitan municipalities, which in addition to district mayors have a provincial mayor who is responsible for the coordination of all district municipalities in the entire province and for supplying necessary services at the provincial scale. Village administrations are responsible for the rural villages and have almost no planning authority, except in allowing construction in the settled area of the village and regulating the use of the commons of the village. The special provincial administrations are the representatives of the central government at the provincial level. They are governed by the governors and general secretaries under them, who are appointed by central government. The responsibilities of these administrations start at the rural areas that are outside the boundaries of any municipality. Moreover, these administrative units have the right to prepare the so-called "provincial environmental plans" at scales of 1/100,000 or 1/50,000 that identify the main strategies and development axes of provinces. Hence, the lower-scale plans prepared by municipalities have to comply with the main decisions laid down in the plans prepared by the special provincial administrations.

Two points should be noted at this point, which are further elaborated in the following sections of this chapter. First, the responsibility of preparing environmental plans is borne not only by the special provincial administration but also by the Ministry of Environment and Urbanism. This has caused confusion among authorities, leading to the preparation of some plans being hindered until recently. Second, the existence of special provincial administrations is currently being questioned in Turkey, and recent reforms in public administration have led to these units being abandoned in at least some provinces.

As may be expected, the planning system is characterized by similar features to this top-down, centralist administrative system. A hierarchical, statutory planning system is responsible for land-use planning and development control in Turkey (Türk and Korthals, 2010). Mainstream planning consists of two levels. The first level consists of regional plans and environmental plans, first produced by the newly established Regional Development Agencies (RDAs) and for the NUTS 2 level regions (Figure 12.1), and later produced either by special provincial administrations or the Ministry of Environment and Urbanism for the related provinces or a group of provinces in some cases. The second level consists of development plans and implementation plans produced by the municipalities.

A summary of data regarding the spatial planning system in Turkey is provided in Table 12.2.

Figure 12.1 NUTS 2 level regions in Turkey

Table 12.2 A summary of data regarding the spatial planning system in Turkey

Plan type	Scale	Attributes	Planning responsibility
National development plan	No physical scale The whole country	• Prepared for five-year periods • Includes broad development frameworks or perspectives	Prepared by commissions of experts under the authority of the SPO (recently the Ministry of Development)
Regional plans	No physical scale NUTS 2 regions	• Socio-economic development plans • Planning units are NUTS 2 level regions • Aim to be strategic planning documents for local economic development	Regional Development Agencies of the related regions are responsible for preparing these plans
Environmental plans	1/100,000 1/50,000	• Prepared at the provincial (NUTS 3) or regional level. • Regional level is rarely used and mainly defined by river basin boundaries	Under the authority of the Ministry of Environment and Urbanism or Special Provincial Administrations
		• Physical land-use plans • Prepared due to Special Provincial Administration Law 5302/2005	Can be prepared collaboratively with the related institutions such as metropolitan municipalities, governorships and the Ministry of Environment and Urbanism
Physical development plans	1/25,000 1/5,000	• Local plans • Prepared due to Development Law 3194/1985	Prepared by municipalities at city or metropolitan city level
Implementation plans	1/1,000	• Prepared due to Development Law 3194/1985	Local plans prepared by the district municipalities

Although there is a clear hierarchical organization in the Turkish planning system, there is no vertical or horizontal functional integration and no consistency between scales. The regional plans are not clearly introduced as binding documents for the lower-level plans, and they are also more oriented towards economic development than towards spatial decision-making. Furthermore, planning practices are piecemeal and authority issues are complicated (e.g. bureaucratic delays, lack of coordination between authorities). That is, on a given spatial level there is more than one planning authority. In a related context, for a given spatial unit there is more than one planning document. There are many different levels of plans and the regional level is particularly weak, since the regional development plans were not prepared until 2011.

The interdisciplinary nature of the planning process is not institutionalized. Participatory decision-making tools and mechanisms are insufficient at each planning level. Development plans are mostly physical land-use plans that create and allocate rent; in addition they are incapable of producing sustainable and livable spaces and environments. In order to overcome fragmentation of the planning authority, ministerial restructuring has recently been undertaken. Providing it functions properly, the newly formed Ministry of Environment and Urbanism might be seen as creating an opportunity to coordinate planning practices, since the role of setting standards and requirements for all physical plans is given to that ministry by law (Law 644, 29 June 2011). The same law also allocates the duty of preparing and monitoring the implementation of "strategic spatial plans"; however, this falls to RDAs – hence the preparation of regional plans is under the authority of another newly established ministry, the Ministry of Development.

The *EU Compendium of Spatial Planning Systems and Policies* (EC, 1997) does not include Turkey. However, if we intend to categorize the Turkish planning system of the 1990s in one of the four "ideal types" of the *Compendium*, we would argue that it has most similarities with the "urbanism" planning tradition. This is because it is dominated by the features of a "regulatory" planning perspective (building permissions, land-use, statutory plans) based on hierarchical structures, command and control mechanisms, paternalistic style and a strong legalistic tradition. However, *ad hoc* and *ex post* implementation of statutory planning regulations cannot adequately resolve the problems (e.g. unofficial housing). The challenges in addressing the aforementioned problems could be: adopting contemporary spatial planning principles of participatory planning; environmental concerns; new planning tools; shifting towards strategic spatial planning; linking spatial planning and regional socio-economic development; and overcoming the fragmentation of different planning authorities.

3 Dimensions and directions of change in the planning system

Brenner (2001, p. 603) discusses understanding geographical scale and distinguishing it from other major dimensions of socio-spatial structuration:

> Recent contributions to the analysis of scale production and scale transformation thus hold the promise of providing scholars with a still more precise, differentiated and rigorous theoretical vocabulary for socio-spatial analysis than that which had been developed during the preceding two decades. To realize this theoretical potential however, it is crucial to distinguish what might be termed scalar structurations of social space – which involve relations of hierarchization and rehierarchization among vertically differentiated spatial units – from other forms of socio-spatial structuration, such as place-making, localization and territorialization, whose theoretical foundations are currently relatively well developed within human geography.

The transformation of the spatial planning system in Turkey has arguably been taking place for some considerable time and is associated with a wider framework that is broadly defined as the "public administration reform." Influenced by neoliberal discourses of new public management, a major reform of public administration and spatial planning has been implemented in Turkey since the 2000s. In the last decade, as a response to wider concerns about sustainable development, globalization and Europeanization and the related changing institutional context, new visions have been set up for planning that attempt to increase efficiency at the regional level. Among the major components of this change are the introduction of the NUTS system for the definition of regions, the establishment of regional development agencies for the regions at NUTS 2 level, changing the statutes of 13 municipalities to create larger (metropolitan) municipalities so that there is now a total of 29 greater municipalities, abandoning the special provincial administration units in these provinces with Law 6360 dated 12 November 2012 and the redefinition of the status of TOKI, thus allowing it to construct mass housing projects and introduce urban renewal projects throughout Turkey without having to comply with any plans. Through amendments to the TOKI Law 2985/1984, TOKI was furthermore given the authority to clear or rehabilitate squatter areas and to develop squatter transformation projects.

The spatial planning agenda in Turkey thus changed, also in accordance with the EU territorial policy in the light of a multidimensional framework. There is strong emphasis on strategic planning and communicative planning. City councils are supporting public participation and collaborative planning. In a related context, the decentralization of public administration has been considered a key priority in Turkey since the early 2000s. New public administration was proposed in the draft Public Administration Basic Law and later came into force with Municipality Law 5393/2005, Metropolitan Municipality Law 5216/2004 and Special Provincial Administration Law 5302/2005 (published in the Official Gazette).

Although there is increasing interest in and support for legislative reforms, the scale of "region" as an administrative unit is still problematic, due to political issues related to national sovereignty. In a related context, an administrative system that strengthens the role of regions and tends towards more fiscal and political autonomy is considered as a separatist threat by central government.

Directions of change in spatial planning thus concern the institutional capacity, central–local relations and public–private partnerships. A tendency to move from a comprehensive to a strategic planning approach could also be observed.

The legislative reforms related to metropolitan governance and urban and regional development management focus on the following issues:

- Institutional capacity building, and better management through strategic planning at the institutional level

The RDAs are responsible for preparing strategic development documents for their regions. Moreover, the new public administration laws such as Municipality Law 5393/2005, Metropolitan Municipality Law 5216/2004 and Special Provincial Administration Law 5302/2005 necessitate that all public institutions as well as municipalities and local governments should prepare strategic plans. Tewdwr-Jones and McNeill (2000) assess four key components that have engendered this sense of strategic policymaking over the past few years: central government funding opportunities through partnerships; the emergence of regional planning; the creation of regional development agencies with an urban remit; and opportunities provided by European Union funding mechanisms.

- Decentralization of competences and fiscal power to local authorities

New laws enable local municipalities to enjoy more local tax income generated by the real estate market and other local financial resources, which provides the necessary funds to implement a local strategy of development and enhance fiscal autonomy. The new law for metropolitan municipalities has transferred a substantial amount of central government responsibilities to the metropolitan municipalities. Previously, the provincial administration was responsible for planning the whole area of the province. This has not only broadened the spatial borders of authority, but also increased spheres of responsibility. The need for strategic planning within new extended boundaries (functional urban/metropolitan areas) has been acknowledged.

- Enabling private–public, non-governmental organization partnerships

Though the municipalities could already in the past establish different types of partnerships with the private sector, the new Municipality Law 5393/2005 (item 76) provides that a city council should be established in a way that enables the representation of different socio-economic groups. The recent Regional Development Agency Law 5549/2006 enables an organizational form of private–public and non-governmental organization partnership that might be the key to successful strategic planning at the urban region level.

Although such legal and institutional change has paved the way for better conditions for decision-making and the implementation of strategic plans, the planning approach itself has remained relatively conventional, without clear identification of the roles of actors or forms of cooperation between these actors

In Turkey, a major setback is that national development planning and spatial planning systems and strategies are not related. The national development plans have been harmonized with the EU system; the 9th National Development Plan for 2007–2013 has been prepared with the use of information from Community Strategic Guidelines (CEC, 2005). However, there has been no consideration of the spatial perspective – hence their influence on the lower-tier spatial plans is limited.

The spatial planning context in Turkey, together with all the institutional transformations experienced in the past two decades, brings to mind Brenner's (2001) paragraph cited at the beginning of this section. The "hierarchization and rehierarchization among vertically differentiated spatial units" could be argued to be the best way of describing the current condition. On the one hand, there are the attempts to decentralize public administration, as could be observed in the introduction of RDAs, their responsibility for the preparation of regional development plans and the increases in the jurisdiction areas of many municipalities and their financial resources. This tendency increases the necessity and the importance of the regional level and of the preparation of spatial regional development plans. However, on the other hand, these decentralization attempts are clearly diminished in favor of central government when high amounts of urban rent are involved. This is seen by the emergence of central actors (e.g. TOKI) with permission to bypass local spatial development plans. Equally indicative are large-scale and impulsive decisions on the part of central government, such as the construction of a new settlement for one million inhabitants, the building of an international airport in the north of Istanbul and the Canal Istanbul project that is to create an artificial channel from Marmara Sea to the Black Sea (Kundak and Baypınar, 2011). A further current example that is highly criticized by the public is the decision to build a third bridge across the Bosphorus. Such a massive transportation decision was not taken in the current Plan of

Istanbul, mainly due to environmental concerns, but was decided upon by the Ministry of Transport in Ankara. This decision indicates the power of central government over the institution of planning. Figure 12.2 indicates large-scale urban development projects that are not included in the Istanbul Environmental Plan but are imposed by central government.

A functional classification of these projects is displayed in Table 12.3. These projects caused much public discussion and were criticized by professionals; however, central government insisted on their construction despite negative public opinion. Such large-scale urban development projects, as indicated by Swyngedouw et al. (2002), are usually poorly integrated with existing plans and are used for central government takeovers of local authorities with the purpose of intervening in urban policies at first hand.

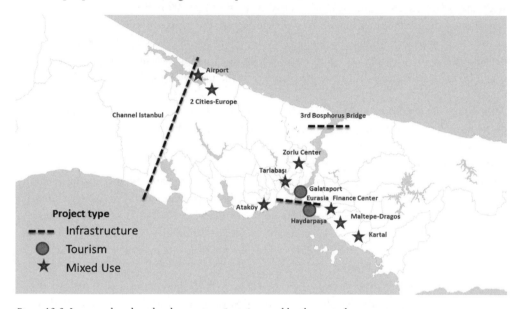

Figure 12.2 Large-scale urban development projects imposed by the central government

Table 12.3 Recent large-scale urban development projects in Istanbul

Type of project	Name of project
Infrastructure projects	Third bridge over Bosphorus
	Third airport
	Eurasia Tunnel Project
	Channel Istanbul
	Taksim Pedestrianization Project
Tourism projects	Haydarpaşa
	Galataport
Mixed projects (Housing + Office + Service + Culture)	Zorlu Center
	Ataköy Tourism Center
	Finance Center – Ataşehir
	2-Cities Project

Regarding spatial planning, bureaucrats, academics and professionals at the Urbanization Council (UC) in March 2010 agreed that a national spatial planning approach is needed to guide spatial development patterns and lower-tier spatial plans (UC, 2010). Another point raised by the UC is that the national spatial strategies should be related to the strategies set up by the National Development Plan.

On this point, it is promising to see one of the priorities in the 9th Development Plan's (2007–2013) annual program for 2012 (Ministry of Development, 2011, p. 134) was as follows:

socio-economic development policies and spatial development policies will be more integrated, and a strategic planning structure will be formed to direct the physical plan, its implementation and the built environment. Spatial strategic plans will be prepared in order to strengthen the relationship between regional and spatial development planning and urbanization and physical development.

In mid-2012, the Ministry of Environment and Urbanism commissioned a new project for the preparation, implementation and monitoring of strategic spatial planning.

4 Emerging actors and their influence on decision-making and urban/regional change

Which key actors have emerged as a powerful influence on major planning decisions and urban/regional change? What are their relations with the comprehensive and integrated planning approaches? This section aims to focus on these questions by giving examples from both spatial and strategic planning practices within a multi-level administrative and spatial framework, and project implementation on the level of the metropolitan region of Istanbul.

Istanbul has been one of the fastest-growing metropolitan regions both in Turkey and among other OECD member countries (OECD, 2008). Traditionally, from the 1950s onwards, the city attracted internal migrants from Eastern Anatolia and the Black Sea area. As a consequence, unauthorized housing, called *gecekondu* in Turkish, emerged as a specific type of land-use in Istanbul and other big cities. After the 1990s, when international migration emerged as a new phenomenon in Turkey, immigrants from Africa and the Middle East moved to these settlements too.

With the largest concentration of high value-added productive activities in the country, Istanbul is the leading economy in Turkey and generates almost one-quarter of the country's GDP. The concentration of output in Istanbul contributes to the large regional disparities in the country. Following the enlargement of the boundaries of the Greater Municipality to cover provincial boundaries, the Istanbul Metropolitan Municipality and Provincial Special Administration both became responsible for the planning issues of Istanbul. This was the first instance of the boundary enlargement of a metropolitan municipality in Turkey. Later, planning responsibility was transferred solely to the Metropolitan Municipality of Istanbul, a development towards a unified planning approach. The province of Istanbul is at the same time an administrative unit at NUTS 3, NUTS 2 and NUTS 1 levels.

In 1995, the Istanbul Metropolitan Area Master Plan (a comprehensive master plan focused only on land-use) was cancelled due to legislative limitations (the mismatch between legislative borders mentioned above) on the authority of the metropolitan municipality. Four years later, in 1999, the European Spatial Development Perspective (ESDP) was introduced (EC, 1999). The necessity of establishing vertical and horizontal relationships between local and governmental authorities was a key concern of the document. It was also mentioned that job creation should be a main priority in order to overcome regional inequalities. However, due to the 1999 earthquake, the main planning priority became disaster prevention and risk management. Lack of a legislative background and institutional capacity also prevented the integration of the ESDP policies in the planning agenda in Istanbul. Such a complex situation engendered a chaotic environment where planning practices go hand in hand with the involvement of more and more societal, private and governmental actors whose actions are not easily controlled by formal and binding spatial plans whatever the scale (Dühr et al., 2010, p. 58).

As cited by Loewendahl-Ertugal (2004):

> The lack of a planning approach is closely related to the existence of rent-economy in Istanbul (Tekeli, 1994, p. 37). It is argued that certain interest groups have expectations of rent, which is causing reluctance to do planning. There are politicians and administrators who depend on these certain interest groups, who therefore do not want plans that will restrict their freedom of manoeuvre in sharing the rent with these interest groups.

The current (2007) metropolitan planning experience of the Istanbul Metropolitan Area provides some basic information that is vital for the future of the urban and regional planning system in Turkey and its links with related European policies. The successful integration of Turkey into the European Union depends not only on effective macroeconomic policies, but perhaps even more on the successful integration of Turkish urban and regional systems into those of the EU, creating value and increased quality of life for both citizens of Turkey and the EU. This section thus aims to draw attention to some of the problems related to the real position of Istanbul within the global and European urban system, and the challenges of targeting competitive strategic decisions coherently in line with the local needs of urban society and of the nation.

One of the challenges lies in the analytical problems related to the lack of international data at the city level that focus on the particular relation of cities in specific economic sectors, cultural systems and socio-demographic changes. Although there is a pool of data at the scale of the nation state, the current global urban–regional system imposes a need to better understand interrelations between cities in different countries.

Another challenge lies within the very heart of the national policy which focuses on export-oriented industrial growth, although elsewhere many policy decisions demonstrate that the development of producer and distributive services has also become vital for the on-going competitiveness of the country. This establishes a field of conflict between ideas of decentralization and the re-clustering of industrial activities, and interests (especially in Istanbul) to develop the (financial) service sectors and high-quality distributive services such as telecommunication services, high speed rail systems, etc.

It all becomes additionally complicated for local urban–regional planners who have to face these challenges when the legislative base for planning and territorial management changes quickly, in line with that in other EU or OECD countries. The complexity of these problems is exacerbated by continuous decentralization of administrative authority to local governmental systems and the strengthening of the Ministry of Development (former SPO) as an institution that establishes the informative and financial background for development policies. Nonetheless, it is the case that the Ministry of Development provides the basic grounds for strategic planning that enable urban–regional governments to adapt better to the challenges imposed by the new competitive domains of the global environment.

The latest (2007) plan for the Istanbul province was prepared by the newly established Istanbul Metropolitan Planning Office (IMP) and BİMTAŞ, a public–private partnership of the municipality. The background research and analysis of the metropolitan plan was drawn up with contributions from academics and a large number of planners. NGOs such as the Human Settlement Association and pressure groups such as the Chamber of Planners and Chamber of Architects criticized the lack of participation in the planning process as the contribution and role of the actors were not programmed in advance.

Many other strategic plans have been simultaneously made for Istanbul, due to changes in the law. Though these strategic plans are corporate strategic plans, they will usually have a spatial influence. There are also the current master plans (spatial) of districts, the new corporate strategic plans of these district municipalities, and thematic plans such as the Earthquake Master Plan and the Historical Peninsula Area Management Plan. The OECD Territorial Review of Istanbul (2008) takes up the visions of all these plans by suggesting that strategies towards development in tourism, logistics and finance are of key importance for authorities involved in the strategic spatial development of the city.

Both the lack of institutional capacity at the local level and the legislative framework has handicapped the preparation and implementation of a spatial strategic plan for Istanbul. At the local level, considering typologies of urban projects, Ünsal (2007) named four different categories of projects that involve actors from various backgrounds:

- "Imposed projects" by powerful actors such as developers and real estate agencies. For instance the Galataport project, a cruise ship marina surrounded by shopping centers, hotels and recreational spaces; Haydarpaşa Port, which aims to transform the major historical train station into a seven-star hotel surrounded by a marina, a yacht club, a cruise ship port, office buildings and shopping centers; and Dubai Towers.
- "Macroform stretching projects" by TOKI.
- "Benefit for all projects" such as projects by the Pendik municipality.
- "Community-based projects" such as those in Gülsuyu realized with the participation of some academics.

Despite the decentralization of planning to the local level, a contradiction can be seen in the increasing impact of central government on the metropolitan city of Istanbul, which in the case of some tools can be evaluated as re-centralization. For example, the imposed projects are realized by TOKI (through the law governing mass housing), the Ministry of Culture and Tourism (through the law regarding tourism incentives) and the Directorate of Privatization (through the Privatization Law). Another tool is the Redevelopment Law, which came into force by changing an item in the Municipality Law. Through this law it became possible to designate transformation zones and proceed with project-based implementations in urban renewal areas. The key actors here were district and metropolitan municipalities. For the historical areas, another law came into force, namely the Urban Regeneration Law 5366/2005, which should be implemented by the related municipalities.

Lovering (2009) states that the architectural and urban design fashions are associated with the "neoliberal era," and he evaluates the actors involved in the mega-projects of Istanbul: "the developers and local politicians get on with business as they like it … The lack of public information about major developments is extraordinary from a West European viewpoint, as is the general lack of public concern about it."

As evidence of public concern, we can mention the *ad hoc* urban resistance groups formed to resist the relocation of vulnerable groups of Romany residents from Sulukule and Tarlabaşı.

5 Perspectives for and new challenges to the fostering of regional and urban development and strategic spatial planning

What could be the obstacles to the fostering of regional and urban development in the near future? What are the key technical/professional and institutional problems related to the planning system that might hamper urban and regional development? What intervention points could be suggested for the future of the Turkish planning system? This section will try to elaborate on these questions with the help of a study by Erkut et al. (2007), which provides some important insights to the issue, based on a case study about cross-border cooperation and strategic planning in the West Marmara region. The study briefly demonstrates that the impacts of administrative reforms are not clearly observable in practice and that the issues related to territorial dimensions mentioned in the Cohesion Policy are problematic in the case of the West Marmara region. As an ex-ante analysis on the RDAs, it also points out that neither public nor private institutions have sufficient knowledge about RDAs. Some key findings of the study suggest that:

- The local governments are not completely aware of problems in their own regions related to growth and employment, economic diversification of rural areas and cooperation with local, national, transnational and interregional partners to enhance competitiveness, achieve economies of scale and increase innovativeness.
- They also face significant difficulties in achieving financial support, experience problems related to human resources and know-how, and do not follow spatial development strategies established collaboratively.
- The RDAs are not integrated within the administrative system and planning context of Turkey. The regional plans produced by development agencies contribute to the existing confusion of overlapping authorities within a defined region.

In the case of Istanbul, some planning challenges and institutional problems also arise. Through the beginning of the twenty-first century, Istanbul was the largest financial center in Turkey, and the largest industrial agglomerate together with the surrounding settlements. Though Istanbul's role in the Turkish economy has regained much weight, its role in the global city-region system has not attracted much attention until recently.

While decentralization of governance has been a key policy concern, the result is the emergence of multiple actors at different hierarchical levels that claim power in this global city region, using strategic planning frameworks to validate their roles. This is one of the sources of conflict based on place, locality and identity. The framework of spatial strategic planning is hollow and seems to be used to implement a set of projects that markets support. In Turkey, the strategic planning framework is very new. Since it is in its infancy, it is perhaps not yet hollow but is rather hard to fill with solid strategies based on good regional analysis and collaborative decision-making. Furthermore, the milieu of planning has not yet fully internalized the concept of strategic spatial planning. It is thus open to exploitation by various actors. It can be said that Turkey is trying to participate in the revival of strategic planning in the Western world, since now more local actors have learned about aspects of strategic planning and its potential outcomes, and more voices call for increased social integration and justice. As stated by Lovering (2009), the "problematic nature of urban development in Turkey manifests in the built environment and the weakness of political culture." In the case of Istanbul, it is still not clear whether it will be possible to establish a network of actors that will be able to provide a full framework of spatial strategic planning which incorporates not only market-oriented projects but also socio-economic and ecological strategies that will help the integration of this global city region with either international or national development priorities and with regional and sub-regional development priorities.

Finally, to draw some conclusions from the previous sections, at the regional level it could be argued that in Turkey regional plans prepared by RDAs are not perceived as statutory, their spatial dimension is underestimated and they only provide a basis for regional economic strategies. The short-term agenda of these institutions seems to be the allocation of national and EU pre-accession funds and investment promotion rather than the provision of strategic development frameworks and regional plans. But there are attempts to overcome this problem, as indicated in the annual program of the Ministry of Development.

Apart from the RDAs, the strategic planning concepts are extensively used but not internalized among planning institutions. Strategic planning thought still needs to be understood by stakeholders. In these terms, a new understanding of planning is needed. A National Spatial Strategic Plan should be developed with the participation of all relevant parties. A new law on "Urbanization and Planning" has to come into force with the sole target of coordinating and harmonizing the planning system. There is urgent need for a National Spatial Strategy and spatial strategies at lower levels, as was also mentioned by the UC. The participation mechanisms of the planning process should also be clearly defined.

6 Conclusion

In Turkey, the planning agenda focuses on looking for ways of integrating the traditional comprehensive land-use planning approach with strategic spatial planning. The forthcoming years are critical for Turkish local governmental institutions to learn how to incorporate different stakeholders in the implementation of strategic decisions, and how to integrate institutional strategies with those strategies necessary for regional development and competitiveness. Though the new legislative foundation provides a much better environment especially for metropolitan governments such as that of Istanbul, the learning process in terms of inter- and intra-institutional relations seems to constitute a challenge to those involved in strategic planning processes (Erkut et al., 2006).

Another major limitation for the successful development and implementation of strategies at the metropolitan level is the lack of data on international and cross-border relations. It seems to be one major obstacle that will continue to hamper the strategic planning processes under current conditions.

This is a critical moment for Istanbul, as the city is likely to be the Turkish region most affected by the integration process with the EU. The planning system thus needs to incorporate a research and development agenda that focuses on the precise positioning of Istanbul within south-eastern European space, on its contribution to the stability and welfare of the region, and on adding value to Europe as a competitive urban region. Some of the focuses of such an agenda should cover a better understanding of cross-border relations, international law that enables and limits cross-border cooperation, local development priorities and their compliance with international interests, and better identification of the roles and capacities of local actors.

For Turkey, with regard to the obstacles and developments discussed above, there are then five major areas in the planning agenda that require immediate intervention (Erkut, 2008). First is urban and regional governance and its institutional background. Certain setbacks that have been identified are the lack of human resources, analytical tools and a knowledge base, inter-disciplinarity and professional diversity. The institutions concerned should therefore employ planners and other professionals involved in the issues, and should provide necessary organizational change to accommodate such technocrats.

Second, a better integration of local actors into the strategic spatial planning system is required, as this will ease communication between these actors and local governments. Institutions should seek for and demand reliable knowledge and expertise, and concentrate this on the issues mentioned above, in the EU Cohesion Policy and EU Neighbourhood Policy, as well as in the document on the "Territorial State and the Perspectives of the EU."

Third, in relation to the transformation of the planning system, there is a demand for new roles for planners. Turkish professionals should be able to satisfy the sophisticated demands of local governments, requiring that the profession accommodate a more inter-disciplinary approach and not just employ those with traditional educational backgrounds. Geographers (both physical and economic–cultural), sociologists, development economists, environmental planners, public administrators and others should be able to find ways to participate in a spatial strategic planning system with a solid legislative and institutional basis. The current stock of planners should develop new skills and learn new knowledge through contact with other disciplines and through professional certification programs. To provide such a workforce, universities should implement necessary reforms in their academic programs, approaches and organization, employ those capable of executing research in these fields and disseminate knowledge through undergraduate or postgraduate programs as well as certificate programs for professionals. Universities should be able to execute research to support such strategic spatial planning activities and to support the professionals as well as the technocrats and public administrators involved in these activities. Universities should also create more knowledge available to the public to facilitate the better functioning of city councils and NGOs.

The fourth major concern requiring urgent action is that the critical actors in society should be more aware of the issues at stake. While there is plenty of tacit knowledge that could be used effectively to attain the objectives identified in the 9th National Development Plan and EU Cohesion Policy, the absence of capable actors poses a barrier to the transfer of this tacit knowledge into knowledge useful for strategic spatial planning. In this sense, central government, local governments, professionals, universities and NGOs should feel responsible and disseminate knowledge.

Last but not least, to support all such activities, Turkey should not face difficulties in achieving financial and technical support. The Instrument for Pre-Accession Assistance (IPA) that allocates the EU integration funds to Turkey could be used effectively in strategic spatial planning.

Overall, the evaluation of the planning system in Turkey indicates trends towards decentralization and re-centralization at the same time. The driving forces of the changes are globalization, Europeanization and the neoliberal intervention of the central government at different scales. Concerning power relations, multi-actor planning practices in the form of new coalitions have emerged. The private sector has gained a new role in planning. An increasing need and efforts to integrate the planning system and other sector policies such as regional development policy can be observed. As the analysis of Istanbul planning activities indicates, the coexistence of different planning practices such as statutory planning, strategic planning and project planning is practiced. The planning system is trying to find ways to cope with new problems and challenges.

Note

1 The 9th development plan was prepared for seven years (2007–2013) with the purpose of harmonizing the Turkish planning system with the EU.

References

Boratav, K. (2007). *Türkiye İktisad Tarihi 1908–2005* [*Economic History of Turkey 1908–2005*]. Istanbul: Imge Kitabevi.

Brenner, N. (2001). The limits to scale? Methodological reflections on scalar structuration. *Progress in Human Geography*, *25*(4), 591–614.

CEC – Commission of the European Communities. (2005). Communication from the Commission, Cohesion Policy in Support of Growth and Jobs: Community Strategic Guidelines, 2007–2013. Brussels: Commission of the European Communities.

Dühr, S., Colomb, C. and Nadin, V. (2010). *European Spatial Planning and Territorial Cooperation*. London/New York: Routledge.

EC – European Commission. (1997). *The EU Compendium of Spatial Planning Systems and Policies*. Luxembourg: Office for Official Publications of the European Communities.

EC – European Commission. (1999). *European Spatial Development Perspective*. Luxembourg: Office for Official Publications of the European Communities.

Eraydin, A. (2011). Changing Istanbul city region dynamics: re-regulations to challenge the consequences of uneven development and inequality. *European Planning Studies*, *19*(5), 813–837.

Erkut, G. (2008). EU territorial policy and planning agenda in Turkey. *Town Planning Review*, *79*(1), i–vi.

Erkut, G., Baypinar, M. B. and Özgen, C. (2006, June). Istanbul as part of an emerging EU global connection zone: prospects for strategic metropolitan planning. *International Conference on Shaping EU Regional Policy: Economic, Social and Political Pressures*. Leuven: RSA International Conference.

Erkut, G., Baypinar, M. B., Özgen, C. and Gönül, D. (2007). *Batı Marmara Bölgesi'nde Stratejik Kalkınma ve Sınırötesi İşbirliği* [*Strategic Development and Cross-Border Cooperation in Western Marmara Region*]. Istanbul: Program for International Scientific Research, Istanbul Technical University.

Kundak, S. and Baypınar, M. (2011). The crazy project: canal Istanbul. *Tema Journal*, 4(3), 53–63.

Loewendahl-Ertugal, E. (2004). Regional and European integration: prospects for regional governance in Turkey. *Second Pan-European Conference: Standing Group on EU Politics*. Bologna, Italy.

Lovering, J. (2009). The mystery of planning in Istanbul: three impressions of a visitor. *Megaron*, 4(1), 96–100.

Ministry of Development. (2011). 9th Development Plan, 2012 Programme. Ankara.

OECD – Organisation for Economic Co-operation and Development. (2008). Territorial Reviews, Istanbul, Turkey. OECD Policy Brief (March, 2008). Retrieved from www.oecd.org/regional/regional-policy/40317916.pdf.

Swyngedouw, E., Moulaert, F. and Rodriguez, A. (2002). Neoliberal urbanization in Europe: large-scale urban development projects and the new urban policy. *Antipode*, 34(3), 542–577.

Tekeli, İ. (1994). *The Development of the Istanbul Metropolitan Area: Urban Administration and Planning*. Istanbul: Kent Basımevi.

Tewdwr-Jones, M. and McNeill, D. (2000). The politics of city-region planning and governance: reconciling the national, regional and urban in the competing voices of institutional restructuring. *European Urban and Regional Studies*, 7(2), 119–134.

Türk, Ş. Ş. and Korthals, W. K. (2010). Institutional capacities in the land development for housing on greenfield sites in Istanbul. *Habitat International*, 34, 183–195.

UC – Urbanization Council. (2010). *Spatial Planning System and Institutional Structuring Commission*. Ankara: Ministry of Resettlement and Housing.

Ünsal, F. (2007, September). The evaluation of project typologies in Istanbul: from conspiring dialogues to inspiring trialogues. *43rd ISoCaRP Congress*. Antwerp, Belgium.

Further reading

Dulupcu, M. A. (2005). Regionalization for Turkey: an illusion or a cure? *European Urban and Regional Studies*, 12(2), 99–115.

Erkip, F. (2000). Viewpoint global transformations versus local dynamics in Istanbul: planning in a fragmented metropolis. *Cities*, 17(5), 371–377.

Lovering, J. and Evren, Y. (2011). Urban development and planning in Istanbul. *International Planning Studies*, 16(1), 1–4.

Pinarcioglu, M. and Oguz, I. (2009). Segregation in Istanbul: patterns and processes. *Tijdschrift voor Economische en Sociale Geografie*, 100(4), 469–484.

13

SPATIAL PLANNING IN POLAND BETWEEN EUROPEAN INFLUENCE AND DOMINANT MARKET FORCES

Giancarlo Cotella

Chapter objectives

The chapter:

- describes the evolution of spatial planning in Poland since the fall of the Soviet bloc in 1989;
- reflects upon the various driving forces that influenced this evolution, among which is the transition from plan to market, the growing influence of foreign investors and the increasing influence of the European Union;
- informs the reader about the legal and institutional framework for spatial planning in the country;
- presents the main actors responsible for spatial planning at the various territorial levels (national, regional and local);
- presents the various spatial planning tools produced at various territorial levels;
- provides a qualitative description of the main spatial planning concepts and ideas that characterize spatial planning discourse in Poland at the various territorial levels, pointing out how Polish experts and policymakers are increasingly engaged within the European spatial planning discourse;
- reflects upon the horizontal and vertical integration of the Polish spatial planning system, pointing out the fracture existing between National and regional strategic activities, that highly reflect the influence of the EU discourse and expenditure policy, and local practices, that keeps being dependent on market forces; and
- suggests how, at the local level, a weak civic sector and limited community participation are combined with the intensive pressure executed by private sector developers on local authorities, often leading to the realization of interests of powerful groups at the expense of inhabitants' quality of life.

1 Introduction

Among the post-socialist nations that entered the European Union (EU) in the last enlargement round, Poland is the one boasting the strongest spatial planning tradition, as a

consequence of the incremental consolidation of scientific and practical experience that originated in the inter-war period and evolved into one of the most significant experiences of the
twentieth century with the advent of socialism. After 1989, the socialist planning structure
was rapidly dismantled by a macro-economic reform that paid little attention to any spatial
considerations. Within a few years, the territorial disparities exacerbated by the neoliberal
macro-economic approach called for a revival of regional policy and the reintroduction of
spatial planning at the national level. At the same time, the growing role played by foreign
investors and the progressive accession into the EU constituted many pressures that encouraged the coherent development of Polish spatial planning in line with the emerging economic
conditions, contributing to the incremental shaping of the present context on – and often
with – the ruins of the previous one. The result is a system characterized by a strong fracture between the strategic activities undertaken at the national and regional levels – highly
influenced by the EU discourse and expenditure policy – and local development practice –
strongly embedded in market forces and dominated by private interests.

Building on the above discussion, the chapter reflects upon the evolution of spatial planning in Poland since the fall of the Soviet bloc. After a brief description of the legal and
administrative reforms that led to the consolidation of the present spatial planning system,
it focuses on the main challenges and drivers of change the system has had to face in the
past two decades. The dimensions and directions of change at the different territorial levels
are then examined. Particular attention is devoted to the actors involved in the process of
change, the planning ideas, doctrines and concepts that shaped the policy agenda in the different time periods, the new and evolving planning tools and the critical aspects at stake. A
conclusion rounds off the chapter, elaborating on the effectiveness of the analyzed changes
and on the future perspectives for spatial planning in Poland.

2 Spatial planning in Poland after 1989: a state of the art

Due to the high contextual uncertainty common to all transition countries, contributions
dealing with the evolution of spatial planning in Central and Eastern Europe had, until
recently, mainly focused on the transitional character of the changes (Newman and Thornley,
1996; Balchin et al., 1999; Altrock et al., 2006; Cotella, 2009a). Similarly, the numerous
attempts developed in the past two decades to consolidate an agreement on general spatial
planning "traditions" or "styles" either ignore Central and Eastern European countries or treat
them as one all-embracing category (Nadin and Stead, 2008). However, despite the similarities that emerged in the reform process, the former socialist bloc presents a high degree of
heterogeneity, with each country having worked out its own path towards the establishment
of a spatial planning system that could effectively perform vis-à-vis overall market economy
requirements and endogenous conditions.

At the end of the 1980s, Poland was characterized by a highly centralized administration,
featuring a two-tier system that included 49 regions (voivodships) and some 2,450 municipalities (gminy). The Communist Party was responsible for selecting the candidates for local
elections, and councilors, once elected, had to implement the Party's national program
according to central economic planning rules (Regulski and Kocan, 1994). First pressures
towards decentralization occurred in parallel with the worsening of the economic crisis in the

1980s (Regulski, 1989). Overwhelmed as it was by the dramatic socio-economic situation, the government progressively abandoned the complex system of central economic planning that had characterized the previous decades (Korcelli, 2005). When the Communist government entered into discussion with the Solidarnosc opposition, local government legitimacy suddenly became a major theme. Eight Parliamentary Acts and amendments to nearly 200 other Acts were rushed through (Swianiewicz, 1992; Regulski and Kocan, 1994) and new democratic elections took place even before detailed regulations were issued through the Self-Government Act in 1990. Following the common post-socialist tendency to react against the highly centralized past, the Act adopted a very decentralized approach, transforming municipalities into completely autonomous legal entities (Regulska, 1997).[1]

However, the political energy released by the sudden collapse of Communism did not automatically generate either the experience necessary for actual government or the political stability needed for the effective establishment of a new institutional structure.[2] The context of political experimentation led to a decision-making lock, in particular in relation to contested fields such as planning, which has often been regarded as being in contradiction with the free market. This situation contributed towards preventing the government from undertaking any regional reform for almost a decade, with *voivodships* that continued to exist in subordination to the central level until 1999. From the second half of the 1990s, under pressure from the EU, the government started a regionalization process aimed at both reducing the number of *voivodships* and providing them with self-elected government bodies (ESPON, 2006a). Enforced in January 1999, the regional reform provided the nation with a three-layer administrative division very similar to the one in force before 1975 (Figure 13.1), dividing Poland into 16 NUTS (Nomenclature of Territorial Units for Statistics) 2 units that host both central government representation (the *voivod* and its office) and a self-government unit (the *voivodship* parliament, elected every four years and managed by the Marshal).[3] While the role of the *voivod* is to ensure fruitful cooperation between the regional administration and the central government, the Marshal Office is responsible for regional development policy, acquisition of financial resources, environmental protection, culture and tourism.

After the municipalities regained autonomy in 1990, the uncertainty over the legal arrangements for spatial planning needed to be sorted out, as the 1961 Planning Act continued to constitute the main reference for territorial governance despite the end of its ideological preconditions (Judge, 1994). Whereas this somehow allowed municipalities to perform their day-to-day practice, plans were rather rigid and neither suited to guiding market processes nor to performing land-use regulation under the new economic conditions. Parliament therefore started to progressively reform territorial governance activities through subsequent legal amendments until the Spatial Management Act[4] was approved in 1994. The Act definitively abolished the centralized, hierarchical system of planning through the institution of a new spatial planning system pivoted on two levels and corresponding actors: the state and the municipalities. The state was responsible for spatial planning at the national level, as well as for the preparation, through its decentralized bodies, of development programs constituting summaries of state activity in a given region. Local physical planning operated by self-elected municipalities became the foundation of the planning system, with local physical plans gaining the status of legally binding documents (Sykora, 1999).

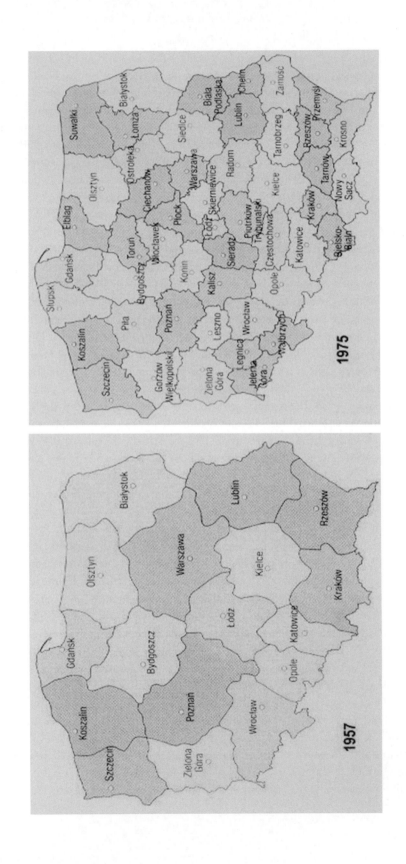

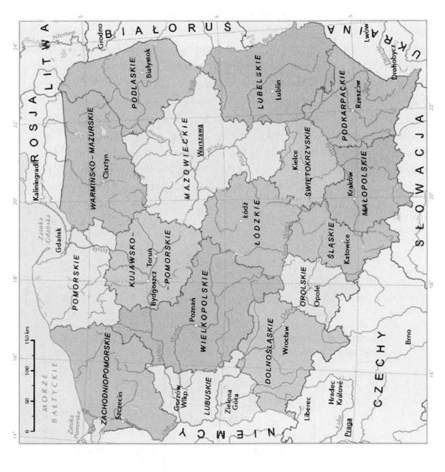

Figure 13.1 Regional administrative division of Poland 1957–1975; 1975–1999; 1999 to today

The weaknesses of the reform emerged almost immediately as spatial planning activities became in some sense overtaken by market actors (Lendzion and Lokucijewski, no date). A substantial share of land-use plans was carried out with the financial assistance of private investors that, in turn, exerted a strong influence over plan preparation. Furthermore, foreseen public participation was administered using a rather formal and legalistic approach, virtually hampering any influence of civil society with disputes settled in most cases in the name of "higher public interest." The 1999 administrative reform sped up the debate on a further revision of the spatial planning legal framework, eventually leading to the approval of the Spatial and Territorial Development Act that replaced the old law in March 2003.

According to the present Act, spatial planning is to be managed at all the levels according to the territorial division of the country (see Figure 13.2). This happens through planning concepts, studies and documents approved by the appropriate institutional bodies, i.e. the parliament, the regional parliaments and the communal councils. At the national level, planning competences lie in the hands of the Council of Ministers together with the Ministry of Regional Development, while at the other levels the respective self-government authorities are provided with similar competences. The national level is responsible for the preparation of the National Concept of Spatial Development, the National Development Plan, the Sectoral Operative Programs and a series of periodic reports on the territorial development state of the nation. For their part, each *voivodship* is responsible for the drafting of the Voivodship Development Strategy, the Voivodship Development Plan and the Voivodship Operative Program. Finally, municipalities are responsible for the preparation of the Study

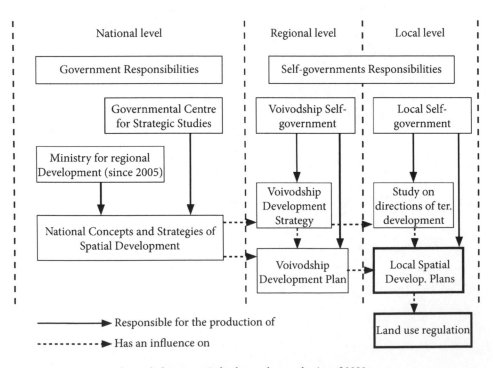

Figure 13.2 Organization of spatial planning in Poland according to the Act of 2003

on the Development Conditions and Directions for Municipality Spatial Development and the Local Spatial Development Plans. Approved documents constitute binding acts of internal management for the administrative bodies that concur their approval while providing only non-binding guidelines to third parties. The only exception are the Local Spatial Development Plans, whose regulations are binding on the territory of a commune.

3 Main challenges and drivers of change

The reforms that have occurred in Poland since 1989 have been driven by a combination of external forces (the influence of the EU and international monetary institutions, the impact of increasing foreign direct investments) and internal factors (the chosen macro-economic path, the emergence of socio-economic imbalances, etc.). This has, in turn, influenced the evolution of the spatial planning system.

While the removal of Communism was immediate, its replacement has been a much slower and tortuous process (Newman and Thornley, 1996). Inspiration could be drawn from a number of alternative market models each presenting its own institutional support structures and set of values, and various foreign and international agencies advocated the virtues of their own particular brand of market economy, often linking financial support to the undertaking of specific measures (Newman and Thornley, 1996; Cotella, 2007). In particular, the International Monetary Fund (IMF) and the World Bank influenced the pursued reforms through credits and loans ensuring the necessary economic stability for changes to be implemented and for market actors to operate, thus reducing the scope of governmental maneuvering in policy definition (Shields, 2004).[5] The experts were polarized between two alternative families of approaches. A more cautious group argued for the need of semi-protectionist measures favoring the adaptation of people and enterprises to the new economic model (Murrel, 1993). However, under the pressure exerted by the international institutions claiming the necessity of realizing macro-economical reform as quickly as possible, the Polish government opted for so-called *shock therapy*, a drastic anti-inflationary program combined with the fast liberalization of the economy through rapid privatization, transition towards global market prices and reduction of state aid (Lipton and Sachs, 1990; Swianiewicz, 1992; Newman and Thornley, 1996).[6]

A second driver of change, strongly entwined with the former one, is represented by the neoliberal flavor of the adopted reforms. Whereas the weak priority attributed to planning and social policies has often been assumed as the litmus test of a withdrawal of the public sector, the collapse of the old communist structure did not limit the influence of the state, but only changed its mechanisms (Paul, 1995; Shields, 2004). In particular, state apparatuses assumed a leading role in the sphere of production and finance. Agencies directly connected to the national economy, such as the Ministry of Finances, began to progressively subordinate the role of the Ministries of Industry, Labour, Housing, etc. to one of international economic forces. The minimal state philosophy adopted nationally found strong justification in the resurgent cultural beliefs of self-reliance and individualism, caused by 45 years of imposed uniformity (Sykora, 1999), and the slogan "the less government the better" was used to support the abolition of taxes on foreign capital and the privatization of the welfare sectors.

The adopted neoliberal economic project aimed at fully enabling the functioning of international capital and allowed for the exponentially growing impact of foreign direct investments on the economy and, in turn, on territorial development (Blazyca, 2001). Foreign enterprises started to invest their capital and relocate their own productive structures within Polish borders, permeating practically all sectors, in particular the car industry, trading, the food industry, furniture, consumer electronics and, since the second half of the 1990s, banking and financial services (Śleszyński, 2006; Cotella, 2007). Several sectors of the economy were gradually transformed from state-owned strongholds to transnational capital monopolies, in a process where privatization, instead of bringing about competition and de-monopolization, perpetuated and exacerbated market domination and concentration (Shields, 2004). This led to the development of a complex network of cross-ownership, self-ownership and ineffective small shareholding via investment funds connected with state-owned banks (Stark, 1996), and to the consolidation of a new "power elite" controlling the command positions of political and economic institutions at the expense of the consolidation of a new "Polish bourgeoisie" in a scenario where the only distinct owners were the state and foreign capital (Eyal et al., 1997).

Once the economic and political barriers that sheltered the Polish economy from international competition were removed, the old patterns of economic production could no longer be maintained and new patterns of socio-economic and political organization began to emerge. The relation between public and private actors changed in favor of the latter, turning cities and regions from objects of public planning into locations for private investments (Sykora, 1999; Śleszyński, 2006). The impact on the labor market was dramatic, with pauperization and unemployment hitting wide strata of the population.[7] The standards of living of most of the workers worsened, mainly due to the growing polarization of incomes and the precariousness of jobs. Moreover, as workplaces and professional organizations were the main locus of social provision, social welfare was further undermined by the crisis of the Polish state industry (Gorzelak, 2001).

Within a macro-economic framework enabling rapid socio-economic polarization (Paul, 1995; Gorzelak, 1996), the growing intra- and inter-regional disparities have constituted the main challenge for Polish spatial planning for much of the past two decades. The economic competition valorized the strengths of some areas, exposing the weaknesses of others at the same time. Economic benefits affected large cities and metropolitan areas, particularly Warsaw, Poznan, Cracow, Wroclaw and the Gdynia-Gdansk conurbation, as well as some smaller towns that managed to attract large shares of foreign investment. In contrast, areas dominated by traditional heavy industry and extensive farming experienced dramatic socio-economic decline, with most of the eastern *voivodships* performing far below the national average.[8] Whereas the strong polycentric character of the country's settlement system, inherited from the previous historical period, partly counteracted this tendency, specialized activities traditionally associated with medium and small centers increasingly concentrated in main cities, worsening intra-regional disparities as well as unemployment, service accessibility and income polarization (ESPON, 2006b).

The shortage of transport infrastructures is still today perceived as constituting a further territorial emergency, and has generated many conflicts between the improvement of road transport on the one hand and environmental protection on the other. The same is true for the regeneration of the huge socialist *kombinats*, a challenge both with regard to the reuse of contaminated soils as well as in relation to the economic decline of their surrounding regions. Alongside the need to counteract spatial inequalities, at the local level growing demands from market actors quickly became the basic contextual characteristics to be integrated within the establishing spatial planning system. A first step towards the creation of a land and property market was undertaken through the restitution of land to former owners. However, this process has been slow and contested, due to difficulties related to the evaluation of ownership claims as well as to agreeing on how far back to go in the process[9] (Newman and Thornley, 1996). Problems have also been encountered in cases where compensation was to be awarded instead of actual possession, as neither the government nor the municipalities had the finances to back up the compensation vouchers.

Last but not least, the EU constituted another important driver of change during the whole transition period. As Piazolo (2000) underlines, ever since the prospect of accession became real, the transition started to assume a growing European flavor, as membership was always linked not only to the adoption of the EU's vast *acquis communautaire*, but also to political conditionality in the establishment of a functioning market economy. More importantly in relation to spatial planning, the pre-accession period brought with it a series of financial measures that contributed to exert a direct influence on spatial planning reforms through economic conditionality (Cotella, 2009a). At the same time, since the end of the 1990s the "European spatial planning agenda" has increasingly influenced spatial planning changes through the diffusion of spatial planning concepts and ideas.

4 Dimensions and directions of change

4.1 Evolution of spatial planning at the national level

4.1.1 The first years of the transition

At the beginning of the 1990s, the basic ideological assumption of transformation policies was that market forces should be the only principle of regulation. The Polish government barely undertook any form of spatial policy, allowing the widening of regional disparities (Paul, 1995; Gorzelak, 1996). In order to limit the territorial concentration of social and economic problems, a few years after the start of the transition a first set of *ad hoc* territorial policy responses was introduced on the national level. Sectoral in nature, most of these interventions derived from trade union pressure in favor of regions that were experiencing dramatic decline and varied from the promotion of infrastructures to economic subsidies for enterprises in crisis.

In 1993, the Ministry of Labour and Social Policy was responsible for the most advanced regional policy concept of the beginning of the transition, launching a program supporting spatially defined areas affected by structural unemployment that targeted as many as 412 municipalities, accounting for almost 15 percent of the national population and 20 percent of the unemployed (Sykora, 1999). In the following year, all areas facing increasing unemployment benefited from accelerated amortization rates of fixed assets, infrastructure grants for local budgets, income tax relief for private businesses which run vocational training and tax exemption for firms employing school graduates directed by Employment Offices, etc. (Gorzelak, 1996, p. 134).

Whereas it is hard to evaluate the described measures, mostly due to the impossibility of establishing causal relations between them and the economic recovery and reduction of unemployment, it is possible to notice how they have been characterized by the absence of comprehensiveness, scarce transparency in terms of institutional competences and lack of coordination between the different ministries.

4.1.2 The growing influence of the EU

From the second half of the 1990s, a crucial input for regional policy was provided by the EU accession negotiations. The financial support and the knowhow attached to the pre-accession programs stimulated the resurgence of national spatial planning and provided it with a strong European flavor in terms of concepts, priorities and procedures (ESPON, 2006a). A first repositioning of national spatial planning activities occurred in 1995, when the Governmental Centre for Strategic Studies (GCSS) was entrusted with the preparation of the National Concept of Spatial Development (NCSD) (GCSS, 2001). Approved by parliament in 2001, the document constitutes the first comprehensive spatial planning document produced after the end of socialism and defines the conditions, aims and direction for the sustainable development of the nation (Korcelli, 2005; ESPON, 2006a). The NCSD has limited legal value and constitutes a set of guidelines for territorial development, to be taken on board more or less voluntarily by the lower levels (ESPON, 2006a). Since its institution in 2005, the Ministry of Regional Development has been responsible for enhancing the coherence between the NCSD and the Voivvodship Development Strategies as well as for the preparation of the NCSD's periodic update reports.

Moreover, since 2000 the government has been responsible for preparing National Development Plans (NDPs), as requested by the EU.[10] The first NDP was produced for the period 2000–2003 in order to manage the pre-accession support. Subsequently, a similar document was prepared for the period 2004–2006 in the context of the negotiations with the European Commission on the Community Support Framework that would have defined the magnitude of structural support to the nation (IGPNDP 2004–2006, 2003). Although with scarce results, the document also aimed at the integration of sectoral and regional perspectives at the national level through the provision of indicative guidelines addressing the development of the Polish territory after accession. The NDP 2004–2006 was complemented by a set of Sectoral Operative Programs (SOPs) that focused on the achievement of sectoral goals of national relevance and defined the budget devoted by each of the involved government sectoral agencies.

Interestingly, the influence exerted by the EU during the second half of the 1990s favored the emergence of several parallelisms between the aims declared by national spatial documents and the contents of the main EU spatial orientation documents. In particular, the priorities of the NCSD and the NDP 2004–2006 overlap substantially with the policy aims listed in the European Spatial Development Perspective (ESDP) (CEC, 1999; ESPON, 2006a). While some authors impute this coherence to the several channels of communication opened between the ESDP process and the knowledge arena within which the NCSD was being shaped,[11] others believe it is a consequence of the contribution of Polish planners to the development of some of the key concepts that now underpin the European spatial planning discourse[12] (ESPON, 2006a; Adams et al., 2011).

Several criticisms of Polish national spatial planning documents have been voiced. On the one hand, dependence on EU financial support has been seen as over-conditioning the definition of national goals. This is especially evident in the NDP 2004–2006, which seems to focus exclusively on the appropriate way to obtain and manage the highest possible share of EU funds (Grosse and Olbrycht, 2003; Grosse, 2005; Korcelli, 2005). Similarly, the priorities underpinning the NCSD have also proved to be strongly hegemonized by the EU discourse, and are often inadequate or even contradictory once translated into the national context. This is clearly the case with the tensions generated by the equipollence of economic growth and territorial cohesion, where the majority of the cases are solved in favor of the development of stronger areas, thus leading to further spatial polarization (Korcelli, 2005; Cotella, 2007, 2009b). Last but not least, it is important to underline how national spatial planning has been characterized, until recently, by a low degree of sectoral coordination (Grosse and Olbrycht, 2003; Grosse, 2005). As central economic planning was based on a highly sectoral organization of power, this legacy is not surprising: post-1989 spatial policies remained weak vis-à-vis sectoral interests as inflexible, sectorally organized government institutions were ill-prepared to respond to horizontal integration demands (Gorzelak, 2001, p. 323, Sagan, 2010). Despite the required coherence between the NCSD, NDP and SOPs, the different ministries therefore undermined any attempt at coordination, often generating duplication or even contradiction of policies. A recurring example is the clashes between infrastructural interventions and environmental policy objectives, as for instance in the case of Via Baltica and the Cracow-Gdansk highway (ESPON, 2006a).

4.1.3 Towards the forefront of the European debate?

In recent years, the newborn Ministry for Regional Development has introduced several measures aiming, on the one hand, to overcome the sectoral mentality and, on the other hand, to free national priorities from the hegemonic influence of the EU discourse. As a consequence, the NDP 2007–2013 represents a step towards the growing integration of the different sectoral priorities as well as of the different territorial levels. In contrast to its predecessor, it aims not only at the appropriate use of EU support, but at the integration of European and national resources within a coherent, comprehensive strategy for the development of national space (Grosse and Olbrycht, 2003; IGPNDP 2007–2013, 2005). To do so, it includes several goals of national importance that do not necessarily match EU goals and priorities, hence constituting an innovative tool for coordination of supranational and national goals. In addition, it delegates the preparation of Regional Operative Programs to the *voivodships* for the first time, thus aiming to counteract the tendency of the national ministries to autonomously pursue sectoral policy and favoring greater integration and complementariness between national, sectoral and regional priorities (Grosse, 2005).

Moreover, the Ministry of Regional Development has recently supervised the preparation of the National Spatial Management Concept for the years 2008–2030 (NSMC, 2011), which is intended to constitute the main reference for Polish spatial development in the years to come. The document has been drafted by a team of experts originating from numerous circles (societal, academic, ministerial, self-governmental) and disciplines (geographers, planners, economists) and, also as a consequence of the recent economic crisis, clearly reflects the competitive turn that characterizes contemporary EU spatial discourse on territorial development, interpreting the objective of territorial cohesion as functional to economic growth (Czapiewski and Janc, 2011; see also Tewdwr-Jones, 2011). Its vision is pivoted on the network of the largest Polish cities – Warsaw, Cracow, the Upper Silesian conurbation, Wroclaw, Poznan, Lodz and the Tri-City (Gdansk/Sopot/Gdynia). The multi-nodal infrastructure connections of these cities form the so-called "Central Exagon," creating synergies that the National Spatial Management Concept (NSMC) hopes to use to foster the competitiveness of the Polish urban system within the regional networks of metropolitan centers in Europe (NSMC, 2011).

It is important to stress how the NSMC builds on most recent attempts to identify main development trends and challenges in the EU (the Territorial Agenda and Barca's Report, respectively DE Presidency, 2007; Barca, 2009). However, it emancipates itself from the acritical transposition of EU concepts and aims, complementing them with distinct domestic priorities (Szlachta and Zaleski, 2005, p. 81). In particular, while striving to consolidate the existing polycentric network and to improve the accessibility of the main cities of the Hexagon from the peripheral regions, it partially challenges EU development scenarios – as depicted by the ESPON 3.2 project – that indicate the future extension of the advanced knowledge-based economy axes as bypassing the territory of Poland to the north and south (Czapiewski and Janc, 2011, elaborating on ESPON, 2007a). This recent critical engagement of Polish experts and policymakers with the European spatial planning debate may be read as an attempt to emancipate Polish spatial planning discourse from EU hegemonic pressures. In fact, as detailed analyses of the ongoing territorial cohesion debate show, Polish actors are progressively positioning themselves at the forefront of the debate, having been involved in as many as 46 of the responses to the consultation launched by the European Commission Green Paper on Territorial Cohesion (Cotella et al., 2012) as well as having played a crucial role in the drafting of the new Territorial Agenda of the European Union 2020 (HU Presidency, 2011).

4.2 The resurgence of regional planning

4.2.1 Regional planning in the 1990s

Until 1999, regional authorities constituted a mere outpost of the central administration. Regional development was managed through specific central budget allocations and through the institution of specific Regional Development Agencies (RDAs) (Gorzelak, 1996; Balchin et al., 1999). Socialist *voivodship* plans were abrogated in 1989 and substituted by two new documents: the Spatial Arrangement Study and the Regional Development Program. Prepared as they were by decentralized government units, these documents promoted the central view on the development of the various regions. The interventions incorporated in the studies and in the programs were negotiated with the representatives of the main municipalities of each *voivodship* (which were much smaller than the present ones) and each agreement had to be incorporated in local planning documents, thereby assuming legal validity (Gorzelak, 1996). The Council of Ministries was responsible for deliberating on cases where agreement was not reached, providing the system with a strong hierarchical flavor.

The goals promoted by the different *voivodship* instruments were characterized by a highly sectoral character, with the *voivodship* offices favoring the trickling down of sectoral priorities from the different ministries. The pursued interventions had little or no spatial content, with the exception of limited actions fostering economic restructuring and employment in specific declining areas (Gorzelak, 1996, 2001).

A more specific spatial dimension characterized the goals pursued by the RDAs, the majority of which were created by the mid-1990s by the Governmental Agency for Industrial Development, in cooperation with regional administrations, local authorities, chambers of commerce and various associations of enterprises, banks, etc. (Gorzelak, 2001). RDAs provided consulting services to local enterprises and public administrations during the compiling of regional and local development strategies and they were often involved in the management and realization of projects sponsored by EU pre-accession funds.[13] Among the objectives pursued by RDAs, it is worth mentioning the exchange of methods to fight unemployment, the promotion of initiatives towards the creation of low environmental impact jobs, the coordination of activities focusing on the restructuring of industrial heritage, the promotion of actions to counteract labor market problems, the education and relocation of existing labor forces, the promotion of public-private cooperation, the support to SMEs and the promotion of international cooperation initiatives aimed at ensuring the participation of foreign partners in local and regional development (ESPON, 2006b).

4.2.2 The administrative reform and the 2000s

The administrative reform approved in 1999 favored a resurgence of autonomous spatial planning at the regional level. The new administrative configuration called for a decentralization of planning and development competences, which occurred through specific amendments to the 1994 Spatial Management Act and eventually through the promulgation of the new Act in 2003, introducing new regional spatial development tools under the responsibility of the Marshal Office: the Voivodship Development Strategy (VDS) and the Voivodship Development Plan (VDP). Furthermore, the *voivodships* are responsible for the agreement of Regional Contracts with the national administration and, since the present programming period, for the preparation of the Regional Operative Programs in the framework of EU cohesion policy.[14]

The VDS and the VDP constitute the framework for the development of a given *voivodship*. The VDS defines the conditions, the objectives and the direction of the development of the *voivodship* according to the objectives defined in the 1999 Voivodships Self-Government Act and in the Spatial and Territorial Management Act of 2003. The VDP aims to realize the VDS, defining the guidelines of the *voivodship* territorial policy on the basis of the latter. The directives concerning public interest interventions of supra-local concern included in the VDP are binding for municipalities and must be incorporated in the respective local planning documents.

The reform allows each region to promote development according to autonomously formulated spatial goals and visions. Immediately after the first election round, the government bodies of every *voivodship* undertook analyses and studies in support of the elaboration of the VDSs. Despite presenting substantial heterogeneity in terms of aims and approaches, the 16 documents are characterized by a strong European flavor, with many of them explicitly referring to the EU discourse. This is evident in the emphasis attributed to concepts such as the wise management of natural and cultural resources, the improvement of infrastructure and knowledge accessibility, and the development of multifunctional rural areas. The concept of polycentric development is a key element in 15 of the 16 VDSs, the exception being the strategy of the Mazowieskie *voivodship*, where the capital city of Warsaw is located (ESPON, 2006a).

As an attempt to further define the relations between the national and the regional levels and, more particularly, between sectoral and spatial policy domains, the so-called Regional Contracts were introduced. These take the form of contractual agreements defining the share of central budget devolved for the realization of the objectives of a given *voivodship* as specified in the VDS and VDP. On the basis of documents elaborated by the various ministries, the government elaborates a Support Program that specifies the main objectives of national regional policy and the related resources. These objectives are then included in the VDSs through measures focusing on the realization of the five main priorities underpinning the Contracts: (1) development and modernization of the infrastructure system; (2) restructuring and diversification of the economic structure; (3) development of human resources; (4) support to declining areas; and (5) development of interregional and intraregional cooperation. Regional Contracts defining the scope, procedures and conditions of the implementation of the different interventions are then negotiated and signed by the Council of Ministries and the *voivodship* governments (ESPON, 2006b).

4.2.3 Critical aspects of regional planning

Throughout the 1990s, Polish planners criticized the inadequateness of a regional planning system whose only aim was to transfer ministerial priorities to the regional level, thus reinforcing sectoral autonomy and leaving little or no room for the interpretation of regional interests. After the 1999 reform, the devolution of powers and competences to the regional level and the introduction of new spatial planning tools provided new hope for the future coordination of sectoral and regional priorities. However, despite the regained autonomy, regional governments were subject to the influence of the central government until at least 2006. Due to the lack of financial independence of regional budgets, which were constituted to almost 80 percent by central subsidies, the majority of the *voivodships* were obliged to integrate sectoral priorities defined at the national level in order to obtain the financial resources required to achieve their own goals (Gorzelak, 2001; Grosse, 2005).

The influence of national priorities is very much evident in the various regional strategies approved with the signature of the Regional Contract for the period 2001–2006, clearly showing how the central government was able to negotiate with the *voivodship* from a stronger position through its Support Program. The presence of a considerable sum of money linked to issues listed as being at the top of national priorities (e.g. the completion of the highway network) forced the adoption of such priorities by the majority of the *voivodships*, eager to obtain a higher amount of resources (Gorzelak, 2001). Aiming at developing a more transparent definition of sectoral and regional priorities, the NDP 2007–2013 redesigned the general framework for regional policy with the introduction of Regional Operative Programmes (ROPs), in so doing contributing to further decentralization (Grosse, 2005). However, the evidence suggests that the management of ROPs proved to be a complex task for the *voivod-ships*, in many cases requiring the adjustment of their internal organizational structure. As a result, several *voivodship* administrations are now characterized by a fracture in responsibilities, with the VDS and the ROP being managed by different departments, this constituting an obvious coordination barrier.

4.3 Spatial planning at the local level

4.3.1 New planning under old rules

With the promulgation of the Self-Government Act in 1990, Polish municipalities all of a sudden became responsible for managing the development of their respective territories, were the only bodies entitled to produce legally binding planning documents and therefore found themselves at the fulcrum of the Polish spatial planning system. However, financial decentralization did not proceed in parallel with the devolution of competences, and local government activities were undermined by the dramatic financial situation. Limited skills and the pressure of everyday matters as well as many other factors further hampered the municipalities in performing their new role (Gorzelak, 1996). The old law of 1961 was still valid and this generated a series of challenges associated with the scarce ability of the old tools to cope with development processes under the new economic conditions. The lack of political stability and the low priority given to "regulative" themes led to conspicuous delays in the establishment of a market-oriented planning system. As a consequence, local administrations had to deal with day-to-day practices of land-use management, building regulation and management of property rights in the absence of any general guidance.

Within this scenario, each city started to adopt its own approach in an attempt to relate to the new political reality and market orientation, and under pressure from foreign developers and investors affirming the irrelevance of the planning system (Judge, 1994). For the whole of the 1990s, the main roles played by local administrations have involved, on the one hand, dealing with contingent challenges related to ownership claims and building permission and, on the other hand, continuously exploring ways to attract foreign economic subjects to invest within the municipal borders, in order to stimulate local economic development and employment and to benefit from the revenues that the new activities would provide.

This climate of competition between cities led the newborn public administrations to develop a prevalently entrepreneurial mentality. They started to undertake an increasing number of urban marketing initiatives – in the majority of cases following logic borrowed from Western urban contexts without considering in advance how such strategies would fit the local reality (Dimitrovska Andrews, 2004; Capik, 2011) – and favor foreign investors through localization incentives and the progressive deregulation of the building process. In Lodz, for example, the new 1993 general plan explicitly aimed at showing local authority commitment to establishing a "vision" based on the strengths of the city that would allow it to compete for investment (Markowski and Kot, 1993). Similarly, in Poznan a document was prepared aimed at attracting hotel investments and setting out all the possible locations, costs and benefits of such developments (Poznan Municipal Town Planning Office, no date). Special "business promotion zones" were also included in the new city plan (Poznan

Municipal Town Planning Office, 1992), as well as in those of several other Polish cities, indicating a trend where marked mechanisms started replacing spatial planning.

4.3.2 The new spatial planning acts

In the attempt to set up a new framework for spatial planning in the country, the Polish government approved the new Act on Spatial Management in 1994, after a series of parliamentary debates and legislative proposals. As mentioned above, due to some serious weaknesses and, most importantly, as a consequence of the administrative reform of 1999, an alternative legislative act was approved in 2003, substituting the previous one. Both laws defined two main instruments of local planning, i.e. the Study on the Condition and Direction of Municipal Territorial Development (Study) and the Local Spatial Development Plan (LSDP) (ESPON, 2006b; COMMIN, 2007).

In the first place, a municipality elaborates the Study, a strategic document related to the scope of the spatial policy of the local authority, prepared for the whole communal area. The document does not have legal character, but it is binding in the process of drawing up the LSDP and plays a coordinating role in this respect. Among other things, the Study includes indications of:

1   directions of change in the spatial structure of the municipality;
2   directions concerning land-use, with indication of areas excluded from construction development;
3   a list of protected areas;
4   the development of the infrastructure systems;
5   areas chosen for investment projects of local public interest;
6   areas chosen for investment projects of supra-local public interest in conformity with the VDP;
7   areas for which the municipality intends to elaborate specific LSDPs.

The Study, whose preparation has to take into account the NCSD principles and the VDP development directions, is approved after negotiation with the Voivodship Council and public discussion, where each citizen is entitled to present observations. Upon its approval, the municipality draws up the LSDP for selected areas of the municipal territory, including those areas that include specific projects of supra-local interest, as defined by the NCSD and the VDP. For each of the areas covered, the LSDP generally defines directions concerning land-use, zoning and development principles, the principles of protection and definition of spatial order, the variables related to the definition of public spaces, the parameters related to building interventions, and the borders and development indications for protected areas. The procedure for elaboration of the LSDP resembles that of the Study. During the procedure, the mayor is responsible for obtaining the consensus of the municipal architecture and planning boards, and the mayors of bordering municipalities are responsible in the case of projects that interest more than one municipality.

Compared to the 1994 Act, the one approved in 2003 introduced more efficient instruments of public interest protection, limiting the right of ownership. It also strengthened the role and the legal status of the Study as the most essential document for municipal spatial policy, including a more precise description of its relations with the LSDP. However, as will be explained in detail, the present law still leaves too much room for arbitrary decisions by administrative authorities.

4.3.3 Spatial development "in vacuum"?

Despite the new legal spatial planning framework, two decades of reforms have resulted in a strong limitation of municipal planning activities, shifting towards a merely strategic role, rather than a prescriptive and regulative one, in line with mainstream neoliberal orientations as well as with cities' entrepreneurial approach to spatial development (Sagan, 2010). Although city planning has ceased to be a tool for implementing central goals, it seems to have swung too far the other way, and is now almost completely neglected (Izdebski et al., 2007). Due to the freedom left to municipalities to decide which portions of their territories should be covered by LSDPs, local spatial development processes are mainly unregulated, as the majority of the municipal governments find it easier to directly negotiate with private investors in the absence of the cumbersome presence of legally binding planning tools. Under these conditions, investors are shaping urban spaces, often with the silent complicity of local public authorities driven by the short-term interests of investment returns and political re-election, rather than longer-term concerns about urban quality (Kafka and Nawratek, 2004).

This spatial development "in vacuum" accounts for as much as almost 80 percent of building interventions and is realized on the grounds of the so-called "decisions on building conditions of site development" (decyzja o warunkach zabudowy – WZ). WZs operate virtually as plan substitutes for those areas that are not covered by the LSDP, and are basically carried out through case-by-case consideration of investors' proposals by the municipality. Whereas they are often perceived by municipal leaders and private investors as the ideal instrument for soft urban development governance (Sagan, 2010), in reality their simplified procedure and the lack of control over the decision endanger the spatial and functional order of local development.[15] As site development decisions are not applicable for areas covered by local development plans, the plan coverage of city areas is significantly limited.[16] While in 2009 as much as 95 percent of Polish municipalities were covered by Studies, only 26 percent of the national territory was covered by LSDPs. For instance, in Warsaw only 15.9 percent of the city area was covered by the current plans in 2006. In the same year, the percentage of Cracow subject to LSDPs was even smaller, equal to 10.7 percent.[17]

One example from the city of Sczecin confirms the very unclear practical principles steering present local spatial planning in Poland. Through WZ procedure, in 2005 the Mayor of Sczecin sold a plot of 5.28ha (named Gontyka) to an investor, who announced his intention to build a hypermarket on the site. Eventually, the investor decided to deliver an aqua park in return, on a plot rented for 25 years, and immediately the municipality allowed the development, responding to the needs of the investor. Although the City Board rather aimed to sell the area, they had to accept the new conditions as the municipal budget already included the foreseen revenues from the development (Matuszczak, 2005). Similarly, at the end of 2000 Cracow municipalities agreed with Carrefour the redevelopment of an old industrial plant devoted to the production of soda. Beside the creation of a new shopping mall, the investor was supposed to be responsible for the regeneration of the polluted land and to finance the arrangement of infrastructural and public space interventions in two bordering neighborhoods. Eventually, this failed to materialize as the company claimed that the pollution removal costs were too high, and the only intervention that was actually realized was the mall (Cotella, 2005).

5 Conclusion

Capitalism did not fall on Poland fully formed from the sky in 1989. Several variables and driving forces contributed to influence the adoption of certain solutions over others and, more generally, the redefinition of the national system of governance. The state has acted as the architect in the transition process, establishing new "rules of the game" in a wider scenario characterized by the presence of strong international forces. The neoliberal paradigm was a main driving force underpinning the reforms undertaken during the first years of the transition, when the focus was on instituting the necessary conditions for the new economic model to work properly, thus favoring the growing influence of foreign investors in the Polish economy. Furthermore, as soon as accession into the EU became a real perspective, the negotiations started to exert a growing influence on Polish patterns of transformation, triggering Europeanization processes based on the transposition of the *acquis communautaire* and on mechanisms of economic conditionality.

The evolutionary patterns of Polish spatial planning are a consequence of all these elements. During the first years of the transition, the macro-economic reform did not feature any spatial planning dimensions, if one excludes the few *ad hoc* interventions intended to contain unemployment levels in regions affected by economic decline. In the meantime, at the local level the newly established self-governments had to continue to manage land-use regulation and development as well as to deal with the new challenges accompanying the systemic change, all this under old legal provisions that led to the preparation of planning tools ill-equipped to operate under the new economic conditions.

From the mid-1990s onwards, increasing spatial polarization and the growing influence of the EU led to the approval of a new Spatial Planning Act aimed at establishing a market-oriented spatial planning system. Regional policy resurged and the first comprehensive national planning document was eventually produced. Ideas and priorities developed within the European spatial planning discourse started to trickle down to the domestic debate and to influence the spatial strategies produced by the national government, which was striving to maximize EU structural support. Similarly, the growing participation of Polish experts and policymakers in transnational epistemic communities led to a growing process of discursive integration favoring domestic Europeanization (Adams et al., 2011).

Whereas from 1995 onwards national spatial initiatives grew exponentially, regional planning had to wait for the 1999 administrative reform, after which the self-elected *voivodship* governments were entrusted with the spatial planning competences for their respective territories. However, the strategies and plans produced by the various *voivodships* continued to suffer under the strong influence of national sectoral ministries that were able to ensure that their respective priorities were included in regional strategies by using the high financial dependence of the *voivodships'* budgets on the central level as leverage. The domination of the vertical sectoral division of administrative structures persisted until recently, when the Ministry of Regional Development and the National Development Plan 2007–2013 somewhat limited the influence of sectoral goals and priorities over spatial planning through the promotion of an innovative system of governance aiming at the spatial re-composition and further coordination of national, sectoral and regional priorities. The new family of regional policy documents and spatial guidelines produced at the national level also enabled a partial emancipation of national priorities from the hegemonic pressures of the EU discourse. This is the result of the increasing engagement of national experts and policymakers with the EU planning discourse and may be interpreted as an indication of the Polish will to play a growing role in the definition of the concepts and principles that will determine future EU support (Cotella et al., 2012).

Be that as it may, a strong fracture still persists between these activities and local spatial planning and development practices. Despite the introduction of new legal foundations for spatial planning in 1994 and subsequently in 2003, local spatial planning seems to have progressively lost importance. The original intention to dismantle the communist legacy of a centralized, extensive planning system led to the establishment of a local spatial planning system characterized by the high discretionality of municipalities when it comes to deciding what to include under the regulation of binding spatial plans. As a result, city mayors are reluctant to extend local development plan coverage in their municipalities, claiming that local development plans are a hindrance in the dynamic governance of the city, and preferring to conduct and allow development interventions through case-by-case site development decisions.

The widespread slogan among municipalities of being "investor-friendly" clearly suggests an admission of dependency on investors' goodwill (Sagan, 2005, p. 53), indicating how municipalities are ready to "bend over backwards" to accommodate the interests of private capital, even if this involves sacrificing other long-term goals and ideals. Under these conditions, pressure and lobbying from investors significantly shape the spatial development of municipalities, opening the gates to corruption and speculative functions. This tendency to keep as much of development decision-making as possible governed by the *ad hoc* verdicts of local government bodies is very strong. The common opinion prevails that it is actually impossible to achieve any consensus with or within local communities and that they need enlightened leaders. This provides an excuse for eliminating community participation from planning practice, in a scenario where a weak civic sector and limited community participation is combined with the intensive pressure exerted by private developers on local authorities, often leading to the interests of powerful groups dominating at the expense of those of inhabitants.

In conclusion, the chapter suggests how the Polish government, under the influence of the EU, has been pressing forward in the creation of a "comprehensive integrated" spatial planning system, with "strong vertical (between levels with competences in spatial planning) and horizontal (between policies with territorial impact) coordination" of policymaking (ESPON, 2007b, p. 41). However, whilst the policy discourse and legal framework have changed substantially over the past two decades, practice has not always followed suit. In other words, as the ESPON Governance report recognizes, "legislation and policy are valuable as pointers to change but can be misleading" (ESPON, 2007b, p. 285). Even if the legal requirements are in place, progress in the development of new policy instruments is variable and the influence of adopted plans and policies is clearly limited in an environment where the position of the public is weak in the face of strong private interests which often dominate over elected representatives. Progress has been made since the late 1990s in overhauling planning legislation and institutional structures, but what is still to be developed is "good governance": transparent, accountable decision-making processes and clear political leadership at the urban and regional levels that could support effective planning (OECD, 2001).

Notes

1 Since the 1990 Self-Government Act, the basic administrative unit in Poland is the *gmina* (NUTS 5). In 2009, there were 2,478 *gminy*: 306 urban *gminy* (whose borders include a single municipality), 1,586 rural *gminy* (whose borders include several villages, one of them hosting the administrative office) and 586 urban–rural *gminy* (whose borders include a main municipality and a set of smaller rural villages). Rural *gminy* are subdivided into smaller sub-units (*solectwo*), while the urban ones are usually subdivided into districts. These sub-units perform specific administrative functions and could be considered as an additional territorial level.

2 As ironically pointed out by *The Guardian* (1 April 1992, cited in Newman and Thornley, 1996, p. 25), the numerous parties set up for the 1991 elections represented all shades of opinion, including the Polish Beer Lovers Party which won 16 seats before splitting into the Big Beer and the Little Beer factions!

3 Since 1999, Poland has also been divided into 314 *powiaty* (NUTS 4) and 65 *powiat*-cities (cities with county rights), responsible for executing statutory public tasks which are beyond communal scope (e.g. advanced social and technical infrastructure, nature preservation at the extra-communal level, organizational activity aiming at solving local problems, etc.). For statistical purposes, two additional levels were introduced: six macro-regions composed of different *voivodships* (NUTS 1) and 45 sub-regions including several *powiaty* within a *voivodship* (NUTS 3).

4 The exclusion of the word "planning" from the name of the Act is evidence of the government's will to demonstrate a clear break with socialist "central planning" principles. Amongst other things, the new Act highlights "the scope and way of procedure in cases concerning the intended use of terrain for specific purposes and settling the ways of development," thus promoting a crucial shift from "complex planning supported by legal acts" towards "regulative planning based, among other things, on title to property" (Matuszczak, 2005).

5 Several critics arose here, as the Polish government often used the need to obtain IMF approval (but also to respect EU Accession Treaties) as a cover excuse to undertake the most controversial measures (Paul, 1995; Szul and Mync, 1997).

6 As Gorzelak (1996) points out, different approaches were chosen in the other post-socialist countries, ranging from the less radical and more pragmatic Czechoslovak program to the more cautious Hungarian macro-economic policy of a "soft landing" into capitalism.

7 The total number of jobs lost in Poland in the period 1990–1993 amounted to over 2 million, and in 1994 the unemployment rate reached 16 percent of the economically active population.

8 Lubelskie and Swietokrzyskie shared the position as the EU's poorest regions until 2007.

9 For instance, some argued for going back to the expropriation made during the Nazi's military occupation, and the Polish church claimed that restitution should go as far back as the expropriations made by Alexander I.

10 NDPs are mid-term instruments presenting a more concrete and pragmatic character than the NCSD.

11 It is worth pointing out the role of the Institute of Geography and Spatial Organization of the Polish Academy of Science as a crucial link between the European spatial planning debate and these government bodies deputed to the preparation of national spatial strategies and programs.

12 In particular, the concepts of polycentrism and urban–rural partnership were already introduced by K. Dziewoński in 1964, in a paper titled "Urbanization of contemporary Poland," then cited and reprinted in numerous scientific publications (Dziewoński, 1964).

13 Even after the administrative reform, RDAs continued to play a role in the promotion of local economic initiatives and in the provision of technical expertise in the preparation of EU applications.

14 At the same time, specific policies that are still under the direct control of the state through the *voivod* office exist, such as those dealing with national parks, military areas and areas identified for the localization of interventions of supra-regional importance.

15 This is due to the fact that they do not necessarily have to conform to the Study, and might be issued for plots of land that have no adjacent developed plots, no access to a public road and no connection to any land infrastructure (Izdebski et al., 2007, p. 49).

16 This situation has been worsened by the fact that all the spatial development plans prepared before the approval of the 1994 Act have been abrogated by the promulgation of the 2003 planning law.

17 According to the Union of Polish Metropolises, in 2005 there were 6,175 site development decisions issued in Warsaw, 3,510 in Krakow and 1,104 in Gdansk.

References

Adams, N., Cotella, G. and Nunes, R. (eds) (2011). *Territorial Development, Cohesion and Spatial Planning: Knowledge and Policy Development in an Enlarged EU*. London/New York: Routledge.

Altrock, U., Güntner, S., Huning, S. and Peters, D. (eds) (2006). *Spatial Planning and Urban Development in the New EU Member States: From Adjustment to Reinvention*. Aldershot: Ashgate.

Balchin, P., Sykora, L. and Bull, G. (1999). *Regional Policy and Planning in Europe*. London/New York: Routledge.

Barca, F. (2009). An agenda for a reformed cohesion policy: a place-based approach to meeting European Union challenges and expectations. Independent report prepared at the request of Danuta Hübner, Commissioner for regional policy. Retrieved from www.interact-eu.net/news/barca_report/7/2647.

Blazyca, G. (2001). Poland's place in the international economy. In G. Blazyca and R. Rapacki (eds) *Poland into the New Millennium* (pp. 249–273). Cheltenham: Elgar.

Capik, P. (2011). Regional promotion and competition: an examination of approaches to FDI attraction in the Czech Republic, Poland and Slovakia. In N. Adams, G. Cotella and R. Nunes (eds) *Territorial Development, Cohesion and Spatial Planning: Knowledge and Policy Development in an Enlarged EU* (pp. 321–344). London: Routledge.

CEC – Commission of the European Communities. (1999). European Spatial Development Perspective: towards balanced and sustainable development of the territory of the EU. Luxembourg: Office of the Official Publications of the European Communities.

COMMIN. (2007). Promoting spatial development by creating COMmon MINdscapes: the Republic of Poland, Baltic Sea Region Interreg IIIB. Retrieved from www.commin.org.

Cotella, G. (2005, October). Interventi di Riqualificazione Urbana a Cracovia. *Città e Regioni del Sud Europa*. XXVI AISRE Conference, Naples.

Cotella, G. (2007). Central and Eastern Europe in the global market scenario: evolution of the system of governance in Poland from socialism to capitalism. *Journal für Entwicklungspolitik, XXIII*(1), 98–124.

Cotella, G. (2009a). Governance territoriale comunitaria e sistemi di pianificazione: riflessioni sull'allargamento ad est dell'Unione europea [EU territorial governance and spatial planning systems: reflections on the eastwards enlargement of the European Union], Ph.D. thesis in Spatial Planning and Local Development (discussed in May 2009), Politecnico di Torino.

Cotella, G. (2009b). Exploring the territorial cohesion/economic growth multidimensional field: evidences from Poland. In T. Markowski and M. Turala (eds) *Theoretical and Practical Aspects of Urban and Regional Development* (pp. 71–95). Warsaw: Polish Academy of Science.

Cotella, G., Adams, N. and Nunes, R. J. (2012) Engaging in European spatial planning: a central and Eastern European perspective on the territorial cohesion debate. *European Planning Studies, 20*(7). pp. 1197–1220.

Czapiewski, K. and Janc, K. (2011). Accessibility to education and its impact on regional development in Poland. In N. Adams, G. Cotella and R. Nunes (eds) *Territorial Development, Cohesion and Spatial Planning: Knowledge and Policy Development in an Enlarged EU* (pp. 346–372). London: Routledge.

DE Presidency. (2007). Territorial agenda of the European Union: towards a more competitive and sustainable Europe of diverse regions. Agreed at the occasion of the informal ministerial meeting on urban development and territorial cohesion on 24/25 May 2007. Retrieved from www.eu-territorial-agenda.eu/Reference%20Documents/Territorial-Agenda-of-the-European-Union-Agreed-on-25-May-2007.pdf.

Dimitrovska Andrews, K. (2004). La gestione della città post-socialista: impatti sulla pianificazione e sull'ambiente costruito. In G. Caudo and G. Piccinato (eds) *Territori d'Europa* (pp. 83–104). Firenze: Alinea.

Dziewoński, K. (1964). Urbanization in contemporary Poland. *Geographia Polonica*, *3*, 37–56.

ESPON. (2006a). Application and effects of the ESDP in member states – national overview: Poland. ESPON Project 2.3.1. Luxembourg: ESPON.

ESPON. (2006b). Governance of territorial and urban policies from EU to local level – national overview: Poland. ESPON Project 2.3.2. Luxembourg: ESPON.

ESPON. (2007a). ESPON Project 3.2: scenarios on the territorial future of Europe, final report. Luxembourg: ESPON.

ESPON. (2007b). Governance of territorial and urban policies from EU to local, final report. Luxembourg: ESPON.

Eyal, G., Szeleny, I. and Townsley, E. (1997). The theory of post-communist managerialism. *New Left Review*, *222*, 60–92.

GCSS – Governmental Centre for Strategic Studies. (2001). Koncepcja polityki przestrzennego zagospodarovania kraju. *Monitor Polski*, *26*, 503–595.

Gorzelak, G. (1996). *The Regional Dimension of Transformation in Central Europe*. London: Jessica Kingsley Publishers.

Gorzelak, G. (2001). The regional dimension of Polish transformation: seven years later. In G. Gorzelak, E. Ehrlich, L. Faltan and M. Illner (eds) *Central Europe in Transition: Towards EU Membership* (pp. 310–329). Warsaw: Regional Studies Association.

Grosse, T. G. (2005). Assessment of the National Development Plan for 2007–2013. *Analysis and Opinions*, *31*. Warsaw: Institute of Public Affairs.

Grosse, T. G. and Olbrycht, J. (2003). Preparing for the absorption of structural funds in Poland: critical overview and recommendations. *Analysis and Opinions*, *7*. Warsaw: Institute of Public Affairs.

HU Presidency. (2011). Territorial agenda of the European Union 2020: towards an inclusive, smart and sustainable Europe of diverse regions. Agreed at the Informal Ministerial Meeting of Ministers responsible for Spatial Planning and Territorial Development on 19 May 2011, Gödöllő, Hungary. Retrieved from www.eu2011.hu/files/bveu/documents/TA2020.pdf.

IGPNDP 2004–2006 – Interministerial Group for the Preparation of the National Development Plan 2004–2006 (2003). National Development Plan 2004–2006. Warsaw.

IGPNDP 2007–2013 – Interministerial Group for the Preparation of the National Development Plan 2007–2013 (2005). National Development Plan 2007–2013. Warsaw.

Izdebski, H., Nelicki, A. and Zachariasz, I. (2007). *Land Use and Development: Polish Regulatory Framework and Democratic Rule of Law Standards*. Sprawne Państwo, Program ErnstandYoung, Warsaw.

Judge, E. (1994). Poles feeling good on the road to market. *Planning*, 21 January.

Kafka, K. and Nawratek, K. (2004). Przegrana gra w miasto. *Gazeta Wyborcza*, 8 września, 15.

Korcelli, P. (2005). The urban system of Poland. *Built Environment*, *31*(2), 133–142.

Lendzion, J. and Lokucijewski, K. (no date). Compendium of spatial planning systems in the Baltic Sea Region. Retrieved from www.vasab.leontief.net/teams.htm.

Lipton, D. and Sachs, J. (1990). *Creating a Market Economy in Eastern Europe: The Case of Poland*. Brookings Paper on Economic Activity, 1. Washington: Brookings Institution.

Markowski, T. and Kot, J. (1993). Planning for strategic economic development of Lodz: concepts, problems and future vision of a city. In T. Marszal and W. Michalski (eds) *Planning and Environment in the Lodz Region* (pp. 28–42). Lodz: Zarzad Miasta Lodzi.

Matuszczak, K. (2005). *Brief Overview of Planning Legislation in Poland 1994–2005*. ECORYS Research and Consulting.

Murrel, P. (1993). What is shock therapy? What did it do in Poland and Russia? *Post-Soviet Affairs*, *2*, 111–141.

Nadin, V. and Stead, D. (2008). European spatial planning systems, social models and learning. *disP*, *44*(1), 35–47.

Newman, P. and Thornley, A. (1996). *Urban Planning in Europe*. London: Routledge.

NSMC – National Spatial Management Concept. (2011). *Koncepcja przestrzennego zagospodarowania kraju do roku 2030*. Warszawa: Ministerstwo Rozwoju Regionalnego.

OECD – Organisation for Economic Co-operation and Development. (2001). *Cities for Citizens: Improving Metropolitan Governance*. Paris: OECD.

Paul, L. (1995). Regional development in central and eastern Europe: the role of inherited structures, external forces and local initiatives. *European Spatial Research and Policy*, *2*(2), 19–41.

Piazolo, D. (2000). The significance of EU integration for transition countries. In G. Petrakos, G. Maier and G. Gorzelak (eds) *Integration and Transition in Europe* (pp. 200–216). London: Routledge.

Poznan Municipal Town Planning Office. (1992). *The Guidelines for the General Physical Plan of Poznan City*. Poznan: Municipal Town Planning Office.

Poznan Municipal Town Planning Office. (no date). *Proposal of Hotel Sites in Poznan*. Poznan: Department of Information and Development.

Regulska, J. (1997). Decentralization or (re)centralization: struggle for political power in Poland. *Environment and Planning C: Government and Policy*, *15*(2), 187–207.

Regulski, J. (1989). Polish local government in transition. *Environment and Planning C: Government and Policy*, *7*, 423–444.

Regulski, J. and Kocan, W. (1994). From Communism towards democracy: local government reform in Poland. In R. Bennett (ed.) *Local Government and Market Decentralization* (pp. 41–66). Tokyo: United Nations University Press.

Sagan, I. (2005). The policy of sustainable development in post-socialist cities. In I. Sagan and D. M. Smith (eds) *Society, Economy, Environment: Towards the Sustainable City* (pp. 45–57). Gdańsk-Poznań: Bogucki Wydawnictwo Naukowe.

Sagan, I. (2010, December). Soft space governance: the case of Poland. Draft paper presented at the *ESF Explanatory Workshop Planning for Soft Spaces across Europe*.

Shields, S. (2004). Global restructuring and the Polish state: transition, transformation or transnationalization? *Review of International and Political Economy*, *11*(1), 132–155.

Stark, D. (1996). Recombinant propriety in East European capitalism. *American Journal of Sociology*, *101*(4), 993–1027.

Swianiewicz, P. (1992). The Polish experience of local democracy: is progress being made? *Policy and Politics*, *20*(2), 87–98.

Sykora, L. (1999). Local and regional planning and policy in East Central European transitional countries. In M. Hampl (ed.) *Geography of Societal Transformation in the Czech Republic* (pp. 153–179). Prague: Charles University, Department of Social Geography and Regional Development.

Szlachta, J. and Zaleski, J. (2005). *Approximate Assessment Preliminary National Development Plan on Years 2007–2013, Final Report*. Varsavia: MGiP.

Szul, R. and Mync, A. (1997). The path towards European integration: the case of Poland. *European Spatial Research and Policy*, *4*(1), 5–36.

Śleszyński, P. (2006). Socio-economic development. In M. Degorski (ed.) *Natural and Human Environment of Poland* (pp. 109–124). Warsaw: Polish Academy of Science.

Tewdwr-Jones, M. (2011). Cohesion and competitiveness: the evolving context for European territorial development. In N. Adams, G. Cotella and R. Nunes (eds) *Territorial Development, Cohesion and Spatial Planning: Knowledge and Policy Development in an Enlarged EU* (pp. 84–102). London: Routledge.

14

CONCLUSION

Multiple trends of continuity and change

Panagiotis Getimis, Mario Reimer and Hans Heinrich Blotevogel

The previous country chapters focused on the transformations of planning systems, mainly during the past two decades, highlighting a broad variety of planning practices between and within each system. At the very beginning of our comparative research (see Chapter 1), we set the initial hypothesis that we do not expect to find one dominant direction of change, but multiple trends of change and continuity that correspond to the different path-dependent and path-shaping practices prevailing in each country.

The 12 country chapters in this book cover a variety of planning systems across Europe. At least two countries have been chosen to "represent" the four different "ideal types" or "planning traditions" identified in the *EU Compendium* (CEC, 1997): (1) comprehensive/integrated (Denmark, Finland, the Netherlands, Germany[1]); (2) regional–economic (Germany, France); (3) urbanism (Italy, Greece); and (4) land-use planning (Belgium/Flanders, UK). Three more countries that were not included in the *EU Compendium* in 1997 have been analyzed, focusing on the recent developments in eastern European countries (Czech Republic, Poland) and in a pre-accession country in south-eastern Europe (Turkey).

Our primary intention was not to construct a new typology of planning systems with regard to the present situation, but to detect common and diverse trends of change and explain the inertia, rigidity and resilience of planning systems and practices, especially since the 1990s. Focusing on common and diverse trends of planning transformation, we can highlight hidden aspects of convergence and divergence, emphasizing the multiplicity of change and continuity.

Whether or not these multiple trends of spatial planning transformation in the 12 examined EU countries reflect common patterns of change, either among all countries or among countries of the same ideal type (*EU Compendium*), is an open question to be answered on the basis of the comparative analysis of the country-specific findings. Following the structure of a methodological framework, we focus our comparative analysis on three main topics:

1   problems, challenges and driving forces;
2   dimensions of change: objectives, planning modes and tools, scale, actors of change and policy/planning style; and
3   an evaluation of change and continuity.

1 Problems, challenges and driving forces

Analyzing the findings of the country chapters, differences among spatial problems in the countries are at a first glance not very significant. In all the 12 countries examined, more or less similar spatial problems and challenges existed already in the 1990s, which had developed during the previous decades of urbanization and urban growth. Problems of urban sprawl, uncontrolled land-use development, regional inequalities and demographic problems, lack of sufficient infrastructure and transport, environmental degradation, energy supply issues and urban decay in old city districts are common in nearly all analyzed countries, therefore operating at a macro level (see Chapter 1).

It is striking that, even in countries belonging to the "comprehensive/integrated" ideal type such as Denmark and Finland, the problems of controlling urban sprawl ("Fenosprawl") or even the "illegal" parceling of land are prevalent, as is the case in southern Europe (e.g. Greece).

However, different manifestations of spatial problems emerge and different understandings and priorities are allocated. Local embeddedness and the "intrinsic logic of place" matter (Selle, 2007, 2009; Getimis, 2012). While for example in southern European countries, such as Italy and Greece, illegal settlements at the fringe of urban centers and in the coastal zone areas constitute a major problem, in central and northern European countries other spatial problems prevail, such as a lack of control of the expanding demand of the retail sector outside the cities (such as in Denmark, Finland, Germany and France).

Accordingly, problems concerning the inefficiency of the mainstream planning system to tackle and "process" spatial problems (i.e. the adaptive capacity on the meso level; see Chapter 1) are conceived differently by the planning community in different countries. For example, in Greece the inefficiency of the statutory, hierarchical, mainstream land-use planning is seen mainly in terms of "ex-post" and "emergency" features of planning implementation, which is delegitimized (e.g. ex-post legalization of squatters through legislation). In central and northern European countries (e.g. Denmark, Finland, the Netherlands, Germany), the critique focuses mainly on the maturity and inertia of the institutional architectures, on bureaucratic planning procedures, on the inadequate mobilization of participatory and deliberative mechanisms and on the lack of coordination among levels and policy sectors (for the latter see especially the contribution on the German planning system).

Evidence-based findings from different countries indicate different understandings and action logics concerning spatial planning priorities. Apart from the unresolved spatial problems, which have accumulated during past decades, in the 1990s and 2000s new common challenges emerged in all European countries that all spatial planning systems had to face. Comparing the findings from all countries, the most important challenges are:

a) The need for better coordination with economic programming and sector policies

The lack of coordination of spatial planning with other sector policies at all levels (national, regional, local) is well documented as a major problem in all country chapters. Even in planning systems belonging to the "comprehensive/integrated" type, in which the goals of coordination and integration are at the core of the agenda, there is evidence of deficits of coordination, the overwhelming dominance of sector planning goals (e.g. Germany) and a lack of cooperation among planning departments and departments of economic development, even in the same public institution. Moreover, in countries with strict hierarchical and bureaucratic planning procedures, there is not only a lack of coordination, but mainstream planning is actually considered to be a "burden" for local and regional development opportunities (e.g. Greece).

b) The need for simplification of the planning system: towards flexible planning

The challenge to overcome rigidities and complexity is common to all planning systems, both in "regulatory/statutory" planning regimes with legally binding plans and in "discretionary" types of planning actions.

Massive bureaucracy and delays emerge not only in strict hierarchical planning systems with a dominant central state (such as in Greece and Poland), but also in more decentralized planning systems in which the regions and/or the municipalities have gained more planning competencies and power during a long process of incremental reforms (e.g. Denmark, Finland, UK, the Netherlands). Administrative delays on the part of spatial planning function as "barriers" to the implementation of important investment projects by the private and public sector. Furthermore, conflicts and litigations are time-consuming, with negative effects for economic development.

Responding to the challenge of reforming and simplifying planning procedures by introducing "flexible planning" in "soft spaces" with "fuzzy boundaries" (Allmendinger and Haughton, 2009) has gained more and more supporters in the planning community (i.e. cross-border cooperation programs and projects initiated by EU funding like Interreg). Furthermore, the challenge of organizing "mega events" (e.g. Italy, Greece) and complying with strict timetables has called for reforms of the existing planning systems and for new planning tools, "bypassing" the obstacles of mainstream statutory planning.

c) The prerogative of effectiveness and competitiveness

Balancing "efficiency" and "legitimacy" was and still is a major concern in all planning systems. On the one hand, planning has to effectively fulfill objectives related to spatial development and needs to coordinate sector policies on all levels. On the other hand, spatial planning activities need to be legitimated by the citizens and other involved actors through transparency, accountability and participation mechanisms. The "argumentative turn" of spatial planning in the 1990s (e.g. Fischer and Forester, 1993; Healey, 1997) even increased the need for legitimacy and accountability.

This balance between efficiency and legitimacy has been better achieved in planning systems with integrated participatory mechanisms (e.g. the Netherlands, Germany, Denmark, Finland) than in top-down hierarchical planning systems (e.g. Poland, Greece). However, even in these consensus-oriented planning systems, claims of "underuse of the deliberative and participatory potential" (e.g. Finland) have been raised.

In the 1990s and 2000s, the prerogative of effectiveness and competitiveness for all public policies, including spatial planning, became a major concern. This was due to the overwhelming priority given in all EU countries to strengthening the competitiveness of regions and cities with less public resources and positioning them in the framework of Europeanization and the dominance of neo-liberal policies. Spatial planning was subordinated to these principles, while legitimacy lost ground. The recent financial and economic crisis following 2008 (austerity policies and cuts in public spending), together with negative impacts on spatial planning, further enhanced this trend.

d) The upgrade of environmental concerns

Spatial planning systems have been challenged by the increase of environmental concerns, especially during the 1990s and 2000s. Already in the 1980s several EU countries started paying more attention, through early legislation and policies, to the protection of the natural environment (e.g. Denmark, UK, Germany, the Netherlands). These were the "initiators" of the formation of the EU environmental policy. However, the incorporation of environmental principles and tools in the different spatial planning systems (e.g. sustainability principles, climate change, sustainable land policies, environmental impact assessment tools, participatory and consultation processes) is not only a matter of EU pressure (legal compliance), but a dynamic process of change, also dependent on various citizen movements and local demands and on the various responses and "openness" of the different planning systems (i.e. on the adaptive capacities of planning systems). Thus, countries with more flexible and integrated planning systems seem to more easily adopt the "environmental *acquis*" than other countries in which more rigid planning systems prevail (e.g. Greece, Poland, Turkey).

e) The rise of "territorial governance"

Spatial planning, formerly considered as an exclusive public domain, is being challenged to open up to negotiations with public and private stakeholders. Multi-actor and multi-level territorial governance arrangements enhance new networks of "bargaining" and "arguing," challenging close and formally defined legal planning systems. Again the EU-financed programs and the Open Method for Coordination (OMC) have functioned as "vehicles" for the introduction of new principles of "governance" in planning systems and practices (e.g. participation, coherence, accountability).

Thus, the implementation of "territorial governance" practices depends on the flexibility of the planning system in each country. In countries with more flexible and decentralized planning systems (e.g. Denmark, Finland, UK, Germany), which already in the past incorporated similar principles (e.g. social and territorial cohesion, discretion, participation of stakeholders), "territorial governance" principles have more easily penetrated the planning systems. A contrasting situation is found in countries where the rigidity of hierarchical planning systems prevailed (e.g. Greece).

2 Dimensions of change

2.1 Objectives

In all examined countries, in the past two decades there has been a common shift towards a more *strategic, development-oriented* spatial planning approach, aiming at better coordination with economic planning, regional development and sector policies (especially infrastructure networks). This shift represents the need to facilitate investments (economic-led planning) and to involve private stakeholders in the framework of territorial governance. Furthermore, strategic objectives refer to the incorporation of sustainability principles and to territorial cohesion, improving horizontal and vertical coordination of public policies across sectors and jurisdictions.

However, it should be noted that spatial planning systems in all countries in the past had to balance general strategic objectives on the one hand and more specific objectives on the other hand, focusing on land-use, permit regulations and project planning. In this sense, the shift towards strategic planning in the 1990s and 2000s is a matter of new priorities, concerning the *specific content* and *meaning* of "strategic" goals, which vary from country to country.

In *Denmark*, strategic planning is mostly connected with local strategies towards "holistic" local development related to economic planning. Given the great power of municipalities in planning, which has increased following the recent radical decentralization reform (2007), municipalities undertake a variety of strategies coordinating spatial planning with sustainable development.

In *Finland*, the shift to strategic planning is connected, on the one hand, to the shift towards territorial governance (public–private partnerships, decentralization, communicative planning styles and networking) and, on the other hand, to the scope to strengthen urban and regional competitiveness and sustainability within neo-liberal conditions. Strategic planning at all levels (national, regional, local) aims at increasing local dynamism in the framework of Europeanization and globalization (e.g. Greater Helsinki Vision 2050, "bargaining" networks for local urban development with global players).

In *the Netherlands*, strategic planning mainly focuses on fostering the competitiveness of the country. While in the past national spatial planning was more comprehensively integrated and strategic, after the recent rescaling and decentralization reform (2011) it shifted more towards economic development for the most competitive areas of the country (regional economic approach).

In *Germany*, several strategic concepts have since the 1990s been developed to strengthen the competitiveness of the country, i.e. the so-called "European Metropolitan Regions." Today, 11 regions have been positioned by the Ministerkonferenz für Raumordnung (MKRO); they aim at strengthening social, economic and cultural development and are meant to accelerate the process of European integration. Furthermore, informal strategic planning instruments and concepts have gained importance on all spatial levels (especially on the regional and local levels) in order to cope with old and new spatial challenges. Nevertheless, they only complement existing formal instruments. Although a general trend towards growth, competitiveness and development-oriented strategies can be perceived, a traditional strong paradigm of balancing spatial inequalities persists.

In *France*, the main scope of the spatial planning reform (1999–2000) focuses on the strategic goal of "territorial coherence and coordination." This strategic objective includes spatial planning coordination of cities and regions, based on a non-binding national strategic development perspective (SNADT). Furthermore, it refers to coherence between planning documents and policies at different levels and to inter-municipal cooperation in terms of common spatial visions and strategies that extend beyond and across administrative borders in designated "geographically coherent" spaces, overcoming statutory plans.

In *Italy*, the shift to strategic planning is mainly connected to territorial governance (*governo de territorio*), including multi-actor planning actions, public–private coalitions and participatory networking for strategic local and regional development. It is thus expected to overcome the dominant spatial planning tradition ("Urbanistica") and its rigidities. The rise of territorial governance (Single Act 1999, Constitutional Reform 2001) is strongly influenced by the need for strategic programming capacity (EU programs, effectiveness criteria) and neo-regionalism (devolution of planning competencies to regional and local levels).

In *Greece*, the shift to "strategic planning" in the 1990s and 2000s focuses on the promotion of economic growth, social cohesion and sustainability, along with the implementation of major infrastructure projects (e.g. Athens international airport, motorways, etc.). This shift from the dominant type of mainstream "physical" planning (statutory urban plans, fragmented and ex-post land-use regulations) towards a more strategic and development-oriented approach is strongly influenced by the Europeanization principles and directives (territorial cohesion, competitiveness, sustainability, coordination).

In *Belgium/Flanders*, strategic planning operates in the framework of "structure planning" at all levels, aiming at coherence and coordination among spatial planning, transport, regional and rural development, environment and housing. "Structure planning" functions as a counterbalance to the fragmented land-use and permit planning system, which lacks integration and cohesion. It is interesting to stress that in Belgium "structure" planning has gained importance in certain historic phases (1972–1983, 1991–1999), while it has been weaker at other times when project-oriented planning practices and a liberal planning permit system prevail (e.g. recent phase 1999–today).

In the *United Kingdom*, although planning can in no way be described as strategic or "comprehensive/integrated," during the 2000s there were significant efforts towards strategic planning, bringing forward "the spatial planning approach" on all levels: planning in the "devolved administrations" (Northern Ireland, Scotland and Wales), regional spatial strategies (abolished in 2011) and "local strategic partnerships" involving business interests and civil society and intended to improve coordination through voluntary arrangements of local governments, especially in metropolitan areas. However, this attempt has a weak record of creating efficient spatial strategies.

In the *Czech Republic*, strategic planning was introduced initially on the city level as an attempt to make spatial planning a more flexible and more proactive alternative to territorial planning. Regional strategies have been connected to Europeanization, mainly to EU accession procedures. However, the use of strategic plans is often limited to a single election period.

In *Turkey*, strategic planning has been closely interlinked with concerns about sustainable development, globalization, Europeanization and the altering institutional environment. Since the 2000s, a major reform of the public administration has occurred as a response to influences from new public management. Emphasis has been given to communicative planning, decentralization of public administration and participatory processes.

In *Poland*, the orientation towards strategic planning is mainly interlinked with a process of harmonization with the EU spatial planning agenda (ESDP principles) and is dominated by a development-oriented (and investor-friendly) planning approach.

Having presented the various contents and specific objectives of the shift towards strategic planning in the examined countries, it is obvious that various meanings and interpretations prevail in each country, depending on the different planning agendas of the reform periods, the different spatial problems to be tackled and the challenges to be met.

Furthermore, concerning the main objectives of the spatial planning reforms, there is evidence that there is not only one homogenized trend of change in mainstream planning systems (no matter what the ideal type might be) towards "strategic planning," nor can a linear development be detected.

The most characteristic case of different trajectories, even within the same country, is Belgium/Flanders. A 150-year-old system of planning permits within a framework of multilevel land-use planning (zoning) has shifted towards "structure" planning with more strategic goals in the reform periods of 1972–1983 and 1991–1999, while contrasting shifts towards predominance of the permit system, urban design and project planning emerge in the periods of 1983–1991 and after 1999 until today. Another notable shift with regard to modes of planning is seen in the UK: while in the 1990s a "plan-led system" prevailed (having emerged from the prior *ad hoc* "muddling through" planning system), in the 2000s a more strategic spatial planning approach was attempted, followed in the 2010s by a more centrally oriented and less strategy-oriented planning system.

This multiplicity of changes concerning the main objectives of spatial planning confirms our initial hypothesis on the different path-dependent and path-shaping planning practices in a development-oriented framework. This trend reflects the need for an increased flexibility of spatial planning in designating and regulating land-use and project planning, without creating obstacles to economic development but at the same time integrating environmental and sustainability concerns.

Depending on the specificity of spatial problems in the different countries, specific objectives of spatial planning practices emerge. It is worth mentioning the following:

- The challenge to organize effectively "mega" events such as the Olympic Games (Greece 2004, Italy 2006) led to specific planning regulations intended to overcome and "bypass" obstacles set by the main spatial planning system. Especially in the case of the Athens Olympics (2004), specific regulations allowed "fast-track" and *ad hoc* solutions (deviations from the rigid procedures of urban plans, shifting regulatory powers for granting permits to the central state) that thus effectively achieved the initial goals.
- The emergence of crisis situations (e.g. earthquakes) and the acute problems of illegal parceling and squatter settlements at the urban fringe and in coastal areas (e.g. Greece, Italy) led to specific planning regulations (e.g. legalization of illegal settlements, new planning instruments and tools).
- The urbanization processes in many big and medium-sized cities across Europe and the new challenges of coordination and cooperation between urban and neighboring municipalities led to the emergence of new schemes for metropolitan strategic planning, with specific objectives in agglomeration areas (e.g. Germany).
- Specific planning regulations for steering and controlling the expanding demands of the retail sector, a phenomenon that is emerging in most countries (e.g. Denmark, Germany, France, the Netherlands).

- In countries under pressure due to the current financial and economic crisis (e.g. Greece, Italy, UK) specific regulations facilitating private investments and "bypassing" traditional statutory planning are being promoted (e.g. through outsourcing, privatization).
- The reunification process in Germany led to an enhancement and "revitalization" of the historically rooted principle of social and spatial equality in the 1990s, as the differences between western and eastern parts of Germany were, and still are, remarkable. Thus, the tendency towards competitive spatial agendas was cushioned.

2.2 Planning modes and tools

Changes in planning objectives are accompanied by changes in planning modes and tools foreseen in the framework of institutional planning reforms. These emerged in different periods in each country, involving a variety of regulations: incremental amendment of planning legislation, new planning laws, acts, decrees or new administrative acts. Planning reforms depend on more general administrative reforms, concerning the central–local relations in every country, e.g. decentralization reforms and new public management reforms in public policy. Overall, the new planning modes and tools are more strategic and proactive, enabling multi-actor negotiations, participation and networking at different levels. New planning modes and tools can be formal or informal; they enhance flexibility and incorporate economic-led programming and management principles. They are introduced as more innovative planning modes, without overwriting the existing modes and tools of the mainstream planning systems.

There is a variety of different planning modes and tools emerging in each country. These can be categorized into two main types: (1) planning regulations and documents; and (2) new institutional settings for "territorial governance."

1) Planning regulations and documents

New planning regulations and relevant documents mainly concern the replacement, restructuring, renovation or amendment of the existing planning system at different levels (national, regional, local). They refer either to more general issues (e.g. strategic spatial plans, general guidelines, spatial visions) or to specific issues (e.g. land-use and permit system, building regulations, special emergency crisis regulations, metropolitan planning, spatial management tools).

Examples of *general strategic planning regulations* can be found in almost all countries.

In *Denmark*, following the incremental planning reforms of 1992, 1997 and 2000, the decentralization reform of 2007 enhanced further strategic planning in relation to economic planning and sustainability at the regional level (non-binding regional plans, visions) and at the local level (possibility for local spatial development plans).

In *Finland*, the National Land Use Guidelines (advisory) and the National Regional Development Targets, formulated by central government, aim at steering land-use issues that are important for the whole country in accordance with the priorities for regional competitiveness and growth.

In *the Netherlands*, after the recent shift in spatial planning, the newly formed Structure Vision on Infrastructure and Spatial Planning (2011) constitutes a spatial policy aimed at decentralizing the main responsibilities to sub-national governments and targeting simplicity and integration within the field of spatial policy.

In *Germany*, the amendment of the Federal Spatial Planning Act in 1998 has led to an adaptation of general spatial planning principles, i.e. the introduction and institutionally bound regulation of sustainable development as a superordinate, overall principle of spatial planning. The so-called *Föderalismusreform* of 2006 meant that the federal government lost its competence to pass and implement a framework law with regard to spatial planning; the states (*Länder*) can derogate from the federal provisions. However, another amendment of the Federal Spatial Planning Act in 2008 strengthened the position of the federal government as it introduced the option to implement national spatial plans for certain nation-wide issues. Currently, the federation has hardly made use of these rights.

In *France*, within the framework of the Spatial Planning Reform (1999–2000), the renovation of planning documents focuses on enhancing coherence and coordination (Plan Local d'Urbanism (PLU), Scheme de Cohesion Territoriale (SCOT) 2003).

In *Italy*, the reform of the "Single Act" of 1999 foresees strategic planning regulations aiming at territorial governance, while important administrative reforms (e.g. directly elected mayors) have increased municipal planning power (also through the Constitutional Reform 2001).

In *Greece*, the General Spatial Planning Framework for the whole country and Regional Spatial Planning Frameworks (RSPFs) for the 13 regions have been prepared and approved.

In *Belgium/Flanders*, the integration of a subsidiary system of three-level "structure" plans and legally binding implementation plans is foreseen (Decree of 1999). Furthermore, a Spatial Structure Plan for Flanders (2009–2010) enhancing economic development opportunities and a Spatial Policy Plan (2009) have been prepared.

In the *United Kingdom*, in the 2000s the first strategic "national plans" were prepared for Northern Ireland, Scotland and Wales, aimed at integrating social, economic and environmental objectives in spatial strategies. Strategic planning is strongly market-led and development-oriented and aims at redressing market failure and enhancing economic growth through strategic projects.

In the *Czech Republic*, regional policy was introduced with the Regional Development Act (2000) which was adapted to the EU *acquis communautaire* through later adjustments. The Planning and Building Act of 2006 deals with spatial planning, promoting sustainable development as the main target of planned development. Moreover, the 2006 Act foresees the intervention of lower levels in matters of local development, as well as monitoring as a fundamental process of planning. Strategic Plans exist at all levels; however, they have no legal base and no statutory power.

In *Turkey*, a new public administration was proposed through the Municipality Law 5393/2005, Metropolitan Municipality Law 5216/2004 and Special Provincial Administration Law 5302/2005. These laws foresee that all public institutions, municipalities and local governments should prepare their strategic plans. Furthermore, more competencies have been allocated to local authorities and they have obtained fiscal power.

In *Poland*, the new comprehensive Spatial and Territorial Development Act (2003) introduced spatial development plans at all levels: at the national level, the National Concept of Spatial Development (NCSD) in coordination with the National Development Plan (NDP); at the regional level, the Voivodship Development Strategy (VDS) and the Voivodship

Development Plan (VDP) – strongly influenced by Europeanization (ESDP discourse and principles) – and at the local level, the Local Spatial Development Plan (LSDP).

The above examples of general planning regulations and planning documents reflect the common trend of changes in all countries towards more strategic, proactive planning modes and tools compatible with economic programming and sustainability.

Examples of *specific planning regulations and tools* of strategic character can be found in most of the analyzed countries referring to:

- strategic planning for metropolitan areas (e.g. Greater Helsinki Vision 2050, Master Plan for Athens and Thessaloniki, Strategic Planning for metropolitan areas in Italy and Germany, "Fingerplan" for the Copenhagen region, spatial strategies for the Paris greater area);
- spatial planning regulations and tools for specific issues and sectors (e.g. special spatial planning frameworks for tourism and renewable energy sources in Greece 2008, retail trade sector planning in Denmark, National Land Use Guidelines in Finland);
- "emergency" planning (e.g. legalization of illegal settlements as well as earthquake emergency planning practices in Italy and Greece); and
- specific planning tools for new investment areas (e.g. outsourcing of inspection, privatization of planning processes).

2) New institutional settings for territorial governance

New *institutional settings*, enhancing coordination and multi-actor involvement at different levels, are very important tools currently being introduced. They are complementary to the planning regulations and documents mentioned above and reflect the more general shift from "government" to "governance." They focus on multi-actor participation (private and public stakeholders) and networking ("bargaining" and "arguing" networks), enhancing effectiveness and legitimacy while making spatial planning practices flexible and proactive.

Different types of institutional settings emerge, varying according to the specific actor constellations in each country and to the level at which planning practices are implemented (local, regional, national, cross-border).

In *Denmark*, after the 2007 decentralization reform, the enhancement of the planning competencies of municipalities has led to increased multi-actor participation in various planning practices at the municipal level (traditional land-use plans, broad spatial development plans, land-use planning as a strategic management tool).

In *Finland*, alongside the devolution of planning power to municipalities, the enhancement of Public–Private Partnerships (PPPs), the participation of relevant stakeholders and the emergence of planning networks has taken place.

In *the Netherlands*, the shift of spatial planning towards a regional economic approach and competitiveness has enhanced the involvement of public and private stakeholders in new partnerships, whilst foreign investors are encouraged to participate in major public infrastructure projects.

In *Germany*, the institutional architecture itself (institutional tiers) is stable and has not been markedly changed due to the high political costs of such changes. The established institutional structures have existed for about four decades and have reached a certain degree of maturity and therefore inertia. Gradual adaptations of laws and programs rather than radical shifts are therefore characteristic of German planning.

In *France*, a variety of new institutional settings have emerged, intended to enhance territorial collaboration and multi-actor participation. The most important ones are inter-municipal cooperations (Établissement Public de Cooperation Intercommunale (EPCI)) and the "Development Councils." Furthermore, these institutional settings aim at tackling problems in "geographically coherent" spaces, beyond and across jurisdictions ("soft" planning and "fuzzy boundaries").

In *Italy*, several new instruments in the form of contractual agreements have been introduced to enhance territorial governance:

- Institutional Program Agreements (*Intesa Instituzionale di Programma*);
- Framework Program Agreement (*Accordo di Programma Quadro*);
- Territorial Pact (*Patto Territoriale*);
- Program Contract (*Contratto di Programma*);
- Area Contract (*Contratto d'Area*).

The Territorial Pact and the Program Agreement have been used in specific domains, mobilizing multi-actor networking and PPPs.

In *Greece*, examples of multi-actor participation (public and private NGOs, academic actors) in specific planning practices (e.g. Athens Olympics) and at the national level (e.g. the establishment of inter-ministerial committees and the National Council for Spatial Planning and Sustainable Development) can be found.

In *Belgium/Flanders*, with the dominance of the "land-use permit system" and the recent further development of "project" planning, new instruments and tools are being employed (e.g. PPPs, project subsidies, city-marketing).

In the *United Kingdom*, during the devolution period in the 2000s, the strengthening of local government and the accent on coordination among municipalities was accompanied by "place-based strategies" that have enhanced PPPs and multi-actor participation (public, private, NGOs).

In the *Czech Republic*, where planning processes are far from being communicative or collaborative, the balance of power and conflict resolutions among main stakeholders (investors, business interests, developers, municipalities) are located behind the scenes, and there is a lack of new institutional settings for territorial governance.

In *Turkey*, the new Municipality Law 5393/2005 stipulates that a city council should enable the representation of the different socio-economic groups of society, while the recent law of the Regional Development Agency 5549/2006 enables an organizational form of private–public and NGO partnership that empowers strategic planning at this level.

In *Poland*, in the framework of Europeanization and the shift towards economic-led and investor-friendly development, it is worth mentioning the new instrument of "Regional Contracts," even though dedicated resources are scarce and regional budgets have low financing independency.

It should be stressed that in parallel to the above-mentioned new formal institutional settings that move towards territorial governance, "informal" arrangements also exist, facilitating planning implementation. We refer, for example, to the case of Finland, where an "unofficial land use agreement" had existed since 1964. This "unofficial" arrangement functions as a filter for claims and dispute resolution in cases of land-use and development, giving landowners opportunities to develop their own land (dominant landowner's right in Finland). In southern European states, unofficial arrangements often exist that tolerate illegal parceling and housing in order to meet acute housing needs, while planning regulations are absent or emerge ex-post, legalizing even whole settlements in emergency situations.

2.3 Scale

Spatial scales are not ontologically fixed geographical configurations but are socially constructed arenas in which economic, social, ideological and political power is exercised. Scales are restructured, redefined and contested, depending on the socio-spatial transformation and the actor constellation that prevails in each country. We are focusing on the scale of planning power and on processes of restructuring, not necessarily in the preordained conventional hierarchical framework (local, regional, national) but also with regard to new "soft spaces" that overcome institutional boundaries. Changes in planning systems are strongly dependent on broader institutional administrative reforms concerning local–central relations (decentralization and recentralization reforms). With regard to the case studies in this book, we can define both common and diverse trends of change concerning scales of planning power.

Since the 1990s, devolution of planning power from the central level to lower administrative tiers has taken place in all countries. However, parallel to this decentralization trend, an opposite trend had emerged: a recentralization of planning power to the central state, involving crucial policy areas such as environment, water resources, crisis management, retail planning, coastal zone management and housing.

Concerning the vertical restructuring of planning power and especially the strengthening or weakening of the regional and local levels, differences emerge among the examined countries. While in some countries (e.g. Greece, Italy, Poland) the regions are gaining planning power, in other countries (e.g. Denmark, UK) they have lost planning competencies in favor of the local level (municipalities). These differences reflect both the different historic roles of the regions (or other intermediary tiers, e.g. counties, provinces) and the priorities and scope of the institutional planning and administrative reforms, which differ from country to country.

In *Denmark*, in the framework of the decentralization reform (2007), regions lost planning power (leaving only non-binding regional plans and spatial visions), while the local level gained new planning competencies. However, parallel to the devolution of planning power to the merged 98 municipalities, there emerged a contrasting shift towards the enhancement of planning power at the central state level through the exercise of veto rights in crucial issues (environment, water resources, retail sector, taking over the strategic planning responsibilities of the Greater Copenhagen Region).

In *Finland*, the shift of strategic planning and governance was accompanied by the devolution of planning power mainly to the local level. The former hierarchical three-tier planning system has been transformed. The national level keeps a steering role providing general "national land-use guidelines" and regional development targets, while the role of the regions focuses on specifying goals for regional development (18 regional councils as statutory bodies coordinating EU Structural Fund Programmes, binding regional plans); planning power has been transferred to the local level (optional "jointmaster plans" and binding "detailed plans"), which disposes a variety of planning initiatives (defining land-use, negotiating with developers, enhancing participation). Regional planning and networking of urban areas constitute important issues of recent planning practices, referring to new "soft spaces" of functional metropolitan areas and city networks.

In *the Netherlands*, since the early 1990s planning has intended to simplify governance and aimed to become more practical. In 2008, the reform of the Spatial Planning Act resulted in the redistribution of powers and responsibilities between different government levels in order to speed up planning processes. In addition, the Structure Vision on Infrastructure and Planning (SVIP) brings spatial planning closer to those affected by it (citizens and businesses), leaving the main competencies to provinces and municipalities and intervening only when necessary.

In *Germany*, spatial planning is characterized by the very strong position of sectoral policies. One major and difficult task of federal spatial planning is the vertical coordination of scales and responsibilities and the horizontal coordination of sectoral interests. The capacity of spatial planning to control and regulate spatial developments sometimes seems to be overestimated. Sectoral policies have more financial resources at their disposal and are closely interlinked with the world of politics. Thus, they can mobilize support better than spatial planning. Nevertheless, vertical and horizontal coordination can be achieved through strategic guiding principles, aims and visions with regard to spatial planning. Scale-shifting processes can be observed in two directions: the decentralization of competencies (recent planning reforms and the strong position of federal states and regions as well as municipalities) on the one hand and the "upscaling" of planning tasks exceeding "traditional" administrative boundaries of single municipalities on the other hand. This does not mean that spatial planning at the national level is obsolete. Rather, rescaling processes are leading to new spatial and institutional fixes, trying to identify suitable combinations of formal and informal governance arrangements (e.g. new processes and instruments with regard to retail development on a regional scale).

In *France*, with a strong hierarchical "Jacobin" state tradition, each institutional level of the planning system preserves its competencies (legal obligation for compatibility). The need for horizontal and vertical cooperation and complementarity prevails. The national level sets general guidelines and directives (non-binding national strategic development perspectives), while the regions are responsible for spatial planning and regional development. The "departments" are in charge of important matters (e.g. roads), while "inter-municipal cooperation schemes," taking advantage of the new institutional settings (EPCI, Development Councils), implement not only their mainstream planning competencies but also develop common spatial visions and strategies for "geographical coherent spaces." Furthermore, deep transformations emerge at different scales and within "soft spaces" (functional urban areas (*aires urbaines*), metropolitan regions, middle-size cities, rural areas, cross-border areas).

In *Italy*, decentralization reforms since the 1990s have shifted planning power to the already strong regions (neo-regionalism) and to the municipalities, which also became more politically powerful after the reforms regarding the direct election of mayors. However, the contrary shift towards the recentralization of planning power to the state has also emerged, concerning especially the coordination of sector policies and the management of "crisis" situations (e.g. illegal settlements regulations, earthquakes).

In *Greece*, in the framework of decentralization reforms (1994, 1998, 2010), planning competencies have been transferred to the 13 regions and to the municipalities. However, due to legal objections from the Council of State, planning power has again been concentrated in the central state (recentralization trend). Nevertheless, during the past two decades, especially in the spirit of Europeanization, the regions have gained important powers concerning regional and spatial development (EU Structural Fund Programmes, European Initiatives, cross-border programs). Furthermore, planning practices are implemented in new "soft spaces" (e.g. cross-border areas and metropolitan areas).

In *Belgium/Flanders*, the three-tier subsidiary planning system remains (Flemish government, five provinces and 308 municipalities), shifting towards strategic planning at all levels (e.g. three-level structure plans), while a liberalization of the land-use permit system and project planning has emerged in successive time periods after the 1990s.

In the *United Kingdom*, the main planning powers belong to the central government, which allocates certain competencies to local authorities (the regional level of planning was abolished in 2011). However, local government's competencies are limited and, most importantly, there is no constitutional safeguard for their power. Even in the 2000s, when an extensive devolution of competencies took place, central government intervention in the planning reform towards "simplification and streamlining" was very crucial. The recent reform in 2011, although it claims to emphasize localism, reinforces central planning procedures, especially when delivering major transport and energy infrastructures.

In the *Czech Republic*, the planning system is a mixture of different approaches. The "urbanism" tradition still exists, along with land-use management in local planning and comprehensive planning at national and regional levels.

In *Turkey*, apart from the national level, spatial planning is exercised on three more levels: the regional level with Regional Plans, the provincial level with Environmental Plans and the local level with Physical Development Plans. However, even after the 2000s, with decentralization reform and the transfer of planning power to the municipalities (e.g. local taxation) and to the 16 metropolitan governments, the regions remain weak due to political reasons (avoidance of the risk of devolution by the central state).

In *Poland*, administrative reforms (1999) modified the centralized hierarchical planning system, especially after the comprehensive Spatial and Territorial Development Act (2003), moving towards a complementarity of economic-led development and spatial planning. However, although there is a shift of planning power to the regions and municipalities (*Voivodship* development strategies and plans, local spatial development plans), the hierarchical top-down system still persists (low financial autonomy, dependence on central state financing, non-binding plans at the local level).

It is worth mentioning that further differences among countries exist, concerning the rescaling of planning power, according to the following criteria:

1 binding or non-binding/optional planning regulations to the lower tiers; and
2 latitude and flexibility of content of spatial planning at all scales.

While in some countries (e.g. Denmark, Finland) regional plans are non-binding for the municipalities (spatial visions, indicative planning guidelines) and wide latitude has been given to municipalities (enabling flexibility and diversification of planning practices), in other countries (e.g. Greece, Poland, Turkey) planning of higher levels is binding for lower administrative tiers (hierarchical dependencies).

2.4 Actors of change

Multi-actor involvement in planning practices at all levels has been one of the main objectives in all planning reforms since the 1990s, reflecting the shift from government to governance. Main actors triggering changes to the existing mainstream planning system are forming "reform coalitions" stemming from politicians, public servants, mayors, planners, experts, academic community, private stakeholders (e.g. landowners, developers, building companies, industrialists) and NGOs. The scope of territorial governance implies the active involvement of all interested parties, enhancing networking and bargaining in order to achieve effective solutions. The initiative is often taken by political personnel (politicians, mayors, parties of the ruling majority) and by associations of planners, planning schools and experts. Opposed to the planning reforms, we find actors mainly in the traditional bureaucratic planning hierarchies who often express rigidity when it comes to incorporating innovation and change. Individual economic interests (e.g. property owners, building constructors) often oppose broader planning reforms. Political parties of the opposition, especially in "pendulum democracies," may also express resistance to change.

Depending on the prevailing governance model, the central–local relations and the specific objectives of the planning transformation in each country, different actor constellations emerge during the initial phase of preparation of the planning reform, the decision-making and the implementation process of various planning practices. For example, in hierarchical, top-down planning systems (such as in Poland and Greece), the central state is the "architect" of the planning reform, while in more decentralized planning systems with a long tradition of strong municipal power (e.g. Denmark, Germany), associations of municipalities and planners have very decisive roles at all stages of planning reform (initiative, agenda setting, implementation).

In *Denmark*, important actors initiating the decentralization and rescaling of planning power to the merged municipalities were the Association of Danish Municipalities and the Danish Town Planning Institute (professionals, planners, experts). A reform coalition of local politicians and MPs of the governing majority, without strong opposition, succeeded in shifting spatial planning towards strategic management and enabled the strengthening of municipal planning. The high degree of diversity of local strategies enables a variety of actor constellations in planning practices, including multi-actor participation (increased role of private stakeholders, i.e. landowners, developers, NGOs and planning experts). It should be noted that although an extended decentralization at the local level has taken place (parallel to the weakening of the regions), the central state is still a very important actor, exercising a veto in crucial issues.

In *Finland*, the shift to strategic and sustainable planning through the decentralization of power to the regions (responsible for regional development and EU programs) and to the municipalities (responsible for master and detailed plans regulating land-use and permit systems) enhanced local actors, public–private partnerships and global investors taking advantage of local dynamism. However, tension and clashes emerged among actors (e.g. among different public administration departments) concerning priorities and the complementarity of different objectives.

In *the Netherlands*, civil society and chambers have a strong voice and power to influence decisions, especially since competencies have been handed over to municipalities and provinces. Private stakeholders (developers, investors, landowners and business agents) have decisive influence in the planning process.

In *Germany*, since the 1980s new forms of cooperative governance have been established on regional and local scales (experimental regionalism). Important impulses have come from government employees and planning professionals as well as from other stakeholders (public and private organizations, civil society). Powerful local elites are able (even based on formal law) to prevent innovation and change of established practices, as the example of sustainable land policy at the local scale shows. However, it seems to be more than difficult to identify the main actors of change, as Germany consists of 16 federal states with different political and administrative cultures and therefore also with diverse local planning styles.

In *France*, the shift towards territorial governance and to a more comprehensive and integrated planning type emerged with the mobilization of multi-actor participation. Three-fold governance arrangements enable political actors to take political decisions: (1) via municipalities, EPCIs/inter-municipal cooperation; (2) through cooperation with experts, consultants and planning schools (expert knowledge); and (3) in cooperation with private stakeholders and NGOs (civil society), in the framework of the new institutional settings (e.g. development councils, urban schemes, PLU, SCOT, PPPs).

In *Italy*, the regions had a decisive role in the decentralization reform (neo-regionalism) along with the central state and the municipalities with their directly elected mayors. However, the planning experts and relevant institutions, such as the National Town Planning Institute, were also an important influence. Furthermore, given the enhanced planning power of the local level towards territorial governance, multi-actor participation emerged (private sector actors, NGOs and municipalities, public–private networking).

In *Greece*, the decentralization reforms of the mainstream hierarchical planning system have mainly been initiated by the central state, governing party majorities and the Municipalities Association, while the Council of State (Court) and the planning and academic community have played a decisive role. Multi-actor constellations also emerged in specific planning practices and episodes (e.g. Athens Olympics, specific frameworks for spatial planning), in which a variety of stakeholders from the public and private sector and civil society actors participated.

In *Belgium/Flanders*, in the reformist periods, a coalition of actors stemming from political forces (politicians, mayors, ministers), the planning community (planning consultants, schools, experts) and the public administration (public servants) succeeded in introducing strategic planning principles ("structure plans") into the dominant "land-use" spatial planning system. In the context of balancing conflicting interests, such as land-use and property claims and project development on the one hand, and securing strategic planning on the other hand (preservation of public space, green zones, social infrastructure and environmental and sustainability concerns), multi-actor constellations emerged, constituted by groups of different interests: landowners, building companies, planners, consultants, law firms, sectoral economic actors, municipality councils, mayors.

In the *United Kingdom*, government reforms have led to the involvement of a wide range of actors and interests in the planning system. Public agencies, quasi-public sector bodies, private companies and NGOs exert influence on the policy process, but not with the same gravity. Nevertheless, although planning processes are open and participatory in the framework of the discretionary system of regulation, spatial planning is strongly driven by central government and business and industry interests (recentralization after 2011), despite the rhetoric of localism and opposing interests from NGOs and civil society.

In the *Czech Republic*, while the state remains a key player in spatial planning defining main priorities, economic global actors greatly influence the game. Municipalities have gained power and responsibilities for local development. The market is another important actor as multinational investors have a loud voice. The role of civic society, although legally defined at all stages of planning processes, is usually downgraded, especially in cases of large projects and major investments. Finally, planners who are actively involved in planning execution are not always asked for their professional opinion.

In *Turkey*, since strategic planning is still in its inception, it is not easy to establish a clear network of actors. Nevertheless, multi-actor planning practices have emerged in the form of new coalitions, the private sector has gained a significant role in planning and more and more actors whose actions are not easily controlled by binding spatial plans are engaged in planning procedures.

In *Poland*, the shift from a hierarchical and centralized planning system towards devolution of planning power to the regions and the municipalities was initiated through the central state within the framework of Europeanization. However, even after the devolution of power, the central state remains the main "architect" of the market-oriented reforms. Private stakeholders (e.g. developers, building companies) have gained an increasing role in local development.

From the above comparative analysis, it is evident that a multiplicity of actor constellations has emerged, depending upon the central–local relations and the scope of the planning reform that prevails in each country. Although in all planning reforms there is a common trend to enhance multi-actor involvement in planning practices, there is broad variety in the different roles and the composition of main actors influencing both the phase of initiating the planning reform and the phase of implementation (planning practices).

2.5 Policy/planning style

Planning practices are influenced by the different policy styles and political cultures, mainly in terms of the dichotomy between "command and control" and "consensus oriented" policy styles (Richardson et al., 1982; Fürst, 1997, 2007).

Planning reforms in all countries were oriented towards strategic objectives, decentralizing planning power and enhancing multi-actor participation. A common trend concerning the changes of planning style can be observed: the emergence or the enhancement of consensus features of planning process and an "opening" of planning processes to new stakeholders.

Even in hierarchical, command and control planning systems (such as Greece and Poland), a new orientation of policy styles towards consultation, networking and collaboration is taking place, although the mainstream planning system has not been abandoned. However, "bargaining" networks prevail (negotiations mainly with private stakeholders, e.g. Poland, Italy, Belgium/Flanders, Denmark, Greece), while "arguing" networks are lagging behind or do not even exist. Thus, even in countries with a long tradition in communicative planning cultures such as Finland and Denmark, there is a lack of deliberative participation and "arguing" networks, and mainstream statutory planning systems have not been radically transformed. Meanwhile in strong central states (such as Greece and Poland), the command and control planning style still persists.

There is evidence for the coexistence of heterogeneous planning styles not only among countries, but even among regions and localities in the same country. In *Italy*, we find strong diversification of policy styles and different speeds of change at the regional level. In *Denmark*, there are diversities of local strategies (physical/land-use planning, development plans, holistic local plans) and there is also heterogeneity in planning styles across municipalities (local level). It is obvious that the stronger the local/regional autonomy, and the broader the options for local actors to exercise planning power, the more diverse the planning practices and styles.

In *Denmark* and *Finland*, the shift towards decentralization and rescaling of planning power has further enhanced the consensus-oriented planning style. The communicative planning paradigm developed before the 1990s; however, even in these countries, the lack of deliberative participation networks and the predominance of "bargaining" networks have been highlighted.

In *the Netherlands*, planning is characterized by a systematic and formal hierarchy of plans from the national to the local level, coordinating public sector activities across different sectors. Nevertheless, although a recent shift towards the regional economic approach emerged, at least at the national level, the consensus-oriented planning style (*polderen*), negotiation and consultation are catalysts in planning processes (national plans are not binding, since lower levels of government have the power to reinterpret them).

In *Germany*, planning is based on a systematic and formal hierarchy of plans as well. Spatial planning has changed since the 1970s (from reactive to proactive modes of spatial planning), today being more strategic and communicative in nature. It combines hard and soft modes of governance, i.e. hierarchical steering and communicative and consensus-based forms of interaction.

In *France*, the shift in planning has enhanced features of the consensus planning style. Regulatory planning modes have not been abandoned, but coexist with the new participatory and cooperative mechanisms (e.g. EPCIs, Development Councils, PPPs) that work towards territorial governance and territorial cohesion. New planning ideas of "soft spaces" are combined with the consensus-oriented planning style. A shift from a "Jacobin" to a "Girondin" approach has emerged, with multi-actor involvement and a new need for horizontal and vertical cooperation and complementarity. A new balance among "effectiveness" and "legitimacy" is intended, while the coexistence of different policy styles (command and control, consensus and networking) prevails.

In *Italy*, the shift from top-down hierarchical approaches towards multi-level territorial governance enhanced the consensus-oriented planning style (collaborative and negotiative). Diversification and heterogeneity of planning styles at the regional level have emerged, given the alternative options that exist concerning horizontal networking and cooperation schemes between the participant stakeholders.

In *Greece*, planning reforms (decentralization, shift to strategic planning) introduced new elements of the consensus-oriented policy style (e.g. national councils and fora, horizontal and vertical networking, new participation schemes), implemented in innovative planning practices. However, these elements have not overwritten the dominant command and control ("paternalistic") planning style.

In *Belgium/Flanders*, the alternate shifts from hierarchical land-use planning, permit systems and project planning towards strategic planning (e.g. three-level structure plans) and vice versa reflect a coexistence of different policy and planning styles (command and control, consensus-oriented and networking).

In the *United Kingdom*, planning is characterized by the "land-use management tradition"; however, it entails elements of "comprehensive/integrated" planning, such as the voluntary coordination of local governments (mainly in metropolitan areas). In general, spatial planning in the UK is discretionary, with more emphasis given to negotiated solutions during development proposals. Moreover, although local governments' competencies are rather limited and overshadowed by the four central governments, public involvement (large number of NGOs with great influence) in planning is central in the UK. A tension emerges between shifts towards a more deliberative planning style ("soft spaces" with "fuzzy boundaries") and towards a more technocratic and centralized planning style.

In the *Czech Republic*, the planning style could not be characterized as communicative or collaborative. The state's command and control style has shifted towards competing interests among the state, municipalities and investors. According to the criteria of flexibility and certainty of the *EU Compendium*, Czech planning is "indicative," characterized by the notion that any decision on land-use should be based on a binding legal regulation. Moreover, planning is "value-free," with planners fulfilling the needs of their clients and not setting goals for sustainable development.

In *Turkey*, incremental steps from a planning tradition with many similarities to "urbanism" (hierarchical structures, command and control mechanisms, paternalistic style) towards decentralization are also accompanied by recentralization trends (e.g. Istanbul metropolitan area), due to the powerful central government and the hierarchical central state tradition.

In *Poland*, the decentralization process (shifting power to the regions and municipalities) and the introduction of new multi-actor participation schemes (with an important role played by private stakeholders) have not overwritten the dominant command and control planning tradition under the shadow of the central state.

Two main concluding remarks can be made. First, the emergence of a heterogeneity of planning styles among countries and even regions and, second, the slow pace of change of embedded planning styles and the coexistence of consensus-oriented features with command and control planning styles.

3 Evaluation of change and continuity

The comparative analysis has highlighted both common and diverse features of spatial planning transformations in the 12 European countries during the past two decades, focusing on

296

spatial problems, driving forces and directions of change (planning scope, models and tools, scales, actors and policy styles). Evidence-based outcomes show that there is no dominant direction of change ("homogeneous" path of planning transformation) but multiple trends, corresponding to different path-dependent and path-shaping factors. However, there are similarities and common features of change and continuity that lead to partial convergent and divergent trends, which will be further evaluated.

3.1 The multi-faceted impact of Europeanization and globalization

The diversity and heterogeneity of spatial planning systems in Europe was already highlighted in the early 1990s. Spatial planning systems are rooted in "the specific histories and geographies of particular places, and the way these are interlocked with national institutional structures, cultures and economic opportunities" (Healey and Williams, 1993, p. 710).

This diversity is not only due to the different national legal and administrative frameworks, but also to different socio-economic, political and cultural conditions prevailing in each country. However, the different planning systems are not "static" structures bound by the historical context, but rather dynamic in nature (Nadin and Stead, 2008) and are subjected to incremental change and innovation. "Norm entrepreneurs" ("actors of change") respond in different ways both to "internal" domestic needs for spatial planning reforms and to "external" influences of Europeanization and globalization.

Europeanization, a dynamic and contradictory process of "top-down" and "bottom-up" European integration, is the main driving force for the different institutional and policy transformations in EU, accession and neighboring countries (Risse et al., 2001; Giuliani, 2003; Radaelli, 2003, 2004; Paraskevopoulos et al., 2006). "Europeanization might lead to convergence in policy outcomes, but at least to clustered convergence and continuing divergence with regard to policy processes and instruments, politics and polities" (Börzel and Risse, 2003, p. 72). The domestic planning systems have responded in different ways to the Europeanization challenges and therefore have different adaptive capacities (see Chapter 1). Challenges stem both from the EU regulatory framework (e.g. EU directives, rules pertaining to structural funds, EU sector policies) and from the voluntary mechanisms and tools of cooperation and coordination (e.g. OMC, White Paper on Governance).

As the empirical evidence has shown, there are different intensities and paces of adaptation and different priorities in domestic planning agendas and in concrete planning practices, supported by new measures and financing tools (e.g. cross-border projects, Interreg, European initiatives). There are countries and regions that have taken full advantage of these opportunities (e.g. Germany, France, the Netherlands, Finland, Baltic countries), while others are lagging behind (e.g. Italy, Greece, Balkan countries, south-eastern Mediterranean countries).

It is important to stress that the influence of Europeanization was much greater in all countries from the 1990s to the mid-2000s, during the period of European "euphoria" and high expectations of European enlargement (2004–2005). Thus, countries under transition from central planning to market economies (Poland, Czech Republic) were, at least in the first phase, more open to including the EU spatial planning agenda in a domestic planning discourse, supporting the designed planning reforms and facilitating the absorption of EU funding (pre-accession and structural funds).

Although the emergence of the EU spatial planning agenda played an influential role in the domestic planning reforms, this has not led to a "harmonization" of spatial planning systems and practices across Europe. The multi-faceted impact of Europeanization is reflected in the different responses of the planning systems to the common spatial problems and new challenges, which emerged during the 1990s and 2000s in all EU countries (Farinos Daci, 2006. The differential empowerment of domestic actors, either to push forward and facilitate planning reforms or to oppose and even blockade reform attempts, enhances a continuing divergence of planning systems and practices across EU countries. However, there is evidence that a partial convergence is emerging alongside the "European language" (European meta-narratives) and the main objectives of liberalization and deregulation. Core objectives such as liberalization and deregulation have been imposed in many policy sectors (e.g. transport, telecommunication, energy, European Monetary Union) with important impacts on spatial planning processes. The increasing marketization of the public sphere, through privatization, outsourcing, public–private partnerships and "agencyfication," has enhanced the market orientation of spatial planning and the variety of its manifestations.

Globalization processes, parallel to the Europeanization project, enhanced the dominance of neo-liberal imperatives and further opened up the exposure of national economies to the world markets (trade and financial) and to global players (investors, lenders). New asymmetries, risks and differentiated responses on the part of member states emerged. A characteristic example of the different responses of the EU member states is the global financial crisis (2008) and the public debt crisis of the southern EU countries (from 2009 until today). Countries being hit by the global economic crisis, with reduced public resources, are under strong pressure to move towards "market-led" planning, in order to facilitate private investments and to overcome planning burdens through outsourcing specific planning services. Greece, for example, which since 2009 has represented the weakest part of the economic and public debt crisis of the EU countries, has recently imposed important radical changes in the "rationale" of spatial planning: orientation to "market-led" and pro-growth strategies, facilitating investment, outsourcing and marketization of planning services, weakening of strict environmental and planning regulations and "bypassing" of planning burdens through specific planning regulations.

Globalization and the recent economic crisis have further deepened neo-liberalization and the market orientation of planning, with a variety of manifestations. The pace and intensity of neo-liberal influence on spatial planning and the focus on economic growth and competitiveness differs among the examined countries ("temporal, spatial and scalar variegation"; see Allmendinger and Haughton, 2012). While in the UK and the Netherlands (forerunners in terms of neo-liberal policymaking) the shift towards market support planning is more radical, in Germany and France it is more balanced (see also Waterhout et al., 2012).

3.2 Values, "rationale" and policy priorities: the prerogative of "market-led," pro-growth spatial planning

The common shift towards "strategic" planning objectives in all examined countries in the past two decades is combined with changes in the normative framework and the policy priorities of the different modes of governing. Spatial planning systems have always had to balance values and goals that are not always compatible or are even contradictory: efficiency vs. legitimacy, comprehensive/holistic vs. selective, spatial equity vs. spatial fragmentation, cohesion vs. competitiveness, authoritative/command and control vs. participatory/consensus, top-down vs. bottom-up.

The common shift towards "strategic" planning in the examined countries encompasses different values, contents and meanings. While in some countries it is associated more with the coordination of spatial planning with sector planning, leading to "territorial cohesion" and spatial equity (e.g. Germany, France), in others it is more focused on the efficiency of planning, facilitating growth and responding to tailor-made local development needs (e.g. UK, the Netherlands, Denmark, Poland, Czech Republic). Furthermore, while in countries with a "communicative" planning tradition (e.g. Finland, Germany, Denmark, the Netherlands) the values of participation and legitimacy through "bargaining" and "arguing" networks are inevitably connected with strategic planning, in countries with strong hierarchical structures (e.g. Poland, Greece) strategic planning is implemented through top-down processes and command and control planning practices, even if participatory mechanisms are formally and legally foreseen.

However, the shift to "strategic" planning, with all its different manifestations and meanings across countries, is not a linear evolutionary process of progress and triumphs of planning without tensions and contradictions. It includes experimental episodes, success and failure, "U-turns" of planning reforms and a multiplicity of changes and continuities, dependent on the spatial problems, challenges and modes of governance and policy priorities in each country (see also Allmendinger and Haughton, 2012). In periods when neo-liberal policies dominate, the market orientation of spatial planning is much more intense than in periods of social-democratic policies, when a more balanced combination of competing planning discourses is pursued (efficiency and legitimacy, cohesion and competitiveness, sustainability and growth, environmental and development tasks).

Overall, it is significant to stress that the prerogative of competitiveness, pro-growth and market-led spatial planning is gaining ground and dominates recent transformations of spatial planning systems across all examined countries. The "rationale" of spatial planning changes: not only does it incorporate, as in the past, the values of economic and regional development alongside other values such as sustainability and environmental and social goals, but it is exclusively subordinated to the logic of market-led principles, economic investments and selective growth. In an era of increased competition among cities and regions in Europe, and with much more limited financial resources, both from the member states (under fiscal pressure) and from the EU structural funds (reductions in redistributive regional policy programs), spatial planning is under new pressure to transform.

The political position of strategic planning is becoming weaker in relation to the imperatives of economic policy and other sector policies. Spatial planning is called upon to abandon existing burdens caused by inflexible administrative jurisdictions (rigid boundaries of planning competencies), to bypass statutory regulations and longstanding bureaucratic processes and delays, and to overcome "spaces of resistance" to growth that emerge from local protest and social movements. The prerogative of "market-led" planning requires a new flexibility to be able to respond effectively both to macro-economic imperatives and to tailored local growth needs, which emerge in non-statutory functional areas ("soft spaces" with "fuzzy boundaries").

The "strategic" character of planning is reduced to a soft coordination of single "projects" and sector planning, while other policy priorities, which formerly ranked high in the planning agenda (such as territorial cohesion, sustainable development, social housing, public services, environmental protection), are underestimated and absorbed by the dominant "market-led" and "competitive" principles. However, as the empirical evidence of the comparative analysis shows, "strategic planning" has not been abandoned; rather, it has changed its contents, "rationale" and priorities, with different manifestations among the countries.

A common trend in all planning reforms during the past two decades is the shift of strategic planning towards "territorial governance," which involves new institutional settings and planning tools enhancing coordination of private and public sector actors (e.g. territorial contracts, PPPs). Territorial governance arrangements open up new development opportunities and can lead to win–win situations for all involved stakeholders (public, market, civil society), exploiting the endogenous potential of localities and regions. Ideally, they can promote both effectiveness and legitimacy and equal distribution of policy outcomes, demonstrating that beneficiaries are not only the powerful stakeholders (e.g. investors, business enterprises, developers and landowners) but also other less powerful actors from civil society (e.g. associations, NGOs, local initiatives, etc.). In the framework of territorial governance, the new planning tools are more flexible and proactive, enabling multi-actor networks to achieve the initially self-defined and agreed-upon goals. Different institutional settings and planning tools, varying across the examined countries, lead to specific actor constellations and mixtures of policy goals, as the empirical evidence shows. While in some countries "bargaining" networks with dominant private actors in market-led planning practices prevail (e.g. UK, the Netherlands), in others a more balanced mixture of policy priorities is attempted, including both competitiveness/pro-growth goals and legitimacy and accountability through public participation (e.g. Finland, Germany, Denmark). Overall, "arguing" networks and participation of less powerful actors lag behind, since the neo-liberal agenda and its priorities towards "competitive," "market-led" and/or "project" planning increasingly influences the spatial planning reforms.

3.3 Rescaling planning power and "actors of change"

The rescaling of planning power has shown both common and diverse trends. In all countries, devolution of planning power from the central state to lower administrative tiers has taken place during the past two decades. More analytically, we observe in all countries devolution of planning competencies to the regional and local level. This devolution is strongly dependent on broader institutional administrative reforms (functional and/or territorial decentralization), which have been implemented in different periods in the countries examined. The dominance of a neo-liberal agenda has been seen to enhance the rescaling of planning power mostly to the local level (e.g. new "localism" in the UK in 2010, decentralization reform in Denmark in 2007, liberalization of the land-use permit system and project planning in Belgium/Flanders in 1999 and 2008).

However, devolution of planning power in all countries is combined with a contrary trend, the recentralization of power on the central level concerning important policy areas, such as major infrastructure investments, protection of environment and water resources, retail planning or coastal zone management. Central state intervention in core planning fields is suggested to be a necessary response to the fragmented and differentiated landscape, which emerges due to devolution. Pressures towards a "centralized decentralization" (Allmendinger and Haughton, 2012; Baker and Wong, 2012) are due to spatial problems that cannot be resolved at the local level. These problems refer to the economic and environmental crisis, "emergency" situations, property development cycles, house price inflations, lack of housing land and so on. The strengthening of planning powers at the central level, parallel to decentralization, corresponds to the differentiated development needs of the markets and to the policy priorities of various scales of governance.

While searching for the "perfect" market supportive scalar and institutional fix, planning reforms foresee different roles and planning powers for the intermediary levels (regions, provinces and municipalities). While in some countries (e.g. Greece, Italy, Poland) the regions are gaining planning power, in other countries they have lost planning power or have been abandoned (e.g. UK) in favor of the local level. These differences reflect both the historic role of the regions and of the other intermediary tiers (e.g. countries, provinces), and the different scope and priorities of the administrative and planning reforms prevailing in each country. In countries with strong hierarchical state traditions (e.g. France, Belgium, Greece, Poland, Turkey), the preordained conventional hierarchical planning system is maintained even after administrative and planning reforms.

It is worth mentioning that diverse trends exist among the countries in terms of the features of rescaling planning power (binding or non-binding/optional planning regulations to the lower tiers) and the latitude and flexibility of the content of planning competencies at all scales. While there are countries such as Denmark in which regional plans are indicative and non-binding for the municipalities, there are other countries such as Greece, Poland and Turkey with hierarchical planning regulations that are strictly binding to the lower tiers and reduce flexibility and latitude of planning practices at the local level.

The rescaling of planning power not only refers to the vertical relations of administrative jurisdictions, but also to the horizontal relations among multiple actors in voluntary cooperation schemes. The shift towards strategic planning and "territorial governance" requires the activation of multiple stakeholders in multi-scalar arenas in order to tackle spatial problems that emerge across and over existing planning jurisdictions. Functional problems refer to local and regional labor markets, travel to work areas, housing areas, river catchment areas, risk areas, metropolitan areas and cross-border areas. These problems cannot be solved within the preordained rigid boundaries of existing administrative planning authorities. New "soft spaces" with flexible boundaries emerge, and planning practices tailored to specific needs are experimented with.

The rescaling of planning power (horizontal and vertical) is triggered by "actors of change" and facilitating institutions. These "change agents" or "norm entrepreneurs" (Börzel and Risse, 2003) are persuaded of the necessity of the planning reforms and try to overcome "multiple veto points," either through persuading opposed actors to redefine their goals and interests in processes of social learning or through authoritative, top-down policy measures that impose planning transformations. "Change agents" can be epistemic communities (networks of authoritative claims to knowledge), advocacy coalitions or "principled issue networks" with common beliefs, values and identities, policy networks (bound together by common goals for planning reforms) and communities of actors in specific planning practices. "Actors of change" differ in terms of the composition of the main initiators of the planning reform and the contents, values and priorities of planning transformations (Adams et al., 2011).

Successful planning reforms are based on "reform coalitions" of actors stemming from political forces (politicians, ministers, mayors), the epistemic community (planners, consultants, experts), the public administration (public servants), private stakeholders (landowners, developers, investors) and civil society (NGOs). Planning reforms are not simply passed down from above; they are processes always filtered, contested and negotiated with opposing interests. Actors, mainly in the traditional bureaucratic planning hierarchies and in political parties, express resistance to change and rigidity towards incorporating innovation. It is a dynamic process of balancing conflicting interests, such as land-use and property claims and project investments on the one hand, and securing strategic planning and territorial governance on the other (territorial cohesion, equity, sustainability, participation principles).

To sum up, all planning reforms have been initiated by a multiplicity of "actors of change," forming coalitions with different compositions, roles and paths of transformation. Variations in actor constellations also emerge in the phase of the implementation of planning reforms, as they are manifested in the differentiated planning practices of territorial governance.

3.4 Planning practices, policy styles and political cultures

Planning reforms in all countries have introduced not only the "opening" of planning processes to multiple stakeholders, but also enhanced consensus policymaking in territorial governance arrangements. At the discursive and rhetoric level, the principles of consultation, bargaining, arguing and cooperative decision-making are included in the agenda of the planning reforms, both in countries with hierarchical planning systems (e.g. Greece, Poland, Turkey) and in countries with a long tradition of communicative planning (e.g. Denmark, Finland). However, during the implementation of these planning reforms, we find divergent trends concerning the pace and the intensity of change. An important factor for this heterogeneity of planning practices is the policy style, which is connected with the type of political culture that dominates in each country.

The political culture can be coalitional or contradictive (Lijphart, 1999). The coalitional political culture refers to an integrative democratic tradition, where decisions are taken on the basis of consensus (non-majoritarian), while the exercise of power is open and inclusive (Loughlin et al., 2011). The contradictive or confrontational political culture refers to an aggregative democratic tradition, where decisions are taken on the basis of the majoritarian principle ("pendulum democracy") (March and Olsen, 1989). In the second case, the exercise of power is mostly exclusive ("Westminster democracy," "winner takes it all").

There is evidence that in countries with a coalitional political culture and integrative democratic tradition based on consensus and cooperation, policy and institutional change occurs more efficiently. Multiple veto points are easier to overcome, since bargaining and arguing processes can secure a better distribution of the transformation costs. Furthermore, socialization and learning through persuasion can be achieved; "winners of domestic change compensate the losers" (Börzel and Risse, 2003 p. 72). In contrast, in countries with a contradictive/confrontational political culture with power excercised exclusively, polarized and conflicting interests slow down, impede or even blockade policy and institutional change. In fact, the Mediterranean countries are characterized by a contradictive political culture in a framework of antagonistic relations between the central state and society (Loughlin and Peters, 1997) and strong multiple veto points that weaken or block institutional and policy reforms.

Political culture is related to national policy style (Richardson et al., 1982) and the "steering" style of policy (Fürst, 1997, 2009). Thus, contradictive political cultures are combined with command and control steering styles, while coalitional political cultures are related to consensus steering styles. In countries with a coalitional political culture (e.g. Germany, Nordic countries) a consensus policy style prevails in planning practices. In countries with a contradictive political culture (e.g. Greece, Italy, Poland), the domination of command and control planning styles is maintained, even after new consensus and participation elements have been introduced by planning reforms.

As the comparative analysis of the 12 countries shows, there are different planning styles, deeply rooted in the different political cultures and national policy styles, that decisively influence the path of the planning reforms in each country. There is evidence of heterogeneous planning styles not only among countries, but even among regions and localities in the same country (e.g. Italy, Denmark). This is due to the different discretionary roles of the regions and municipalities in exercising planning power in different ways (inclusive/exclusive, command and control/consensus).

The coexistence of heterogeneous planning styles is reflected in the broad variety of planning practices: on the one hand territorial governance arrangements in "soft spaces," through "bargaining" and "arguing" in multi-actor networks (consensus-oriented), and on the other hand via statutory, regulatory practices of hierarchical mainstream planning systems (command and control). Planning reforms that attempted to introduce innovative planning practices with consensus-oriented planning styles have not overwritten the mainstream statutory planning approach; these two approaches coexist. Dominant planning styles, being rooted in the different national policy styles and political cultures, are difficult to change. Planning transformations that are concerned with policy style are very slow, while a multiplicity of changes and continuities emerge.

4 Summary

The cross-national comparison of the spatial planning systems and practices in the 12 examined countries during the past two decades highlighted the main changes and continuities of planning transformations and the main trends of convergence and divergence of the planning systems. Based on the above conclusions, we argue that there is no "homogeneous" direction of planning transformation, but multiple trends of continuity and change and an increased "heterogeneity" of planning transformations, corresponding to different path-dependent and path-shaping factors.

Common trends refer to the challenges and driving forces of Europeanization and globalization, the adoption of the European spatial planning agenda "rhetoric," the neo-liberal imperatives of deregulation, the prerogative of pro-growth spatial planning and its subordination to market-led values and policy priorities, the shift towards strategic "planning and territorial governance," the rescaling of planning power (devolution to lower tiers combined with a recentralization of power on the central level), the search for new "soft spaces" with flexible boundaries to tackle spatial problems that emerge across and over jurisdictions, the activation of multiple "actors of change" (norm entrepreneurs) and facilitating institutions in order to implement planning transformations, the need for multi-actor involvement (public and private sector) in horizontal and vertical cooperation networks in planning practices and the introduction of consensus-oriented policy styles at the "discoursive" level in the intended planning reforms.

Different trends refer to the multi-faceted impact of Europeanization and globalization reflected in the different responses of the domestic planning systems, the new asymmetries and differential responses to the global economic and financial crisis and public debt crisis of the southern EU countries, the pace and intensity of neo-liberal influence on spatial planning systems, the variety of contents, meanings and understandings of "strategic planning" and "territorial cohesion" among the countries, the diverse trends of rescaling planning power concerning vertical and horizontal relations, the composition, the role and the enactment of the "actors of change" of planning reforms and the dominance of the different policy styles and political cultures, influencing in different ways the implementation of planning reforms.

Future comparative planning studies should focus further on more specific aspects of the direction of change than the five topics selected in this study (scope, modes and tools, scale, actors, policy style). Given the diversity of spatial planning systems and practices and the multiplicity of changes and continuities, there is an increased demand for specific knowledge of how planning is conducted and implemented in concrete and comparative planning practices.

Note

1 The German planning system is characterized by elements of both types.

References

Adams, N., Cotella, G. and Nunes, R. (eds) (2011). *Territorial Development, Cohesion and Spatial Planning: Knowledge and Policy Development in the Enlarged EU*. London/New York: Routledge.

Allmendinger, P. and Haughton, G. (2009). Soft spaces, fuzzy boundaries, and metagovernance: the new spatial planning in the Thames Gateway. *Environment and Planning A, 41*, 617–633.

Allmendinger, P. and Haughton, G. (2012). The evolution and trajectories of English spatial governance: "neoliberal" episodes in planning. *Planning Practice and Research, 28*(1), 6–26.

Baker, M. and Wong, C. (2012). The delusion of strategic planning: what's left after the Labour Government's English regional experiment? *Planning Practice and Research, 28*(1), 83–103.

Börzel, T. A. and Risse, T. (2003). Conceptualising the domestic impact of Europe. In K. Featherstone and C. M. Radaelli (eds) *The Politics of Europeanization* (pp.57–80). Oxford: Oxford University Press.

CEC – Commission of the European Communities. (1997). *The EU Compendium of Spatial Planning Systems and Policies*. Luxembourg: Office for Official Publications of the European Communities.

Farinos Dasi, J. (2006). *ESPON Project 2.3.2, Governance of Territorial and Urban Policies from EU to Local Level, Final Report*. Esh-sur-Alzette: ESPON Coordination Unit.

Fischer, F. and Forester, J. (1993). *The Argumentative Turn in Policy Analysis and Planning*. Durham/London: Duke University Press.

Fürst, D. (1997). Humanvermögen und regionale Steuerungsstile: Bedeutung für das Reginalmanagement? *Staatswissenschaften und Staatspraxis, 6*, 187–204.

Fürst, D. (2007). Planungskultur: auf dem Weg zu einem besseren Verständnis von Planungsprozessen? *PND online*, *III*, 1–15.

Fürst, D. (2009). Planning cultures en route to a better comprehension of "planning process." In J. Knieling and F. Othengrafen (eds) *Planning Cultures in Europe* (pp. 23–48). Farnham: Ashgate.

Getimis, P. (2012). Comparing spatial planning systems and planning cultures in Europe: the need for a multi-scalar approach. *Planning Practice and Research*, *27*(1), 25–40.

Giuliani, M. (2003). Europeanization in comparative perspective: institutional fit and national adaptation. In K. Featherstone and C. M. Radaelli (eds) *The Politics of Europeanization* (pp. 134–156). Oxford: Oxford University Press.

Healey, P. (1997). *Collaborative Planning*. London: Macmillan Press.

Healey, P. and Williams, R. (1993). European urban planning systems: diversity and convergence. *Urban Studies*, *30*(4/5), 701–720.

Lijphart, A. (1999). *Patterns of Democracy: Government Forms and Performance in Thirty-Six Countries*. New Haven, CT: Yale University Press.

Loughlin, J. and Peters, B. G. (1997). State traditions, administrative reform and regionalization. In M. Keating and J. Loughlin (eds) *The Political Economy of Regionalism* (pp. 1–62). London: Routledge.

Loughlin, L., Hendriks, F. and Lidstroem, A. (2011). *The Oxford Handbook of Local and Regional Democracy in Europe*. Oxford: Oxford University Press.

March, J. G. and Olsen, J. P. (1989). *Rediscovering Institutions: The Organizational Basis of Politics*. New York: Free Press/Oxford: Maxwell Macmillan.

Nadin, N. and Stead, D. (2008). European spatial planning systems, social models and learning. *disP*, *44*(1), 35–47.

Paraskevopoulos, C. J., Getimis, P. and Rees, N. (2006). *Adapting to EU Multi-Level Governance: Regional and Environmental Policies in Cohesion and CEE Countries*. Aldershot: Ashgate.

Radaelli, C. M. (2003). *The Europeanization of Public Policy*. In K. Featherstone and C. M. Radaelli (eds) *The Politics of Europeanization* (pp. 27–56). Oxford: Oxford University Press.

Radaelli, C. M. (2004). Europeanization: solution or problem? *European Integration Online Papers*, *8*, pp. 1–23.

Richardson, J. J., Gustaffson, G. and Jordan, G. (1982). The concept of policy style. In J. J. Richardson (ed.) *Policy Styles in Western Europe* (pp. 1–16). London: Allen and Unwin.

Risse, T., Caporaso, J. and Cowles, M. G. (2001). *Europeanization and Domestic Change: Introduction. Transforming Europe: Europeanization and Domestic Change*. Ithaca, NY: Cornell University Press.

Selle, K. (2007). Neustart: vom Wandel der shared mental models in der Diskussion über rämliche Planung, Steuerung und Entwicklung. *PND Online*, *III*, 1–15.

Selle, K. (2009). Gruppendiskussion über Planungskultur. *PND Online*, *II*, 6–7.

Waterhout, B., Othengrafen, F. and Sykes, O. (2012). Neo-liberalization processes and spatial planning in France, Germany and the Netherlands: an exploration. *Planning Practice and Research*, *28*(1), 141–159.

INDEX

General terms

Specific terms